Socio-syntax

How do we adapt our grammar to communicate social detail? Do all working-class people have a local dialect or are we free to use language in ways that transcend our place in the social hierarchy? Seeking to answer these questions, this pioneering book is the first to exclusively and extensively address the relationship between social meaning and grammatical variation. It demonstrates how we use grammar to communicate alignments and stances *and* to construct our social style or social identity. Based on an ethnographic study of high-school girls in Northern England, it also uses the author's own experiences as a working-class student, to argue for change in how we conceive of grammar and how grammar is taught in schools. Lively and engaging real-life examples from the study are included throughout, bringing to life new contributions to debates in variationist sociolinguistic and linguistic anthropology.

EMMA MOORE is Professor of Sociolinguistics at The University of Sheffield. She was a British Academy Mid-Career Fellow in 2020–2022. Recent publications include *Language and a Sense of Place* (co-edited with Montgomery, 2017) and *Social Meaning and Linguistic Variation* (co-edited with Hall-Lew and Podesva, 2021).

Socio-syntax
Exploring the Social Life of Grammar

Professor Emma Moore
University of Sheffield

CAMBRIDGE
UNIVERSITY PRESS

Shaftesbury Road, Cambridge CB2 8EA, United Kingdom

One Liberty Plaza, 20th Floor, New York, NY 10006, USA

477 Williamstown Road, Port Melbourne, VIC 3207, Australia

314–321, 3rd Floor, Plot 3, Splendor Forum, Jasola District Centre, New Delhi – 110025, India

103 Penang Road, #05–06/07, Visioncrest Commercial, Singapore 238467

Cambridge University Press is part of Cambridge University Press & Assessment, a department of the University of Cambridge.

We share the University's mission to contribute to society through the pursuit of education, learning and research at the highest international levels of excellence.

www.cambridge.org
Information on this title: www.cambridge.org/9781108826198

DOI: 10.1017/9781108921299

© Emma Moore 2024

This publication is in copyright. Subject to statutory exception and to the provisions of relevant collective licensing agreements, no reproduction of any part may take place without the written permission of Cambridge University Press & Assessment.

First published 2024
First paperback edition 2026

A catalogue record for this publication is available from the British Library

Library of Congress Cataloging-in-Publication data
Names: Moore, Emma, 1976- author.
Title: Socio-syntax : exploring the social life of grammar / Emma Moore.
Description: Cambridge, United Kingdom ; New York, NY : Cambridge University Press, 2024. | Includes bibliographical references and index.
Identifiers: LCCN 2023019007 (print) | LCCN 2023019008 (ebook) | ISBN 9781108843973 (hardback) | ISBN 9781108826198 (paperback) | ISBN 9781108921299 (epub)
Subjects: LCSH: Speech and social status–England. | English language–Syntax. | English language–Spoken English–England. | English language–Social aspects–England. | English language–Variation–England. | Working class–England–Language. | High school girls–England–Language.
Classification: LCC P40.5.S632 G766 2024 (print) | LCC P40.5.S632 (ebook) | DDC 306.442/21042–dc23/eng/20230607
LC record available at https://lccn.loc.gov/2023019007
LC ebook record available at https://lccn.loc.gov/2023019008

ISBN   978-1-108-84397-3   Hardback
ISBN   978-1-108-82619-8   Paperback

Cambridge University Press & Assessment has no responsibility for the persistence or accuracy of URLs for external or third-party internet websites referred to in this publication and does not guarantee that any content on such websites is, or will remain, accurate or appropriate.

For Hilda and Frank Moore,
who wanted more for me and Sarah, and gave
it unconditionally.

Contents

List of Figures	*page* ix
List of Tables	xii
Acknowledgements	xiv

1 Why Does the Social Meaning of Grammar Matter? — 1
  1.1 What Is Grammatical Variation? — 7
  1.2 How Will This Book Examine the Relationship between Grammar and Social Meaning? — 10

2 The Social Landscape of Midlan High — 15
  2.1 Situating Midlan High — 17
  2.2 Places and Spaces within Midlan High — 19
  2.3 The Process of Ethnography — 20
  2.4 The Social Groups at Midlan High — 28
  2.5 Reflections and Limitations — 44

3 How Do We Study the Social Meaning of Grammatical Variation? — 46
  3.1 Interpreting Social Meaning — 49
  3.2 Grammatical Variants and the Development of Social Meaning — 61
  3.3 Types of Grammatical Variant and Types of Social Meaning — 67
  3.4 Investigating the Social Meaning of Grammar — 71
  3.5 Establishing Sociolinguistic Meaning — 74

4 How Free Are We to Vary the Grammar We Use? — 75
  4.1 Children and the Acquisition of Local Dialects — 77
  4.2 Children, Peers and School — 80
  4.3 Levelled *Were* at Midlan High — 81
  4.4 What Constrains Our Use of Grammatical Variation? — 105

5 How Do We Use Grammar to Design Our Talk? — 111
  5.1 The Semantics of Negative Concord — 115
  5.2 Negative Concord at Midlan High — 117
  5.3 The Discourse Context of Negative Concord — 125
  5.4 The Social Meaning of Negative Concord — 129
  5.5 Highly Stigmatised Grammar, Pragmatics and Social Association — 136

6	**Does Everyone Use Grammar to Make Social Meaning?**	138
	6.1 What Types of Right Dislocation Are Possible?	140
	6.2 What Are the Functions of Right Dislocation?	143
	6.3 How Were Right-dislocated Tags Analysed?	149
	6.4 How Are Right-dislocated Tags Distributed at Midlan High?	151
	6.5 How Are Personal Pronoun Tags Distributed at Midlan High?	157
	6.6 The Social and Interactional Functions of Right Dislocation	160
	6.7 What Is the Relationship between Form, Frequency and Function?	167
	6.8 Syntactic Variables, Semantics and Social Meaning	168
7	**How Does Grammar Combine with Other Elements of Language?**	171
	7.1 The Tag Questions Dataset	174
	7.2 How Are Tag Questions Distributed at Midlan High?	175
	7.3 How Do Tag Questions Vary at the Discourse Level?	179
	7.4 How Do Tag Questions Vary in Their Linguistic Content?	186
	7.5 Summary: How Do Tag Questions Vary?	190
	7.6 Tag Questions and Social Meaning	195
	7.7 Do Tag Questions Have Character-type Social Meanings?	204
8	**What Does It Mean to View Grammar as a Fluid, Flexible Social Resource?**	207
	8.1 What Are the Key Findings of This Study?	210
	8.2 What Are the Wider Implications of Foregrounding the Social Meanings of Grammar?	223
	8.3 The Educational Consequence of Recognising the Social Meaning of Grammar	225
	8.4 Final Words	232
	References	233
	Index	253

Figures

2.1 The location of Bolton, in relation to the city of Manchester, the county of Greater Manchester, and the rest of England, Scotland and Wales. (This work is based on data provided through EDINA UKBORDERS with the support of the ESRC and JISC and uses boundary material which is copyright of the Crown. © Crown Copyright/database right 2017. An Ordnance Survey/EDINA supplied service.) *page* 17
3.1 The three components of a sign, using the example of coat-wearing at Midlan High. 49
3.2 A hypothetical indexical field for the tag question *innit*. [Grey cogs indicate stance-related social meanings and black cogs indicate character-type social meanings (with persona-linked meanings in small capitals, and social-type meanings in italicised small capitals).] 57
3.3 Type SM: Trajectory of social meaning rooted in semantics. 61
3.4 Type CT: Trajectory of social meaning derived from a character-type index. 62
3.5 Type SS: Trajectory of social meaning derived from sound symbolism. 62
3.6 A simplified representation of inter-related social meanings of *innit*. 67
4.1 Distribution of levelled *were* by social class. 89
4.2 Distribution of levelled *were* by parental place of birth. 90
4.3 Distribution of levelled *were* by community of practice. 91
4.4 Average distribution of levelled *were* by year of recording. 93
4.5 Average distribution of levelled *were* by year of recording for each community of practice. 93
4.6 Pairwise comparisons of EMMs between the levels in the clause-type factor group. 101
4.7 Pairwise comparisons of EMMs between the levels in the subject-type factor group. 102

4.8	Pairwise comparisons of EMMs between the levels in the community of practice factor group.	103
4.9	Pairwise comparisons of EMMs between the levels in the social class factor group.	104
4.10	Pairwise comparisons of EMMs between the levels in the community of practice factor group, by year of recording.	104
4.11	The Townies' use of levelled *were* over time.	107
4.12	A hypothetical indexical field of levelled *were*, showing how social meaning may develop for an individual over time.	109
5.1	Mean use of negative concord over time, by community of practice.	120
5.2	Distribution of negative concord according to community of practice. Bars show group means; circles show individual speakers.	121
5.3	Distribution of negative concord by social class membership. Bars show group means; circles show individual speakers.	122
5.4	Raw frequencies of topics discussed in the instances of postverbal negation with indeterminates, by community of practice.	125
5.5	Percentage distribution of topic for instances of standard negation (e.g., *I don't like anything*), by community of practice.	126
5.6	Percentage distribution of topic for instances of negative concord (e.g., *I don't like nothing*), by community of practice.	127
5.7	A hypothetical indexical field of negative concord, showing how social meaning may be rooted in semantics (black circle), association with character types (dark grey circle), and embodiment of character types in local space.	133
6.1	Frequency of right dislocation by social class. Each dot represents one individual. Bars represent group averages.	151
6.2	Frequency of right dislocation by community of practice. Each dot represents one individual. Bars represent group averages.	153
6.3	Use of right dislocation by tag type for each community of practice.	154
6.4	Use of right-dislocated personal pronoun tags by community of practice.	156
6.5	Distribution of verb processes by personal pronoun type.	157
6.6	Distribution of stance according to personal pronoun types.	159
6.7	Distribution of right-dislocated tag types for the two outliers in the analysis (Michelle, Geek, and Georgia, Popular).	163

List of Figures xi

6.8	Use of first-person pronoun tags as a proportion of all personal pronoun tags, over time.	165
6.9	Use of second- and third-person pronoun tags as a proportion of all personal pronoun tags, over time.	166
7.1	Frequency of tag questions by social class. Each dot represents one individual. Bars represent group means.	176
7.2	Frequency of tag questions by community of practice. Each dot represents one individual. Bars represent group means.	177
7.3	Use of tag questions over time, by community of practice.	178
7.4	Proportional differences in the type of response to turn-final tags, by social group.	181
7.5	Proportional differences in the type of response to turn-medial tags, by social group.	182
7.6	Proportional occurrence of overlap with tag question usage, by social group.	183
7.7	Topic of talk used in tag questions by social group.	185
7.8	Use of personal pronouns in tag questions, by social group.	186
7.9	Proportion of /h/-dropping within tag questions, by social group.	188
7.10	Proportion of /t/ variants, by social group.	189
7.11	Use of morphosyntax within tag questions, by social group.	189
7.12	Populars' use of tag questions over time. Smoothies are shown in black.	202
7.13	Responses to turn-final tags in Year 10.	203
7.14	Responses to turn-medial tags in Year 10.	203
8.1	Type CT: Trajectory of social meaning derived from a character-type index.	221
8.2	Type SM: Trajectory of social meaning rooted in semantics.	222

Tables

1.1	Types of grammatical variation studied by sociolinguists	*page* 7
2.1	Participants included in the linguistic analysis, by social group	28
2.2	Number of words included in the corpus for the data analysis, by social group	29
3.1	Types of grammatical variation	68
4.1	Agreement patterns for past tense BE in English, with example clauses	82
4.2	Distribution of levelled *were* by social class	89
4.3	Distribution of levelled *were* by parental place of birth	90
4.4	Distribution of levelled *were* by community of practice	91
4.5	Distribution of levelled *were* by year of recording	92
4.6	Linguistic factors considered in the analysis of levelled *were* at Midlan High	95
4.7	Results of the generalised linear mixed-effects modelling for use of levelled *were*	99
5.1	Results indicating the effect of indefinite type on the occurrence of negative concord (Fisher's Exact, two-sided, $p = 0.004$)	118
5.2	Results indicating the effect of negative element on the occurrence of negative concord (Chi-square, $\chi^2(3) = 8.36$, $p = 0.004$)	119
5.3	Results indicating the effect of position of the indeterminate on the occurrence of negative concord (Chi-square, $\chi^2(1) = 5.64$, $p = 0.018$)	119
5.4	Use of negative concord by community of practice	120
5.5	Use of negative concord by social class	122
5.6	Use of negative concord by parental place of birth	123
6.1	Types of right dislocation found in British English	141
6.2	Verb process types used in the analysis of personal pronoun tags according to Halliday (1985)	150
6.3	Evaluative stances expressed in the context of right dislocation use	150

6.4 Log likelihood comparisons for social class groups	152
6.5 Distribution of right dislocation at Midlan High by tag type	154
7.1 Significant pairwise log likelihood comparisons with the High social class group	177
7.2 Significant pairwise log likelihood comparisons for communities of practice	178
8.1 Types of grammatical variation and their likely trajectories of social meaning	220

Acknowledgements

This book started as a conversation with one of my wonderful PhD supervisors, the much-missed Richard Hogg. I was complaining to him about the dominant depiction of working-class people: as unfulfilled, feckless and ignorant, with brutal family lives and hopeless futures. Sociolinguists did not seek to perpetuate these stereotypes, but the social meanings relied on to explain patterns of variation (that working-class speech was 'tough', 'rough' and 'masculine') did little to challenge the dominant narrative. Everything felt a little one-sided: it wasn't that people didn't perceive working-class speech in these ways, rather that it was just one way of perceiving working-class speech. Richard pointed me to sociological literature that more richly nuanced the heterogeneity of working-class existence and then, one day, he handed me Penny Eckert's *Linguistic Variation as Social Practice*. In a typically understated Richard way, he said, 'I think you might like to read this.'

The world shifted on its axis and – perhaps for the first time – I started to see how I could bring my own life experience with me into academia. It has been a long journey, though – it's taken me twenty years to write this book. I write about the reasons for this in the book itself – something I couldn't have done twenty, even ten, years ago – so I won't reiterate them here. Instead, I use this space to thank the people who helped me to do it.

Richard Hogg and David Denison kept me afloat at university. They were also the perfect double-act (Richard was a bit anarchic, David was steady) and they were both patient, encouraging, thoughtful and inventive in finding ways to keep me engaged. I don't think we ever talked explicitly about how university made me feel but you seemed to know what I needed. You were generous (especially with the KitKats, David), and continued to support, encourage and cheer-lead, even when I chose sociolinguistics over historical linguistics. I now realise how significant this was, given how some top linguistics departments perceived sociolinguistics in the 1990s.

It is not an exaggeration to say that Penny Eckert changed my life. I read her book and Richard encouraged me to email her. Knowing very little about me, Penny invited me to meet her at UKLVC2 in Essex. I was terrified. I drove

Acknowledgements   xv

there (scared the whole time that I was going to run out of petrol as there was a petrol shortage at the time), spent two hours talking to Penny, stayed one night, and drove home. I wasn't even brave enough to attend the conference properly in case someone asked me what I did or what I thought. For some reason best known to Penny, she then invited me to attend Stanford as a visiting scholar. I spent April–June 2001 in the Linguistics department. It was an opportunity of a lifetime. I learnt so much in those three months, and not just about linguistics and anthropology. Thank you, Penny, for showing me a different world, being my fiercest critic, and becoming a valued friend. Thank you also for not flinching (too much) when I asked you to cook that very expensive tuna steak 'well done' when I stayed with you and Ivan that time.

Stanford introduced me to some brilliant minds who continue to challenge what I think and how I articulate it. Rob Podesva, I love you, and I forgive you for only accepting me into your cool gang in the last month of that first Stanford visit. You've made up for it since. Thank you for working with me on my tag question data, which was published as Moore and Podesva (2009). The UK has wonderful minds too. My friend and colleague, the brilliant Sarah Spencer, continues to provide tea and thoughtful, perceptive insights. Thank you to you, and to Julia Snell, for challenging me to properly articulate the theory, and for being my working-class allies. Julia, thank you for working with me on my right-dislocation data, which was published as Moore and Snell (2011). Jenny Cheshire helped me in many different ways as I was working on this book. I think I may have finally read everything that you've ever written and the seeds of what I say in this book were planted in your brilliant work on morphosyntax and discourse. I've tried really hard to show where you led the way in the following pages – but everyone should just read everything you've written for themselves.

I wouldn't be an academic without the funding I received as a graduate student from the AHRC. The writing of this book was supported by a British Academy Mid-Career Fellowship which bought me out of teaching and admin and allowed me to focus solely on writing and speaking to people about my ideas. It was a huge privilege that I am very grateful to have received. Helen Barton and Izzie Collins at Cambridge University Press have been helpful, encouraging and – most importantly – patient. The reviewers of the book proposal and the final manuscript were clearly not of the 'Reviewer 2'-type and provided thoughtful, useful and articulate feedback. Holly Dann and Sarah Tasker got all of my data into LaBB-CAT, and Holly, in typically affable and calm fashion, supported my mangled attempts to use R. I really have had some of the most wonderful postgraduate students, who have taught me a great deal.

Marie Feltham saved me twice. Once as a young lecturer, out of my depth in a new job, in a new city; and once during the COVID-19 pandemic when I was trying to write this book. Marie: thank you for helping me to realise that happiness is a choice, and that being a perfectionist can be a superpower if used well. You only have to read this bit of the book.

To Mum and Dad, Hilda and Frank Moore, and my sister, Sarah: I know you don't always know what I'm doing or why I'm doing it, but I love you so much for always doing everything you can to help me all the same. Chris, thank you for helping me to build a life where it is possible to raise a wonderful, quirky, happy child, whilst also spending hours in the attic writing a book. I love that we are a pair of equals and an equal match. Lara, thank you for being patient when I've been in the attic and you wanted to play, and for coming in for impromptu cuddles. You really are the best chimp, and I love our little family more than anything.

Finally, as Penny Eckert once said to me, you can theorise all you like, but it's the data that matters. My data came from some amazing young women, who allowed me to step into their lives. To be honest, you were often slightly terrifying, but always uplifting. I imagine that you scarcely remember those months when that weird woman came into your school and tagged along at lunchtime. Thank you for trusting me. I've worked really hard to try and make you sound like the real, interesting and engaging people you were. Your words are important and they can make a difference.

1 Why Does the Social Meaning of Grammar Matter?

> For some who may want to forget or downplay their class backgrounds, 'class is never simply a category of the present tense. It is a matter of history, a relationship with tradition, a discourse of roots' (Medhurst 2000: 20). Indeed, it is important that sociolinguists' own classed identities and backgrounds also be addressed and foregrounded in their work on class, to further 'encourage reflexivity about the role of the researcher in data collection and analysis and the politics of representation in scholarly writing' (Bucholtz & Hall 2008: 406).
> (From: Chun, Christian W. 2019. Language, discourse, and class: What's next for sociolinguistics? *Journal of Sociolinguistics* 23. 332–345; p. 341.)

Before I went to university, I didn't think about how much of the grammar I used diverged from standard English, never mind why I might be using it. Non-linguists generally don't spend a lot of time thinking about how or why they use language – until someone points out that their speech is 'unusual' or that it needs 'correcting', of course. But not being able to identify the relative clause in a sentence like 'I read this book, *which was fun*', doesn't mean that you aren't capable of using a relative clause to add information about your attitude towards reading a book. People adapt their language to subtly communicate social detail all the time. They might be able to say how they were trying to sound but, rarely, how they used language to try and sound that way.

The extent to which people are able to adapt their grammar to communicate social detail is the focus of this book. There are many, many studies which show a correlation between the use of localised grammar and low socio-economic status, but far fewer interrogate the extent to which our use of localised grammar is constrained by our class status. Does being working class mean you can't help but use localised grammar, or are we free to use language to develop styles and personas which transcend our place in the social hierarchy? This book seeks to answer this question.

The volume of research on social class in sociolinguistics can give the impression that we are all constantly and consciously working to present our classed selves to the world. But, just as people don't think about the language they are using, people who aren't social scientists or social activists don't tend to think about social class much either. We're all too busy just being, day-to-day. We know that there are people who are different from us and that can make us feel many things about ourselves and them, but it takes social mobility or encounters with 'others' to make us reflect on our precise place in the social order. I didn't know what linguistics was until I went to university, and I didn't know that I was working class either. I just knew I wanted to learn some more and that going to university involved stepping outside the norms of my everyday experience and usual ways of being (my *habitus*, Bourdieu 1990: 12–15). I had signed up for a degree in English Language and Literature, without really understanding what it involved. The English Language and Literature A level I had taken was relatively new, and the language component had taught me how to precis texts and what kinds of language to use in debates, but I don't remember learning anything about phonetics or grammar or linguistic theory. I'd always enjoyed reading and had done well at writing. I wrote stories and poems, and people said I had a good imagination. I wanted to be a teacher. The only person I knew who had been to university was my sister, who had trained to be an occupational therapist. Both of my parents left school aged fifteen. My mum became an office clerk, but stopped working when my sister was born (she subsequently retrained as a nursery nurse when both me and my sister were at school). My dad had an apprenticeship which trained him as an electrical engineer. He'd wanted to be a teacher. They both valued education enormously and had not wanted to leave school at fifteen. Our house was full of books.

Encouraged by my parents and my school teachers, I thought I was good at literature but, on arriving at university, I quickly learned that I wasn't. Everybody else in the classes seemed to know more than me, and it wasn't just because they had read the texts before (although many of them had). They seemed to understand how the texts connected to history and culture, and they identified references that I missed. The other students also seemed to know how to talk about the texts and how to talk to the lecturers. I wrote copious notes and never missed a class, but the books we read didn't make me feel anything and I only talked in class when I was picked on to answer a question. Then I found it hard to get my words out. I tried to focus on creative writing because I was confident about that, but I was told that my writing was parochial (a word I had to look up) and that the things I wanted to write about weren't relevant. I stopped being confident about it.

The linguistics classes that formed the English Language component of my degree were different. We had done bits of work on grammar at school, but mostly in my French class. I loved the grammar classes at university – there were rules to follow and puzzles to unpick about why certain structures were grammatical and others weren't. The lecturers were interested in – and often pleasantly surprised by – my judgements about which kind of sentences were possible in my dialect. Nobody minded that I transcribed things in my own accent when I learnt the International Phonetic Alphabet in my 'Sounds of English' classes. I loved Old English too because we had to learn the grammar to understand what we were reading. It was another problem to solve and one that wasn't dependent upon what I did (or, rather, didn't) know about the current zeitgeist (another word I'd learnt in my literature classes).

My inability to engage with the English Literature curriculum was bewildering. I thought I was clever (there are a lot of geeks in this book, and I was one of them) but I felt stupid. It felt personal. It was only in the final year of my degree, when I took a class in Sociolinguistics, that I realised that how I felt in my classes *was* deeply personal. As I learnt about the ways in which my language could be structured by my social class, my gender, and the location of my upbringing, I began to realise that these factors provided a framework for all of my experiences. I wasn't engaged by the literature classes because I didn't have the collection of social assets, including credentials, tastes, style of speech, forms of social engagement (*cultural capital*, Bourdieu & Passeron 1990) to engage with them. I didn't feel like I could talk in class because I knew my style of speaking was different. I didn't know how to position myself as a legitimate participant in the seminar discussion.

My experience of the two components of my degree, English Language and English Literature, illustrate something about what is required for people to adapt and change (and, ultimately 'to learn'). I didn't enjoy my literature classes and I felt like my access to them was inhibited by some deficit in me (the lack of cultural capital). On the other hand, I enjoyed the challenge of the linguistics classes (a subject which was mostly new to everyone in my cohort) and the encouragement of my linguistics lecturers supported me to succeed, despite the fact that I felt like I didn't belong in the university. Three factors determined my success in linguistics: *access* to the university environment, *opportunity* to engage successfully with it (facilitated in a large part by supportive lecturers) and *motivation* to become involved in the institution. As Eckert and Wenger (1993) have noted, all three are necessary to learn successfully (as suggested above, this definition of 'learning' is broader than 'schooling'). Motivation is determined by the individual (although it can be conditioned by other factors, like confidence or sense of legitimacy), whereas access and opportunity can be externally controlled. Sometimes, individuals may want to learn, but they may not have obtained the necessary qualifications to enrol on a particular course, or they may not be able to find a course they can afford, or one which fits around other obligations like caring responsibilities. Sometimes opportunities to learn have gatekeepers who deny access to individuals who aren't considered legitimate. People may not consciously exclude others – there is a long literature describing how implicit biases can affect the decisions people make about who is or isn't the right fit for a job or a place on a course (see Brownstein & Saul 2016 for an overview) – but if individuals are perceived to lack the qualities required of a legitimate participant, then they can be excluded. In their examination of apprenticeships, Lave and Wenger (1991: 37) note that apprentices only learn successfully when they achieve a state of 'legitimate peripheral participation' (where the peripherality refers, not to position in relation to an abstract group centre, but to 'an opening, a way of gaining access to sources of understanding through growing involvement'). Consequently, what matters in gaining access to a site of learning is the achievement of legitimate status.

Acquiring new language styles or adapting how we use language in our day-to-day interactions is a form of learning too. Consequently, if we want to understand why people use the language they do, we need to understand what they have been able to learn and the extent to which they are able to modify that learning. Social class is a place to start – it is central to the social order (Eckert 2019b: 2) and gives us access to certain linguistic variants and styles – but social class is not the place to stop. Opportunities and motivations shape what we learn too. Precisely how they do so will be explored in this book.

So this is a book about social class that is not about social class. In addition to using language to index certain social qualities, we also use language to undertake social action. Whilst we might infer something about a speaker's social background from how they speak, a speaker's utterance may also communicate more nuanced social detail. It might communicate subtle information about when a person is speaking, what their preferences are, what their alignment is to what they are saying, and what their feelings are about who they are saying it to. Whether or not a speaker uses a particular linguistic form may be guided by these consideration as well as, or even in spite of, their social background.

Consider Extract 1.1. It comes from a conversation between me and two girls who feature heavily in this book, Georgia and Jennifer. They are discussing Georgia's relationships with boys.

Extract 1.1[1]

1	E	Who's Danny?
2	J	Her boyfriend.
3	G	It's not. [(INAUDIBLE)]
4	J	[It used to be Mike.] But now she likes Danny.
5		
6	G	Mike was.. a bad, bad mistake for me. We were –
7	J	Oh, she's talking all heartache. Can you tell? It's like,
8		[(SIGHS AND MOCK SWOONS)].
9	G	[It's cos my cold's coming back!]
10	E M	[(LAUGHS)]
11		
12	L	No, he were bad, though, weren't he?

(Georgia and Jennifer, 48A:402–415)

---

[1] In all extracts, transcription conventions have been kept to a minimum for clarity. Non-speech is shown in round brackets (e.g. '(LAUGHS)'). Transcriber comments/notes are shown in arrowed brackets (e.g. '<content omitted>'). The first instance of overlap in a turn is marked by single square brackets (e.g. '[ ]'); subsequent overlap in the same turn is marked by double square brackets (e.g. '[[ ]]'). Latching is shown using '='. Line spaces are used to distinguish overlap from the surrounding discourse.

To understand the meaning of these utterances, we need to be able to decode the content conventionally associated with the words that are used and the way they are structured. For instance, to understand the sentence 'he were bad, though, weren't he?' on l. 12, we need to know that *he* refers to Georgia's ex-boyfriend, that *were* is a localised variant of past-tense third-person singular BE, and that the verb BE can depict a state or condition (importantly, we don't need to describe grammar in this way to understand it). We also need to know that *bad* is a word used to describe something that is not good and *though* is typically used to qualify something said previously (in this case, Georgia is qualifying why her ex-boyfriend was a bad mistake). It's also necessary to know that these words are assembled to make a declarative statement, 'he were bad, though', and a tag question, 'weren't he?', following the conventions of English. Decoding this information gives us the *semantic meaning* of Georgia's utterance: it enables us to perceive the reality and truth about what she is attempting to describe. But we don't just use language to decode propositions or truth conditions. Our understanding of Georgia's utterance also relies upon our ability to understand meanings that are not abstractly entailed by the words and structures she uses. Some meanings are recoverable from the fact that words and structures are used in particular ways at particular moments of interaction. For instance, we might wonder why Georgia uttered a tag question at this point in the discourse. We'll learn much more about tag questions in Chapter 7 but, for now, it is enough to note that their structure invites an interlocutor to attend to the proposition expressed in the preceding declarative statement. Unlike regular questions, they rarely constitute requests for truth-conditional information; Georgia is not asking whether Mike is bad news – she knows full well that he is. Rather than establishing whether her statement is true or false, her tag question seems to be seeking to establish that this is an opinion shared with Jennifer. It is seeking to establish common ground.

That Georgia's utterance includes a tag question, as opposed to being a simple declarative, could be interpreted as marked. The markedness of an utterance can help us to determine what a speaker is inferring beyond what is said in a purely semantic-referential way (Horn 2004; Acton 2019). This is *pragmatic meaning*: it requires us to consider what is implied or presupposed by an utterance, beyond its referential content. Utterances may be marked for many reasons: they may require more interpretative effort, or they may indicate something about a speaker's alignment with the content of their talk. In Extract 1.1, the syntactic configuration of the tag question (as opposed to a less marked form) may serve to emphasise Georgia's evaluation of Mike and conduce agreement around this evaluation. If people in our speech community use a lot of tag questions in this way, it may be that we will come to associate tag questions with especially evaluative personality types.

But utterances can be marked for reasons beyond the interpretative effort required to decode them. They may be heard less frequently than alternative utterances, or they may violate dominant social norms. In constructing the tag question on l. 12 of Extract 1.1, Georgia uses a form of verbal agreement that differs from standard English: 'he *were* bad, though, *weren't* he?'. I've previously referred to this variant as nonstandard *were* (Moore 2010), but to avoid unnecessarily stigmatizing variants that differ from the standard, I refer to it here as levelled *were* – to reflect how the use of *were* is levelled across all persons in the past tense. We'll learn a lot more about it in Chapter 4, but for now, it is sufficient to observe that it is not a speech error, but a local variant that is common in Georgia's dialect. The *were* has the same semantic referential meaning as the *was* in 'he *was* bad' and '*wasn't* he', in that they are alternative ways of marking past-tense third-person BE. But does Georgia's use of *were* have any other kind of meaning? Acton (2021) has argued that utterances can gain meaning from their sociohistorical use. That is to say, we may infer something about an utterance based upon what we associate it with and our beliefs about this association. For instance, levelled *were* is more frequently used by people in lower-social-class groups. If a listener is aware of this association they may decode Georgia's use of levelled *were* as a symbol of working-class status or, at least, as a symbol of her alignment with working-class practice. In turn, the listener may infer that Georgia has any number of social characteristics that are associated with working-class status. These might include traits like resilience, toughness, or friendliness, dependent upon the listener's precise beliefs about working-class people. In this way, levelled *were* may index *social meaning* associated with being working class, i.e., being resilient, tough or friendly. I define 'social meaning' as what can be inferred about a person's interactional position or character on the basis of how they use language in a specific interaction. This is distinct from pragmatic meaning, which I define as what is implied or presupposed by an utterance, beyond its referential content. Acton (2021) argues that social meaning is a form of pragmatic meaning (see also Hall-Lew, Moore & Podesva 2021), however, it is important to note that whilst all kinds of social meaning entail pragmatic meaning (as defined above), pragmatic meaning does not necessarily entail all kinds of social meaning. For instance, it is possible to presuppose something about a person's interactional position *without* presupposing something about their character. The range of meanings that different grammatical variants can carry, and how these meanings are generated, will be a central concern of this book. In Chapter 3, we further explore different levels of meaning and consider how social meanings develop by exploring issues of ideology and indexicality. For now, it is important to note that the term 'grammar' can encapsulate a wide range of different variants. If we are to understand how social meaning attaches to grammatical variants, we need to be explicit about how we define those variants. In the next section, grammatical variation, and the range of grammatical forms that can vary, is more precisely defined.

1.1 What Is Grammatical Variation?

Grammar is the way in which we structure our utterances by (i) combining meaningful units of language (morphemes) into words and (ii) putting strings of words into interpretable units (clauses). In sociolinguistics, grammatical variation is often referred to as 'morphosyntactic' or just 'syntactic' variation, but these labels can depict a broad and diverse range of linguistic units. Table 1.1 provides a simplified representation of some of the types of grammatical variation discussed by sociolinguists (Romaine 1984: 419; Winford 1984: 272; Cheshire 1987: 261–262).

It is not equally easy to identify sociolinguistic variation across these different grammatical types. To evaluate why one linguistic variant is used over another, sociolinguists have endeavoured to decipher the linguistic choices available for communicating a given state of affairs (Labov 1978: 5). This is a relatively straightforward process if we can easily determine the alternative forms and compare their social value. For linguistic units like phonemes, identifying alternatives requires us to know which phonemes can denote which sounds. For instance, in British English, there are – broadly speaking – four different ways to pronounce the 'th' sound in a word like *thing*:

Example 1.1 [θ] (the most 'standard' pronunciation: 'thing');

Example 1.2 [f] (found in many different varieties; e.g., Levon & Fox (2014): 'fing');

Example 1.3 [t] (often attributed to young people in urban multicultural communities; e.g., Drummond (2018a): 'ting');

Example 1.4 [h] (in certain Scottish communities; e.g., Stuart-Smith *et al.* (2007): 'hing').

Table 1.1 *Types of grammatical variation studied by sociolinguists*

Type of variable	Example	Example study
Morphophonemic	Definite article reduction: where *the* is pronounced as, e.g., [t] or [θ] ('I went t' shop', 'The bird lives in th'oak tree')	Tagliamonte & Roeder (2009)
Morpholexical	Negation with deleted auxiliary in Scots, e.g., *I na like it* ('I don't like it').	Smith & Durham (2019: 136–148)
Morphosyntactic	Negative concord: where both verb and indeterminate are negated but only one would be negated in Standard English, e.g., *I didn't do nothing* ('I didn't do anything').	Burnett *et al.* (2018)
Syntactic	Variation in the strategies used to mark discourse new entities, e.g., *my friend went to a garden centre* vs. *it was a garden centre that my friend went to* (where 'garden centre' is discourse new – i.e., it hasn't been mentioned in the preceding discourse).	Cheshire (2005a)

It is easy to see the four forms in Examples 1.1–1.4 as alternatives because, whichever of them occurs, the same word is still articulated. They are, quite literally, alternative ways of referencing the same *thing* (Winford 1984: 269). Importantly, the forms in Examples 1.1–1.4 have no inherent value in themselves. They reference a sign vehicle ('th'), but not because they have any underlying properties that intrinsically mean 'th'; they are arbitrary pairings of sound and sign vehicle (Romaine 1984: 410). This arbitrariness frees phonemes up to be carriers of social meaning. Although not all alternates necessarily carry social meaning, if forms are used variably in discourse and across communities of speakers, they are potential carriers of social meaning. In the absence of any intrinsic meaning, linguistic variants like those in Examples 1.1–1.4 can take on social meanings via associations with who uses them and when.

However, unlike phonetic variants, grammatical constructions are composed of contentful morphemes and words. And the way in which these are ordered determines how constructions function. For instance, in the expression *Georgia's boyfriend*, the word 'Georgia's' is comprised of the proper name 'Georgia' and the morpheme 's', which denote a person and her possession of 'a boyfriend', respectively. Similarly, in a sentence like *He were bad*, the verb *were* denotes 'being', but its form also references tense (past) and person (third person in Georgia's usage). Furthermore, there are grammatical rules about where *were* can appear in the string of words that contain it.

Nonetheless, some grammatical variants involve alterations in what is produced in a clearly circumscribed linguistic 'slot'. For instance, in the case of Definite Article Reduction (DAR), we are dealing with different ways in which the word *the* is articulated. Similarly, with morpholexical variants, like the use of *na* in Scots, there may be a simple process of deletion at work, rather than an alternation or substitution of linguistic form(s) (Smith 2001). To some extent this makes these types of grammatical variants similar to phonetic variants in that it is a discrete and isolatable unit that varies (i.e., internal word structure or lexeme) rather than any kind of complex syntactic structure. However, the lower we get down Table 1.1, the harder it is to determine what 'slot' the variation falls into, and what the linguistic alternatives to a particular form might be. It also becomes more difficult to talk about the semantic equivalence of anything we might consider to be an alternative. If we think about morphosyntactic variation, this, by definition, involves some kind of structural alternation to form. For instance, with negative concord, there is repetition of negation via the use of multiple negative particles. Although, early on, Labov (1978: 5) argued that negative concord is 'by definition multiple negation with the same truth value as single negation', elsewhere, he has argued that the repetition of negative particles is intensifying (Labov 1984; Eckert & Labov 2017: 469) – something that could be argued to affect

1.1 What Is Grammatical Variation?

the state of affairs that is communicated. If negative concord communicates something different to standard negation by virtue of its grammatical structure, it becomes more difficult to think about standard negation and negative concord as functioning as simple linguistic alternatives.

As we move to the bottom of Table 1.1, the effects of grammatical configuration make it even more difficult to discern what counts as viable alternatives. The syntactic example in Table 1.1 references a study by Cheshire (2005a), who observed variation in how speakers introduce something new into their discourse. Imagine an interaction, where a garden centre is mentioned for the first time. There are many ways of introducing this discourse new entity. These could include the following:

Example 1.5 *it was a garden centre that my friend went to*

Example 1.6 *a garden centre, that was where my friend went to*

Example 1.7 *my friend went to a garden centre*

Examples 1.5 and 1.6 are both marked ways of highlighting that the garden centre is a discourse new entity. Example 1.5 uses an existential construction (*it was a garden centre that my friend went to*), and Example 1.6 has a left-dislocated component (*a garden centre, that was where my friend went to*). Cheshire found that the type of marked strategies illustrated in Examples 1.5 and 1.6 were used in similar ways (to highlight new information) by all speakers irrespective of their social background. However, most commonly, speakers didn't explicitly mark discourse new items – instead simply presenting them as bare noun phrases as in Example 1.7: *my friend went to a garden centre*. Unlike the marked discourse new strategies, the use of bare noun phrases did pattern sociolinguistically – with girls and working-class speakers more likely to use examples like those in Example 1.7 than boys and middle-class speakers. Cheshire argues that this is because boys and middle-class speakers tend to use marked discourse new strategies to highlight the discourse moments when key, factual, information is revealed, whereas girls and working-class speakers tend to be more focused on the affective content of their discourse, rather than its information structure.

Cheshire's study shows that decoding the social meaning of syntactic variants requires us to focus on the function of expressions rather than their form. In Cheshire's study, there is no clear 'linguistic slot' that bare noun phrases or marked discourse new entities fill. What makes these two strategies alternates is that they are both ways to present discourse new information. Furthermore, when Cheshire compares these forms, she finds that the sociolinguistic variation is rooted in pragmatics – it occurs where speakers are communicating different messages about their orientation to the discourse and their interlocutors. Unlike phonological variants, syntax can come with inbuilt dispositions to certain pragmatic functions. For instance, many of the constructions that Cheshire identifies as marking discourse new entities avoid placing the grammatical subject of the main clause in an initial position in the utterance. This violates the general principle of given-before-new information (Cheshire 2005a: 486). Consequently, the syntactic configuration itself (placing the new information at the beginning of the utterance) facilitates the articulation of certain pragmatic inferences (in this case, Cheshire's analysis suggests that the speaker is focused on communicating new, key, factual, referential information rather than on building interactional rapport).

The ability for syntactic constructions to encode pragmatic meaning by virtue of their grammatical configuration makes them quite different from phonological variants. It is a difference that has long been recognised (Lavandera 1978; Dines 1980; Romaine 1984; Cheshire 1987, 1999, 2005a; Cameron & Schwenter 2013), but the focus on phonetics and phonology in sociolinguistics has hindered our understanding of the relationship between grammatical variation and social meaning. In the next section, I outline the way in which this book attempts to explore the relationship between grammatical variation and social meaning.

1.2 How Will This Book Examine the Relationship between Grammar and Social Meaning?

So far, the vast majority of work on grammatical variation in sociolinguistics has focused on morpholexical and morphosyntactic variation. This work has been important in demonstrating how these types of grammatical variable correlate with macrosocial categories such as social class, gender, age and ethnicity (see Tagliamonte 2012 for an overview). However, the extent to which grammatical variation can encode these and other types of social meaning remains unclear. For this reason, the social meanings associated with different types of grammatical variable will be explored in Chapters 4–7, which form the analysis chapters in this volume. In order to increase our understanding of a wider range of grammatical variables, Chapters 4 and 5 will apply new methods to the study of traditional morpholexical and morphosyntactic variables, whereas Chapters 6 and 7 will focus on less frequently studied and more 'purely' syntactic phenomenon.

The research that has been undertaken on morpholexical and morphosyntactic variation has suggested that these variables are less subject to social evaluation than phonological variables (Labov 1993; Labov 2001: 28; Levon & Buchstaller 2015) and that the types of social meaning they index are more restricted than those typically found for phonological alternatives (Eckert 2019a: 758–759). In particular, it has been suggested that, because these variables are the focus of educational attention in a way that phonological variation is not, they develop social meanings directly associated with social class and institutional orientation (Eckert 2019a: 758–762). However, few studies of syntax have given serious consideration to the local contexts in which language operates. This means that our understanding of the social meaning of syntax is dominated by correlations between linguistic forms and demographic categories (to the extent that variants are depicted as being 'working-class', for instance). More significantly, the social meanings of categories have been inferred in line with dominant ideologies about class. That is to say, research has highlighted outsider perspectives on the meaning of working-class practice. This is despite the fact that the notion of covert prestige (coined by Labov as far back as 1972) implies that speakers orient to localised linguistic variants on the basis of social meanings which differ from overt prestige norms. Whilst it may well be the case that the social meanings of grammatical items are more likely to be limited to those associated with social class and institutional orientation, we simply do not have sufficient data to evaluate the extent to which this is true.

Part of the focus on category-linked social meanings stems from research suggesting that whilst we can continue to acquire lexical and morphologically conditioned changes across our lifespan, syntactic change is more difficult to acquire as we age (Kerswill 1996). If there are psycholinguistic conditions on the acquisition of syntax, then what we learn in childhood may constitute a default style of speech: 'the form first learned, most perfectly acquired, which we use automatically and unthinkingly' (Labov 2013: 3). This style will reflect the circumstances (place/time) of our acquisition. Although there is evidence for the 'cognitive primacy' of what we acquire in childhood (Sharma 2018: 26), there also remains insufficient data about the extent to which we can adapt or change our use of grammar, irrespective of the social meanings it encodes.

By focusing on the range of social meanings that can be articulated by a linguistic variant of the type most frequently studied in sociolinguistics (what I have earlier referred to as 'levelled *were*'), Chapter 4 will consider the extent to which speakers use morpholexical/morphosyntactic variation in stylistically sophisticated ways. More specifically it will suggest that speakers can adapt their use of these variables providing that (i) they have access to them (i.e., they are available in their input) and (ii) that they are motivated to use them by virtue of their utility as a social symbol.

The variant studied in Chapter 4, levelled *were*, is situated on the boundary between morpholexis and morphosyntax. What other factors do we need to consider when we examine a variable that is more firmly morphosyntactic in character? Recall that the social meanings of grammatical variants which are structurally embedded are likely to be tied to their semantics. This makes it vital that any exploration of social meaning includes consideration of the pragmatic meanings that a form's semantics and structure permits it to portray. Earlier, we noted that the repetition of negation via the use of additional negative particles in negative concord can be intensifying. But we also know that negative concord is 'arguably the most common stigmatized variable in the English language' (Eckert 2000: 216). Does the pragmatics of the repetition of negative particles have any role to play in the social meaning of negative concord, or has its social stigma bleached out this pragmatic function? We will explore the balance between social association and pragmatics in Chapter 5 via a study of negative concord.

Both of the variables studied in Chapters 4 and 5 match the profile of the highly stigmatized grammatical variant. However, Chapters 6 and 7 will move beyond this prototypical variant type to explore more purely syntactic variation that does not easily conform to notions of stigma and nonstandardness. The pragmatic utility of syntactic forms – like those used to introduce discourse new entities – may be common to all speakers, even if they are used at varying frequencies. For these linguistic forms, variation is not necessarily driven by the variety one acquires in childhood and how this variety is placed along the axis of prestige and stigma, but by pragmatic utility and communicative need. That is to say, differences in social meaning that are rooted in the pragmatics of a construction may engender differences in how frequently certain groups use a linguistic form. Put more simply, whether or not an individual uses a particular syntactic item might depend upon 'what speakers choose to talk about' (Cheshire 2005b: 99) and, perhaps more importantly, *how* they choose to talk about it. The linguistic form studied in Chapter 6 is right dislocation. This structure consists of a tag at the right periphery of a clause, such as *She's fun, my mum*. The tag ('my mum') is co-referential with the preceding subject or object pronoun (the subject pronoun 'she' in the example). Right dislocation is very common in informal spoken language – even people who do not consider themselves to have a local dialect will use it from time to time. However, its precise grammatical composition can vary. Consequently, Chapter 6 will consider how the precise grammatical environment in which these forms occur may intensify or attenuate their pragmatic effect, such that – despite the universality of their occurrence – different social groups interact with this variable in socially meaningful and socially nuanced ways.

Chapters 4–6 focus on occurrences of discrete grammatical items. However, syntactic variants are contentful: they don't just differ by their syntactic structure, they also differ by their lexical content and, in speech, by their phonetic content. Do these different levels of linguistic architecture work individually or synergistically to create social meaning? The focus on phonetics and phonology in sociolinguistics has meant that we are a long way from understanding how different elements of language might work in related ways to affect social meaning. As Eckert and Labov (2017: 485) note, 'the

1.2 The Relationship Between Grammar and Social Meaning 13

realization of a phonological variable is a short (and frequent) event in a syntactic series of events'. Consequently, it is likely that the nature of 'a syntactic event' will constrain the precise social meaning articulated by any of its constituent parts. For this reason, we will think about the relationship between syntax and other types of linguistic structure in Chapter 7. By examining tag question constructions (like the example, *He were bad, though, weren't he?*, in Extract 1.1), Chapter 7 will show how grammatical environment can work synergistically with other levels of linguistic architecture – including phonetics – to create social meaning. This chapter will attempt to propose recommendations for how to better integrate the study of syntactic variation into a wider understanding of the social meaning of language more generally. In this chapter, we will also think about whether the universality of syntactic variables like tag questions (i.e., variables that everyone uses to some extent to express interactional positioning), means that they do not acquire the types of social meanings found for other linguistic variables.

The chapters described so far, (Chapters 4–7), form the data analysis chapters in this book. But, of course, sound empirical analysis relies upon good quality data. Chapter 2 will present the ethnography on which this book is based. The ethnography took place in a school, Midlan High, and this institution will be contextualised socially and geographically. The social groups within the school will also be described. This chapter will reflect upon the fieldwork process and the intricacies of doing fieldwork within an educational context. It will also discuss the types of linguistic data collected during the ethnography, and reflect upon their relationship to other types of data typically collected in variationist research, and ways of categorising speakers in studies of linguistic variation.

Sound empirical analysis also draws upon (and refines) theories about a particular set of concepts. Understanding the social meaning of linguistic variation requires that we study language as it relates to social practice and forms of social engagement. Chapter 3 will more deeply interrogate how we study social meaning and the processes involved in meaning making. What concepts do we need to know to understand how social meaning develops and what techniques are required to understand how these concepts operate? The ways in which variationist sociolinguists have examined the social meaning of linguistic variation, with a specific focus on how these have been applied to the study of grammatical variation, will be considered in Chapter 3. Given that social meaning may interact with pragmatics, this chapter will also highlight the need to combine research on the pragmatics of spoken language with variationist work on the social embedding and social distribution of linguistic variables.

The research described in Chapters 4–7 will demonstrate how grammatical variation contributes to the social meanings and styles that the young people of

Midlan High articulate in everyday interaction. Drawing upon the range of grammatical variables studied in the preceding chapters, Chapter 8 will argue that grammatical variables are subject to social evaluation just as phonological variables are, but that the type of grammatical variable may affect the types of social meaning associated with the specific variable studied. Consequently, the final chapter of this book will reflect upon what it means to view grammar as fluid, flexible and as a social resource. Educational linguists have pointed out the benefits of teaching grammar explicitly to school pupils, but have noted that this teaching is most effective when grammar is presented as a semiotic resource for meaning making (Myhill *et al.* 2012; Myhill 2018). However, it has been argued that current educational policy not only shapes how teachers conceptualise grammar (as rigid and inflexible), it also encourages negative and potentially damaging responses to any deviations from the standard variety of a language (Cushing 2019a, 2019b, 2020; Hudson 2016). This is despite there being no significant evidence that speaking in a localised dialect affects literacy (Snell & Andrews 2017), or that children's literacy improves by decontextualised grammar teaching (Elley 1994; Hudson 2001; Wyse 2001; Andrews *et al.* 2004). This chapter will reflect upon the wider implications of foregrounding social meaning in our understanding of grammar. What are the potential benefits of viewing style shifting as a form of linguistic skill that children already have at their disposal? In this way, the final chapter of this volume will seek to apply the theoretical discussion of previous chapters in order to evaluate (and generate) the impact of the research. I began this chapter by talking about social class, and this final chapter will demonstrate how misconceptions about grammar and its social meaning help to perpetuate class-based social inequalities.

The following pages contain discussions of data I collected, but my analysis is rooted in the words of the lively, fascinating, vibrant young people of Midlan High. As I hope to make apparent in what follows, their discourse doesn't just facilitate our understanding of the social meaning of language; the young people of Midlan High use language to actively animate their social world. In order to redefine models of grammatical variation on the one hand, and better inform debates about how children use language to make social meaning on the other, we need to properly appreciate the social and pragmatic functions of the grammatical features embedded in ordinary people's everyday use of language. With this in mind, the next chapter introduces the young people of Midlan High.

2   The Social Landscape of Midlan High

It's lunchtime at Midlan High and I'm in the corridor outside one of the Year 8 form rooms, chatting with Tanya, Scarlet, Melanie and Susan. Tanya's trying to persuade me to join them in the canteen for lunch, but Melanie is anxious to get to the IT room because she needs to finish a piece of coursework. As I'm talking to these girls, we hear a disruption in the form room. It's centred around a table of girls who are sitting by the radiator at the front of the room. Tanya tells me that one of the girls at the table, Katie, has been causing trouble and telling lies. Katie said that Helen, another of the girls at the table, has really muscly legs, and Helen is not happy. It turns out that Katie is annoyed because she has not been invited to Helen's house at the weekend; the other girls have all been invited to have pizza and watch a video. Katie was supposed to be going to the cinema with Alex, but Alex is now planning to go to Helen's and she did not tell Katie why she had changed their plans. As the arguing intensifies, a group of about ten girls wearing coats adorned with sports' labels, who have been sitting on tables at the back of the room, get up and make a circle around Helen, Katie and Alex. They are chanting, 'Fight, fight.' Helen leaves them and comes over to me. She tells me the argument isn't her fault; she had not not invited Katie – she had just happened to mention the party to Alex because she didn't want to leave anyone out, but now it has just escalated into a big row (although when challenged later by Alex, Helen is not willing to issue an invite to Katie). Her friend Catherine gives her a big hug and tells her it's not her fault – she is just too nice and trying to please everyone. Helen goes back to her friends at the table near the radiator; they hug her and tell her Alex is a drama queen. A dinner lady appears and, ignoring Alex and Katie, who are still arguing, tells the girls from the back of the room to calm down, sit on the chairs and take off their coats. Some of them take off their coats (some don't), but those who do put them back on again as soon as the dinner lady has left the room.

(adapted from fieldwork notes, p. 60)

I had been visiting Midlan High for about six weeks when this scene unfolded. It was the Autumn term. The colder weather meant that students were allowed into their form rooms at lunchtime (the time I typically visited the school each day), but not all of the students used the form rooms in the same way. Girls like Tanya, Scarlet, Melanie and Susan went in there to drop off their bags after their classes, but they did not typically linger there. They went for lunch in the snack bar, often using a dinner pass to jump the queue because they had a sports' practice, were helping a teacher with an administrative task, or – as with Melanie – they had some work to finish in one of the school's workrooms. Other people called these girls 'Geeks'.

Unlike the Geeks, the other two groups of girls used the form rooms territorially. If they weren't getting lunch in the canteen, girls like Helen and Alex would sit at the same table, at the front of the room, near the radiator (sometimes complaining about the lack of heat it emitted, or the state of the curtains adorning the windows which lined the same wall as the radiator). Most of the girls sitting at this table lived in a small settlement, 'Eden Village', which was a few miles bus ride from the school. Their home address was elite and rural. They weren't the only girls in their year who lived in Eden Village, but they were the only girls whose peer networks were almost exclusively limited to friendships with others from their home village.

The Eden Villagers rarely went to the back of the room. This was the domain of a large group, the 'Populars', whose volume and number made them an imposing presence during the lunch break. The Populars were always on the look-out for action. Sometimes they created this for themselves, by flicking elastic bands at each other, or throwing around the bags that had been put in the room for safe-keeping. At other times, they would suddenly get up and rush out at the report of some drama elsewhere in the school. Popular girls tended not to use the canteen or the snack bar (preferring to eat their own food, or food that had been sneaked in from the local chippy), but some would leave the form room to smoke (although sometimes they would just do this through an open window).

These groups – the Geeks, the Eden Villagers, and the Populars (and the group that would later split off from the Populars, the Townies) – embodied distinct forms of social practice. The distinctions between them – which include their variable use of linguistic features – offer a window on the social functions of linguistic variation. To fully understand the dynamism of their social practice, and the semiotic function of their linguistic variation, it is necessary to have a detailed understanding of the world they inhabit. This world is described below. The nature of at least some of these groupings will be familiar to you if you attended a state-funded British high school; there is nothing particularly unique about Midlan High. The institutional context – in which different types of kids orient to differing activities, engagements and relationships – brings about distinctions which echo across time and space. Several linguistic ethnographies document opposing groups which are variously pro- or anti-school (Eckert 2000; Lawson 2009; Kirkham 2013; Alam 2015; Gates 2019; Quist 2021). However, the social and geographical location of the school undoubtedly determines the precise nature of social groupings within it. Young people across time and space continue to be constrained by the same forms of societal structure – perhaps, most principally in Britain, by social class (Hargreaves 1967; Lacey 1970; Willis 1977; Ball 1981) and its intersection with race, ethnicity and gender (Reay 2004; Abbas 2007; Vincent *et al.* 2013). As subsequent chapters will show, young people's response to these constraints is determined by their access to forms of social participation and their motivation to engage with them. Consequently, whilst the local forms of participation and interactional stances detailed in this chapter are linked to social structures, like class (via a process of 'fractal recursivity'; Irvine & Gal 2000: 38), the social groups of Midlan High also create the social order they inhabit on the ground.

2.1 Situating Midlan High

Midlan High is a community secondary school situated in Bolton, a town in the north-west of the English county of Greater Manchester (see Figure 2.1). It provides mixed-gender education for children aged between eleven and

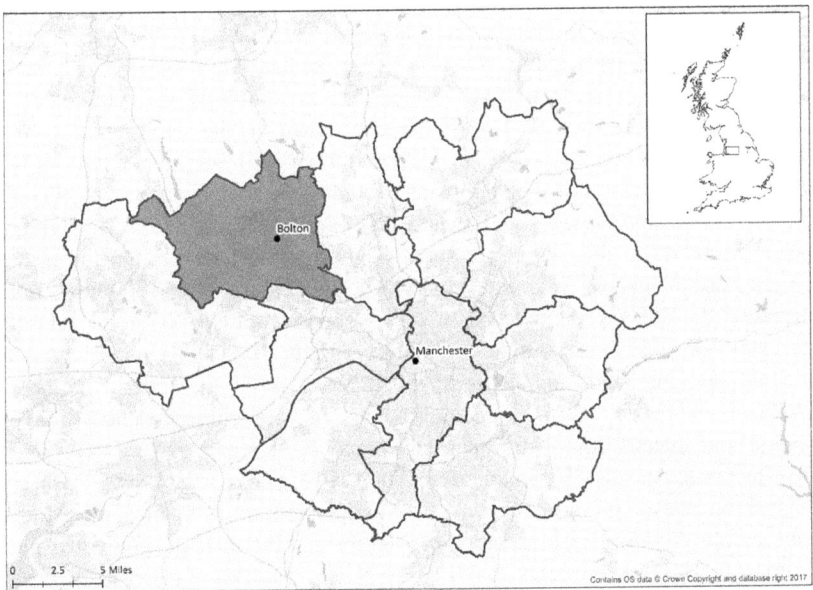

Figure 2.1 The location of Bolton, in relation to the city of Manchester, the county of Greater Manchester, and the rest of England, Scotland and Wales. (This work is based on data provided through EDINA UKBORDERS with the support of the ESRC and JISC and uses boundary material which is copyright of the Crown. © Crown Copyright/database right 2017. An Ordnance Survey/EDINA supplied service.)

nineteen. The school is in the district of Green Vale (a pseudonym, as is Midlan High and all participants' names in this book), an area detached from intense urbanisation. Despite its semi-rural status (the adjacent landscape contains farmland, country parks, reservoirs, heritage centres and moorland), Green Vale contains discreet reminders of Bolton's sociocultural history. During the second half of the nineteenth century and the first half of the twentieth century, Bolton played a key role in the Industrial Revolution. The town was not only one of the chief centres of the UK textiles industry (with over 300 mills operating in 1922), but also a major producer of the coal that supported this activity (Shorrocks 1998: 15). Although Bolton's textiles industry declined in the 1960s (relatively late, considering that the national decline of this industry began in the 1920s), the landscape around Midlan High retains some of the (much sought-after) stone-clad cottages and terraces which housed weavers and, later, mill workers, and old mill buildings (many of which have been converted into prestigious apartments).

Picturesque Green Vale is a desirable place to live because it is close to the modern facilities of Bolton town centre, yet sufficiently distanced to escape the problems associated with inner-city urban areas. A report completed by the Office for Standards in Education, Children's Services and Skills (Ofsted) when the study's participants were attending Midlan High, notes that Green Vale has more families from higher social class backgrounds and with experience of higher education than most schools. However, the same report notes that the school's intake is much wider than Green Vale (it extends into more highly urbanised areas of social housing), making the socioeconomic profile of the pupils broadly average. This means that pupils at Midlan High (including those discussed in this book) are some of the most privileged and the most socially disadvantaged. In contrast, however, the ethnic profile of pupils is not diverse – the Oftsed report recorded only 4.0 per cent of pupils in the school as identifying as Black, Asian or minority-ethnic. The study's participants include one girl with Indian heritage, and one with dual ethnic heritage (African and White British). Ethnographies of multicultural schools have shown that intersections between social practice, race and ethnicity can and do effect language use (Kirkham 2013; Alam 2015; Gates 2019). I urge readers to seek out these ethnographies to better understand issues of race and ethnicity, as the predominantly monoethnic nature of Midlan High precluded me from examining these effects in this study. As I did not want to erase the girls with minority-ethnic heritage from the study on the basis of their heritage, both were included in the data analysed here. Significantly, neither of the two girls spoke English as a second language (the Ofsted report noted that there were no pupils aged eleven to sixteen in the school identified as having language needs resulting from not having English as a first language). I do not identify them further to ensure their anonymity.

2.2 Places and Spaces within Midlan High

Midlan High is well-established: it has stood at the heart of Green Vale for several years. It is made up of a secondary school (providing education for those aged between eleven and sixteen) and a sixth form (educating sixteen- to nineteen-year-olds). When the fieldwork was completed, it comprised one main two-storey building, a sports centre and two temporary outbuildings (one containing classrooms and the other the sixth form block), tennis courts and an all-weather pitch. The school is always oversubscribed and one of the consequences of overcrowding is that every room capable of holding thirty or so pupils is used as a form-room (a room where pupils are registered each day by the same member of staff who is their form tutor). In warmer weather, pupils are made to go outside at break times, but they are permitted indoors in cooler weather. As pupils are banned from science labs and technology rooms, this leaves few classrooms in which pupils may socialise.

As staff discourage individuals from hanging out in the corridors (although these areas are always full of people), many pupils continue to spend time outside, even in the winter months. The main yard area consists of a long avenue between the main building and temporary outbuildings. This avenue leads to a paved area and a grassy incline which itself leads to the all-weather pitch. Young people run about in this area, or sit around on the grass – sometimes alternating between the two. Groups of young people walk up and down the avenue – some stroll up and down, arm-in-arm, others are intimidating in big groups that stride purposefully on their way to their next cigarette. Some pupils hang around the doorways of the main building, sitting on railings and shouting things at their peers as they pass. All of this space is available as a resource to the young people, although it is patrolled by staff.

In addition to this main yard area, there are pockets of outdoor space that are less heavily monitored by the staff because they are located in gaps between sections of the main building. In one section, there are some benches and young people sit together – too many of them squashed onto one seat, some sitting on the floor. Some of the Populars stand around or lean against the outer wall in these areas, cupping cigarettes in their hands, although the usual place for smoking is behind the sixth form block where there are a few trees. This space gives the Populars something to hide behind. The staff don't like them hanging around in big groups, so they break up – a couple of pupils to each tree. They finish their smoke and then group together again to walk back up the avenue. The other place the Populars go to smoke is the all-weather pitch. Although there is nothing to hide behind out there, the pitch is far enough from the main building to discourage the staff from venturing out to it too often; when staff do come out there, it is possible to see them coming.

Very little ground in the school is rejected as a spatial resource. Even the smaller outdoor areas within the main school building are exploited – these include two quads of land between the corridors of this building. The first of these is known as 'the Fence' as there is a walkway alongside a fenced-off grass area. Geeks jostle to stand in the doorway halfway along the walkway or perch themselves on the top of the fence, play-fighting and pushing each other off. The second of the small internal quads, the 'staff room quad', provides a walkway from the main entrance to one side of the school. This walkway runs alongside the staff-room. It should be no surprise that this quad is used almost exclusively as a route from and to the school's main entrance. Sometimes there are younger pupils who sit alongside the opposite wall from the staff-room, but these tend to be just odd couples talking quietly, or even just people sitting alone. None of the young people described in this chapter lingered in this space for long.

How Midlan Highers use the landscape is far from random. As different groups move within the school, preferring one place over another, space takes on meaning, and a key part of the ethnography was understanding how this space was inhabited and by whom. To examine this further, I now turn to a more detailed account of the ethnography.

2.3 The Process of Ethnography

2.3.1 *A Way In*

My arrival into the social fabric of Midlan High was facilitated by my previous associations with some of the school's pupils. Partly as a trial-run at fieldwork, and partly as a way to develop networks amongst young people, I had offered my services to a youth theatre in Bolton town centre three months before I began my visits to Midlan High. The youth theatre was producing a play about the town which involved young people aged between twelve and twenty-five, including pupils from a number of local schools. I explained my research to the group's leaders and they agreed to allow me access to rehearsals, in return for which I helped out backstage during the performances.

I was already familiar with the youth theatre as I had been a member of the group for many years. Consequently, when I was introduced to the members of the youth theatre, they were told that I was someone from the '18+' workshop group (a group for those aged eighteen and over) who was helping out backstage. This meant that the young people perceived me as one of them; that is, a youth theatre member (albeit older), rather than a youth theatre leader. This status was supported by the older youth theatre members who knew me from previous work we had done together.

As the production progressed, and I got to know the young people very well, I started to explain that I was working on a project for university about Bolton

2.3 The Process of Ethnography

and the young people who lived in the town. On the whole, the youth theatre members were interested and enthusiastic about the idea of me coming into their schools to hang out with them and their friends. Once I'd found out which schools were represented at the youth theatre, I wrote to the relevant schools explaining my research and requesting access to their students.

In the end, only two schools replied: Midlan High, of course, and another school, which had been my own secondary school. I went into both schools to meet with senior staff, who agreed to me coming into the schools at lunchtime. My plan was to network through the schools, starting with the young people I knew from the youth theatre, and I spent June and July going into both schools. This was hard work because I had to divide my attention between two focus points. In the time I had to think during the summer holidays, I decided that I had underestimated the demands of ethnography; so when I returned to my fieldwork in September, I only went back to Midlan High. My decision was based on the fact that I had fewer ties to this school than I had to my own old high school, so I had fewer preconceived ideas about the school's social structure. Also, I had no relationships with the staff at Midlan High. This was an important difference as, at my old high school, teachers approached me as an old acquaintance, and this was hindering the development of my relationship with the young people.

2.3.2 My Role as Ethnographer

I was twenty-four years old when I started my fieldwork at Midlan High. I had lived my whole life in Bolton, in an area less socioeconomically prosperous than Green Vale. I was still living at home with my parents and had lived at home all through my university education. This wasn't just for financial reasons, although my parents' income was low enough that I qualified for tuition fee funding. I was too scared to leave home. Nobody in my family had ever gone away to university. Despite their abilities and intellectual curiosity, my parents hadn't gone to university at all, although my older sister had done a vocational course at a local university. I had been offered a place at the University of Exeter but, when it came down to it, I couldn't make myself go. I took up a place at the University of Manchester, where I completed all of my academic degrees.

I did this fieldwork as part of my PhD project. When I started my PhD, I still didn't feel like I fitted in at the University of Manchester. After developing an anxiety disorder during my undergraduate degree, I had developed strategies to cope with the university environment, but I certainly didn't feel like an academic. I also still felt like I would never want to leave Bolton. I was doing a PhD because my supervisors told me I could do it, the Arts and Humanities Research Council had generously funded it, and my parents told me I could do whatever I put my mind to (without pressurising me to do anything). As

I noted in Chapter 1, Sociolinguistics had saved me at university; it explained how I felt in every university classroom and the explanation wasn't that I was stupid or inadequate. I was doing a PhD because I felt strongly about how people wrote about 'the working class' and the dialects associated with them. I wanted to do ethnography because I didn't know how else to make working class people sound real.

Nobody likes to highlight the difficulties they have experienced, but I have written about mine for two important reasons. Firstly, when I entered the university system, I spent a long time trying to hide my background but now I want to be seen. Secondly, and of more relevance to this book, this information helps you to read my ethnography. What follows is not a 'view from nowhere' (Gal & Irvine 1995: 995). What I noted in the school was influenced by my own experience as someone from the same town. It was also influenced by my own experience of education. I had done well at school, but my experience at university helped me to see that this was because I had been lucky enough to have my parents, and to have encountered adults along the way who had taken time to listen to and support me. I might have been trying to hide, but others had seen me.

I tried to see everyone in the ethnography. This was difficult; because of the authoritarian role of staff in schools, young people are deeply suspicious of adults who show interest in their activities. They are aware that adults have privileges to which they don't have access, including the right to determine institutional rules and norms of behaviour. I certainly felt this distrust at the start of my fieldwork at Midlan High. However, this suspicion was alleviated in two ways. Firstly, as mentioned above, I was only twenty-four when I completed the fieldwork and the school had a sixth form, where some students were nineteen. Sixth-form students were allowed to dress in their own clothes and had many of their lessons in the same buildings as the younger students. Consequently, because I was relatively young compared to the majority of teachers and dressed more like a student than a teacher, several younger students just assumed I was a sixth-form student. Although this meant they treated me with some degree of suspicion, they did not associate me with institutional authority. Perhaps more importantly, some of the adults in the school mistook me for a sixth form student. I only ever went into the same spaces that the students were allowed into. I never went into the staff room and only went into staff offices when – much like the school's students – I needed to request something from the teachers. I had to wear a visitor's badge, but even that was confiscated six months into the fieldwork when a dinnerlady[1] didn't believe I was in legitimate

---

[1] Dinnerladies are untrained staff who look after children during the school lunchbreak. The name is clearly gendered but so is the role – I have never encountered a male dinner supervisor. All the dinnertime supervisors were women at Midlan High.

possession of it. Dinnerladies told me to remove my coat, like they told the young people to, and even when I explained to them why I was in school, they would often challenge me if they found us recording in an empty classroom.

I didn't see many of the teachers, as my fieldwork took place during the lunch break when there were no lessons. When I did encounter teachers, I was usually challenged rather than treated like an ally. This had a positive effect on my relationship with the young people as the following excerpt from my field notes indicates:

As we were talking, a teacher approached me and said that she'd seen me around and wondered what I was doing in school. I had to explain about being a student and doing some research. She asked what I was researching and who my point of contact was. Although the teacher was very pleasant, I felt quite uncomfortable about this questioning and how it made me look to the pupils. However, in a way, it was quite a positive experience, because the pupils realised that I was as vulnerable to the authority of the staff as they were. They explained that the woman was one of the deputy heads and that they didn't like her very much. This sparked off a bit of a conversation about the teachers in general. (adapted from fieldwork notes, p. 57)

The second factor that affected how the young people perceived me was my prior acquaintance with some of them through the youth theatre. This meant that I was usually introduced as a friend of a friend. The fact that the young people who I already knew were very comfortable with me meant that their friends were also put at ease. Having someone to vouch for my authenticity and integrity was extremely important to my progress through school networks, but it also determined the way I progressed through the different social groups. Although I mixed well with the individuals introduced to me by my youth theatre associates, other friendship groups then perceived me as a friend of that original group. If there was any animosity or bad-feeling between groups, it was much harder for me to appear neutral if I was already perceived as associated with a rival group. For this reason, I always had to work harder to be accepted by the groups that I met later in my fieldwork, as I discuss below.

That said, the longer I was in school, the more people became curious about my intentions and brave enough to ask questions about it. Information about the project I was working on was more widely disseminated and I had to do less explaining, even if I had to do the same level of convincing at times. I tried various ways to explain my research and quickly discovered which made sense and which didn't. I told individuals that I was working on a project about the school and its students. This in itself was a satisfactory explanation, but young people would occasionally ask why the project was so prolonged. They seemed to have trouble reconciling the amount of time I spent working on the project with their concept of coursework or study requirements. I tried explaining about the PhD but they found this hard to comprehend. In the end, I found it easiest to say that I was writing a book. This had meaning to the young people and was also a reasonably accurate depiction of the PhD thesis that I wrote soon after I finished my ethnography. Of course, as you will now realise, it has taken me many more years to write this book.

I discovered that the young people were happier with a simple explanation. My desire to be as honest as possible with them meant that I would offer protracted explanations that were neither required nor appreciated. More often than I was disappointed by rejection, I was surprised by how much information the young people offered with so few assurances of my integrity. They wanted to talk. I felt privileged to have them share their lives with me, but was always conscious of my responsibility to them. Their eagerness to talk suggested that conversations with non-judgemental, interested adults were hard to come by and were perceived as worthwhile by the young people themselves, even if the adult's credentials were unknown. This eagerness to talk meant that some young people approached me even before I had chance to network into their social niche. More often, though, I would start talking to a particular individual who would introduce me to a group of friends who had been waiting for me to find them. I quickly learnt that the success of my relationship with some groups depended on the position of the individual I found first, and what happened next. I explain the effects of this when I describe the individual groups below.

2.3.3   *The Trajectory of the Ethnography*

At the beginning of my fieldwork at Midlan High, some of the youth theatre members would meet me when I arrived in school at the beginning of the lunchbreak. However, these initial meetings weren't ideal because, although the kids were in the same youth theatre show, they didn't normally hang out together at school because of their differing ages. Over the first couple of weeks of my fieldwork, I found myself spending more time with one girl, Tanya, and her friends in particular. Tanya was in Year 8 when I started my fieldwork. Year 8 students are aged between twelve and thirteen and in their second year of secondary school. The Year group comprised eight different form groups of mixed abilities (although pupils were banded for ability in their Maths, Science, French and English classes). Although I made efforts to interact with as many people from this Year group as possible, the majority of the participants in my study came from two of the Year 8 form groups that I initially met when I started the ethnography. Although it was completely fortuitous, it turned out that this was an ideal group to study. In Year 8, the young people were still a little constrained by who they had known from their feeder primary schools, but they were beginning to shift their friendships in a way which was more firmly consolidated as the ethnography progressed in Years 9 and 10.

2.3 The Process of Ethnography

I spent about a month in the school before the summer break and then resumed my field work when the young people returned as Year 9 pupils in the following September (the British school year runs from September to the following July). I went in almost every school day for the whole of the young people's time in Year 9, with a break between April and June when I was on a study trip overseas (during which, some of the young people wrote to me). Some days I would arrange to meet someone in advance and we would go for lunch, or to wherever their friends were hanging out; on other days, I would just wander around, trying to engage young people in conversation. As time went on, and I met more people, it was easy to just arrive at school and fall in with someone that I knew.

I first recorded interactions with the study's participants in the October when the participants were in Year 9 (so after two months of visiting, not counting the summer vacation). Most of these recordings were completed in the lunch hour, although some took place after school. I returned to the school when the pupils were in Year 10, solely to conduct recordings. In these final stages of the data collection (when the informants were aged between fourteen and fifteen), the school permitted me to take young people out of their Personal, Social and Health Education classes to record them.

Recordings always took place after I had hung out with the recordees on at least one prior occasion. Most participants seemed more at ease talking with their friends and, for this reason, the majority of recordings were with groups of between two and four friends. I always let the young people choose their own recording partners in order to make them feel as comfortable as possible. However, towards the end of the fieldwork, as the young people became increasingly confident, several were happy to be recorded alone; a small number of these one-to-one recordings are included in the dataset. Recordings were made using a tape recorder and an omnidirectional table-top microphone, although wired tie-clip radio microphones were used in early recordings (less successfully, because the young people often moved around). Recordings were subsequently transcribed in full and digitised.

The recordings were an extension of my regular interactions with the young people. My goal was to see each set of individuals in the school in context. The young people knew that I was interested in them, and the recording sessions offered them a chance to give permanence to their accounts of themselves. They clearly used the sessions as a way to record their activities. They would discuss events between themselves and encourage each other to tell me about particular occurrences. Sometimes, groups would approach me and say that they needed to 'do taping' in order to tell me about a specific event which they felt I should be aware of. This suggested that these groups were using the recordings as a kind of diary of their lives. The process benefitted from the advent of reality TV shows – where individuals present their lives to the camera – which provided the pupils with a way to contextualise the recording process. In most cases, my input to recordings was minimal. I would ask questions if I misunderstood the conversation or if there were particular issues I wanted to hear about, but I never questioned individuals using a structured questionnaire. In fact, I sometimes found myself answering the questions of my informants rather than vice versa. As our relationships developed, the young people learnt about me, just as I learnt about them, and this reflects some alleviation of power asymmetries in the data I collected.

2.3.4   The Gender Problem

I recorded all who offered, but I also made efforts to pursue individuals who were under-represented in the dataset. Nonetheless, I found myself spending more time with girls than with boys, and girls were much more willing to be recorded than boys were (none of the students identified as non-binary or gender non-conforming when the study was undertaken – something that would likely be very different if the ethnography were repeated today). The majority of boys that I came into contact with were those who had girls as friends. I found it extremely difficult to break into male-dominated networks. In the middle of the fieldwork, I made a concerted effort to engage with boys at the school, with some success, but even then I felt that our interactions were very different to those I had been experiencing with the girls. The girls – irrespective of social group – became comfortable with me. In January, when the young people were in Year 9, I had a conversation with a Popular girl, Tina, who asked me if I were visiting any other schools. When I said I was just coming into Midlan High, she nodded and said, 'That must be easier, because you fit in here now' (fieldwork notes, p. 238). Conversely, the boys continued to see me as an outsider. A few days after the conversation with Tina, I was speaking to Kara, a Geek girl, who was asking me why I was spending so much time trying to record the boys. She noted how the boys had been talking about me earlier, but that they were struggling to recall my name and kept calling me 'Miss'. Kara thought this was funny because I wasn't 'Miss' – 'just Emma' (fieldwork notes, p. 243). One boy in particular would consistently make pig noises or references to 'bacon' whenever he passed me, despite strong reassurances from the girls that I was not an undercover police officer and that I could be trusted to keep confidences. When I did record boys, they would often mess about or play fight instead of talking to one another – on one occasion a group of boys started writing on the tables during a recording and then chased each other around the room, climbing over the tables as they did so (fieldwork notes, p. 291–292).

This behaviour seemed, in part, to be a consequence of the life stage of my informants, and the emergence of sexual identity. The passage from childhood to adult social spheres, and the subsequent development of a sexual marketplace, is accompanied by an altered awareness of gender-related issues (Thorne 1993; Eckert 2011, 2014). This fact alone brings different psychological conditions to the fieldwork situation. I clearly identified as female and was clearly older than the young people at the school. Whereas many of the girls I spoke to commonly hung out with, and had relationships with, older boys, none of the boys I spoke to hung out with older girls (other than siblings at home). Whereas the girls tended to see me as an older version of themselves (my fieldwork notes record how the girls – irrespective of social group – often assumed that I was more like them than I was like girls from the other social groups), it was clear that the boys didn't know how to position me.

Whilst other researchers have experienced similar difficulties in relating to young people whose gender differs from their own (Lawson 2009), or have chosen to study only those whose gender matches their own (Mendoza-Denton 2008; Alam 2015), the reluctance of the boys to engage with me may reflect a failing in my own skills as an ethnographer. There are several linguistic ethnographies which contrast young male and female participants (Snell 2008; Bucholtz 2011; Kirkham 2013; Fox 2015; Drummond 2018b; Gates 2019). These have exposed telling differences in how males and females use linguistic variation. Eckert (1989, 2000) provides an insightful account of the differences in how male and female adolescents use sociolinguistic variation, suggesting that language is a more significant resource for girls than for boys; whereas boys use their actions and abilities to mark out social differentiation, girls instead focus on self-presentation and linguistic presentation (Eckert 1998). However, other studies have minimised the agency of female speakers and/or questioned their abilities to engage with the range of social identities found for their male peers (Cheshire 1982; Ilbury 2019). Outside the field of linguistics, seminal work in youth cultural studies focused on males exclusively (Willis 1977; Hebdige 1979), to the extent that '[m]any scholars considered youth culture to be a male preserve almost by definition' (Bucholtz 2002: 536). This was despite research in the same era showing girls did indeed construct agentive and coherent stylistic practices (McRobbie 2000).

The predominance of girls in my sample troubled me for a time, but I was more concerned with providing an accurate, vivid, account of young people's sociolinguistic practice. By focusing only on female participants, this study aims to provide a rich account of the many complex and diverse ways in which female speakers use sociolinguistic variation. It seeks to go beyond earlier stereotypes of female students as passive and to explore the extent of female social differentiation within the school system. On these grounds, I make no apologies for my focus upon female participants in this study.

2.4 The Social Groups at Midlan High

In the following sections, I outline the different female social groups that I observed at Midlan High. These groups may be more accurately defined as communities of practice. Communities of practice were introduced into sociolinguistics by Eckert and McConnell-Ginet (1992), but the community of practice was an analytical domain first used by Lave and Wenger (1991) to describe how individuals learn their place as social beings. It describes a group of people who mutually engage in a jointly shared endeavour; the endeavour being such that it leads to the construction of a shared set of resources. It is not a social group who share a particular social characteristic, nor is it a set of individuals who are co-present in the same space; it is a group whose shared activity results in the production of shared practices. Via mutual engagement, a community of practice 'develops ways of doing things, views, values, power relations, ways of talking' (Eckert 2006: 683).

Table 2.1 provides a list of the names of the individuals, according to social group, who were included in the linguistic analysis that is provided in subsequent chapters. This does not include all of the individuals who were identified as members of these groups during the ethnography. This is because not all group members agreed to be recorded and, of those that did, not all were recorded over the two years that recordings took place (when the young people were in Year 9, aged between thirteen and fourteen, and when they were in Year 10, aged between fourteen and fifteen). To ensure continuity across the two years of recordings, only those individuals who were recorded over both years are included in the data analysis presented in Chapters 4–7. The

Table 2.1 *Participants included in the linguistic analysis, by social group*

Eden Village	Geeks	Populars	Townies
Alex	Caroline	Annabel	Amanda
Helen	Faye	Beverley	Ellie
Leah	Jennifer	Cindy	Meg
Lucy	Kara	Georgia	
Ruth	Louise	Kim	
	Melanie	Lindsey	
	Michelle	Marie	
	Susan	Sally	
	Suzanne	Tina	
	Tanya		
N=5	N=10	N=9	N=3

2.4 The Social Groups at Midlan High

Table 2.2 *Number of words included in the corpus for the data analysis, by social group*

Eden Village	Geeks	Populars	Townies
38,667	98,232	75,964	49,244

differences in the number of individuals included in each social group reflect the ethnographic facts rather than sampling bias. As Table 2.2 indicates, substantial data was collected from all groups, yielding sufficient data for quantitative analysis.

2.4.1 Eden Villagers

The Eden Village (EV) girls kept their distance from me for a long time. I was first introduced to them at the very beginning of my research, but five months passed before I recorded a breakthrough in my field notes. In the intervening period, I was aware that the girls were observing and assessing me, and their subsequent questions and requests for reassurance revealed their suspicion of me. I never achieved the easy companionship with the EV girls that I had with the other social groups, but they did warm to me as the fieldwork progressed. Perhaps surprisingly, acceptance from the EV girls seemed to coincide with me becoming more integrated into the Popular community of practice, and spending less time with the Geeks. Although this may have been a coincidence, it did reflect the EV girls' tendency to eschew explicit displays of compliance with school authority. Whilst many of the Geek and EV characteristics overlapped (in particular those related to learning and institutional success), unlike the Geeks, the EV group did not engage in many school-based extracurricular activities. Whilst the people present in the Geek group altered daily, depending on who was helping out a teacher, or finishing some coursework, the EV girls had quite a rigid lunchtime routine. They always ate lunch as a group in the school dining hall – taking over a large table and reserving seats for one another. The rest of the time they could usually be found in their form room. Their desks were at the front of the class and they hung around this area. Occasionally, they would go outside to the main yard area, but only rarely (and usually only if their access to the form room was prohibited for some reason).

Although both the Populars and the EVs exhibited forms of noncompliance with the school's authority, the Populars actively opposed the school's authority by clashing with it, whereas the EV girls articulated a position as being better than, or beyond the reach of, the school authority. They would complain about the lack of nutrition in school food, or the school's inability to maintain discipline. When they committed minor transgressions (for instance, not lining up neatly at lunchtime), they would laugh off the adults' attempts to point them out. The sense that the EV girls were 'above the law' was not without foundation. For instance, in Year 9, Ruth was given a detention for speaking to a boy in class, but she managed to get herself excused from this by simply agreeing to write out a list of dos and don'ts for the teacher (fieldwork notes, p. 279).

This stance did not mean that the EV girls didn't do well at school, or that they didn't prize academic achievement. They were in the higher bands for classes that were streamed and they were proud of their accomplishments. As Extract 2.1 shows, they were ambitious and knew that doing well at school facilitated that ambition, but they also knew the social necessity of not boasting about their accomplishments (ll. 9–12).

Extract 2.1

```
 1  EM  I think there's some people who kind of like do well at school, but are like
 2      embarrassed about it.
 3  H   I'm not embarrassed about – by it, at all.
 4  L   Neither am I.
 5  H   If I do well at school, I tell everybody (LAUGHING).
 6  L   (LAUGHS)
 7  H   I know it's stupid. But I'm really pleased – proud of myself.
 8  L   Yeah.
 9  H   I don't.. brag obviously, cos I'm not that sort of person. But I'm not embarrassed by
10      it, cos why should you be? You know. It's good that you've.. But I'm not – I do care
11      about my school work but it doesn't mean I'm actually good at every subject
12      (LAUGHS).
```
(Helen and Lucy 51A: 806–817)

As this extract indicates, the EV girls were accomplished social engineers (note Helen's cautious addendum mitigating her claim to have done well). Alex told me that a central EV girl, Ruth, had been well-liked at primary school and, when I spoke to Ruth about other girls, she had warm things to say about several of the Popular girls, despite me only ever seeing her interact with one of them (Sally) who went to the same dancing class as her. In contrast, the Geek girls never said anything nice about the Popular girls. One day, the Populars started up a game of flicking elastic bands at other people in the form room. The Geeks would generally just leave the form room (if they were even there in the first place) when this kind of thing happened. On the other hand, the EV girls just got themselves out of the way of the action (by moving their seats) until it blew over (fieldwork notes, p. 170).

In their recordings, the EV girls were reluctant to comment negatively on anyone, and emphasised the closeness of their friendship group. This made them a very visible collective. However, their narrative of group collaboration was undermined by a clear hierarchical structure. Ruth and Leah were at the top of this hierarchy but they had quite distinct roles. Ruth was a clear leader, with lots of authority – Helen and Lucy were always with Ruth, and tended to follow her lead. Ruth was the gatekeeper, who initially inhibited my interactions with the EV girls. In the beginning, Ruth would either explicitly ignore me, or politely say hello but indirectly indicate her hostility:

the [EV] group certainly seems to be quite exclusive and has its own personal jokes, which seem to be led by Ruth. She talked a lot whilst we were at lunch – organising what was going on and criticising people. She had a dig at Katie because she had spent too much on her lunch and now didn't have enough to get the bus. She said, 'Fancy not working out how much your lunch is going to be'. ... She does talk to me sometimes but seems quite reluctant to be around me; for instance, she made a point of telling me that her and the other girls wouldn't be coming outside with me and Tanya because they wanted to stay indoors. She did ask the others what they wanted to do but it was more a case of 'I want to stay inside... What do you want to do?' (fieldwork notes, p. 29)

Leah was much more independent and was always very confident in her interactions with me and others. Unlike the other EV girls, she would sometimes hang out with some of the Geeks, but this didn't seem to affect her standing in the EV group. In contrast, the fifth EV girl in the data analysis, Alex, was more of a loner, and much more peripheral to the EV community of practice. It seemed that the rest of the group tolerated her because she lived near them and had grown up with them, but Ruth would often police her behaviour. For instance, I noted that 'Alex seems to irritate a lot of the girls and has trouble saying the right thing to them. When I was sitting near them, she started messing with a cut on her hand and ... Ruth was pretty disgusted by it and told her to stop being so gross' (adapted from fieldnotes, p. 172). Squabbles tended to be quickly dismissed, however. When Helen was bickering with a peripheral Eden Village girl, Catherine, she told me that their group of friends was always falling out with each other, because they spent too much time together. However, as if to counterbalance this overtly negative statement, Ruth and Helen immediately hugged, then Ruth ran over to mock-fight Catherine before eventually hugging her too (fieldwork notes, p. 181).

The closeness of this group was undoubtedly facilitated by their shared home address. Outside school, they pursued interests such as watching television at each other houses, dancing, or shopping for clothes in the town centre. The geographical isolation of Eden Village meant that these girls were often reliant upon parents for transportation; consequently, shopping, dancing or cinema trips were sanctioned and aided by their parents. They were all regular visitors at each other's houses and were known to each other's families – 'family time' being something they emphasised. The girls were aware of how their home address was perceived: Ruth told me that she knew some thought that people from her village were posh (fieldwork notes, p. 90). Indeed, some of the Geeks explicitly described the EV girls as "quite posh and stuck up and ... well-off financially" (fieldwork notes, p. 15), and one of the Popular girls, Tina, impersonated Ruth and Alex by standardising her dialect and talking about horse-riding (fieldwork notes, p. 242) although, in reality, only Alex rode horses.

Their financial circumstances would sometimes become apparent around engagement in certain activities – for instance, birthdays and present-buying were important. On Lucy's birthday, I was asked which of two bracelets she was wearing I preferred. One had been bought by Leah, and another by someone not in the EV group. My fieldwork notes (p. 289) record that I knew it was a loaded question and all of the girls were quick to assert that Leah's, more expensive-looking present, was the best. Where EV girls were critical of others, they would often be indirect in this way, for instance, by criticising an accessory, rather than the person gifting or wearing a particular item. Ruth, Helen and Lucy's discussion in Extract 2.2 shows how they took care over their appearance and wore lots of 'smart and grown up' (l. 9) 'girly clothes' (l. 1) and colours (l. 22). Although the school had a uniform policy, they also had several non-uniform days when it was possible to more clearly evaluate how different communities of practice dressed. EV girls described their clothing style as 'trendy' and 'girlie' and I observed them dressing in feminine styles.

Extract 2.2

```
1   R    Yeah. Me, Helen and Lucy are into sort of like.. girly clothes and.. [jeans] and boots.
2   H                                                                          [Yeah.]
3
4   L    I don't care [what I wear like] inside the house,
5   H                 [Individual.]
6
7   L    but when I go out, I like.. make an effort (LAUGHS).
8
9   H    I like – I like to [look quite smart and grown up as well.]
10  R                       [Like Kay – Kay likes] wearing like jeans and these=
11  L                                                                          =gothic=
12  R                                                                                 =awful black
13       tops. You know, with the hoods [sort of thing that all the –]
14  H                                   [Yeah. I'm not into that.]
15
16  L    Off-spring.
17
18  H    I like – [I wouldn't –]
19  L            [Umm.]
20
21  R    Oh, they're [horrible. They're so not] flattering at all.. at all.
22  H               [I wear strong colours.]
```

(Ruth, Helen and Lucy 32A: 1541–1558)

If I am honest, the Eden Village girls were the group I felt like I knew the least, but that in itself reveals something about their dynamic: they were an exclusive clique.

2.4.2 The Geeks

The Geeks were the first young people I encountered at Midlan High (via my social ties to Tanya). They were less cohesive than some of the other social groups, but there was no doubt that they constituted a community of practice. Their activities united them in a shared endeavour within the school, but they inhabited a fuzzy area in the sense that they lacked the focused 'cliquiness' of the Eden Village girls, or the mass visibility of the Populars.

The Populars referred to these girls as *Geeks*. The term was clearly derogatory and never used in self-identification (although see Bucholtz 1996 for reclaiming of the 'geek' label in the United States). However, these girls were intensely proud of their orientation. They would talk about their achievements openly, boasting about how hard they worked and about never getting detentions or skiving classes. They explicitly talked about class tests and homework and personal successes in them. Although they had looser networks than some of the other communities of practice, they arose as a community of practice by virtue of their shared disapproval of other groups in the school and shared mutual engagement in school-orientated activity. From this, they developed a joint enterprise as they designed identities that stood in opposition to the Popular group, in particular.

Some of the Geek girls shared networks with Leah and Alex from the Eden Village group, but these networks seemed to be contained within the school day. In fact, even within the wider Geek community of practice, girls did not engage actively together outside school. This was a consequence of a more heterogeneous geographical background, and the fact that many Geek girls were engaged in out-of-school pursuits (sports, drama, dancing, music) which occupied much of their leisure time. Time left after these pursuits was usually spent with the family.

However, within school, Geek girls joined together in their active participation in the school's internal structure, contributing to a variety of school clubs and extracurricular activities (including school bands, orchestras and sports teams). These activities either took place at lunchtime or after school. Two of the Geek girls, Caroline and Michelle, would often do filing and administrative work for one of their teachers at lunchtime. This afforded certain privileges, such as having a dinner pass which allowed them to skip the queue (in Northern England, the lunchtime meal is known as 'dinner'). On one occasion, Caroline and Michelle had been enthusiastic about being recorded and we were trying to find a free room to use, with little success. They suggested using a room that was kept locked and retrieved the key from the teacher's office. When I expressed concern about this, they assured me that they were allowed to do this. When we returned the key, the teacher was back in her office and, although she seemed uneasy about the girls' taking the key, there was no reprimand when Caroline explained the circumstances. The girls also weren't reprimanded when they returned late to registration either. In my fieldwork notes, I observed that '[t]hese two seem to conform to the school rules the majority of the time and receive a lot of trust in return from the teachers. Consequently, they can manipulate this trust to their advantage and seem to reap several benefits from it' (fieldwork notes, p. 144).

As Extract 2.3 illustrates, Geek girls see school as important (ll. 1–2) for social advancement (ll. 4–5) and future growth (ll. 6–7). It is something to be enjoyed and its activities embraced as opportunities.

Extract 2.3

```
1   L   Like school is quite an important [part..]
2   S                                    [Yeah, it's] an important.. thing.
3
4   S   Not only cos you're – you – you – cos you can socialise with people there as well
5       and.. stuff like that and..
6   L   People just see it as a waste of time cos you don't like look ahead and think about the
7       future and that they might need it in the future and..
8
9   S   Um. That's why they just.. They just don't.. like – well, they don't think – I bet – I bet
10      they actually do like school a little [bit, you know..]
11  L                                         [Umm.]
12
13  L   Yeah, [it's] like more of a face they put on.
14  S         [But..]
```

(Louise and Suzanne 39A: 634–644)

Geek girls tended to lunch in the snack bar (but also used the main dining hall on occasion). Later on in my fieldwork (towards the end of Year 9), if the Geek girls were free at lunchtime, they started to hang out in the quad that they called 'the Fence'. This space became increasingly important as a resource in their construction of identity. Geek girls rarely hung out in the form room – preferring the Fence or the main yard area. Some school-orientated boys would also hang out at the Fence. In Year 8, Geek girls had platonic friendships with boys – they would sometimes talk about who they fancied, but interest in boys was quite heavily criticised and policed. This often led to girls falling out; for instance, Faye fell out with Beth and Kara because she perceived them to be flirting with boys (fieldwork notes, p. 32–33). Geeks girls would often fall out with one another and explicitly criticise each other, to the extent that I would sometimes lose track of who was talking to who over any given period.

In Year 9, I had a conversation with the Geek girls in which they asked about my boyfriend. Tanya became very embarrassed when a peripheral Geek (who had moved to Midlan High from another area of Bolton) asked if we had had sex. Tanya said that 'she'd talked to her mum about sex and couldn't imagine why anyone would want to do it' (fieldwork notes, p. 115). Not all of the Geek girls were like Tanya – indeed, I have notes on a conversation where they talked to me openly and candidly about what had happened in a sex education class (fieldwork notes, p. 21) – but the difference between how Geek (and Eden Village) girls talked about boys and how Populars engaged with them sexually was very stark – even late into Year 9 and into Year 10, when some Geek girls did have boyfriends.

The Geeks' contrast with the Popular girls was visible to me, but it was also something that the girls themselves recognised. For instance, when Geek girls discussed their social activities, they would often situate them positively in relation to Popular girls' activities. In Extract 2.4, Michelle and Caroline explain why their family-orientated or home-based activities, like visiting relatives (ll. 16–17) or watching TV (l. 36) are more fulfilling. Note that they are joined in their discussion by Alex (an Eden Village girl).

Extract 2.4

```
1   C    But .. It's all on a Friday night and [you see –]
2   M                                          [(TUTS) God. I he-, I hear them in like] Maths and
3        stuff. I heard them –
4
5   C    ['What you doing on Friday?']
6   M    [Actually I heard them today,] erm, 'Where you going tonight?' and everything.
7
8   C    ['I'll meet you here and..']
9   M    ['Are you going to Dunley?']
10
11  M    'I'll go park at ten o'clock' and all this.. an-
12
13  C    [I – I got back –]
14  M>   [I – I don't] find it like appealing, that, at all – [[going out, freezing cold,]] getting
15       drunk.
16  C                                                        [[ I got back from my auntie and
17       uncle's –]]
18
19  C    I got – got back from my auntie and uncle's at half past eleven on a – on a Friday
20       night and we were driving down the road and there was about a group of about twenty
21       of them stood on a corner like with massive bubble coats
22       on and you [could see –]
23  M                [Of our Year?]
24
25  C    N-, I don't know whether they're our Year – but you could see they were freezing
26       stood there like that
27  M    Yeah.
28
29  C    and what's the point at half eleven at [night,]
30  A                                           [I know.]
31
32  C    just stood there on a [corner doing nothing?]
33  A                          [I'd rather be tucked up in bed with [[a hot chocolate..]]
34  C                                                               [[So would I!]]
```

35	A	[..with – with loads of marshmallows and a flake in it.]
36	M	[Watching *Friends* and stuff.]
37		
38	M	I like doing that.

(Caroline, Michelle and Alexandra 2A: 396–424)

Of course, Geeks were also visibly different from Populars. The way Geeks dressed reflected their orientation towards practicality. As Extract 2.5 shows, they were unconcerned with wearing designer names (l. 38) and their clothing style was influenced by their parents' notions of quality and value (ll. 11–37). In general, they dressed in a mixture of smart tops, jeans and bright colours.

Extract 2.5

1	F	I've got – I've got two pairs of name trainers.. [right.]
2	T	[Oh my God,] I don't have that many.
3		
4	F	But one – one of them I can't wear them cos all the back's fallen down. I get one pair
5		a year for school and then I've got – I get a pair of tracky bottoms.. for school, and..
6		that's it. And I've got – and if I want anything else, I have to pay for it myself
7		
8	T	[My mum don't even – my mum doesn't even –]
9	F	[cos my mum refuses to pay 50 quid for a jumper] or something.
10		
11	T	My mum doesn't even let me buy my own stuff. I'm not allowed to buy my own
12		shoes. My dad – my dad got mad just cos I got these ones, [cos I had Kickers.]
13	J	[My mum doesn't mind]
14		paying like a lot of money, but if it's like 90 pound or something for
15		like a top, or, [like some pants] or something,
16	T	[(INAUDIBLE)]
17		
18	J	[she won't pay that.]
19	F	[My mum won't pay that.]
20		
21	J	She'll pay like – the most she'd pay on s-, on tracksuit bottoms or something – or a t-
22		shirt, is like 30 pound [and that's cos –]
23	F	[30 quid for a] tracksuit bottoms! I know, but all they have is
24		like – if you have Nike ones, they've got a little tick there, which most jumpers cover
25		up anyway, so..
26		
27	J	I know. I've got some Nike pants and the tick..
28		[is like there.]
29	F	[Yeah, the tick's on the seam] there, [[innit?]]
30	J	[[And then]] my top goes over it, so I don't see
31		the point in wearing it.
32		
33	J	But [now like my mum's] started buying me
34	T	[I only like –]
35		
36	J	like some like pants and like tops and everything instead of like tracksuit bottoms and
37		all that, [cos I don't –]
38	T	[I only get them] cos I like the colours. I don't bother doing it for names.

(Faye, Tanya and Jenny 3B: 417–445)

Towards the end of Year 9 and into Year 10, one of the Geek girls started to orientate towards a 'goth' persona, and her personal style influenced how some of the other Geek girls dressed. In expressing this style, Kara started dressing in dark clothes, dyed her hair black, wore dark eye make-up and painted her nails black. There was a group of pupils in the older years in the school who were clearly visible embodiments of this style (in fact, I was told that both the Head Boy and the Head Girl were goths). Had I continued my ethnography beyond Year 10, I suspect there would have been a more expansive adoption of this style amongst some of the Geek girls. Sadly, this development was not captured by this study. Nonetheless, the evolution of the Geeks was not surprising. As mentioned at the beginning of this section, this group was diverse and, as they aged, they seemed to settle into more subgroups. In Year 10, I even witnessed an emerging friendship between a Geek girl, Jennifer, and a Popular girl, Louise, as the Populars themselves were reorganised in response to the emergence of the Townies.

I had a really good relationship with the Geeks throughout the ethnography. We enjoyed each other's company and there was an easiness between us. This wasn't surprising: I had been a Geek in another time and place.

2.4.3   *Populars*

The Popular girls' attraction to, and involvement in, trouble meant that I heard about members of this group some time before I learnt to recognise who constituted this community of practice. The Popular community of practice only became visible to me in Year 9 with the arrival of the Autumn term when pupils were allowed back into the school buildings during the lunch break. These girls tended to hang around at the back of the form rooms and always seemed to be in large groups of anything up to ten girls. However, they never stayed in this area for long. In the early days of my interactions with these girls, I would often be chatting comfortably with them, when someone would rush in with a report of an altercation, and everyone would rush off and I'd be left alone (e.g., fieldwork notes, p. 64). Girls were constantly on the lookout for action – even during recording sessions. On one occasion, when I was recording Lindsey and Ellie, 'the room that we were taping in looked out onto the driveway of the school and ... the girls got really distracted by the number of people outside as this usually means that a fight is about to take place. They were both really excited about this prospect and became very animated' (fieldwork notes, p. 86). The girls also told me about fights that took place outside school, like the one described below:

Kim asked me if I had heard about the fight on Friday. She explained that there had been a fight on the park between some boys from Midlan and some boys from High Wood [another nearby school]. Kim said that Midlan didn't get on with High Wood and that the main boy involved was disliked by the Midlan boys. She said that he had ended up being really badly beaten and had to be taken to hospital. Everyone had pushed him and Kim said, that because he was so drunk, he had fallen back really sharply and smashed his head when everyone had pushed him. Kim explained that her and her friend had gone to tell his parents what was happening to him because he was getting beaten up so badly. His uncles had come to defend him and Kim said that they were carrying metal bars and the like. She said that they had gone mad at everyone and were trying to find out who had been involved. Kim didn't know what had happened to the boy since, but said that she knew he was badly enough beaten to go to hospital ... Although Kim was quite animated when she was talking about the fight, it was clear that she disagreed with its severity – this was clearly demonstrated in her going to the boy's house to get his parents. (fieldwork notes, p. 149)

Although fighting was an accepted practice, responses to fights would often include evaluations of their (unnecessary) severity and consideration of whether or not they were just or fair fights, as Kim's response to the fight described above suggests. In addition to getting help for the boy in the schools' fight, I witnessed Popular girls breaking up other fights that they considered to be unfair (fieldwork notes, p. 246). This suggested that fighting was exciting to them, but it also had to be fair – in the sense that the conflict needed to be justified and of a scale warranted by its cause.

The search for drama meant that the girls would often cruise around the school, filling the width of the corridor as they walked. Unlike the Eden Village and Geeks girls, these girls eschewed the 'official' lunching arrangements at the school; if they did use the snack bar or dining hall, they rarely lingered – simply grabbing food and moving on. Some of these girls smoked; consequently, they inhabited areas of the school where they could pursue this activity. I mentioned earlier that smokers often clustered behind the sixth-form block or out on the all-weather pitch and these were both areas used by the Popular girls.

Despite their orientation towards trouble, some of the Popular girls also engaged in school-related activities; the most significant of which were the regular talent shows held in the main hall at lunchtimes. Some Popular girls participated in dance classes outside school and, in Year 9 at least, those who did not were supportive of their friends (attending the competitions and cheering from the back row). Girls would practise dance routines in the sports hall, or even in the classroom, with their friends looking on. Other girls participated in school sports teams. However, Populars' participation in school activities was very much on their own terms. For instance, one of the Popular girls, Sally, talked enthusiastically about dancing, but also admitted that she was 'supposed to go to orchestra and PE activities' but that she didn't go to these (fieldwork notes, p. 89).

When I first associated with these girls in Year 9, they all regularly hung out together outside school – especially on a Friday night, which was the big night out for the group. The girls would meet up, usually in Green Vale, and hang out drinking around the local shops, on a nearby field, on in some of the back alleys behind the main street. These were local landmarks which were mentioned again and again in their narratives. The girls would also often sneak alcohol into the cinema. On one occasion, my parents had been to the cinema at the weekend, and told me about a bunch of young people being thrown out for being disruptive. When I went into school the following Monday, I found out it had been the group of Popular girls in my ethnography.

As Caroline's comments in Extract 2.4 suggest, Popular girls had a very recognisable style. The girls all dressed in branded sportswear (this could be top-to-toe gear, or a shirt/jumper mixed with jeans and trainers). Coat-wearing was also a highly significant practice. Pupils were not allowed to wear their coats inside the school and the dinner-staff would attempt to confiscate the coat of any pupil if she refused to remove it. I rarely saw the Popular girls without their coats on. If dinnerladies asked them to remove their coats, they typically would, but as soon as the member of staff had left the room, they would put the coat back on. This constituted a visible form of resistance against school policy. The Popular girls told me they felt harassed by the dinnerladies, who did seem to upbraid them for the smallest infraction. In fact, my acceptance by this group was facilitated by an incident involving a dinnerlady (fieldwork notes, p. 61). I was in the form room and different dinnerladies were persisting in coming in and telling the Popular kids to sit down and be quiet (it didn't strike me that they were being particularly rowdy). I suddenly found myself implicated when a dinnerlady approached me to ask me what I was doing. At the time, I was annoyed about this happening in front of this group, but it seemed to help as it aligned me with them. The girls then went on to talk about how the dinnerladies threw them out of the form-room if they weren't seen to be behaving, but they then complained that if they went outside as a result they were accused of smoking if they were in a big group. Their sense of injustice was a little undermined when one of the girls pointed out that they usually *were* smoking. This reveals that, whilst the dinnerladies' reactions to the Populars often seemed excessive, the girls did frequently and explicitly go against the school rules.

In addition to challenging school authority, Populars were also adept tricksters. One trick was asking people for a small amount of money (ten pence or even two pence). The amount was so small and the justification so reasonable (for instance, that it was needed to supplement lunch money), that the girls were often successful at gathering large sums of money. I soon realised that this was actually a competition, where girls would boast about having collected the most money (fieldwork notes, pp. 74, 106, 236, 244). Popular girls developed savvy strategies to prevent having to give over money to their peers – for instance, Lindsey once hid money in her shoes so that she couldn't be accused of not helping out a friend (fieldwork notes, p. 215).

After spending a long time anxious about how I would break into this group, when their acceptance came, it was swift, and the girls were friendly. They had clearly been waiting for me to talk to them. They were immediately open and talked about smoking, drinking, sex and boys. Nonetheless, it is important to note that whilst the Popular girls enjoyed drama, they often just sat around, talking to one another or engaging in witty sparring. They could be compassionate (for instance, by standing up for a girl who was being publicly humiliated by a teacher – fieldwork notes, p. 154), and they were loyal to their friends. On one occasion, Tina had been quite badly injured when a boy had flicked an elastic band in her face because she wouldn't give him some money. Despite clearly being in pain, Tina refused to report the incident or to seek medical attention because the boy 'had already been suspended and would be expelled if he was in more trouble' (fieldwork notes, p. 239). This generated a long discussion amongst the girls, who evaluated Tina's moral dilemma carefully. Tina didn't tell in the end, but the girls were overt in expressing their disapproval of him directly. This method of dealing with disagreements 'in-house' was typical of the Popular girls. It conflicted with how other girls resolved disagreements, for instance, by involving teachers to arbitrate over disagreements between them.

Whilst all the practices discussed above were shared between the group, girls participated in them to differing degrees. Towards the end of Year 9, shifts in behaviour allowed small differences to take on new significance. Three girls – Amanda, Ellie and Meg – started to hang around with a group of older boys and their Friday night social behaviour became more extreme, involving both sexual activity and drug-taking. This caused splits to emerge in the group as individuals took various stances towards this behaviour. Some girls started to avoid 'Friday night' altogether. On other occasions, girls would go out, but end up splintering off when the behaviour of others in the group became too extreme for them. In Extract 2.6, Lindsey and Beverley discuss the change in the Popular group between Years 8 and 9 and their location between the emerging subgroups (ll. 1–12). They then go on to talk about an occasion when some of the girls had been intimidated by the older boys with whom other group members were associating (ll. 18–36).

Extract 2.6

```
1  L   In Year 8, we'd all just sit round that table in our form. We'd all just have this
2          massive table to sit round. And now, it's changed into all – we're all set – sat in like
3          the groups that we hang around with. There's like Meg, Ellie and Tracy sit next to
4          each other, and then we sit – cos.. we're in between them all, aren't we?
5  B   Um.
6
7  L   Like    [we'll go out with Ellie and Meg..]
8  B           [We're sat between the two groups.]
9
```

```
10  L    ..but then we'll go out with Tina and Paula as well. So we're not either in one or the
11       other. We're both. But, erm.. Tina and that lot don't go out with Ellie and that, do
12       they? And then last week it was so annoying, right. Was it last week?
13       [Pete's?]
14  B    [What?] Pete's? Yeah.
15
16  L    Right, we went out on Friday night.. instead of going to the cinema. And we said..
17       And Paula said, 'Right, I'm coming out tonight' cos she never,
18       [ev-, ever comes out. And – and we seen] Pete, right.
19  B    [Ohh. This – this done – did my head in and all.]
20
21  L    And he said, 'Oh, I've got a free house.' So we went up to his house. We're just sat
22       there. And then all Roughley crew came down. There were about thirty people, so
23       [we were all just sat there, like that.]
24  B    [They're quite fit,] the Roughley [[crew.]]
25  L                                      [[So we]] just quickly ran up to his room, right. We
26       looked so sad. We were just sat in his house, like that.
27
28  E    (LAUGHS)
29  L    And then they said, 'You can come down, you know. We're not gonna twat you or
30       anything.' So we're like that, (LOOKING AROUND). So we came down, and then – then
31       Georgia, Sonia and, erm..
32  B    (LAUGHS)
33  L    Georgia, Sonia and Paula said, 'Aw, I wanna go,' so we all went, and then we were
34       just soot – s-, like sat in the middle of the road for about half an hour, deciding what
35       we were gonna do. And me, her, and.. Tina wanted to go back, and they were saying,
36       'No, no. I don't wanna go back.'
```
(Beverley and Lindsey 41A: 375–410)

By the time I returned to school after the summer vacation, as the participants were entering Year 10, this split had been reified: people were calling Amanda, Ellie and Meg *Townies*.

2.4.4 The Townies

People talked about Townies long before anyone participating in my study was identified as one. At the outset of the ethnography, I was worried that I wouldn't find different social groups, and this led to me asking my youth theatre contacts very direct questions about what social groups existed. They immediately talked about Townies, describing them as 'people who were a bit rough', who tended to 'wear a lot of gold jewellery and sports' labels' and 'baggy pants and puffer jackets', and that they were 'scrubbers' and 'slags' (fieldwork notes, p. 8). These contacts also told me explicitly that people only started to become Townies in Year 10. These early descriptions of Townie dress and adornment matched what I observed of Ellie, Meg and Amanda's style in late Year 9 as they started to split off from the Popular group, although the descriptions of Townie practice were subjective and pejorative evaluations of the assumed social class status and sexual morals of Townie girls more generally.

When other groups talked about the emergence of the Townies, they would identify Meg and Amanda as members of this group, but Ellie was always marked out as the iconic Townie. Her standing amongst her peers and her influence was notable from my first encounter with her:

Lindsey shouted over a girl called Ellie and said that I should talk to her because she always had lots of opinions. Ellie seemed to be very excited when she found out that I was interested in finding out people's opinions and was very keen to talk to me. As she showed more interest in me, other people began sitting closer and paying more attention, and even adding things to the conversation. People seemed to relax quite quickly and were soon talking about issues such as smoking and teachers... Ellie and Meg were talking quite openly about a friend of theirs smoking weed. I got the impression that this was quite a normal thing for these girls... (adapted from fieldwork notes, p. 60)

During that encounter, Ellie took responsibility for introducing me to everyone else in the group and facilitated my initial breakthrough into the Popular group. However, her influence with the wider Popular group waned somewhat as her Townie style developed. Whilst the Townie group were inevitably the focus of negative comment from Geek girls, who described them as 'bitches' (fieldwork notes, p. 71) – they were often unpleasant to the Geek girls: pushing past them, and attempting to intimidate them (e.g., fieldwork notes, p. 98) – the Populars also described the behaviour of the Townies negatively, as shown in Extract 2.7.

Extract 2.7

```
1   T   Actually, like I've got quite an attitude to some of my teachers.
2   C   Yeah you have, ant you?
3
4   (ALL LAUGH)
5
6   T   I've – I've only – I'll stick up for myself if they [say something.]
7   C                                                      [Yeah, she'll stick –]
8
9   C   She's not like –
10  T   And – and like they <i.e. Ellie, Meg & Amanda> do that as well, so it's not –
11  C   Yeah, but Ellie can go a bit over the top, like she'll sometimes throw a chair or
12      something if she gets angry.
```
(Tina and Cindy 37B: 483–494)

As Extract 2.7 suggests, whilst the Populars would stand up for themselves when challenged by teachers (ll. 1–7), Populars like Tina and Cindy considered the Townies to be too extreme (ll. 11–12). The Townies were often in trouble: one of them was internally suspended (this meant she was in ongoing detention for a period of time and not allowed to go to classes with her peers) after an incident where she injured a friend (fieldwork notes, p. 129). They could be disruptive in classes and physically fought with boys (fieldwork notes, p. 248). They had an especially bad relationship with the dinnerladies. The following occurred when I was recording them in a classroom:

The dinnerlady came in to see what we were doing. Ellie was extremely abusive and offensive – she showed no respect at all for the dinnerlady. Ellie spoke to her like she would speak to any other pupils she disliked. The dinnerlady came in again and tried to get Ellie to apologise for her behaviour, but Ellie wouldn't budge. Very embarrassing for me, but I didn't want to alienate Ellie by getting involved. (adapted from fieldwork notes, p. 222)

After this incident, I felt like I had to go and speak to the dinnerlady in case the incident jeopardised the ethnography. She told me that Ellie 'was a problem' and that they had yet to find a way to get her to behave (fieldwork notes, p. 223).

The Townies were also open about taking drugs: they carried drug paraphernalia and smoked cannabis in school. Their separation from the Popular group was, in large part, a consequence of this drug use and also their engagement with older boys. Just as the Populars critiqued Townies' 'extreme' behaviour, the Townies criticised their Popular peers for not being rebellious enough – for instance, when some of the Popular girls were planning to get drunk at the cinema, Meg described this 'as a waste of time', and talked instead about getting older boys to buy alcohol for her on a night out (fieldwork notes, p. 236). As the following shows, as time wore on, the Townies did not just criticise the Popular girls, but began to actively exclude them:

As we [me, Ellie and Amanda] are talking, Kim comes over. Ellie is very blunt and asks Kim to leave as are having a private conversation. Kim doesn't say anything but leaves looking angry and upset. (fieldwork notes, p. 271)

Amanda, Ellie and Meg were very conscious of the shift in their behaviour. They were keen to talk about their new activities and proud of their innovative status. This is clear in Amanda and Meg's attempt to distinguish themselves (l. 11) from the Popular girls (named in l. 5) in Extract 2.8.

Extract 2.8

1	EM	The question I've been asking everybody is, erm, d'you reckon you've changed since
2		I first came in in Year 8?
3	M	Yep.
4	A	Yeah... Well bad... God.
5	M	No, everyone like – all like Lindsey and Beverley and Paula and everybody, they've
6		all been saying, 'Oh, everybody's really changed,' because like this time last year, we
7		were all like proper good friends and everything. And we were all like, 'Ooo!' and all
8		that lot. And then, we all changed. It's us who's done it.
9		
10	A	[Yeah.]

44   The Social Landscape of Midlan High

11 M   [Me,] Ellie, Mandy, Tracy..
12
13 A   Sharon.
14 M   Now Sharon.
15 A   (LAUGHS)
16 M   Like, we're just fucked off our faces (LAUGHING).
17 A   I know.
18 M   No, because like I had my party and then we got in with all everybody at Green Vale
19   and.. and you just see how immature them lot all are.

(Amanda and Meg 40A: 76–94)

There was plenty not to like about how the Townies conducted themselves. They could be bullies, and their volatile behaviour was frightening at times. But they could be witty, intelligent, and self-aware. Whilst I did not always agree with their behaviour, I recognised that it reflected their need to use the resources available to them in order to assert their independence as autonomous young women.

2.5   Reflections and Limitations

This chapter has attempted to depict the social landscape of Midlan High in order to contextualise the language practices described in subsequent chapters. It reflects my personal experience of that landscape but it also draws upon extensive observation, fieldwork notes, and recordings and – where possible – on the participants' own interpretations of people, places and spaces.

When we attempt to make sense of any social landscape, the classification process can serve to reduce the extent of heterogeneity within that space. That is to say, in explaining the communities of practice at Midlan High, I risk giving them 'a concreteness they do not actually possess' (Wenger 1998: 61). Put another way, in outlining the prototypical activities, clothing and school orientation of each social group in this chapter, to some extent, I have abstracted away from the internal complexity of each community of practice. It is important to recognise this abstraction for what it is (an attempt to capture what is an essentially fluid concept) and remember that communities of practice are not fixed categories but 'organizing principles' (Eckert 1989: 20). Consequently, each group member will orient herself to the traits I have depicted in individual ways. I have tried to highlight where differences exist between group members, especially where differences relate to the composition and nature of the social group itself. For instance, the Eden Villagers are hierarchical (so girls differ in how they influence group norms), the Geeks are relatively diverse (and their shared practices are mostly contained within the school day), the Populars are reasonably consensual (but not all of them smoke, and only some of them are committed dancers, for instance), and the Townies are not all equally extreme in

2.5 Reflections and Limitations

their behaviour. Nonetheless, these social groups are salient because they are constructed by individuals who share a social enterprise; that is to say, each social group collectively constructs a way-to-be that differs enough from that constructed by the other groups to be recognised as something distinct. The analysis that follows seeks to test the extent to which these social groupings determine, constrain and explain linguistic behaviour.

This chapter has essentially focused on the distinct *styles* of each community of practice. Style can be defined 'as an emergent system of distinction (Irvine 2001), constituted by linguistic and other semiotic resources and practices that make distinction meaningful; it is ... mediated by ideologies of differentiation' (Zhang 2021: 268). The next chapter unpacks some of the processes which mediate the relationship between language and style. It does so in order to better understand the processes of meaning-making that occur in relation to language at Midlan High.

3 How Do We Study the Social Meaning of Grammatical Variation?

It took me months to learn how to fully interpret what was going on in the Midlan High landscape. Like every social space, Midlan High was packed with signs which provided clues about the people there, their relationships to one another, and to the space they inhabited. We can perceive or embody signs; they may be present in the things we sense, hear, say or do. For instance, on my first day at Midlan High, I noticed that some of the young people were wearing their coats indoors and others weren't. It turned out that the type of coat and, more specifically, when and where coats were worn, was highly significant.

Extract 3.1 provides information on how the Eden Village girls identify Populars and Townies according to their dress. Helen initially notes that this entails wearing 'weird stuff' (l. 5) but she quickly reframes this judgemental observation to one which focuses on the 'expectedness' of a dress code (l. 5). This discussion then moves to focus on the branding of the clothes and a number of fashion labels ('Fred Perry', l. 11; 'Henry Lloyd', l. 13; 'Rockport', l. 15; 'Helly Hanson', l. 21) and a sportwear shop (JJB, l. 35) are mentioned. The discussion then moves to focus on coat-wearing, with the Eden Villagers keen to disassociate themselves from the design and the brands identified as linking to the Populars and the Townies (ll. 25–39). Notably, Ruth implies that the dress-codes are linked to different concerns: Eden Villagers couldn't wear pull-over coats because it would mess up their hair (l. 38). This comment suggests that the Eden Villagers value a particularly neat personal appearance, and it carries the presupposition that the pull-over coat-wearers (the Populars and the Townies) are not concerned with orderly self-presentation.

Extracts 3.2 and 3.3 provide an alternative view of the stylistic choices discussed by the Eden Villagers in Extract 3.1. Both of these extracts discuss Townie Ellie's 'obsession' (Extract 3.2, l. 3) with a boy called Will. Will's coat is central to how he is identified and evaluated in both extracts. Both the colour and the brand of the coat are noted in Extract 3.2 (l. 9). The same information is used to identify him in Extract 3.3 (l. 16, l. 21), despite Extracts 3.2 and 3.3 involving different girls. Will's coat is further praised as 'boss' ('good, stylish'; Extract 3.3, l. 22) – a comment which seems to lead Ellie to subsequently focus on his attractiveness (being 'fit'; Extract 3.3, l. 23).

Extract 3.1

```
1   H    And there's like this thing that everyone should be wearing –
2        [everyone thinks you've gotta be wearing that.]
3   R    [Everyone should be wearing pants,] with their socks tucked in.
4
5   H    And all this weird stuff, and – well, not weird stuff, but, you know – what's expected,
6        you know.
7   L    Like when Chris dyed his hair –
8   R    Yeah.
9   L    – they were all asking why he'd done it. He was just going, 'Cos I want to,'
10       (LAUGHS).
11  R    And you're s'posed to be wearing like Fred Perry or –
12  L    Um (LAUGHS).
13  R    Henry Lloyd or (LAUGHS)..
14  H    Yeah.
15  L    Rockports.
16  H    Yeah.
17  L    (LAUGHS) Helen's got Rock Valley.
18  H    No, I don't, alright! (LAUGHS)
19
20  EM   They all have those coats – you know the ones that you put over your head
21       [and] they've got like Helly Hanson [[and –]]
22  R    [Yeah.]                              [[Yeah,]] Fred Perry.
23
24  R    Hair [on top.]
25  H         [I've just got an] Adidas fleecy-thing.
26
27  R    My Pilot coat [(LAUGHS).]
28  H                  [Yeah, that's nice, [[that.]]]
29  EM                                     [[It is nice.]]
30
31  R    It's my sister's.
32
33  (ALL LAUGH)
34
35  H    I have got a denim jacket. I don't really wear all these pull-over stuff from J [JB].
36  R                                                                                   [No].
37
38  R    It messes your hair up when you have to take it off (LAUGHS).
39  H    Yeah.
                               (Helen, Lucy, Ruth, Eden Village 32A: 1616–1655)
```

Extract 3.2

```
1   EM   Who is – who's Will? Cos Ellie's always talking about him and
2        [I don't know who he is.]
3   M    [Oh, she's obsessed.]
4
```

```
5    ... <identifying info omitted>
6
7   M    Erm –
8   K    He's –
9   M    He's got a blue Helly Hensen coat.
```
(Kim and Meg, Popular, Townie 10B: 36–46)

Extract 3.3

```
1   L      (LOOKING OUT THE WINDOW) Oh, is there [a fight?]
2   E                                              [Dinner –]
3
4   E M    Uh, there's summat going on. Are there a lot of fights?
5
6   E      Oh, yeah. [They're like every week.]
7   L                [It's good when there's fights. The whole] school'll just come out.
8
9   E      Scott Ward's there.
10
11  L      Yeah, [there'll be a -]
12  E            [(GASP) Will's there!] That's Will, that's Will!
13
14  E M    Which one?
15
16  E      You see the one in the blue coat? He's turning round now. He's just stopped and he's
17         facing us. [He's got –]
18  E M               [Oh, yeah, yeah.] [[He's got a red bit on him.]]
19  E                                  [[That's him, there.]]
20
21  E      The Helly Hanson coat, yeah. That's him, there. He's turning round now.
22  L      Oh, it's boss, his coat.
23  E      Oh, he's well fit.
```
(Ellie and Lindsey, Townie, Popular 6A: 704–728)

These interactions suggest that certain coats function as components of particular styles. However, it is not just the appearance of the coats that is significant, but also when and where coats are worn – that is to say, the wider practice around coat-wearing is important to decoding social meaning. The school didn't permit coats to be worn indoors but the Townies and several of the Populars did wear coats indoors. These girls were not cold. Their act of coat-wearing simultaneously signalled their disregard for the school as institution, and differentiated them (via appearance and practice) from the girls who embraced educational norms.

This chapter seeks to interrogate how social meaning is enacted via social and linguistic practice. It begins by deconstructing the components of signs, before considering how signs cluster to make actions and identities discernible. It then goes on to explore the role of ideology in mediating the relationship between signs and social meaning. Finally, the discussion moves to consider how all of these processes specifically operate in relation to the use of grammatical variants. Does the social meaning of grammar emerge in the same way as the social meaning of phonetic variation? Does the precise formulation of a grammatical variant determine the types of social meanings associated with it? To address how we answer these questions, this chapter also considers the types of data analysis required to decode the social meaning of grammar.

3.1 Interpreting Social Meaning

Peirce (1895: 13) describes signs as consisting of three parts: the sign vehicle, the object, and the interpretant. In the example discussed above, indoor-wearing of particular kinds of coats is the *sign vehicle*, the idea that this marked rebelliousness is the *object*, and the process by which this meaning was construed is the *interpretant*. Notably, Gal and Irvine (2019: 88) relabel the interpretant as *conjecture* to emphasise that it is the process through which we make guesses or hypothesise about possible social meanings. Understanding the social practice of coat-wearing required me to gain knowledge of the locale in which the coats were worn. I also needed to understand the relationship between coat-wearing and non-coat-wearing and, finally, I needed to appreciate the values or beliefs that framed the act of coat-wearing. Put another way, I needed to learn about the local context, and the contrasts and ideologies that circulated within it. Figure 3.1 schematises the three components of the sign for this example.

But, of course, coat-wearing was not the only behaviour that differentiated the young people at Midlan High from one another. The ability to interpret the social meaning of coat-wearing was dependent upon its co-occurrence with other social and linguistic practices which, collectively, constituted the interpretable *styles* described in Chapter 2. The concept of style has a particular history in sociolinguistics (see discussions in Eckert & Rickford 2001;

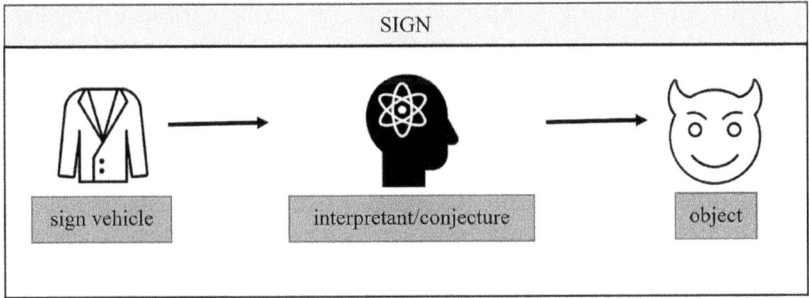

Figure 3.1 The three components of a sign, using the example of coat-wearing at Midlan High.

Coupland 2007; and Schilling 2013). The definition used in this book follows research in linguistic anthropology which characterises style as *distinctiveness* (Irvine 2001). In the example above, the Popular and Townie practices around coat-wearing were differentiated by their contrast with Eden Villager practices.

It is common to think about how we dress as a presentation of our distinctive taste in fashion, and style can reach into all aspects of our existence: the way we dress, how we move, the way we engage in certain activities and, importantly, how we vary our language. Perceiving a style is about recognising an identifiable way of being; we need to make sense of how semiotic material and practices combine. At Midlan High, coat-wearing practice became meaningful in the context of the divergent larger styles in which coats were worn or not worn. Some of the girls who wore their coats indoors also tended to wear make-up and items of gold jewellery. They tended to walk slowly, in groups, taking up the whole width of the corridor. They more frequently used grammatical constructions in their speech that differed from the ones they were taught to write down in their lessons. Ultimately, whilst Populars also sometimes wore coats indoors, indoor coat-wearing was most significant when it was readable as a component of Townie style. This style was explicitly labelled, but it's important to note that not all styles are reified in this way.

Personas (the plural can also be personae) are the embodiment of locally specific styles – someone with a Townie persona embodies Townie style. But styles can also be reified in relation to more general societal *social types*. We might recognise certain signs (such as items of clothing, ways of speaking, consumption of social media or spending behaviours) as components of working-class style, for example. The process of conjecture then involves the ideological interpretation of those signs. Importantly, the nature of conjecture is such that one person may end up interpreting a sign quite differently from another person. In the UK, working-class social types are often parodied in the media as feckless, uneducated and coarse (Bennett 2012). People who have that association are likely to link people perceived as working class, and by extension, the signs of working-class social types, to these negative attributes. However, for many people, being working class is associated with attributes such as resilience, honesty and plain-speaking. How we interpret signs, and the styles they constitute, depends upon our worldly experience and knowledge. If I have felt loved and safe in a working-class home, then I will tend to perceive working-class life (and the practices associated with it) in those terms. If all I know of working-class life is a consequence of secondary representations, then I will draw upon hegemonic narratives in my process of meaning-making. As Gal and Irvine (2019: 91) note, 'the presupposed start of any interpretation is attention and contrast within a frame of expected sameness'. If we know working-class life then we normalise it: it fits our frame of expected sameness and we rely on our experience to interpret it. If we don't know working-class

3.1 Interpreting Social Meaning

life, then our attention is heightened when it is encountered and we construe it in contrast to our own life via a process of 'othering' (Bellinger 2020).

The different construals of a sign vehicle and its object can seem quite distinct, but often there is an underlying 'kernel of similarity' (Podesva 2008) across construals. An underlying expression of candour or frankness can be interpreted as 'crude' by one person, or 'truthful' by another; importantly, both crudeness and truthfulness are linked to candour. A concrete example of this is how 'commonness' is construed by different girls at Midlan High. 'Common' is a term which depicts practices and behaviours associated with the working class. All girls recognise this meaning, but they construe it differently. For the Townies, being identified as 'common' can be a source of pride because it relates to toughness and resilience. Extract 3.4 shows that Amanda both values her commonness and prefers it as a designation (l. 3). She also believes she has stylistic control of it (l. 5), suggesting that she uses the signs of commonness to construct a specific persona. Note, Meg's laughter (l. 2, l. 4), though, which indicates that she considers Amanda's conjecture of commonness to be unusual. The unmarked construal of commonness is reflected in a discussion between Populars, Lindsey and Beverley. Extract 3.5 shows that, for the Populars, 'commonness' is something to be kept in check; it reflects badly on a person. Lindsey notes she has started to talk 'more common' because of her association with Beverley (l. 1). Beverley's strongly worded 'You're a cheeky bitch, you' (l. 3; see Chapter 6 for an exploration of this specific linguistic construction) and her horrified intake of breath when Lindsey states that her mum has noted the change in her speech (l. 6) demonstrates that Beverley clearly takes this as an insult as opposed to a source of pride.

Extract 3.4

1 A   I'm common. I know I'm common.
2 M   (LAUGHS)
3 A   I've always been common. I am. I'm no poshie. I'd rather be common than posh.
4 M   (LAUGHS)
5 A   I could get probably worse. So..

(Amanda and Meg, Townies, 55: 348–360)

Extract 3.5

1 L   I've started talking more common since I've been hanging around with you.
2
3 B   You're a cheeky bitch, you!   [You've been saying that non-stop.]
4 L   [You can't – even my] mum's said it.
5
6 B   (GASP)

(Beverley and Lindsey, Populars, 56A: 568–573)

Another example illustrating the importance of the wider style to sign conjecture is apparent in the discussion in Extract 3.1. One of the brands associated with Townies by Eden Villager, Lucy, is Rockport (l. 15). Rockport is a footwear manufacturer that describes itself as producing shoes that combine the comfort of an athletic shoe, with the style of a dress shoe[1]. In this way, Rockport's advertising depicts their footwear as both functional and smart. In a list of the best shoes for the elderly, the WalkJogRun website list them in the top ten.[2] Why would Townies wear shoes also enjoyed by the elderly? The kernel of similarity here is 'utilitarianism', which is drawn upon in quite distinct ways, dependent upon the larger style in which Rockport-wearing resides. In a senior person persona, this utilitarianism links to practicality, health and comfort. For the Townies, it links to toughness and resilience.

The fluidity of social meaning in these examples demonstrates the mutability of signs and the ideological nature of social meaning. The precise meaning of a sign is the outcome of an ideologically mediated interpretative process; what we believe about certain kinds of people determines what we notice as symbolic of their life and how we evaluate it. Importantly, what we notice is selective, and determined by where we are standing in the social landscape. In Chapter 2, it was noted how the Eden Village girls were perceived as 'posh'. A Popular girl, Tina, identified horse-riding (an expensive hobby which requires access to a horse, stabling facilities, specialised equipment and more) as indicative of this status. But, only one Eden Village girl (Alex) actually rode horses as a hobby. Whilst the link between horse-riding and the Eden Village persona was rooted in a grain of truth, the association was based on selective attention to a practice that corresponded with Tina's view of Eden Villagers: it was based on her beliefs about the kind of activities that go along with 'poshness', not empirical evidence of that association. This is, of course, the process of indexicality (Silverstein 1976; 2003; Ochs 1992) as articulated in linguistic anthropology.

Indexicality refers to a process of association, where a particular sign vehicle (e.g., 'horse-riding') is conjectured to co-occur with a perceived object (e.g., 'being posh'). In linguistic research, the object that a linguistic variant is frequently identified as pointing to is the typical user of that linguistic variant. The typical user may be reified as a persona ('Eden Village') or a social type ('Middle class'). Both personas and social types function as *character types* (Starr 2021) or, to use Agha's original term, *characterological figures* (Agha 2005; Johnstone 2017): they are the stereotyped embodiments of a recognised linguistic style. However, as Agha (2005: 38) notes, linguistic variants can index more than character types, they also index the forms of footing and alignment with which they typically co-occur. The term *stance* has been used to describe interactional moves which enact evaluation, positioning and/or alignment (Ochs 1992; Kiesling 2004; Du Bois 2007; Jaffe 2009; Gray &

---

[1] See www.rockport.co.uk/our-story; accessed 07/06/23.
[2] See www.walkjogrun.net/best-shoes-for-elderly-reviewed [last accessed 30 May 2023].

3.1 Interpreting Social Meaning

Biber 2012). Interactional moves may entail criticism or challenge, or they may entail being authoritative or knowledgeable. In language use, linguistic variants can index both stance and character type and, of course, stance and character type can be indexically linked to one another too, as explored further below.

Indexes are just one of the ways in which objects function in signification. Objects can also function as symbols and icons in Peirce's theory of signs. *Symbols* are the consequence of *convention*. Deciphering a symbol relies on reference to a specific delimited system. Grammatical items are symbols in as much as they denote a specific referential meaning. We know that Beverley is calling Lindsey 'a cheeky bitch' in Extract 3.5 because she uses the second-person pronoun 'you' which is conventionally used to refer to the specific person that a speaker is addressing. The sign vehicle 'you' refers to the object 'a specific interlocutor' by virtue of the structure of the English grammatical system. Symbols are the only type of sign recognised in Saussurian semiotics (Yakin & Totu 2014): they denote a relationship brought about through the conventional binding of a signifier and the signified. *Indexes*, on the other hand, are not governed by convention, but by *contiguity*: the co-occurrence of a sign vehicle and a social meaning in time and space – as we have seen. For instance, horse-riding is expensive, which results in contiguity of horse-riding and the presence of those with material resources and economic capital (i.e., those of a higher socioeconomic status). This association is indexical to the extent that horse-riding (the sign vehicle) and having money (the object) are conjectured as significantly contiguous. This contiguity results in horse-riding 'pointing to' having money and vice versa. Importantly, whilst all linguistic variants function as symbols, our understanding of their meaning also requires that we understand the indexical relations between linguistic variants and speech events or personas (what Silverstein (1985: 220) refers to as 'the total linguistic fact'). That Beverley uses 'you' to directly negatively evaluate Lindsey to her face is not socially neutral. This type of aggressive face-threatening act indicates something about the association between direct address (and the grammatical items used to produce it) and social persona, as we explore further in Chapter 6. All language systems are symbolic, but our understanding of spoken utterances also requires the ability to generate indexical knowledge through conjectures about the relationship between language and its place in the world.

In Peircean semiotics, objects can also function as *icons*. A stylised tick is an icon of a sportswear company. A depiction of a piece of fruit is an icon of a computer company. In these instances, both the sign vehicle and the object are used to symbolise one and the same thing. There is nothing 'natural' about the *resemblance*: it is culturally constructed. In the linguistic realm, onomatopoeia is an example of an iconic relation. As Eckert (2017: 1198) notes, a hiss (a prolonged articulation of /s/) iconically resembles a threat in English, most likely because of its association with dangerous creatures that hiss – such as snakes. In this case, the hiss itself seems to inherently depict a threat. However, *sound symbolism* (the association between an aural sign vehicle and an object) is culturally specific: something demonstrated by the fact that different languages construe animal noises in different ways (Kloe 1977). To give another example, smaller bodies are often perceived to emit higher frequency sounds (this is Ohala's (1994) *frequency code*, as discussed by Eckert (2017)). This occurs as a consequence of ideologies about pitch, gender and age. However, this is a cultural construction which is more prevalent in some cultures than others; Drager *et al.* (2021) demonstrate that, in Hawai'i, high pitch is actually associated with a *larger* body size, due to culturally specific ideologies about ethnicity and body size.

However, iconisation in language goes beyond sound symbolism. Linguistic variants can shift ground from being indexes to become icons when 'forms identified *as* linguistic, and taken up by specifically linguistic knowledge, are further construed as similar to (sharing qualia with) nonlinguistic phenomena' (Gal & Irvine 2019: 103). *Qualia* refers to the perception of sensation (Gal 2013): that something is sweet, oily or rough, for instance. Zhang (2008) shows how the 'smooth operator' persona is associated with increased use of rhoticity in Beijing Mandarin. The ideological association between slick smooth operators and rhoticity leads to the iconisation of rhoticity as 'oily' sounding. Here a linguistic variant is taken to resemble the perceived qualities of those associated with its occurrence. This occurs as a consequence of *rhematisation*. According to Peirce, a rheme is a sign 'that could be conjectured as iconic by some guesses, yet taken by others to be indexical, depending on the presuppositions and knowledge of those who make the guesses' (Gal & Irvine 2019: 106).

The tag question *innit* is a sign that is both indexical and iconic (i.e., it is rhematised) at Midlan High. This linguistic variant featured in the discussions of different features of language which took place towards the end of the fieldwork. As Extract 3.6 shows, for Eden Village girls, *innit* resembled Townieness (l. 6), a persona which they agree indexes brash confidence (i.e., 'being cocky'; ll. 33–37).

Extract 3.6

1 LE Ah, we don't really say 'ain't'. We say 'ant' or 'ent'.
2 EM What like – like 'in''e?', like at the bottom of example 4?
3 LE Um ... yeah.
4 EM Or 'innit?'
5
6 LE [No, we don't say 'innit'. That's Townies.]
7 R [(INAUDIBLE)]
8
9 EM Is it?
10 LE Yeah.

3.1 Interpreting Social Meaning

11	R	(LAUGHS)
12		
13	...	
14		
15	R	The things that Townies say are like, erm, 'Aw, the pigs.' [They won't say the]
16		police [[and stuff.]]
17	LU	[(LAUGHS)]
18	LE	[[Or 'blagged'-]]
19		
20	LE	No-one says 'blagged', except Townies.
21	EM	Are there any other kind of words that they use?
22	R	Um .. 'Mint' – 'mintage'.
23	LE	(LAUGHS) Oh yeah.
24	EM	(LAUGHS)
25		
26	R	'Aw, [it's mint,] that.'
27	C	['Sound'.]
28		
29	C	I hate that word.
30	LE	It's just that sentence – like that "he's just told her that if she treats me like shit again
31		then he's going to end it.' And I said, 'Well, that's no – no use to me.' That's just
32		Townie talk.
33	EM	Oh right. So you think it's like a cocky thing?
34		
35	LE	[Yeah.]
36	C	[Yeah.]
37	R	[Yeah,] yeah.

(Leah, Ruth, Lucy, Catherine, Eden Village, 54A: 139–199)

However, as Extract 3.7 suggests, for some Populars, *innit* tag questions more broadly index stances such as being critical (e.g., evaluating something as stupid, l. 11), or being lazy (by virtue of *innit* being perceived as a less effortful articulation of 'is not it', l. 33), as well as character types such as 'common' (ll. 25–26). Lindsey argues that *innit* is avoided by Eden Villagers, like Ruth (ll. 10–11), because it is 'slang' (l. 31) – a term used here to index a number of pejorative social characteristics. This range of qualities suggest a constellation of social meanings, some of which resemble situated conjectures about class ('being common'), and some which only point to certain interactional stances (such as 'being critical').

Extract 3.7

1	EM	Are there like differences – are there like big differences, d'you think between how
2		you lot speak and say how different groups of people speak in the school?
3	L	In the school? Yeah.
4	B	Do you?
5	L	I think there are differences.
6		
7	B	[There's differences,] but they're not big differences.
8	L	[People – if you listen –]
9		

10	L	Yeah, there are, quite. If you listen to like Ruth and everyone speaking, then they
11		don't go around, going, 'Can't be arsed, me. Aw, it's stupid, this, innit?'
12		
13	B	Yeah, but it's not big.. [differences.]
14	L	[Well-]
15		
16	B	[It's different..]
17	L	[If you added] it all up, then it would be quite big. It's not huge.
18		
19	EM	D'you think – do people like think about differences as being sort of like common or
20		posh or..?
21		
22	B	[Yeah.]
23	EM	[Like..]
24		
25	B	[We're more common side.]
26	L	[We sound more common] than them lot.
27		
28	B	Yes.
29		
30	B	[(INAUDIBLE)]
31	L	[We use more] slang.
32		
33	B	It's easier, though, innit? Than saying .. 'not'.

(Beverley, Lindsey, Populars, 56A: 163–197)

Eckert (2008) has described ideologically related constellations of social meanings as an *indexical field*. The notion of the indexical field makes it possible to schematise the inter-relationship of conjectures that may result from a kernel of similarity in meaning. Figure 3.2 demonstrates a hypothetical indexical field for the tag question *innit*. The centre of the indexical field contains the kernel of similarity that goes across social meanings contained within the field. The cogs in Figure 3.2 contain social meanings that are especially interrelated by virtue of ideological construal, and this interrelatedness is schematised by the action of the arrows which move the cogs in step with one another. The figure's label explains how the colour of the cogs and the font type indicate different kinds of social meaning.

As we saw in Chapter 1, and as we'll explore in depth in Chapter 7, the syntactic structure of tag questions predisposes them to a particular pragmatic function: conduciveness. This is because their structure (a declarative, followed by a question) both encourages and implies agreement with the proposition expressed in the declarative. Tag questions, like *innit*, are symbols to the extent that they referentially encode an interrogative state (and, in so doing, constitute the first part of a conventional two-part question and answer sequence). This referential meaning can be used to infer the pragmatic encoding of conduciveness. With an example like 'It's easier, though, innit' (Extract 3.7, l. 33), the declarative which precedes the tag question entails a proposition (in this context, that using *innit* as opposed to *isn't it* or *is not it* is less

3.1 Interpreting Social Meaning

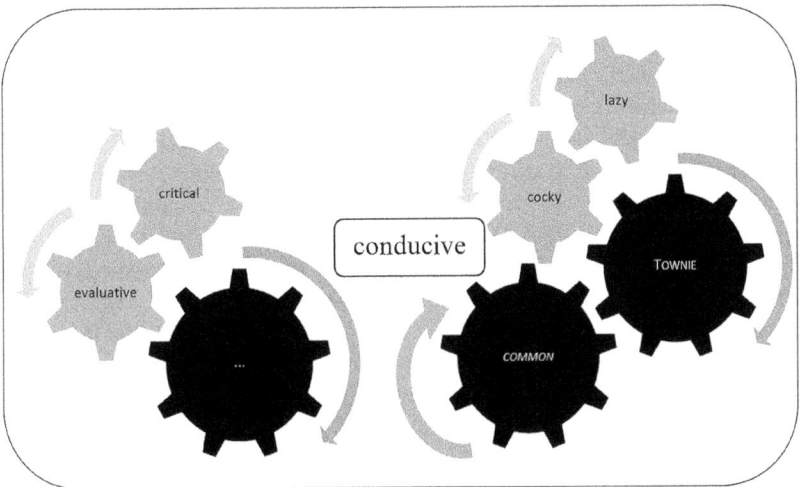

Figure 3.2 A hypothetical indexical field for the tag question *innit*. [Grey cogs indicate stance-related social meanings and black cogs indicate character-type social meanings (with persona-linked meanings in small capitals, and social-type meanings in italicised small capitals).]

effortful), and the tag question structure sets up an expected response to this proposition (with the most felicitous response being 'Yes, it is.'). In this way, the syntactic structure of tag questions (and what this structure referentially encodes) predisposes tag questions to certain pragmatic functions. Some of their indexical (i.e., social) meaning is directly shaped by this semantic meaning, to the extent that 'their performative potential is rooted in that conventional meaning' (Eckert 2019a: 754). This is why 'conduciveness' lies at the heart of the indexical field for *innit*; however else *innit* functions socially, it will always be a conventional symbol for an interrogative clause because of its underlying semantics. In turn, this referential meaning will have an impact on the form's pragmatic potential.

Some of the social meanings of *innit* (i.e., those to the left of the indexical field) seem to derive directly from conduciveness. In Extract 3.7, Lindsey's illustrative *innit* tag in l. 11 seemingly serves to conduce agreement around the stance that something is 'stupid'. This specific *innit* tag expresses a critical stance: it seeks to establish common ground around a particular (negative) evaluation. If *innit* tags are perceived to be contiguous with negatively evaluative and critical stances, then the tag itself may become associated with these social meanings. Further, if Populars are perceived to frequently articulate these specific stances then, via a process of *stance accretion* (Du Bois 2002; Rauniomaa 2003), it may be that this particular character type is itself construed as a social index of *innit* tags. However, the character type cog is empty in the left-hand schematisation in Figure 3.2, because we have not encountered evidence in this example for an indexical link between *innit* tags and the social meaning 'Popular'. This is discussed further below.

If we consider the social meanings on the right-hand side of Figure 3.2, these are less obviously associated with the semantics of 'conduciveness'. Acton (2021: 121) notes that, in addition to being rooted in semantics, social meaning can also be rooted in iconicity and indexicality. Earlier, I noted that iconic meanings can derive from sound symbolism, on the one hand, or from the rhematisation of an indexical association, on the other. Social meanings rooted in sound symbolism derive from the perception that a particular articulation is the consequence of an embodied state. For instance, we noted earlier that body size can be associated with pitch to the extent that, in Western cultures at least, smaller bodies are perceived to emit higher frequency sounds. To give another example, Pratt (2018: 52–83) shows how creaky voice quality, alongside slower speech rate and slouchy posture, correlates with a particular male 'chill' persona. Pratt (2018: 65) suggests that the embedding of creak in this particular style brings about an 'iconic interpretation which associates those irregular, audibly slow vibrations of the vocal folds with low levels of energy or effort.' This is not a natural association, of course – creaky voice has been found to correlate with a wide number of social meanings including those which do not straightforwardly correspond with low levels of effort – e.g., toughness and emotional distance (Mendoza-Denton 2011) – however, the iconic relation between creaky voice and the embodiment of effortlessness makes it appear so.

In her discussion of *innit*, Beverley hints at a similar iconic relation between the use of *innit* and articulatory ease. In Extract 3.7, l. 33, in reference to the use of *innit*, she argues, 'It's easier, though, innit? Than saying .. "not"'. The inference here is that, using *innit*, rather than *is not it* (or the more likely alternative *isn't it*) serves to resemble a speaker's lazy use of their vocal apparatus. This raises the possibility that the orders of indexicality for *innit* start as a sound symbolic relation between sound and embodied human qualities. This starting point can then lead on to associations with categories of speakers based on their perceived propensity to embody any number of qualities associated with a lack of effort.

However, Extract 3.7 also provides evidence of an iconic association arising from a social index shifting ground. As noted above, social meanings rooted in indexicality derive from qualities associated with the categories of speakers who are perceived to use a particular linguistic variant. It is important to note that, as implied above, *innit* is not simply a tag question, but the outcome of a specific morphophonetic articulation of a tag question. Its morphophonetic properties are conventionally bound to interpretable sounds and units of speech, but they have no inherent meaning of their own. Consequently, they are free to take on indexical meaning, and the social meanings they accrue

3.1 Interpreting Social Meaning

depend upon how the social locations of their occurrence are perceived. *Innit* is not the standard pronunciation of 'isn't it' and, as such, it is associated with character types who less frequently use standard English variants. In the context of Midlan High, these character types are Townies and 'common' people. Of course not all Townies are working class (an entailment of 'common'), but these two character types are bound by the ideological link between Townie practices and stereotypes of working-class behaviour. The Eden Villagers' enthusiastic acknowledgement that Townie talk indexes 'cockiness', and Lindsey's observation that *innit* is associated with 'commonness', reveals the indexical links between these character types and social meanings. There is nothing inherently 'common' about *innit*, it is the specific conjecture that Townies are both common and frequent users of *innit* that imbues *innit* with qualities like 'commonness'.

That the Eden Village girls perceive *innit* to depict Townieness, rather than simply pointing to it suggests that, for them, *innit* has shifted ground from an index to an icon via the process of rhematisation. For the Popular girls, on the other hand, *innit* seems to have the potential to function as both an index and an icon. Lindsey portrays *innit* as contiguous with critical and evaluative stances (i.e., it functions as an index), but in noting that it can also depict qualities like 'commonness', she also recognises its iconic relation to lower social class groups and the qualities and stances associated with these social groups.

The distinction between indexical and iconic social meanings is explored further in Chapter 5. For now, though, it is important to note that rhematisation functions as 'a creative moment' (Gal & Irvine 2019: 124) – it involves both simplification of a sign (in that it reduces a sign to a limited set of conjectures) and *erasure* (in foregrounding a particular constellation of social meanings, other social meanings are ignored or disregarded). Rhematisation causes a sign to be perceived as part of a larger scheme of contrast, or what Gal and Irvine (2019: 124) call an *axis of differentiation*. That is to say, in becoming an icon, *innit* is perceived as sharing qualia with the images of the specific character type it is taken to depict (e.g., Townie) and, in doing so, it stands in opposition to the various qualia associated with other schemes of contrast (e.g., in this context, the expressive forms that are seen to index Eden Villagers). This status as part of a larger axis of differentiation enables *innit* to take its place in the enregisterment of Townieness.

Enregisterment is the process through which a set of linguistic resources are perceived to collectively point to particular identities or activities (Agha 2003; Silverstein 2003; Johnstone 2016). As a process, enregisterment is contingent on rhematisation. In order for a particular linguistic sign, like *innit*, to be taken to share qualia with a specific object, like Townieness, it must be encoded as part of a recognised register – the constituent parts of which point to the same social meanings. That is to say, to be able to conceptualise 'Townie' linguistic style, we need to identify a set of semiotic resources and contrast them with an alternative set of semiotic resources. Furthermore, in choosing one axis of differentiation to denote Townieness, we inevitably deny other possible construals: Townies are lazy, cocky, common, as opposed to tough, resilient and efficacious.

As this discussion suggests, enregisterment is not a neutral process; what is typified through this process is culturally specific and embedded in systems of value. For instance, when I became an academic, I started to get invited around to the homes of people from a more diverse range of social classes than I was used to. What I noticed (and noticing is not the same as experiencing) was that some people who came from established middle-class families did not worry about keeping a neat and tidy house. These noticings constituted one or two tokens of an association between being middle class and having a disorganised house. I noticed these houses in particular (rather than the other orderly ones I encountered) because, for many working-class people, having a neat and tidy house is a form of symbolic status in the absence of material resources (Skeggs 1997: 56–73; Kefalas 2003: 95–122; Watt 2006). This is, of course, influenced by the hegemonic view of the working classes and associated institutions (such as schools in working-class neighbourhoods), as unruly and dirty (Reay 2007). Some working-class people seek to counter unconscious bias about their lifestyles and appearance by keeping a neat house. What I noticed was that some of my middle-class colleagues didn't seem to recognise (or at least attend to) the ideological link between cleanliness and the perception of their own moral standing. That they didn't need to attend to this ideological link was a consequence of a larger system of moral values: physical dirt (which, in turn, is linked to lax morals) is frequently enregistered as part of a larger working-class style. In comparison, middle-class style indexes cleanliness by default, even in the absence of this property. That is to say, cleanliness is immaterial to middle-class identity compared to, say, the riding of horses, the size of one's house, the type of car one drives, the history of one's family or the social institutions one engages with.

The indexical links that end up being rhematised are conditioned by the relative salience of 'discourses about the characteristics of categories of people, events, qualities, and actions' (Gal & Irvine 2019: 95). The tokens of untidy middle-class homes were meaningful to me personally, but it is not a widely held view that middle-class people have disorganised homes. The nature and distribution of power in society is such that some categories are scrutinised and objectified, whilst others are not. Thus the stereotype that working-class people are feckless, lazy and unclean, is much more dominant than the perception that they are house-proud and work hard in employment and in their homes. Dirt and unruliness is iconically associated

3.2 Grammatical Variants

with working-class life and enregistered as part and parcel of working-class identity, at least in conjectures that attend to hegemonic discourse around class distinction.

In this section, I have exemplified the processes involved in the interpretation of social meaning. This has entailed a discussion of the tripartite Peircean sign and the processes of indexicality, iconisation, rhematisation and enregisterment. It has also explored how types of social meanings (stance, persona and social type) are encoded in language. As the discussion of *innit* suggests, social signification operates across all types of language structure. However, grammatical variables differ from phonetic variables in their ability to encode referential meaning. We have yet to fully address how this difference might affect the potential social meanings of grammar. This is explored further in the next section.

3.2 Grammatical Variants and the Development of Social Meaning

The discussion in the previous section demonstrated that the social meaning of a grammatical variant can have more than one root. It can develop from:

(1) the semantics of a variant,
(2) an indexical association between a variant and the character types perceived to use it,
(3) sound symbolism.

Figures 3.3–3.5 schematise how social meaning develops from these different roots, using the example of *innit* discussed above. In these figures, evaluative stances are shown with grey-outlined pictures and bolded text, persona types are shown in black-outlined pictures and small capitals text, and social types are shown in black-outlined pictures and italicised small capitals text.

Recent work in pragmatics has focused on trajectories of social meaning rooted in semantics (Type SM). For instance, Beltrama and Staum Casasanto

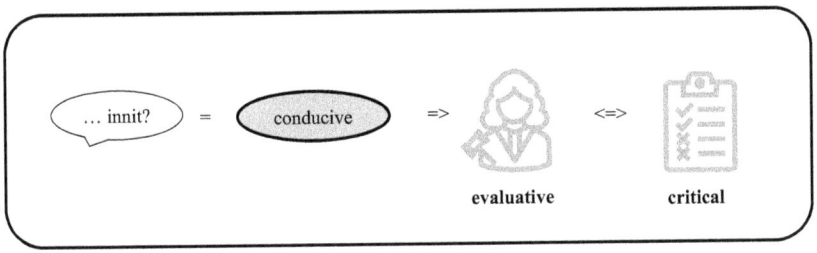

Figure 3.3 Type SM: Trajectory of social meaning rooted in semantics.

Figure 3.4 Type CT: Trajectory of social meaning derived from a character-type index.

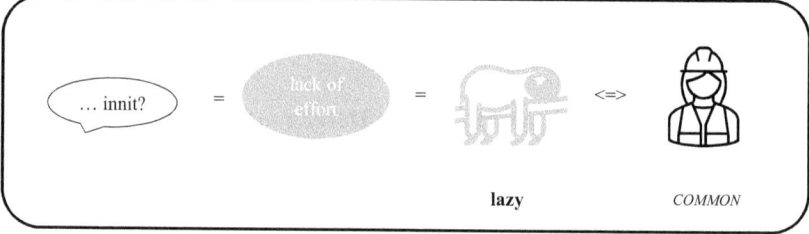

Figure 3.5 Type SS: Trajectory of social meaning derived from sound symbolism.

(2017, 2021) show how intensifiers like *totally* in English index qualities such as being 'excitable' or 'out-going'. Examples of *totally* are given in Examples 3.1 and 3.2.

(3.1)   The bag is *totally* full

(3.2)   I just *totally* blew her out (Beverley, Popular, 30B: 862)

Beltrama and Staum Casasanto hypothesise that these social meanings are linked to the semantics of intensification. For instance, in Example 3.1, *totally* indicates that the bag is as full as it can be. Beltrama and Staum Casasanto (2021: 97) propose that the referential meaning of *totally* (i.e., that it denotes 'reaching of the top', or at least 'reaching the highest region', on a particular scale) 'might trigger the association with attributes that likewise embody an element of extremeness, such as being particularly excitable or outgoing'. In this sense, the semantics of the intensifier leads to a pragmatic specificity, such that it gains a pragmatic meaning of 'extremeness'. This pragmatic meaning may then be ideologically associated with social behaviours that are considered 'extreme' in some way, such as being especially excitable or out-going.

More concretely, Beltrama and Staum Casasanto provide evidence that the intensifier *totally* is more socially salient when it occurs in compositionally

3.2 Grammatical Variants

marked contexts – i.e., when the adjacent expression does not encode a gradable scale, as in Example 3.2. To 'blow someone out' means to dramatically disassociate oneself from them, hence it refers to a definitive, rather than a gradable act (it wouldn't make sense to *'slightly blow someone out' – you either blow them out or you don't). As the predicate does not provide a gradable scale for *totally* to intensify, the intensification is taken to grade the speaker's attitude in this example – such that, in Example 3.2, Beverley is expressing her full commitment to the act she reports. Beltrama and Staum Casasanto observe that, in perception experiments, listeners more readily made links between social characteristics (age, solidarity and status) and *totally* when it was in a sentence like Example 3.2 as opposed to a sentence like Example 3.1. This provides evidence for morpholexical items gaining social meaning when their semantics are exploited to produce new (or less regularly encountered) pragmatic inferences in interaction.

Markedness is also observed as an important criteria in other studies which show morpholexical variants to have social meanings rooted in their semantics. Drawing upon the observation that demonstrative pronouns convey shared understanding of specific referents (Lakoff 1974) (compare *Can you pass me the pencil?* with *Can you pass me that pencil?*), Acton and Potts (2014) show that this presupposition is exploited to achieve solidarity effects in interaction when a demonstrative is otherwise unwarranted (e.g., in examples like 'Can you believe *that* one?' when 'one' refers to a human subject). Similarly, Acton (2019, 2021) analyses the marked use of *the* with plural noun phrases (e.g., 'the Americans') to show how speakers use this form to manage social alignment in interaction. In this case, the morpholexical item, *the*, is used to create a distancing effect from a group portrayed as monolithic, such that the group is depicted as separate from the speaker. Here the semantic distinction between *the*-plurals ('the Americans'), which infer a well-defined collection of individuals, and bare plurals ('Americans'), which do not, is utilised to create social meaning. By analysing data from a corpus analysis of US political discourse, Acton shows that political parties more commonly use *the*-plurals to talk about their political opponents than they do their own political party. In this way, Acton's research reveals how 'differences in meaning beget differences in use along social lines' (Acton 2019: 45).

The relationship between semantics and social distribution is further illustrated in Glass's (2015) work on strong necessity modal verbs. She shows that *need to* is used over *have to* or *got to* to signal that an obligation is good for an addressee's well-being. She subsequently finds that *need to* is more frequently used by speakers who have authority over the addressee, or where they are mentoring the addressee. She argues that this form occurs more frequently in these contexts because it enables the speaker to linguistically articulate their authority over the addressee's priorities. In this instance, we would expect the social distribution of *need to* to reflect the relative power of speakers in particular contexts.

All of these studies show social effects that are rooted in the semantic properties of grammatical items. It is notable, however, that these social effects are predominantly constrained at the level of stance, rather than at the level of character type. This can also be seen in the depiction of the trajectory of Type 1 social meanings for *innit*. Figure 3.3 does not include a character-type association for social meanings rooted in semantics. It may be difficult to imagine any context in which a tag like *innit* is heard as distinct from the identity of its speaker. But imagine that you are a member of a working-class community in which most people use *innit* tags. When you hear these tags from a neighbour over the garden fence, you are unlikely to be focused on their identity as they articulate them (because of the expectedness of your interaction). In this sense, character type is immaterial to the interaction, and to what is socially relevant to it – at least for the people actually engaged in the interaction. In this context, the relevant social meanings perceived are more likely to be at the level of stance (e.g., that the speaker is being conducive, critical, or evaluative).

Does this mean that social meanings rooted in semantics never develop character-type associations? This question has yet to be satisfactorily answered. It seems feasible that such an association could arise. As suggested in the discussion of Figure 3.3, if a particular social group is perceived to more frequently articulate the specific stances facilitated by a grammatical item, then the grammatical item may be construed as indexing a character type commonly associated with that social group. However, given that the grammatical items discussed above (e.g., tag questions, intensifiers, demonstratives, determiners, modal verbs) occur across all language inputs, irrespective of the acquiree's place in the social order, it would take a noticeable distinction in language practice across groups to allow a character-type association to evolve. Understanding the likelihood of this, and what might motivate it, is a major concern of this book.

Figure 3.4 shows a Type CT trajectory: social meaning developing from a character-type association. CT trajectories can occur across all types of linguistic variant; they are not restricted to grammatical variants. Here the social meaning of *innit* derives from the percept that this linguistic form is most typically used by people who embody a Townie persona and/or a 'common' social type that is indexically linked to Townieness. Importantly, social meaning here does not draw upon the semantics of tag questions, but on the socio-indexical meaning that is rooted in the morphophonemic constituents of this tag question. That is to say, it relies upon the way in which *innit* is articulated, and on comparisons with other, alternative, articulations (e.g., *isn't it*). The salience of distinct articulations is sufficient to cause *innit* to 'lose some or potentially all of [its] pragmatic specificity' (Eckert 2019a: 756). That is to say, when heard in isolation, listeners for whom *innit* functions as a rheme, are likely to hear this tag question and think 'that's a Townie voice' or 'that's a "common" voice'. This is not to say that they will not also infer that the speaker is trying to be conducive (or projecting any number of associated stances), but this pragmatic function may be secondary to, or at least conjectured alongside, their evaluation of the speaker's social identity.

Where social meaning develops along a type CT root, stance-related social meanings may also develop. But these stance-related meanings will derive from the qualia and properties associated with the relevant character type. Consequently, *innit* may articulate a 'lazy' or 'cocky' stance precisely because these qualities are ideologically associated with Townieness and working-class status. The stance stems from the character type, not from any underlying semantics of tag questions. Whilst the syntactic structure of *innit* predisposes it to conduciveness and associated stances, conduciveness is decentred by character-based conjectures.

Finally, Figure 3.5 shows a Type SS trajectory for *innit* that is rooted in sound symbolism. As with Type CT trajectories, social meaning here does not draw upon the semantics of tag questions, it relies upon the way in which *innit* is articulated, and on comparisons with other, alternative, articulations. However, rather than drawing upon the association between pronunciation and a perceived stereotypical speaker, the social meaning here is rooted in beliefs about perceived articulatory ease, such that using *innit*, rather than *is not it* (or the more likely alternative *isn't it*) is taken to resemble a speaker's lazy use of their vocal apparatus. This is linked to further social meanings via an indexical association between the perceived nature of an articulation and speaker characteristics and stances. In this example, it results in a belief that the speaker is lazy and, in turn, associated with character types that are considered to most frequently display laziness. As with the Type CT trajectory, the pragmatic functions of tag questions may still be present, but they may be secondary to meanings derived from sound symbolism.

Whilst these three trajectories seem to neatly demarcate the different roots that social meaning may take, it is often impossible to determine the precise trajectory from which social meaning derives. It is particularly difficult to disentangle Type CT and Type SS trajectories. As Figures 3.4 and 3.5 show, there is almost complete overlap in the social meanings encoded in these two trajectories. This point has been observed by Snell (2010) in her work with children aged between nine and ten in Middlesbrough, England. She demonstrates that use of possessive *me* (the articulation of 'my' as [mi]) is highly restricted. It is a minority variant which shows something of a correlation with social class (working-class children use it 7.1 per cent of the time, and middle-class children use it 1.2 per cent of the time). However, its use more clearly corresponds with particular expressions of 'negative affect or transgression, often tempered by playfulness or a lack of commitment to the utterance' (Snell 2010: 647) – irrespective of whether it occurs in working-class or middle-class speech. Snell demonstrates that [mi] only occurs in unstressed positions and hypothesises that this linguistic patterning seems to correlate with a perceived lack of effort. This raises the possibility that the phonetic constraints on this feature's occurrence (i.e., that it only occurs in unstressed environments) is iconically associated with a lack of commitment – such that the speaker's body is conjectured to be performing 'unstressed' (i.e., 'laid-back'). In this way, the social meaning of /mi/ could be rooted in sound symbolism: its status as an unstressed articulation predisposes it to inferences about effort and commitment, and the stances and character types associated with these inferences.

However, as Snell's analysis carefully shows, this picture is complicated by the fact that it is working-class speakers who are frequently depicted as lazy, as we have seen in the discussion of *innit*. Is the conjecture that /mi/ indexes an 'uncommitted stance' the consequence of sound symbolism, or is it a consequence of an ideological association with working-class speech? Although Snell (2010: 650) argues that the 'more immediate indexicalities of stance are relevant for speakers/hearers when they use [possessive *me*] in interaction', she also acknowledges that social class is part of the indexical history of this variant. In particular, she notes that school teachers' characterisation of possessive *me* as 'incorrect' stems from its association with 'non-standardness' and those who typically speak local varieties. Acknowledging Silverstein (2003: 196–197), Snell notes that this makes it impossible to determine where the chain of indexical associations begins and ends.

This discussion suggests that it is better to conceptualise social meaning as deriving from an on-going, iterative process, rather than having a linear trajectory. Figure 3.6 schematises this in relation to the social meanings observed in the Type CT and Type SS trajectories for *innit*. As the two sets of arrows on this figure suggest, given the kernel of similarity ('lack of effort') that goes across all of social meanings in Figure 3.6, it is not possible to deduce whether the social meaning 'lazy' leads to the character-type association 'Townie' or vice versa.

Notwithstanding these interactions between Type CT and Type SS trajectories of meaning, is it possible to make predictions about the specific social meaning trajectories of individual grammatical variants? That is to say, is it equally possible for all grammatical variants to develop social meanings from each of the different roots explored in this section? These issues are further explored in the remaining sections of this chapter.

3.3 Types of Grammatical Variant and Social Meaning   67

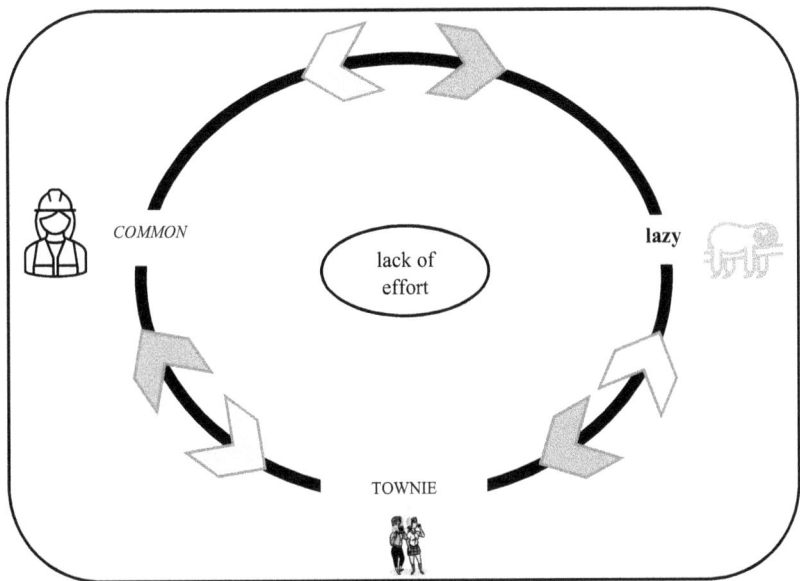

Figure 3.6 A simplified representation of the inter-related social meanings of *innit*.

3.3 Types of Grammatical Variant and Types of Social Meaning

Chapter 1 outlined the different types of grammatical variant we might examine. Do these different types of variant acquire social meaning in the same ways? Furthermore, is type of variant the only factor we need to consider to understand how grammatical variants gain social meaning? We might also wonder about the types of social meaning variants acquire and the extent to which they are socially, or more pertinently, class-, restricted in their distribution. Table 3.1 outlines how we might characterise grammatical variants by their type and their social distribution. In this section, the likely trajectories of social meaning are considered for these different types of variants.

Whilst all grammatical variants carry referential meaning, some types of grammatical variants have clearer linguistic alternatives than others. For instance, a morpholexical variant, like alternation in first- and third-person singular past tense BE, has a circumscribed set of alternative forms (*was, were*). The variants that people use will interact with their place in the social order and what they have been able to acquire in childhood; not everyone will have been exposed to *were* in the first- and third-person singular (referred to in Chapter 1 as *levelled were*). Importantly, variables like levelled *were* are classed as grammatical, but their structural simplicity makes them

Table 3.1 *Types of grammatical variation*

	Grammatical type	Example
Socially restricted	Morpholexical	levelled *were*
		e.g., *It weren't great.*
	Morphosyntactic	negative concord
		e.g., *I didn't do nothing* ('I didn't do anything').
	Syntactic	right dislocation
		e.g., *I'm daft, me.*
Widespread	Morpholexical	intensifier *totally*
		e.g., *the bag was totally full*
	Morphosyntactic	historic present
		e.g., *[He looked at me,] so, I give him the book*
	Syntactic	tag questions
		e.g., *It's good, isn't it?*

akin to lexical and/or phonetic alternatives and, as such, like phonetic variants, they are easily parsed 'in the fast give and take of interaction, as people associate what they articulate and what they hear with aspects of the context' (Eckert & Labov 2017: 481).

Some morphosyntactic variants are similarly restricted in their distribution. For instance, only some children will acquire negative concord in their initial language input. However, the more complex syntactic configuration of morphosyntactic variables provides more potential for pragmatic inferences to arise in relation to that structure. Hence, these types of variant can be readily associated with particular types of speakers, but that is not to say that these speakers don't also exploit semantically grounded pragmatic inferences to make social meaning – especially when a speaker has command of negative concord *and* its standard alternative.

It is difficult to think of more purely syntactic variants that are both socially and regionally restricted, but one example is types of right dislocation like *I'm daft, me*. As discussed further in Chapter 6, these never occur in some varieties of English, but are prominent in others. This restriction in the availability of these grammatical forms means that the social meanings of these variants may also be conditioned by who uses these particular variants and when. However, like negative concord, their more complex syntactic configuration (which includes semantic end-weight, for instance, given the co-referential status of the subject of the main clause – 'I' – and the appended co-referential object – 'me') offers up the possibility of social meaning deriving from their underlying semantics when speakers can vary their use of right dislocation by contrasting it with other resources in their repertoire.

3.3 Types of Grammatical Variant and Social Meaning

These examples demonstrate that morpholexical, morphosyntactic and syntactic variants can all acquire social meanings from character-type associations. However, they also show that, the more syntactically complex their structure, the more likely a grammatical variant is to also index social meanings rooted in semantics.

This chapter has also provided evidence from grammatical items which are not (or at least, much less) socially or regionally restricted in their distribution. That is to say, their acquisition is not a matter of the dialect one is exposed to during childhood. For these items, we can be fairly confident that any social meanings they develop will be rooted in their semantics. For instance, we have encountered the proposal that the distribution of the morpholexical variant *totally* is constrained by its semantics (and, specifically, its reference to 'extremeness'). This may lead to listeners inferring that a speaker is projecting a particularly out-going stance when using this form or that they are particularly excitable. However, Beltrama and Staum Casasanto (2017) also observe that marked uses of *totally* are also associated with younger speakers. This provides evidence that social meanings rooted in semantics *can* develop into character-type social meanings if certain speakers are more apt to make use of their pragmatic specificity. However, evidence for similar developments occurring with more syntactically complex grammatical items is less easy to find. This is because these linguistic forms have not typically been the concern of sociolinguistics – indeed, they have been argued to be beyond the purview of sociolinguistics.

Specifically, Weiner and Labov (1983) argued against the agentless passive being a sociolinguistic variable – precisely because it did not correlate with any macro-social category. Nonetheless, this form has been found to have social meaning at the interactional level. For instance, Henley *et al.* (1995) report that agentless passives are typically used to report violence against women. They found that men (but not women) tended to assign less victim harm and perpetrator responsibility for violence against women when the passive rather than the active voice was used to report sexual violence. Here then, the syntactic suppression of the actor may lead to a pragmatic inference about objectivity. As Eckert (2019a: 755) points out, that agentless passives can encode objectivity may lead them to gain social meaning in relation to individuals or groups (such as lawyers or scientists) who may regularly background agency in their talk. Whilst there is no data to suggest that agentless passives index particular personas or social types (i.e., character-type social meanings), it remains possible that associations like this may arise – even if only within specific communities.

Another widely used morphosyntactic form is the historic present, where a present tense verb form is used to express something in the past tense, e.g., *[He looked at me] so, I give him the book and leave.* The historic present has been found to signal evaluation (Wolfson 1979) and a speaker's movement into full performance (Leith 1995). These interactional functions are undoubtedly linked to the markedness of the historic present and its reference to current time which enables it to infer immediacy. It is conceivable that these functions may lead to increased use by particular speakers who more frequently express stances of evaluation, for instance, but, as with agentless passives, there is insufficient data to test this hypothesis.

However, our discussion of tag questions indicated the possibility of them acquiring social meaning linked to the social groups who most frequently use them within the confines of Midlan High. However, it is necessary to separate out social meaning attached to a tag question as a consequence of its morphophonemic content, and any social meaning derived from its grammatical structure. For instance, the character-type social meaning of *innit* seemingly derives from those aspects of its structure which operate like phonetic alternatives, not from the syntax itself. It remains unclear the extent to which the syntactic structure (as opposed to the morphophonemic content) of tag questions can more acquire social meanings linked to character type. The proposal that tag questions are typical of female speech (Lakoff 1975) hints at an ideological association with character type. Furthermore, the potential association with Popular speech, noted above, suggests that this variable merits further interrogation using the data from Midlan High.

In the analyses that follow, the hypotheses about types of grammatical variant and types of social meaning will be tested. Chapters 4–6 analyse socially restricted grammatical variants, addressing increasingly syntactically complex forms. These variants are the ones most typically studied in sociolinguistics so we know a good deal about their social-type distributions. However, we know much less about their distribution by persona and stance, and even less about how their pragmatic specificity interacts with character-type associations. These chapters will seek to fill this gap in our understanding.

Work at the interface of pragmatics and sociolinguistics (discussed above) has told us a good deal about the extent to which widespread morpholexical items gain social meanings associated with stance. However, we know much less about more widespread syntactically complex forms. Consequently, the final analysis chapter, Chapter 7, considers the social meanings of tag questions with a view to identifying the roots of that meaning. The tag question analysis will empirically test the observations made in this chapter about the distinction between socially restricted and more widespread grammatical forms. In doing so, it will provide a more rounded understanding of the kind of grammatical variables which are pragmatically linked to social action but which are less frequently considered by sociolinguists. In so doing, Chapter 7 will increase understanding of trajectories of social meaning, encouraging a broader definition of social meaning and challenging the limited way in which the sociolinguistic variable has been characterised.

There is excellent guidance on how to study grammatical variables using variationist sociolinguist techniques (Tagliamonte 2006, 2011). These methods have been essential in allowing us to understand how variables are socially distributed amongst different social types. They are also vital for understanding the extent to which this variation is determined by linguistic constraints (an endeavour not always possible with small-scale local analysis, which must rely on macro-level studies to understand where these constraints interfere with social patterning). However, to understand how grammatical variables gain social meanings related to stance, persona and social types, adaptations need to be made to these traditional methods. The final section of this chapter considers how to investigate the social meaning of grammar.

3.4 Investigating the Social Meaning of Grammar

Research on social meaning has sought to understand social evaluations and perceptions of language variation using experimental paradigms (Campbell-Kibler 2011; Pharao *et al.* 2014; D'Onofrio 2015), and some of this work has focused on, or included, grammatical variation (Squires 2013, 2014, 2016; Levon & Buchstaller 2015; Robinson 2021). This research is helping to increase our understanding of the relationship between social meaning and grammatical variation. For instance, Squires (2016) measures the extent to which American participants perceive and notice subject–verb agreement variation in a self-paced reading task. She measured variation in perceptions by measuring reading time, and measured noticing by asking participants if they had observed anything interesting in the grammar using a post-experiment questionnaire. Her results suggest that all participants perceive morphosyntactic variation, but not all explicitly notice it. This adds weight to the argument that morphosyntactic variants encode more than referential meaning – even if all individuals are not able to articulate that knowledge.

Other research has focused on comparing the extent to which grammatical items are socially evaluated with the extent to which phonetic items are socially evaluated. Building on work by Labov *et al.* (2011), Levon and Buchstaller (2015) presented listeners with multiple recordings of the same individual reading a news broadcast. The recordings differed by the degree to which they included (th)-fronting (the pronunciation of *th* as /f/) and the Northern Subject Rule (NSR; the use of a verbal -*s* suffix on plural verbs with a third-person noun-phrase subject – e.g., *they knows the answer*). Listeners were asked to rate the speaker in each recording for professionalism. Their results indicated that listeners were sensitive to both the phonetic and the morphosyntactic variables, although the salience of the NSR was contingent on listener region and respondents' pragmatic language ability (tested using the Broad Autism Phenotype Questionnaire) whereas the response to (th)-fronting was not. They speculate that, whilst listeners do seem to socially evaluate morphosyntax, the process of evaluation may rely upon more complex factors than is the case for phonetic variation. Furthermore, the nature of evaluation may also be constrained by factors such as the regional distribution of a variant, its sociohistorical trajectory, and its contextual relevance.

In more recent work, Robinson (2021) analysed negative concord to discover whether different grammatical configurations affect perception of social attributes. She asked speakers from a range of British and US dialect groups (which variably have forms of negative concord as dialect features) to rate written sentences including negative concord for intelligence, class and education level. Her results indicate that morphological variation (represented by differing polarity conditions, e.g., *I didn't see nothing* vs. *I didn't see anything*) has a larger effect size across different groups of listeners than syntactic variation (whether negative concord occurs with the object [*I didn't see nothing*], subject [*Nobody couldn't see him*] or with auxiliary inversion [*Couldn't nobody see him*]). That is to say, speakers from a wider range of dialect groups consistently rated the negative concord condition as significantly less educated, intelligent and of a lower class than the standard English variant. On the other hand, results were less consistent for the syntactic conditions: for instance, significant differences between ratings for subject-negative concord, on the one hand, and negative concord with auxiliary inversion, on the other, were largely restricted to dialect groups where negative concord with auxiliary inversion is not found. These dialect groups tended to perceive users of negative concord with auxiliary inversion as less educated and less intelligent than users of subject-negative concord. Whilst it may be simplistic to explain these rating differences purely as the consequence of differing grammatical architecture (after all, negative concord with auxiliary inversion is also less frequent and less widespread than subject-negative concord), Robinson's results suggest the precise configuration of a grammatical structure may interact with its social meaning potential. This possibility is further investigated in Chapter 7.

These perception studies have usefully tested hypotheses about whether or not listeners infer social detail when encountering grammatical variation. They also expose factors which may influence whether or not grammatical variation is perceived as socially meaningful. Squires and Robinson's studies show that grammatical variation is found to encode social meaning even in the absence of phonetic detail (both employ a reading-task design). Levon and Buchstaller's study notes the importance of the regional distribution of a variant, its sociohistorical trajectory, and its contextual relevance, alongside its linguistic structure. Finally, Robinson's study emphasises the need to differentiate between different types of structure when evaluating the social meaning of grammar.

Despite these important findings, these studies are limited in their examination of social meaning itself. Squires does not identify any specific social meanings, just the presence or absence of an 'evaluation'. Levon and Buchstaller, and Robinson only consider social meanings that index social class, or qualities associated with social class status ('professional', 'educated', 'intelligent'). In this regard, the nature of social meaning examined in these studies is limited and, as such, they do not allow us to examine the range of social meanings encoded by grammatical variation. To some extent, this is a consequence of the experimental design. In recruiting a diverse set of participants, it is necessary to test only those social meanings which have the widest currency. However, in doing so, the experiments risk reifying the hegemonic social indexes of grammatical variation and neglecting more localised meanings which do not have more widespread reach. It is important to note that is not necessarily the case that experimental work needs to be limited to the testing of social-type meanings. D'Onofrio (2015) shows how persona type can influence perception of phonetic variation, and D'Onofrio and Eckert (2021) provide experimental evidence which suggests that sound symbolism influences how listeners attribute qualities to phonetic variation that are associated with affect. Equivalent work on grammatical variation is yet to be completed.

Furthermore, whilst experimental methods are useful for establishing widespread connections between linguistic forms and their social meanings, they are not suited to answer questions about how speakers construct and exploit interconnected social meanings in interaction. Research examining the localised construction of social meaning has depended on ethnography. Ethnography provides the opportunity to gain an understanding of linguistic variation from the perspective of the language user themself. It requires the analyst to learn how signs are interpreted by others, based on their specific social practices and their experience of social space, rather than relying on their own schemas of interpretation. Without this local view of variation, it is not possible to evaluate social meanings which occur in situated interaction; we can only examine data using general categories. The application of these categories is then filtered through our experience – that is to say, through what our own place in the social order has enabled us to see.

Very few studies have examined grammatical variation from the ethnographic perspective required to understand the local embedding of grammar. The small number of ethnographies that have focused on grammatical variation (Cheshire 1982; Meyerhoff & Walker 2007, 2013; Snell 2008, 2010, 2013; Pabst 2022), or included at least one grammatical variable in a larger ethnographic study (Eckert 2000; Mendoza-Denton 2008; Bucholtz 2011; Fox 2015) indicate that grammatical variants can have a rich array of social correlates and social functions: individuals vary their grammar according to their social affiliations (e.g., friendship groups), aspirations, and to negotiate social hierarchies and manage relationships. These studies have demonstrated the benefits of accessing speakers' social practices and the beliefs (linguistic ideologies) held by study participants and others in their speech community. So, whilst experimental perception work is essential for hypothesis testing (because of its ability to control for a number of potentially confounding factors) and for examining individual linguistic features in isolation, the research presented in this volume turns to ethnography to provide insight into the range of social meanings encoded by grammar. In addition to employing interactional analysis to further develop the sociolinguistic techniques employed by the ethnographic studies noted above, this study also incorporates analysis of the relationship between grammar and semantics and pragmatics, and also considers how phonetics and morphosyntax interact as a consequence of particular pronunciations being 'housed' within grammatical structures. In this way, the analysis in this volume combines ethnography, variationist methods, the study of pragmatic inferences, and interactional analysis to move forward our understanding of the social meaning of grammatical variation.

3.5   Establishing Sociolinguistic Meaning

This chapter has provided a comprehensive overview of the processes involved in the establishment of sociolinguistic meaning. It began with a general discussion about social meaning and semiotics, drawing upon the work of Peirce (1895; Peirce Edition Project 1998) and Gal and Irvine (2019) to develop a theory of signs and an understanding of how signs cluster to make actions and identities discernible. Ideology was a central feature of this discussion and I have been at pains to emphasise the need to recognise how one's perspective influences what it is possible to see in the world and, significantly, in a dataset. In the latter part of this chapter, the discussion moved to focus on how processes of social meaning specifically operate in relation to the use of grammatical variants. This discussion hypothesised about the specific roots through which social meaning emerges for grammatical variants. It also suggested that the precise formulation of a grammatical variant constrains the type of social meanings associated with it. In the final section of this chapter, the methods used to examine grammatical variation were considered, providing a justification for the ethnographic nature of the study reported in this book. The following chapters attempt to provide empirical evidence to support the hypotheses developed in this chapter; namely, that the social meaning of grammatical variants has a number of roots, the social and regional distribution of a grammatical variant interacts strongly with the type of social meaning a form can index, and, finally, the nature of social meaning associated with grammatical variants depends upon the specific configuration of a form.

4   How Free Are We to Vary the Grammar We Use?

Extract 4.1

```
1  EM   So which of them – is there any of them you thought sounded more like you or less
2       like you or..?
3
4  B    There.. with.. ['innit'-]
5  L                   ['There /ðɛː/.']
6
7  B    Shudoop! 'In he' and 'weren't' and, erm – and all that.
8  EM   That sounds like you or not like you?
9  B    Like us.
```
(Beverley and Lindsey, Populars, 56A: 15–23)

After I had finished recording the data that is used in the quantitative analysis that follows, I asked the Midlan High girls some explicit questions about language variation to see how aware they were of the variation I had noticed in their interactions. Extract 4.1 comes from one of these 'language' interviews with two Popular girls, Beverley and Lindsey. They had been asked to look at transcripts and listen to recordings of young people from Bolton using different features of nonstandard grammar. (The recordings were collected from my friends and didn't feature voices the girls would know.) As Extract 4.1 shows, when they were asked if any of the recordings they heard sounded like them, Beverley pointed to the transcription from one which featured the utterance 'He weren't right for them. He's too cheesy, in he?' and specifically noted the instance of levelled third-person past tense 'weren't', and a tag question expressed as 'in he' (standard English would use the form 'isn't he') (l. 7). This was an astute observation: as the analysis below will show, as Popular girls, both Beverley and Lindsey were high users of levelled *were*. Extract 4.1 also shows that the task I had given Beverley and Lindsey functioned to attune them to variation more generally – note how Lindsey mimics Beverley's pronunciation of 'there' in l. 5, which exhibits the NURSE-SQUARE merger (in traditional Bolton English, the vowels in words like 'nurse' and 'square' are pronounced in the same way: as the vowel in standard English 'nurse', see Shorrocks 1998: 212). Note, too, the creativity in their language use – *shudoop*

(l. 7) was a novel way in which the Populars girls told other people to 'shut up'.

Extract 4.1 indicates that levelled *were* is associated with the variety of English spoken in Bolton and, more specifically, that, at least some, young people from the town are able to identify it as a feature of their own speech. Note too, that levelled *were* is identified alongside a phonetic variant (the NURSE-SQUARE merger). This adds some weight to the discussion in Chapter 3 which suggested that the structural simplicity of regionally restricted morpho-lexical variants – like levelled *were* – makes them akin to lexical and/or phonetic alternatives in their ability to attract social meanings that are rooted in character-type indexical associations.

Historical accounts (such as Ellis 1869; Wright 1905; Beal 2004: 121) record *were* across all persons in the Lancashire area, of which Bolton was once a part. The regionally restricted nature of levelled *were,* and its relative stability, suggest an enduring association with place. But just how fixed are these social meanings? Do Bolton children acquire this variant as part and parcel of their language acquisition (such that their use of it becomes fixed), or can speakers play around with features like this to construct locally specific stance and persona-linked social meanings?

In order to answer these questions, this chapter begins by considering how children acquire language variation. Although all humans have an innate disposition to learn language, the precise nature of what we learn is determined by what we hear around us. This could be taken to suggest a kind of sociolinguistic determinism: social structures constrain us to acquire the variety spoken in our local area and, if we are working class, this variety will most likely differ from standard English in significant ways. But how constrained are we to speak the variety most closely associated with our social class status and our geographical locale? Work on phonetic and phonological variation has demonstrated that social practice (a shared patterning of meaningful activity) can be a better predictor of young people's language use than social class (Eckert 2000). Research on grammatical variation has also shown how speakers might adapt their grammar as their social class circumstances change across their lifespan (Buchstaller 2016; Brook *et al.* 2018). But there are far fewer studies that examine whether grammatical variation varies according to a speaker's social practice (as opposed to their place in the social order). This is despite early work by Cheshire (1982) which showed a correlation between use of grammatical items which differ from standard English and engagement in 'vernacular culture'. Cheshire's study suggested that boys were more engaged than girls in vernacular culture and, subsequently, that girls were less likely to use grammatical items to index engagement in local social practice. But what happens when girls *are* engaged in vernacular culture? Do we see similar correlations between their language use and their social orientation, or is the variety that their parents use, or their social class, a better way to explain their use of grammar?

This chapter will address these questions by providing an analysis of first- and third-person past tense BE in the speech of Midlan High girls. The analysis will consider how this variable patterns by social class, parental place of birth, and community of practice. It will show that all of these factors play a role in the use of levelled *were*, suggesting that this variant is strongly embedded in the local community and transmitted to children. However, the analysis will also reveal that the most robust correlation is with community of practice – with Townies, of differing social class backgrounds, using this variant more than other groups. This demonstrates the 'sociolinguistic vitality' (Schilling-Estes & Wolfram 1994: 298) of this grammatical variant; the Townies' use of it simultaneously reflects its traditional social class and geographical roots *and* constructs a more contemporary meaning indexical of the wild and rebellious social practices in which these individuals engage. In this way, the data analysed in this chapter will show how grammatical variants can mark distinctive social styles and personas which extend beyond their social class associations. It will also provide evidence for the extent to which we can adapt the language that we use irrespective of our social class background.

4.1 Children and the Acquisition of Local Dialects

There is a huge amount of research on how children acquire language (see, e.g., Guasti 2002 for an introduction to the field of first language acquisition), but this research has largely focused on how children acquire underlying grammatical structures, rather than the extent to which children acquire variable ways of producing those underlying structures. So, we know that children are capable of producing basic negation in the form of words like 'no' as early as twelve months old, but that more complex forms of negation (which result in expressions like 'that's not a dog') do not begin to emerge until around two years old (Pea 1980). However, we know much less about when children start to vary the forms of negation they use according to the context in which they are speaking (for instance, by alternating between a standard variant like 'I don't like it' and a local one like 'I dona like it' on the basis of the activity in which the child is engaged; see Smith & Durham 2019: 136–148).

The general language acquisition process begins with the acquisition of basic sounds and structures. Initially, children model their caregivers until around the age of four or five. The onset of schooling provides wider exposure to language in use ('input'), such that, between the ages of four and twelve, children begin to develop language that is more in line with their peers than their parents (Kerswill & Williams 2000). However, there is less agreement on when children alternate between variants like 'it was great' and 'it were great' on the basis of the setting or context of the interactions in which these distinct variants more frequently appear. It was initially believed that children acquired the rules of sociolinguistic variation in early adolescence – so at around twelve years old – and that they actively replicate this kind of patterning in late adolescence (Labov 1964: 91–93). However, recent interest in the acquisition of sociolinguistic variation has provided empirical evidence that this process happens much earlier, leading to suggestions that it is part and parcel of the more general acquisition process that begins in the early years (Roberts 1997; Foulkes *et al.* 1999; Chevrot & Foulkes 2013; Jeffries 2019). Most of the evidence in support of this hypothesis has come from studies of phonological variation, but the work of Jennifer Smith and colleagues (Smith *et al.* 2007, 2009; Smith *et al.* 2013; Smith & Durham 2019), Henry (2016), and Shin and Miller (2021) has greatly increased our understanding of how children acquire the sociolinguistic rules of morphosyntax.

Most research on the acquisition of sociolinguistic variation has used experimental data (Barbu *et al.* 2013; Buson & Billiez 2013) or data collected via semi-structured interactions (Khattab 2013), whereas the work conducted by Smith and her colleagues analyses naturalistic data (see also Ghimenton *et al.* 2013; Nardy *et al.* 2014). Smith *et al.* collected their data from a small fishing community in and around the town of Buckie on the north-east coast of Scotland. The data was collected from caregiver/child pairs as they went about their everyday activities using lapel microphones and data recorders. The researchers also collected interview data from the wider community, using a local fieldworker, Moira Smith. This provided a clear indication of the kind of language styles children encountered and used in everyday interaction, and permitted the researchers to identify any significant difference between child-directed speech (CDS) and community norms. CDS refers to the speech patterns that adults use with children, which typically differ from adult-to-adult interactions 'both in terms of *what* is talked about and *how* it is talked about' (Smith & Durham 2019: 8). The Buckie data clearly show that children's acquisition of sociolinguistic variation is affected by the nature of CDS. Most significantly, Smith *et al.* find that the extent to which caregivers style shift (so vary their language use according to whether they are engaged in contexts of *teaching* and *discipline*, versus *routine, play* and *intimacy*) is influenced by the social recognition of different language variants. Importantly, they find that 'whatever the caregivers do, the children do the same' (Smith & Durham 2019: 168). More specifically, they find that caregivers use fewer local forms of negation (i.e., *dona* or *na*) in CDS than in inter-adult interaction, but their use of local agreement patterns (using constructions like *the stones is wet*) patterns the same in CDS as it does in inter-adult interaction. They argue that this is because the variation in the *dona* and *na* is essentially lexical, and lexical variation (variation around word choice) is highly salient in the community (to the extent that community members are aware that the local form is different from the standard and that they can adapt it more readily). On the other hand, community members, in Buckie at least, are less aware of variation around agreement patterns and thus less likely to make adjustments to their speech according to the context of an interaction. This shows us that the shifts caregivers make in CDS speech affect how (and if) children acquire sociolinguistic variation, but it also shows that sociolinguistic variation itself is affected by the type of variable (a point made by Kerswill 1996) and, relatedly, the social salience of individual variables. Importantly, Smith and Durham (2019: 184–188) note that what is socially salient may be community specific: the sociolinguistic variation children acquire reflects what patterns exist in their own wider community, but those patterns may be not replicated across every community speaking the same language.

Ultimately, Smith and Durham (2019: 189) show that once children are exposed to sociolinguistic variation (because caregivers vary in their own use with children), children themselves are able to use it. Put more simply, if children hear that adults speak differently when they are playing versus when they are disciplining, children are also likely to speak differently when they are playing versus when they are being disciplined. This happens with children as young as three years old in Smith and Durham's dataset. Of course, children may not know that these forms have wider social meanings linked to categories of social stratification, but they are able to modulate their speech on the basis of the type of interaction in which they are engaged – in essence, their language use reflects that language is socially embedded and socially meaningful.

The point about social stratification is important here. The pervasiveness of social class patterns in linguistic variation are such that – generally speaking – parents from a lower social class group will use higher frequencies of local variants than parents from a higher social class group. So, a parent whose everyday speech more closely approximates standard English may use very few (if any) local variants ever. Changes in context are likely to be signalled by changes in pitch, intonation or vocabulary, but not by frequency of regionally restricted linguistic variants. On the other hand, a parent whose everyday speech includes many local variants will model a system where changes in context are signalled by changes in pitch, intonation, vocabulary *and* frequency of local variants (at least for those variants which are socially stigmatised according to Smith & Durham 2019). Importantly, the children of these parents will learn that certain local variants index 'playfulness' or 'intimacy', *not* that they index 'working class' – even if their parents' own use is influenced by these social associations. This means that young children learn *stance*-related social meanings first (Kiesling 2009: 176; Smith & Durham 2019: 190). That is to say, they learn to use language to constitute particular interactional positions and to construct alignments to what they are saying or who they are saying it to (Du Bois 2007; Kiesling 2009). Children's understanding of class-linked meanings is only likely to result from exposure to a larger volume of language input and/or when they are exposed to societal language ideologies. So, social class might determine precisely what linguistic variation a child acquires, but young children are not 'doing social class' when they style shift; they are expressing alignments and social positionings. I return to this point at the end of this chapter when reflecting on the social meanings of levelled *were* and how they are indexically linked.

4.2   Children, Peers and School

If children's language acquisition is rooted in and reflects the accomplishment of social action, then what happens when children enter school – an environment much more diverse than the home? Eckert (2003: 112) has described the school as producing 'a social hothouse effect, as groups and categories emerge around defining norms and carving out social meaning.' This effect is at its most intense during secondary schooling. At primary school, children are outside the home more and engage more with peers, but they remain highly dependent on caregivers (this is not to say that primary school children don't engage in dynamic forms of interaction with their peers – see the work of Snell 2008, 2010, 2013, 2018, and Maybin 2006). However, in adolescence, young people start to define their own peer-based social order as a means to appropriate social control from adults (Eckert 2003: 112). There is a sharp increase in the frequency of interaction with peers (Brechwald & Prinstein 2011), as young people become increasingly autonomous, and renegotiate parent/child relationships (Crosnoe & Kirkpatrick Johnson 2011). Furthermore, the confines of the secondary school system – which entails the 'long-term confinement of large numbers of people of diverging backgrounds and interests to a surprisingly small space with considerable constraints on general behaviour' (Eckert 2003: 112) adds a particular intensity to this life stage, given that the catchment areas of secondary schools are typically much broader than those of primary schools. Consequently, we might think of adolescence as a time in which young people are simultaneously seeking to differentiate themselves from their caregivers *and* from the peers they perceive to be different from them.

As noted above, the school places 'considerable constraints on general behaviour' (Eckert 2003: 112) and these include attempts to control the use of language (Cushing 2020). For some children, going to school may be the first time they hear language ideologies being explicitly expressed. The National Curriculum for English, which provides the standards for primary and secondary schools in England, emphasises the use of Standard English across all educational levels. The Key Stage 1 and 2 guidance (for children aged between five and eleven) states that '[p]upils should be taught to control their speaking and writing consciously and to use Standard English' (Department of Education 2014: 5). The extent to which children can control their spoken language 'consciously' is at the heart of this book and will be discussed further in Chapter 8, but the relevant point here is that, as soon as children start school, they encounter discourse which associates standard language forms with educational success and alignment with the school as institution. So, even if, in the preschool years, children vary their use of local language variants in line with stance and social alignment, school-related discourse enables children to acquire associations between distinct varieties of language and different places in the social order. What children do with this knowledge, and how it might affect the way they employ the language variation they have at their disposal, may depend upon how they want to position themselves vis-à-vis the school as institution. Furthermore their success in using language to position themselves in this way will be affected by the extent to which they can use language flexibly in the first place, and the continuing need to use local variants to articulate the range of social meanings initially acquired in the early years.

As noted above, adolescence provides a life stage in which young people are especially motivated to utilise all the linguistic variability at their disposal as they reconfigure their relationships with adults and their place in relation to the other young people around them. The remainder of this chapter will analyse use of levelled *were* in order to explore what adolescents do with the resources made available to them in childhood as they negotiate their place in the social order and continue their development as social actors.

4.3   Levelled *Were* at Midlan High

As noted above, levelled *were* is identified as a feature of Bolton English and, as such we would expect it to be deeply embedded in the community's dialect. This makes it particularly suitable for an analysis exploring the relationship between language, the social order, and social practice. However, nonstandard variation in past tense BE is found across the entire English-speaking world, so just how distinctive is the patterning of past tense BE in Bolton English?

Table 4.1 shows the patterns of past tense BE that have been observed. Note that Table 4.1 shows tendencies, or increased probabilities of certain variants occurring, rather than categorical patterns. So, the most typical local pattern, (i), levelling to *was* across all persons and numbers, could be used to describe a variety where there is proportionally more *was* with plural subjects than there is any other potential alternative to the standard pattern. Pattern (i) is so common that Chambers (1995: 242) refers to it as a 'vernacular primitive' (see Britain 2002: 25 for an extensive list of varieties in which this pattern has been found). As Cheshire and Fox (2009: 2) observe, BE is the only verb in

Table 4.1 *Agreement patterns for past tense* BE *in English, with example clauses*

		Standard pattern	Levelled pattern (i)	Levelled pattern (ii)	Levelled pattern (iii)
Singular	**First person**	I *was* happy I *wasn't* happy	I *was* happy I *wasn't* happy	I *was* happy I *weren't* happy	I *were* happy I *weren't* happy
	Second person	You *were* happy You *weren't* happy	You *was* happy You *wasn't* happy	You *was* happy You *weren't* happy	You *were* happy You *weren't* happy
	Third person	She *was* happy She *wasn't* happy	She *was* happy She *wasn't* happy	She *was* happy She *weren't* happy	She *were* happy She *weren't* happy
Plural	**First person**	We *were* happy We *weren't* happy	We *was* happy We *wasn't* happy	We *was* happy We *weren't* happy	We *were* happy We *weren't* happy
	Second person	You *were* happy You *weren't* happy	You *was* happy You *wasn't* happy	You *was* happy You *weren't* happy	You *were* happy You *weren't* happy
	Third person	They *were* happy They *weren't* happy	They *was* happy They *wasn't* happy	They *was* happy They *weren't* happy	They *were* happy They *weren't* happy

present-day English that makes a person/number distinction (for instance, it uses a different form for *I* than for *you*, and a different form for *I* than for *we*), so it is unsurprising that the verb paradigm has regularised in many local dialects of English.

Pattern (ii) also shows a regularisation pattern, but with levelling to *was* in clauses for positive polarity (so *I was happy, you was happy*), and levelling to *were* in clauses for negative polarity (so *I weren't happy, you weren't happy*). In this pattern, *was* and *were* distinguish between positive and negative clauses – making past tense BE like its present tense counterparts (such as *am/ain't*), and also like other verbs (such as *will/won't, shall/shan't*) that have distinct positive/negative forms (Cheshire & Fox 2009: 2). Pattern (ii) has been observed in several British speech communities: in Reading (Cheshire 1982), York (Tagliamonte 1998), the English Fens (Britain 2002), Birmingham (Khan 2006), London (Levey 2007; Cheshire & Fox 2009) and in corpora collating data from several British English varieties (Edwards & Weltens 1985; Anderwald 2001). It has also been observed in a number of isolated American English speech communities in North Carolina (Schilling-Estes & Wolfram 1994; Wolfram & Sellers 1999; Wolfram & Schilling-Estes 2003). Levelled *weren't* is often extremely circumscribed in these communities. For instance, in York, Tagliamonte (1998: 179) found it to occur predominantly in tag questions with *it* (for example: *Bit scary, **weren't** it, though?*). Cheshire and Fox (2009: 25) find a similar pattern in London; they also find *weren't it* occurring as an invariant tag (for example: *That's a lot of good, **weren't** it?*). However, in some communities, use of levelled *weren't* is more extensive. For instance, Britain's (2002) data from Fenland English finds levelled *weren't* to be used robustly across all persons in his dataset.

Britain's (2002) Fenland data suggests that levelled *were* was once more robust in the Fens, with older speakers exhibiting something more like pattern (iii) in Table 4.1 (so levelling to *were* irrespective of polarity). This is substantiated by the historical record: Ellis (1869–1889) confirms that levelling to *were* across all persons was once more frequent in several counties in the South (including Norfolk and Suffolk), and also across the North of England. Whilst research from the Fens and from York suggests that levelled *were* – pattern (iii) – is gradually losing out to a levelled *was/weren't* pattern – pattern (ii) – in Southern and Northern varieties, Anderwald (2002: 184) has observed resistance to this change in Lancashire in particular, where pattern (iii) persists.

Bolton was a part of the county of Lancashire until boundary reorganisation in 1974, and the data from Midlan High shows levelled *were* to be robust in positive contexts, occurring 17 per cent of the time. We can compare this to a figure of 3 per cent in Tagliamonte's (1998) data from York, and one of 8 per cent in Britain's (2002) data from the Fens. Perhaps more significantly, there is no real evidence for levelled *was* in the Bolton dialect – either historically or in the Midlan High dataset. Although nonstandard *was* occurs 5 per cent of the time in the speech of Midlan High girls, its use is highly circumscribed. Thirty-eight of the fifty-eight instances of nonstandard *was* occur in existentials (for instance, *there was just like loads of people*) – a context in which variation exists even in standardised varieties of English (Cheshire 1999; Hay & Schreier 2004). Indeed, literature on existential BE (for instance, Britain & Eisikovits 1991; Meecham & Foley 1994; Sudbury 2002) has suggested that the uncertainty of case assignment in this context may be leading to lexicalisation of the *there* +'/*is*/*was* collocations (Cheshire & Fox 2009: 8).

This discussion tells us two things about the use of levelled *were* that are pertinent to the analysis of it at Midlan High. Firstly, levelled *were* seems to be holding ground in Bolton, when compared to other varieties which once also exhibited pattern (iii). As noted above, historical accounts show that *were* across all persons is traditional to the Lancashire area, of which Bolton was once a part (Ellis 1869; Wright 1905; Beal 2004: 121). It continues to be noted as a significant feature of the dialect into the twentieth century: it occurs robustly in the Survey of English Dialects' data collected in Bolton in the 1950s (the survey location was actually within the Midlan High catchment area); it is also recorded as being found across the Bolton area in Shorrocks' (1999: 168–169) comprehensive grammar of the Bolton dialect (which uses data collected in the 1970s); and, more recently, Cheshire, Edwards and Whittle (1993: 26) report that participants observed the occurrence of levelled *were* in their 1990s data from the North-West of England, which included Bolton as a survey location.

Secondly, this stability, and the unusual and localised persistence of pattern (iii) in Bolton English, suggests that levelled *were* has the potential to index place. 'Place', here, is not intended to denote a location designated by 'the stroke of a bureaucrat's pen' (Beal 2010: 225), but to something socially constructed, culturally defined, and symbolically meaningful to the girls of Midlan High and their families (Johnstone 2004; Coupland 2010). This social symbolism is apparent in the awareness exhibited about the variant – in Extract 4.1, Beverley and Lindsey don't just identify levelled *were* as being from Bolton, they own it as constitutive of 'them'. Importantly, Beverley and Lindsey weren't the only girls to identify levelled *were* as a local feature found within their own speech. Extract 4.2 shows Geeks, Lara and Michelle, admitting to their own use of the form in the post-data collection 'language' interviews. Michelle does indeed have a reasonably high use of the form (9.2 per cent, 13/141 tokens), although Lara's use (2.2 per cent, 2/86 tokens) indicates that her claim of using it 'all of the time' is an overstatement.

4.3 Levelled *Were* at Midlan High

Extract 4.2

L   [Um,] I say 'weren't' all the time.
M   [Yeah]

M   I say that. All the time.
L   Yeah.

(Lara and Michelle, Geeks, 57A: 131–135)

Extract 4.3 shows another Geek girl, Susan, admitting to using the form – but Susan also tells us something about how the form can be interpreted. Her comment 'The shame of it!' demonstrates that she is not just aware of the form, she is aware that it is stigmatised. Furthermore, Susan's usage seems to reflect her evaluation of it – she only uses levelled *were* 0.9 per cent of the time (2/225 tokens) in the data recorded at Midlan High.

Extract 4.3

S   I say that too.
EM   Yeah?
S   The shame of it!
EM   No, don't be ashamed.
S   Yeah, I do that too.

(Susan, Geek, 54B: 224–229)

The awareness exhibited in Extracts 4.1–4.3 is likely to be replicated in the community more broadly. The salience of the form (particularly, its potential stigmatisation), and its longevity in the community, suggests that levelled *were* is the kind of variant that would exhibit sociolinguistic variability in child-directed speech (see Smith *et al.*). That is to say, there is reason to assume that sociolinguistic variability around the use of levelled *were* was present in the child-directed speech encountered by at least some of the Midlan High girls.

Of course, precisely which girls encountered levelled *were* in their childhood input will have been affected by factors other than its longevity in the Bolton dialect and its social salience. The well-established finding that regionally restricted variants occur more frequently in the speech of lower social classes means that we would expect there to be more levelled *were* in the input received by girls from lower social class groups. Furthermore, if levelled *were* is particularly associated with the Bolton dialect, rather than being a more general 'vernacular universal', then we would expect it to occur more frequently in the speech of caregivers who were also born and raised in the town.

One way to test these hypotheses is to consider whether levelled *were* use correlates with the social class status of Midlan High girls and – more tentatively – the location in which their parents were born (for all girls in the dataset, parents were the assigned caregivers). If location in the social order has determined a girl's exposure to levelled *were* and, if a girl's subsequent use of the form is conditioned by her exposure to it during language acquisition, then we would expect girls with lower social class status to use more levelled *were* than girls with higher social class status. Similarly, if a girl's parent being born in Bolton provides greater opportunities to acquire a local form like levelled *were*, then we might expect girls with at least one parent born in Bolton to use more levelled *were* than girls with parents born elsewhere. Of course, young children also acquire language from their peers after the age of four too – nonetheless, having familial ties to Bolton means that children are more likely to engage in a larger number of social interactions which support the use of local dialect features. So, parental place of birth could be seen as a proxy for access to local social networks, as well as a potential indicator of input.

By examining correlations with social class and parental place of birth, we can begin to build up a picture of the extent to which young people are potentially constrained by the context of their language acquisition. However, we also know that it is possible for young people to reconfigure the linguistic resources at their disposal to create new social meanings. The extent to which the girls of Midlan High do this will be considered by examining the correlation between use of levelled *were* and community of practice membership. Considering the patterns for social class, parental place of birth and community of practice membership will provide a good indication of the ways in which various social factors affect the type of grammar that the young people at Midlan High use.

4.3.1 The Social Factors: Social Class, Parental Place of Birth and Community of Practice

Social class is an incredibly complex phenomena that has been measured in a number of different ways. For recent extended discussion which focuses on work in sociolinguistics, readers are directed to Rampton (2010), Ash (2013), Snell (2014), Block (2014, 2018), and Chun (2019). It is now generally accepted that a person's social class is not just derived from their economic situation but also from their social position and the ways in which the various activities in which they are engaged are valued (with Bourdieu's 1977 marketplace metaphor encouraging us to think about how some cultural activities, including those related to language use, are more highly prized and rewarded than others). Furthermore, the way in which a person inhabits a particular social position and undertakes certain activities will affect how they embody their social class. This indicates the tension between (i) structural conditions (one's place in the social order) which create material and cultural inequalities and (ii) agency (one's ability to engage in forms of social practice which may challenge or transcend the constraints of one's habitus – Bourdieu 1990: 12–15).

4.3 Levelled *Were* at Midlan High

In order to test the correlation between social class and use of levelled *were* at Midlan High, a measure was used which sought to balance the pupils' economic circumstances with the relative social position of their parents. In this way, social class is operationalised here as a fundamentally economic notion, following Block (2014: 56). Of course, it is also important to acknowledge that we respond to similar circumstances in individual ways – as Rampton (2010: 3) has observed, 'people carry class hierarchy around inside them, acting it out in the fine grain of ordinary life'. For this reason, this analysis attempts to distinguish between (i) the potential influence of a person's economic circumstances (the 'social class' category in this analysis) and (ii) the forms of social practice in which an individual engages (essentially how people 'act out' their place in the social order; i.e., the 'community of practice' category in this analysis). In this way, the analysis seeks to answer the following question: Do people's material conditions cause them to behave in accordance with their place in the social order, or do they resist these potential constraints through more agentive forms of social action?

Following Labov (1966, 2001), social class status was assigned on the basis of an index that allocated each girl a score according to parental education, occupation, and house price, using values current when the data was collected. Parental data were used because of the age of the informants involved. The following education levels were considered: (i) high school (up to fifteen years of age only), (ii) high school (over the age of fifteen), (iii) college (age sixteen to eighteen–18), and (iv) university (age eighteen plus). Occupation was rated according to the Office of Population Censuses and Surveys' (1980) Classification of Occupations and Coding Index, and house price was evaluated using the UpMyStreet website,[1] which provided average house prices for postcode areas. The social class calculations initially resulted in five different class groups, but only four are used in this analysis as only one girl was in the lowest class and her data was excluded because she did not provide data across both years of the study. The four social class groups are described as 'High', 'Mid-high', 'Mid-Low' and 'Low', where 'High' refers to those more likely to have better economic and material conditions than those ranked 'Low'. It is important to note that these distinctions are specific to Midlan High and do not reflect how social class may be distributed across the entire British population. Nonetheless, the dataset includes a wide set of circumstances; average house price ranges from c.£30,000 to c.£140,000 (based on prices at around the turn of the twentieth century); all education levels are represented; and occupations range from care assistant and cleaner, to consultant physician and company director.

---

[1] This has now been acquired by Zoopla; see www.zoopla.co.uk [last accessed 30 May 2023].

To test for a correlation between parental place of birth data and use of levelled *were*, data was collected about where mothers and fathers were born. The analysis sought to compare girls who had (i) at least one parent from Bolton, with those who had parents born elsewhere. Girls whose parents were born elsewhere were further categorised into those who had (ii) at least one parent born locally (i.e., within the north west of England), and those whose (iii) parents were born elsewhere (either elsewhere in the UK or overseas).

Finally, the correlation between community of practice membership and use of levelled *were* was considered by testing the correlation between the community of practice memberships observed in the ethnography (see Chapter 3) and the distribution of the linguistic variable.

The presentation of the results below goes through the stages typically applied in a quantitative sociolinguistic analysis. People new to variationist sociolinguistics might find some of the detail confusing, especially as the analysis turns to the more advanced statistical modelling. If you find yourself in this position, try to focus on the key information. This means noting what patterns seem to be occurring and considering the extent to which the patterns are reliable or unreliable (dependent upon the limitations of the manner of data presentation or processing, as noted in the discussion).

4.3.2   The Distribution of Levelled Were

We start by looking at the raw data. Tables 4.2–4.4 and Figures 4.1–4.3 show the frequencies of our *outcome* variable, levelled *were*, by social class, parental place of birth and community of practice respectively. There is a table/figure for each *factor* or *predictor* (social class, parental place of birth and community of practice), and each table shows the *levels* within the factor group (for instance, for the social class factor, the levels are 'High', 'Mid-high', 'Mid-low', and 'Low'). Starting with social class, Table 4.2 and Figure 4.1 suggests that whilst Mid-low and Low social class groups have similar frequencies, these groups differ from the High and the Mid-high groups, in the expected direction (more levelled *were* the lower the social group).

Table 4.3 and Figure 4.2 suggests that parental place of birth also patterns in the expected direction – with the group who have at least one parent from Bolton using more levelled *were* than the groups who have parents born outside Bolton. Finally, community of practice also shows expected patterns of distinction. The Eden Village girls only use two instances of levelled *were*, making their use as low as 0.9 per cent. On the other hand, the Townies use levelled *were* 48.3 per cent of the time. The Geeks and Popular use falls between these two extremes.

The differences across social class, parental place of birth and community of practice seem to suggest that all three of these social factors correlate with use

4.3 Levelled *Were* at Midlan High

Table 4.2 *Distribution of levelled* were *by social class*

	Number of levelled *were*	Total instances of *was/were*	% Levelled *were*
High	39	826	4.7
Mid-high	302	1701	17.8
Mid-low	196	654	30.0
Low	86	280	30.7

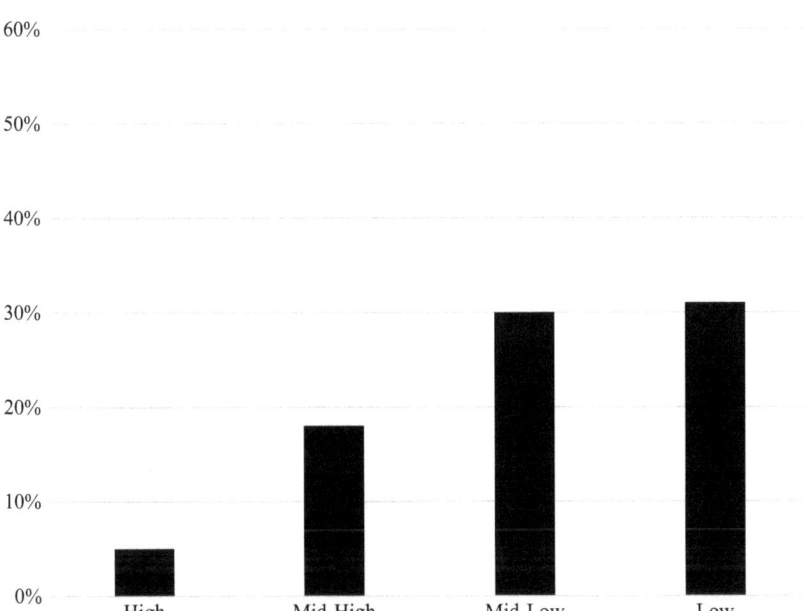

Figure 4.1 Distribution of levelled *were* by social class.

of levelled *were*. However, the data needs to be considered more carefully before we can be confident about this finding. Tables 4.2–4.4 and Figures 4.1–4.3 show only the combined raw data and they do not allow us to evaluate the extent to which any individual might skew the pattern assigned to a particular group. That is to say, how can we be sure that individual members of a group behave in the same way? Is it possible for certain individuals to have a disproportionate effect on the 'group' pattern? Secondly, by viewing each category separately, it is not possible to determine the extent to which data might overlap or be *collinear*. If there is any overlap across social factors, we can't be sure which of them is having the significant effect or, if both

Table 4.3 *Distribution of levelled* were *by parental place of birth*

	Number of levelled were	Total instances of was/were	% Levelled were
Both parents elsewhere	78	1032	7.6
At least one parent local	64	622	10.3
At least one parent Bolton	481	1807	26.6

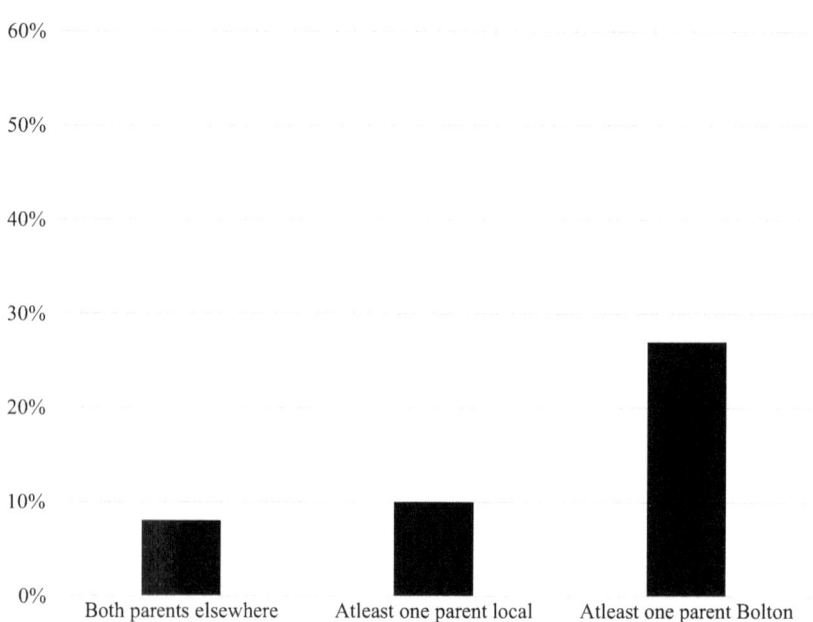

Figure 4.2 Distribution of levelled *were* by parental place of birth.

factors are significant, which is having the most significant effect. For instance, if most of the members of one community of practice all have the same parental place of birth classification, how do we know whether it is their parental place of birth or their community of practice which best explains their use of levelled *were*? In fact, this is precisely the case with the Townie girls: whilst they do not all come from the same social class group, all of these girls have at least one parent born in Bolton. How can we know whether it is their community of practice or their parental place of birth that is having the greatest effect on their language use?

Additionally, studies of language variation and change advise against including levels which show categorical use of one variant over another

4.3 Levelled *Were* at Midlan High

Table 4.4 *Distribution of levelled* were *by community of practice*

	Number of levelled *were*	Total instances of *was/were*	% Levelled *were*
Eden Village	2	573	0.3
Geek	108	1286	8.4
Populars	178	908	19.6
Townies	335	694	48.3

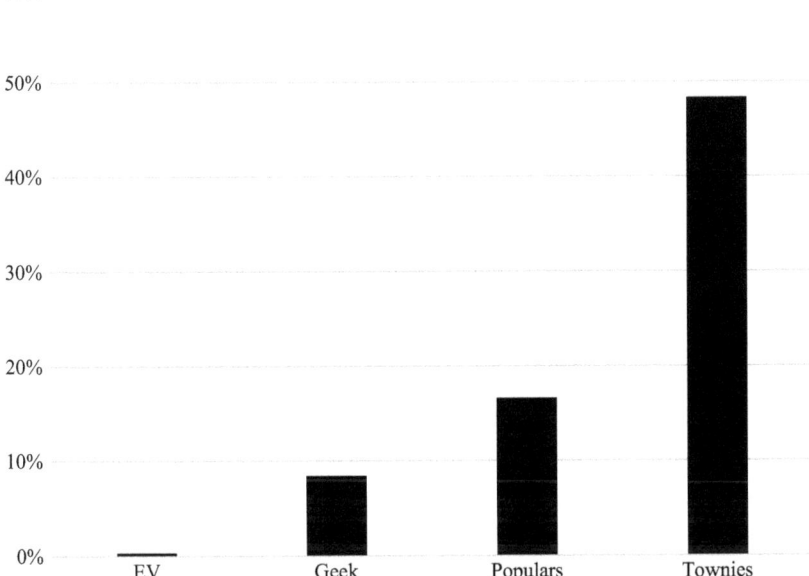

Figure 4.3 Distribution of levelled *were* by community of practice.

(Guy 1988: 132; Tagliamonte 2006: 87) because this can lead to the factors and levels which explain variation (in the data where it does occur) being obscured. In this analysis, the Eden Village girls use only two instances of levelled *were* – and both come from the same speaker, Helen, and from her data in Year 9. By Year 10, she does not use any levelled *were*. This near categorical use of the standard by the Eden Village girls is strong evidence that their community of practice membership conditions their language use – no other factor level within the social class or parental place of birth categorisations exhibits this near categorical status. Consequently, including the Eden Village girls in an analysis testing the effects of other factors on the variation will lead to underestimating or overestimating the effects of certain factors, especially if there is collinearity in the dataset. For instance, all of the Eden Village girls are either in the High or the Mid-high social class groups. Including the members of this near categorical community of practice in the social class analysis might overestimate the effect that being from the High or Mid-high social class group has on the use of levelled *were*. On the other hand, removing the Eden Village girls from the analysis is likely to provide a clearer understanding of the effect of social class on the data (because it will be limited to those speakers who exhibit true variability in their use of levelled *were*). Of course, this does not mean that the way in which Eden Village girls use (or rather don't use) levelled *were* is not important to our understanding of the distribution of the variable, but it does affect how we might want to undertake more complex forms of analysis on the data that seek to determine what best explains the variability.

That Helen, the Eden Villager who produces the two instances of levelled *were*, utters both of these instances in Year 9 also draws attention to something else to consider when seeking to explain the variability in levelled *were*: the year in which the data was collected. It is interesting if the use of levelled *were* changes over time, as it suggests that language use is not fixed according to how an individual is classified socially; or, to put it another way, it suggests that it might be possible to use levelled *were* to signal differences in how a persona is being designed by Midlan High girls. Table 4.5 and Figure 4.4 shows the use of levelled *were* across time. This raw data shows an increase in use of levelled *were* from Years 9 to 10. However, Figure 4.5, which shows the same data broken down by community of practice, suggests that this increase is not universal across all of the communities of practice. Both the Eden Village and the Geek communities of practice actually show a decrease in use of levelled *were* and, whilst both the Populars and the Townies show an increase, the Townie increase is much more dramatic than the Popular one. This raw data suggests that any further data analysis should consider the interaction between community of practice and the year in which the data was collected.

Finally, the raw data shown in the tables and figures in this section does not consider how the distribution of levelled *were* is affected by the types of grammatical constructions or grammatical conditions in which levelled

Table 4.5 *Distribution of levelled* were *by year of recording*

	Number of levelled *were*	Total instances of *was/were*	% Levelled *were*
Year 9	195	1408	13.8
Year 10	428	2053	20.8

4.3 Levelled *Were* at Midlan High

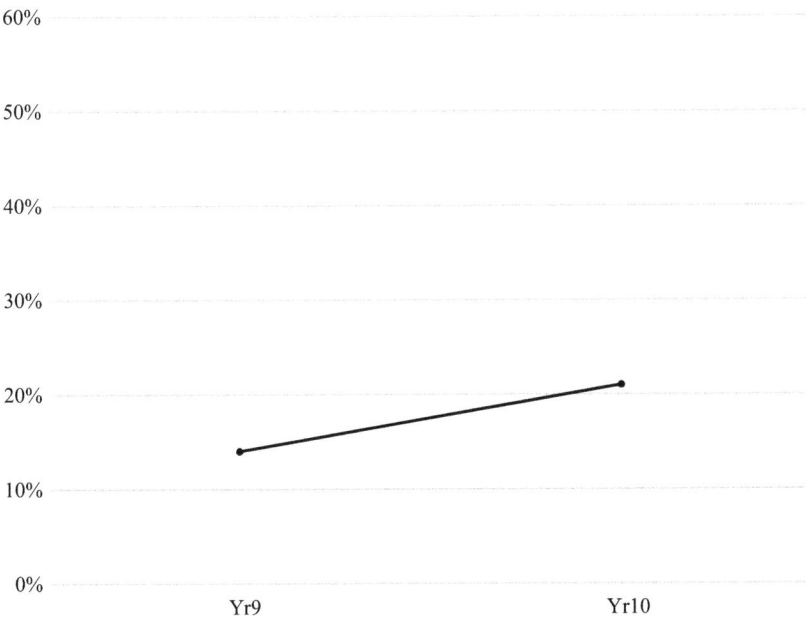

Figure 4.4 Average distribution of levelled *were* by year of recording.

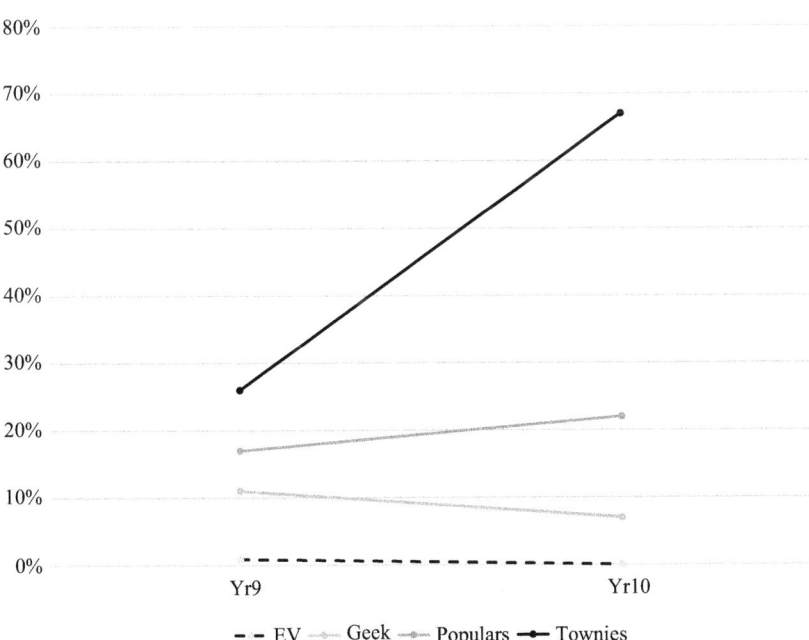

Figure 4.5 Average distribution of levelled *were* by year of recording for each community of practice.

were occurs. That is to say, we know that language has certain properties which predispose it to produce certain patterns – irrespective of how language might be distributed socially. For instance, we saw that polarity (so whether a clause is positive or negative) determined the nature of pattern (ii) – with levelled *were* occurring much more frequently in negative clauses than positive ones. Anderwald (2002: 182) has noted that any language generalisation strategy is strongly preferred in negative contexts over positive ones, so we would expect there to be more levelled *were* in negative contexts no matter what other factors are affecting the variation, or what pattern (i.e., i–iii) past tense BE is exhibiting. Previous studies on past tense BE have noted that structure of the clause containing the instance of past tense BE can also matter: more levelled *were* has been observed in tag questions (Tagliamonte 1998; Anderwald 2002: 178; Cheshire & Fox 2009). Other studies have also shown that the subject type might affect the frequency with which levelled *were* occurs – with existential subjects, in particular, exhibiting more *was* (Cheshire & Fox 2009: 8), and subjects types that are more complex or opaque (like compound indefinites such as *everyone*) potentially occurring more frequently with levelled forms – possibly due to 'general processing reasons' (Tagliamonte 1998: 172). It is vital to consider these kinds of language internal conditions when evaluating the patterning of levelled *were* because we do not want to attribute too much explanatory power to social factors if, for instance, there is an overlap between a linguistic condition (such as use of negative clauses) and the data from one particular social group. Imagine if the Townies happened to use more negative clauses than the Populars, for example. If this were the case, we would want to figure out whether it was the occurrence of negative clauses or someone's status as a Townie that best explained their use of levelled *were* in any one instance. For this reason, the language internal factors are considered in the next section.

4.3.3 *The Distribution of Levelled* Were *and Language Internal Factors*

Table 4.6 shows all of the linguistic factors that were considered in the analysis, and also the raw frequencies with which they occurred with first and third person past tense BE. Note that these frequency counts exclude data from the near categorical Eden Village speakers in order to get the most representative distribution of variability in the data.

Table 4.6 shows some clear and expected patterns. Firstly, the clause type group shows that tag questions occur with levelled *were* 86.8 per cent of the time – making them very different from all other clause types. This is entirely in-line with the previous research discussed above, and also reflects the unique discourse functions of tag questions – something that will be explored further

4.3 Levelled *Were* at Midlan High

Table 4.6 *Linguistic factors considered in the analysis of levelled* were *at Midlan High*

Factor	Example	N	% levelled *were*
CLAUSE TYPE			
Irregular progressive SIT, STAND and LIE	She **was** stood there, like that. (Kim, Popular, 38A: 1107)	63	1.6
Quotatives	I **was** like '(PULLS FACE)' (Kim, Popular, 38A: 1107)	209	3.7
Wh-question	*When was this?* (Kara, Geek, 5B: 792)	43	16.3
Declarative	*He were older* (Amanda, Townie, 40A: 1080)	2481	22.4
Regular question	***Weren't** it like three o'clock?* (Meg, Townie, 40A: 536)	46	37.0
Tag question	She was virtually going around bragging it, **weren't** she? (Caroline, Geek, 46B: 9)	38	86.8
SUBJECT TYPE			
existential *there*	*There **was** a space left* (Amanda, Townie, 40A: 854)	87	11.5
Clausal	*Summat like cycling round and stuff to have a picnic was like dead..weird* (Kara, Geek, 44B: 219)	53	13.2
1sg *I*	*I **wasn't** there all the time* (Melanie, Geek, 42B: 151)	838	14.7
3sg *this/that*	*That **was** really good* (Sally, Popular, 19A: 499)	187	16.6
3sg *it*	*It **was** really artistic* (Marie, Popular, 53A: 323)	656	23.8
3sg NP	*Her phwoar-fit boyfriend **were** there* (Ellie, Townie, 19B: 677)	285	25.6
3sg *s/he*	She **were** feeling sorry for herself (Meg, Townie, 21A: 428)	719	27.0
Compound indefinites	Everyone **were** against me (Jennifer, Geek, 48A: 523)	63	42.9
POLARITY			
Positive	*I **was** still a bit pale* (Caroline, Geek, 46B: 210)	2719	19.5
Negative	*It just **weren't** funny* (Lindsey, Popular, 30B: 318)	169	54.4

in Chapter 7. Regular questions also occur with levelled *were* more frequently than declaratives, but *wh*-questions use levelled *were* less frequently than declaratives. Previous studies do not separate out question types, but the relatively infrequent use of levelled *were* with *wh*-questions may reflect the perception that these question types are relatively formal in comparison with regular questions (Kearsley 1976: 371). The other clause types of note are the irregular progressive SIT/STAND/LIE clauses and quotatives – both of which strongly disfavour levelled *were*. Instead of *I was sitting/standing/lying*, the predominant form used in Bolton English is *I was sat/stood/lay* (see Cheshire *et al.* 1993: 70–71, and Edwards & Weltens 1985: 109, for a discussion of these irregular progressives in North West England). As the example in the table shows, these forms commonly occur in contexts where they introduce some kind of dramatised action or where they express something about the speaker's orientation to the action they have described. This overlaps with the discourse functions associated with quotatives (Buchstaller 2013) – something which can be seen from the examples in Table 4.2. Kim's use of an irregular progressive of the verb STAND introduces a demonstration of bodily stance: *She **was** stood there, like that*. The quotative example, which also comes from Kim and immediately follows the progressive STAND example in her talk, introduces another act of bodily expression: *I **was** like '(PULLS FACE)'*. Elsewhere, researchers have found progressive SIT/STAND/LIE verbs being used to more directly introduce speech: Stein (1990); Rickford, Wasow, Zwicky, and Buchstaller (2007), and Rathje (2009) have suggested these forms may be developing new quotative functions (cf. Stein's (1990) example: 'I'm sitting there, "This is an English test?"'). The parallel patterning of quotatives with the irregular progressive auxiliaries in the Midlan High dataset suggests that these two clause types may serve related discourse functions and that these constructions may have grammaticalised differently from other *was/were* forms (see Buchstaller (2004) for a comprehensive discussion of the grammaticalisation of quotatives). Forms that have grammaticalised may be more likely to use fixed expressions – reducing the likelihood of variability with forms like *was* and *were*.

A closer look within some of the other groups in Table 4.6 reveals differences from other studies on variability in past tense BE. In the subject-type group, compound indefinites (e.g., *everyone*) occur with levelled *were* more frequently than other subjects. This is not surprising, as compound indefinites refer semantically to a mass of individuals so we might predict that they would more frequently take an agreement strategy typical of plural subjects. Nonetheless, this contradicts Tagliamonte's (1998: 169) data, which suggested that these pronouns did not pattern any differently to other third-person pronouns. The order with which the other subject types more frequently take levelled *were* seems to pattern most closely with what Britain (2002) observed in his study of Fenland English, rather than with other studies of past tense BE. This is unsurprising if we consider that Britain (2002) described his dataset as typical of pattern (ii) but with a relic pattern (iii) system. The Midlan High data also patterns more like the Fens data with regard to existential subjects, which occur with levelled *were* less frequently than any other subject type (that is to say *there was a space left* is much more likely than *there were a space left*, with the latter pattern occurring only 11.5 per cent of the time). Previous discussion of existentials and past tense BE have suggested that analogy with there's + plural constructions (e.g., *there's loads of examples*) may lead to more levelled *was* in pattern (ii) varieties (Meecham & Foley 1994; Britain 2002: 19). Wolfram and Sellers (1999: 109) suggest that such forms might become lexicalised to the extent that they can even inhibit levelled *were* in

4.3 Levelled *Were* at Midlan High   97

varieties that permit this with other subject types. However, it's important to note that this lexicalisation strategy is not evident in all varieties; the data analysed by Schilling-Estes and Wolfram (1994) and Tagliamonte (1998) suggests that *there weren't* is more likely to be the lexicalised form in the communities they study.

Finally, Table 4.6 suggests that polarity exhibits the anticipated effect: levelled *were* occurs more frequently in negative clauses than in positive ones.

Whilst there seem to be some clear patterns in how language internal factors affect the use of levelled *were* – just as was the case with the social factors – it is difficult to evaluate the relative effects of these factors compared to all the other potential causes of variability. In order to get a clearer sense of the factors governing variability in levelled *were* at Midlan High, the next section describes a statistical model which evaluates the relative effect of any one social or linguistic factor on the use of levelled *were* whilst also controlling for the potential effects of all other factors *and* the ability for individuals to skew the patterns observed in the group categories.

4.3.4   Determining the Significant Effects on Levelled Were: *Generalised Linear Mixed Effects Modelling*

Regression modelling tests the relationship between a group of predictor variables (social class, parental place of birth, community of practice, clause type, subject type and polarity) and an outcome variable (use of levelled *were*). The relationship between any one predictor (say, social class) and use of levelled *were* is tested while holding all other predicators (parental place of birth, community of practice, clause type, subject type and polarity) constant. The contribution of an individual predictor variable (social class in our example) is tested against a null hypothesis of it having no effect on use of levelled *were*. If the null hypothesis is rejected by the regression model then the predictor variable (e.g., social class) is considered to have a statistically significant effect on how levelled *were* varies. In addition to including the social and linguistic factors described above as fixed effects, a mixed-effects model can also include speaker as a random effect (Johnson 2009). Unlike fixed effects, which include categories that can be generalised in wider populations, random effects are less predictable – individuals do not always behave according to the trends of the categories they constitute. Including speaker as a random effect helps to ensure that predictors are only reported as significant when they are strong enough to show an effect over and above the variation across individual speakers. This helps us to be confident that the results for any one factor are reliable and not overly affected by the idiosyncratic language use of any one individual speaker.

Generalised linear mixed-effects regression modelling was carried out using the 'lme4' package in R (Bates *et al.* 2019). The Eden Village group were excluded from this modelling because of their near categorical use of levelled *were*. In addition to excluding categorical and near categorical levels from predictor factors, levels can also be combined, where appropriate, in statistical analysis in order to reduce problems arising from low data counts. The only levels that were combined in this analysis were the quotatives and irregular progressive levels in the clause-type factor, given the similarity in discourse function and raw data patterns of these two levels (as discussed above). A model was then fit with all the predictors, and a variance inflation factor (VIF) test run to check for collinearity. This test suggested that the social class and parental place of birth factors were highly correlated. As parental place of birth was not significant in the original model, but social class was, parental place of birth was removed from the model. This resolved the issue with collinearity in further VIF testing. An ANOVA was run comparing the two models and, as the one including parental place of birth was not significantly different from the one including it, the model without parental place of birth was selected. The data was then tested for interactions between year of recording and social class, and year of recording and community of practice. This showed a significant interaction between year of recording and community of practice. Although the interaction between year of recording and social class was not significant, this interaction was still included in the final model as an ANOVA found the difference between a model with the year of recording/social class interaction and one without the interaction to be significant. This significant difference suggested that including the year of recording/social class interaction improved the model – put another way, even whilst being insignificant, including the year of recording/social class interaction helps the model to better interpret the variation.

Table 4.7 summarises the results of the regression analysis. The regression analysis works by testing one baseline level in each factor group against all of the other levels. In this model the baselines for each predictor were Geek (community of practice), High (social class), first-person levelled *I* (subject type), declaratives (clause type), and negative (polarity).

In the results, the 'odds ratio' statistic refers to the effect of a predictor on the likelihood of levelled *were*. Where the odds ratio is less than 1, levelled *were* is less likely to occur, and where the odds ratio is more than 1, levelled *were* is more likely to occur. Confidence intervals are shown in the CI column. The range here indicates the degree of certainty in the strength of the effect; wider ranges indicate lower confidence, suggesting that the result should be reviewed more cautiously. Whether or not a result is statistically significant is indicated by the *p* value given in the final column: a *p* value of <0.05 is accepted as a significant result and bolded in the p column. The other value to

4.3 Levelled *Were* at Midlan High

Table 4.7 *Results of the generalised linear mixed-effects modelling for use of levelled* were

Predictors	Use of levelled *were*		
	Odds Ratios	CI	p
(Intercept)	0.03	0.00–0.24	**0.001**
Clausetype [quotatives/irregular clauses]	0.16	0.08–0.33	**<0.001**
Clausetype [question wh-]	0.48	0.18–1.28	0.141
Clausetype [question reg]	1.18	0.53–2.62	0.693
Clausetype [question tag]	17.58	3.74–82.55	**<0.001**
subject [comp indef]	3.32	1.62–6.80	**0.001**
subject [3sg NP]	2.19	1.43–3.38	**<0.001**
subject [3sg s/he]	2.02	1.45–2.80	**<0.001**
subject [3sg it]	1.51	1.07–2.14	**0.019**
subject [3sg this/that]	1.67	0.96–2.92	0.070
subject [clause]	1.03	0.37–2.88	0.953
subject [existential]	0.54	0.24–1.22	0.139
Polarity [positive]	0.15	0.09–0.25	**<0.001**
CofP [Townie]	75.66	11.28–507.61	**<0.001**
CofP [Popular]	3.78	0.84–17.10	0.084
SocClass [Low]	23.75	2.45–230.55	**0.006**
SocClass [Mid-Low]	12.46	1.40–111.22	**0.024**
SocClass [Mid-High]	1.98	0.27–14.24	0.499
Year of recording [Yr9]	0.72	0.24–2.17	0.561
Year of recording [Yr9] * CofP [Townie]	0.18	0.09–0.38	**<0.001**
Year of recording [Yr9] * CofP [Popular]	1.05	0.45–2.41	0.917
Year of recording [Yr9] * SocClass [Low]	0.34	0.11–1.01	0.051
Year of recording [Yr9] * SocClass [Mid-Low]	0.91	0.31–2.66	0.869
Year of recording [Yr9] * SocClass [Mid-High]	1.66	0.63–4.38	0.310
Random Effects			
σ^2	3.29		
$\tau_{00\ speaker}$	1.94		
ICC	0.37		
$N_{speaker}$	22		
Observations	2888		
Marginal R^2 / Conditional R^2	0.473 / 0.668		

note is R^2. This refers to the proportion of the data that can be explained by the model, or the model's 'goodness of fit'. The marginal R^2 provides the value based on the fixed effects in the model (social class, community of practice, Year of recording, clause type, subject type and polarity), the conditional R^2 provides the value based on the fixed effects and the random effect (individual speaker). Ideally, values should be greater than 0.5, but lower values are considered acceptable for social science data, because of the difficulty in making firm predictions about human behaviour (Winter 2013, in Dann 2019: 177).

The regression model shows statistically significant results in all factors tested, as can be seen from the bolded *p* values. This suggests that clause type, subject type, polarity, community of practice and social class all have an effect on whether or not levelled *were* occurs. The bolded levels indicate which of the levels within the factor has the significant effect when compared to the baseline level. The model also finds a significant interaction between Year of recording and the Townie group. Note, though, that the model output only shows the extent to which a given level is different from the baseline level. For instance, in the clause type factor, both the quotatives and irregular progressive clauses, and tag questions are significantly different from the baseline declarative clauses, but we can't easily see whether tag questions are significantly different from, say, regular questions. One way to look into this is to conduct post hoc Estimated Marginal Means (EMMs) testing. This analysis is employed in the next section to determine where significant differences lie within particular factor groups.

4.3.5 *Teasing Apart the Significant Levels within a Factor Group*

Table 4.7 shows that three linguistic factor groups are significant: clause type, subject type and polarity. There are only two levels in the polarity factor group, so we can say with confidence that positive polarity disfavours levelled *were* when compared with negative polarity. However, the multiple levels in the clause type and subject type factor groups require further post hoc analysis to tease apart the significant levels. Starting with clause type, Figure 4.6 shows the pairwise EMMs between the levels in the clause-type factor group. The black dots represent the Tukey-adjusted EMMs (this helps to establish which means among a set of means differ from the rest), the light grey bars show the confidence intervals (wider bands means the data should be treated more cautiously), and the arrows allow comparisons across levels (we can interpret differences to exist – with a probability level of 0.05 – where the light grey bars don't overlap).

Figure 4.6 suggests that tag questions are significantly different from all other clause types, and that quotatives and irregular progressive clauses are

4.3 Levelled *Were* at Midlan High

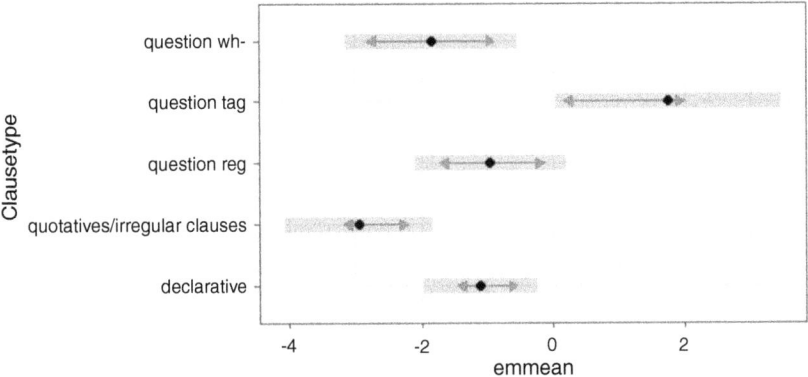

Figure 4.6 Pairwise comparisons of EMMs between the levels in the clause-type factor group.

significantly different from all clause types except wh-interrogatives. The odds ratios in Table 4.7 indicate that levelled *were* is more likely to occur with tag questions, but less likely to occur with the quotatives and irregular progressive clauses. However, note the large confidence intervals for tag questions in Table 4.7 and the large light grey bar in Figure 4.6. This is because there are only thirty-eight instances of first- and third-person past tense BE with tag questions; this compromises the reliability of the statistical models. Nonetheless, given the similar findings of other studies on past tense BE variability, we can assume with some certainty that tag questions do have a significant effect on the use of levelled *were*.

Table 4.7 shows that, in the subject-type factor, compound indefinites are significantly more likely to occur with levelled *were* than with the first-person pronoun baseline level. All of the third-person pronouns are also significantly more likely to occur with levelled *were* than with the first-person pronoun baseline level, with the exception of *this/that* subjects, which are only just below significance. Existential subjects are not significantly different from the first-person baseline, but the EMMs shown in Figure 4.7 suggest that they are significantly different from compound indefinites and most third-person pronoun subjects. Note here that the confidence intervals (the light grey bars) are very wide for some levels – this is no doubt a consequence of the number of levels in this factor group and small data counts for some levels.

We have seen that several language-internal factors affect how frequently levelled *were* occurs, irrespective of any social effects on the data. Tag questions, compound indefinites, most third-person subjects, and negative clauses are more likely to occur with levelled *were*; whereas quotative and

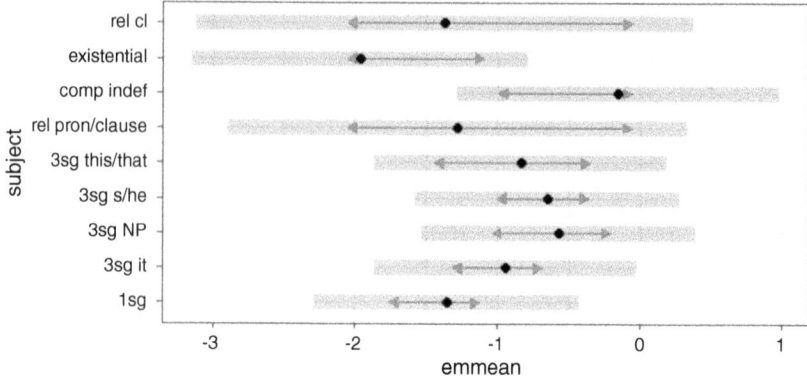

Figure 4.7 Pairwise comparisons of EMMs between the levels in the subject-type factor group.

irregular progressive clauses, existential subjects and positive clauses are more likely to occur with standard *was*. These findings can be summed up as follows:

(i) Polarity: levelled *were* is more likely to occur in negative clauses.
(ii) Clause type: tag questions favour levelled *were*, quotatives and irregular progressive clauses favour standard *was*.
(iii) Subject type: compound indefinites and most third-person pronoun subjects are more likely to favour levelled *were* than existential subjects.

Turning now to the social factors, this modelling – which takes into account the effect of each social factor, whilst also controlling for all other factors, allows us to more confidently interpret the descriptive statistics discussed in earlier sections. First, recall that parental place of birth was collinear with social class and was removed in the preliminary modelling of the data. To double check that parental place of birth was not a significant predictor, a model was also created that removed social class and ran parental place of birth in its place. Parental place of birth was still not significant in this second model. This provides us with fairly clear information that, whilst the descriptive statistics show a relation between having a parent from Bolton and greater use of levelled *were*, the variance in levelled *were* is better explained by other social and linguistic factors which happen to correlate with parental place of birth. To understand this, it might help to think about an individual token of levelled *were*, like the bolded example in the following utterance from Townie girl, Amanda (45B: 323): *That's the only reason she found out, **weren't** it?* Amanda's dad is from Bolton, so she was included in the 'at least one parent from Bolton' category. However, Amanda

4.3 Levelled *Were* at Midlan High

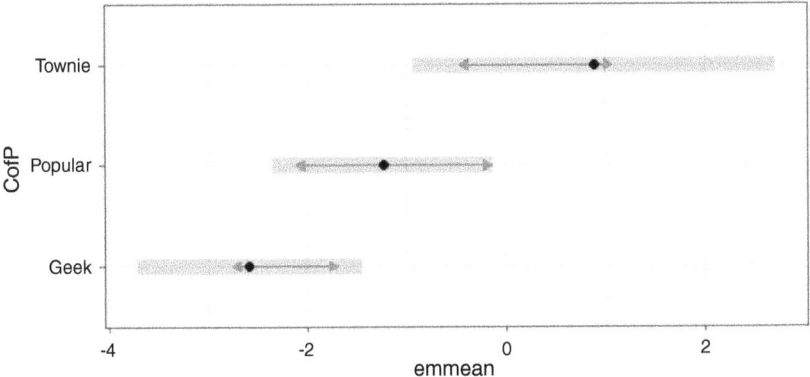

Figure 4.8 Pairwise comparisons of EMMs between the levels in the community of practice factor group.

is also a Townie, and she is in the Mid-high social class group. Furthermore, her utterance has a third-person subject and is a negative tag question. When all of these factors are considered across all of her potential instances of levelled *were* and all the other instances in the dataset, parental place of birth does not stand up against other potential predictors to explain why levelled *were* occurs here and elsewhere.

Nonetheless, other social factors did show up as statistically significant. We already know that the Eden Village group are different from the other groups. The statistical model tested the other communities of practice against each other and found significant differences. Table 4.7 shows that the Townies are significantly different from the baseline Geek level, but Populars are not (although they are not far from significance). The EMMs in Figure 4.8 show this more clearly. The arrows show significant overlap between the Populars and the Geeks, but only marginal overlap between the Populars and the Townies. Again, note the very large confidence intervals for the Townie data in both Table 4.7 and Figure 4.8. This is most likely because there are only three girls in the Townie group and, because the Townies so frequently use levelled *were*, there are empty cells in the analysis for several levels. Nonetheless, the Townies use of levelled *were* is so distinct from the other girls at Midlan High that we can be fairly confident in this result.

Turning now to the social class results, we can see that both the Mid-low and the Low levels were significantly different from the baseline High level. This is confirmed by the EMMs in Figure 4.9. Again, there are some broad confidence intervals for this data, but it shows similarity between the two highest social class levels when compared to the two lowest levels.

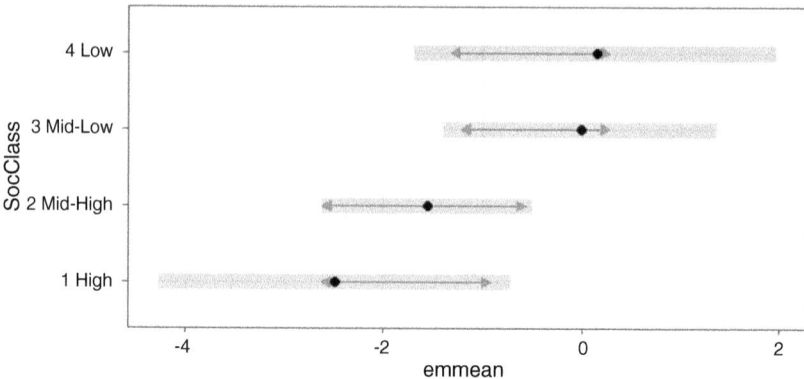

Figure 4.9 Pairwise comparisons of EMMs between the levels in the social class factor group.

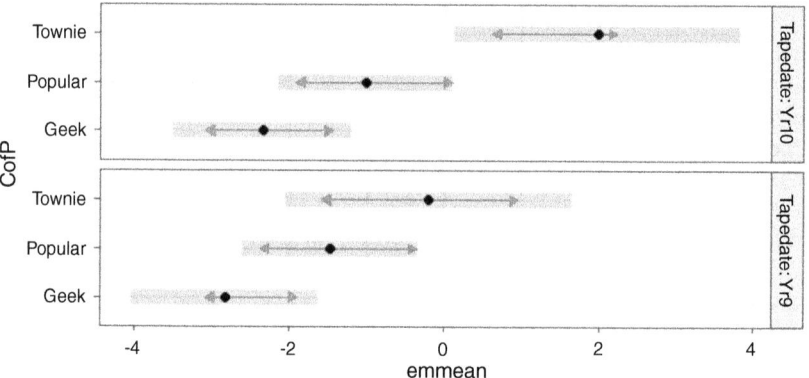

Figure 4.10 Pairwise comparisons of EMMs between the levels in the community of practice factor group, by year of recording.

Finally, the data in Table 4.7 shows that we were right to be cautious about the relationship between Year of recording and use of levelled *were*; Year of recording was not a significant predictor of levelled *were* use in this model. However, the model did find the interaction between Year of recording and community of practice to be significant. The EMMs in Figure 4.10 show this. In Year 9, only the Geeks are significantly different from the Townies but, by Year 10, both the Geeks and the Populars are significantly different from the Townies.

Using a mixed effects regression model on this data has allowed us to see where the social factors affect use of levelled *were* when language internal

4.4 What Constrains Our Use of Grammatical Variation?

effects are held constant. Parental place of birth did not have a statistically significant effect on the data, whereas both community of practice and social class did. Furthermore, we also saw that the year in which the data was recorded interacted with use of levelled *were*, with Townies using significantly more levelled *were* in Year 10 than in Year 9. These findings can be summed up as follows:

(i) The Eden Villagers are different from other social groups in having no consistent use of levelled *were*; the Townies are more likely to use levelled *were* than either the Geeks or the Populars.
(ii) The highest social class group is significantly less likely to use levelled *were* than the Mid-low or Low social class group.
(iii) Townies are more likely to use levelled *were* in Year 9 than in Year 10.

In this section, mixed effects regression modelling was used to better understand how social and linguistic factors constrain the use of levelled *were* at Midlan High. But what do these results tell us about how social factors affect our use of linguistic variation? We turn to this question in the next section.

4.4 What Constrains Our Use of Grammatical Variation?

We started this chapter by thinking about social class and how our place in the social order might affect the language that a person acquires and how they might use that language. The analysis suggested that the social class of the girls at Midlan High does play a role in constraining the language that they use, with those in the lower social classes using more levelled *were*. This is not a surprising result. There are decades of sociolinguistic research showing correlations between social class and language use for all kinds of sociolinguistic variables. The more interesting finding is that social class does not seem to be the only, or even most, significant social factor determining use of levelled *were* at Midlan High. The preliminary review of the raw data revealed that the Eden Village girls showed near categorical use of standard *was*, despite coming from two different social class groups (albeit both at the upper end of the socioeconomic hierarchy: Helen and Leah are in the High group, and Ruth, Lucy and Alex are in the Mid-high group). Perhaps more convincingly, membership in the Townie community of practice significantly correlated with use of levelled *were*, despite none of the Townie girls coming from the lowest social class group (Amanda and Ellie are in the Mid-high group, and Meg is in the Mid-low group). So, whilst the results for social class support the idea that those with parents in the lower social class groups may have been more likely to acquire and use levelled *were* by virtue of their place in the social order, the results for community of practice suggest that place in the social order does not necessarily constrain how children use language in adolescence. The 'not necessarily' is important here; what is it that determines how free someone is to adapt their speech beyond what their place in the social order might predict?

Here we can go back to those principles of access, opportunity and motivation that were introduced in Chapter 1. The Townie girls, Amanda, Ellie and Meg, are situated somewhere in the middle of the socioeconomic hierarchy at Midlan High. All of them have at least one parent from Bolton. At some point in early childhood, it's likely that they will have come across levelled *were* in their input, even if it did not occur at a high frequency. However, we saw that parental place of birth was not a significant predictor of levelled *were* use at Midlan High. This is most likely because of the age of the girls in the study. As discussed earlier, whilst young children initially acquire language from their caregivers, young children also acquire language from their peers after the age of four. For most children, with the exception of those who live in highly homogeneous communities, school will provide more heterogeneous input than what was provided at home. Consequently, parental place of birth will have an initial effect on children's language use, but what matters as childhood language acquisition continues is input in its totality. So long as some of their peers use levelled *were*, girls like Amanda, Ellie and Meg will have *access* to it; and, so long as there are *opportunities* to interact with those who use levelled *were*, girls like Amanda, Ellie and Meg can potentially acquire it – even if it was not in their initial pre-school language input. This leaves us with the matter of *motivation*. What might motivate the Townie girls to use levelled *were*?

In subsequent chapters, we will think more about how grammatical items gain their social meaning, but we've already encountered clues about the symbolic potential of levelled *were*. In the language interviews discussed above, levelled *were* was associated with how people from Bolton speak and it was also considered to be stigmatised by some. Chapter 3 illustrated how a key part of the Townie persona was their engagement with older boys. These older boys tended to live in predominantly working-class areas outside the immediate catchment area of Midlan High, making the Townies' experience of 'Bolton', and the full range of its linguistic resources, more complex and diverse than that of other girls. Secondly, Townie girls are rebellious; they embrace things that subvert polite norms. As Susan illustrated in Extract 4.3, using levelled *were* could be considered 'shameful' by those who were invested in the school as institution. Consequently, one potential use of levelled *were* (but by no means its only use) seems to be its ability to symbolise rejection of institutional norms (and, indeed, a wide range of social meanings indexically linked to the subversion of hegemonic standards). Perhaps more positively, as we'll discuss more in Chapter 5, linguistic resources that are associated with working-class groups can also symbolise more positive attributes associated with working-class culture, including being

4.4 What Constrains Our Use of Grammatical Variation?

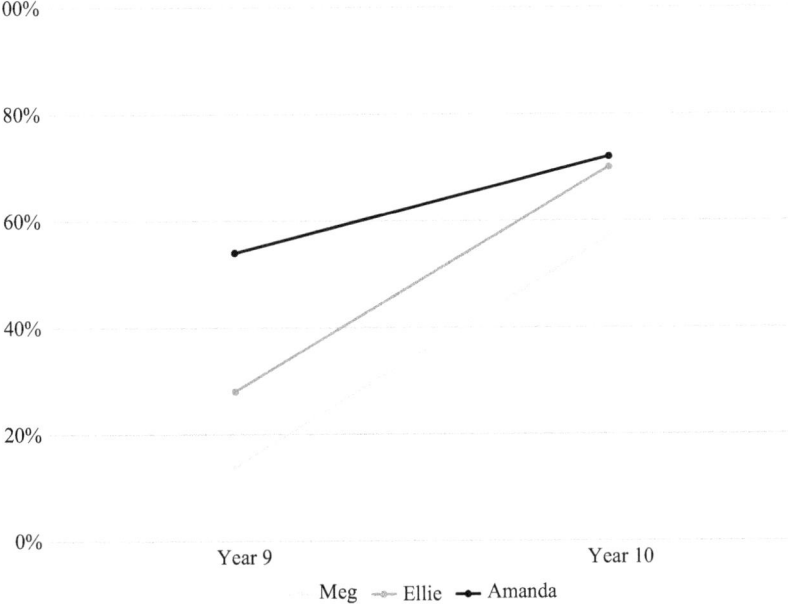

Figure 4.11 The Townies' use of levelled *were* over time.

laid-back, being straight-talking, or being resilient. The Townies' increasing use of levelled *were* over Years 9 and 10, shown in Figure 4.11, hints at the diverse utility of this local grammatical item as they fashion themselves as the most socially extreme group at the school.

The Townies' ability to exploit levelled *were* in this way comes from their social and spatial mobility, and their motivation to exploit all of the resources at their disposal. They have access, opportunity and motivation to use levelled *were* as a symbol of their social distinctiveness. Furthermore, as Figure 4.11 shows, this is an enterprise they are collectively engaged in.

The Townies' social circumstances can be contrasted with those of the Eden Village girls. All of the Eden Villagers come from the same small village, which is a bus ride away from Midlan High. Their elite home address, with its elevated house prices, means that they are all in the High or Mid-high social class group. Unlike girls in the other communities of practice, all of the Eden Village girls went to the same primary school. They began to more regularly encounter girls from other locations on starting Midlan High, but they do not wilfully interact with girls from outside their local clique. Helen's use of two instances of levelled *were* indicate that she is capable of using this form, but the fact that she does not use this form at all in the Year 10 recordings indicates her entrenchment in the Eden Village group and her alignment with their values and practices. The Eden Villagers are all in the two highest social class groups, which may have impacted the extent of variation in their input, but this cannot be the only factor explaining their language use; plenty of other girls at Midlan High are in high social class groups but use more levelled *were* than the Eden Villagers. This suggests that their language use must also be conditioned by their limited spatial and social mobility (reducing access to the form, and opportunities to use it) and the absence of any motivation to align themselves with the symbolic potential of levelled *were*.

This chapter began by posing the question of whether being working class meant that an individual could not help but use nonstandard grammar. To what extent have we observed individuals using language to develop identities which transcend their place in the social hierarchy? The results clearly indicate that the linguistic resources available to us may be determined by the situation of our upbringing and our language input – including what we get from caregivers and, later, from peers. However, the discussion of how young children acquire sociolinguistic variation indicated that, even at a very early age, children are able to use language variability in nuanced ways if their language input varies by social context. This work suggested that children start by learning to use language variability to construct stances and personae. Nonetheless, the stances they learn in relation to variants like levelled *were* are likely to reflect a wider social system, given that they are learning this behaviour from adults, who have experienced social stratification and related systems of value. This means that young children's linguistic behaviour may reproduce the wider social schemes of meaning associated with levelled *were* but their metalinguistic awareness of variables like levelled *were* is likely to be lower than adults if they have had limited engagement with the institutions and discourses in which those schemes of meaning circulate.

The data from Midlan High provides some insight into the point at which children gain increased metalinguistic awareness of social meanings associated with character types. The Townies' use of levelled *were* seems to draw upon the meanings that this variant carries in relation to the wider social class hierarchy. That is to say, by Year 10, their actions (including what they do linguistically) are affected by the ways in which levelled *were* is evaluated in establishment discourse and how it is linked to character types. That is to say, the change in the Townie's linguistic behaviour over time reflects a shift from using levelled *were* to articulate stance and alignment in line with their language input, to using levelled *were* in more agentive ways to index the social meanings that this form has in wider societal discourse. Of course, in using levelled *were* in these ways, the Townies also add to the indexical field of levelled *were* by using it to construct a wild, daring and rebellious locally salient persona.

4.4 What Constrains Our Use of Grammatical Variation? 109

In Chapter 3, it was hypothesised that, as a regionally restricted morpholexical variant, the social meaning of levelled *were* is rooted in character-type associations, which are indexically linked to stance-related meanings. These stance-related meanings derive from the qualia and properties linked to character-type associations. The analysis in this chapter suggests the process through which these social meanings are acquired and adapted, and this process is schematised in Figure 4.12. The black inner circle exemplifies how young children encounter the use of levelled *were* when it exists in their language input. Note that all of these social meanings are stance-related and are determined by the contexts in which they are most likely to encounter the use of levelled *were* in their caregivers' speech. Note too that these social meanings are compatible with positive characterisations of working-class

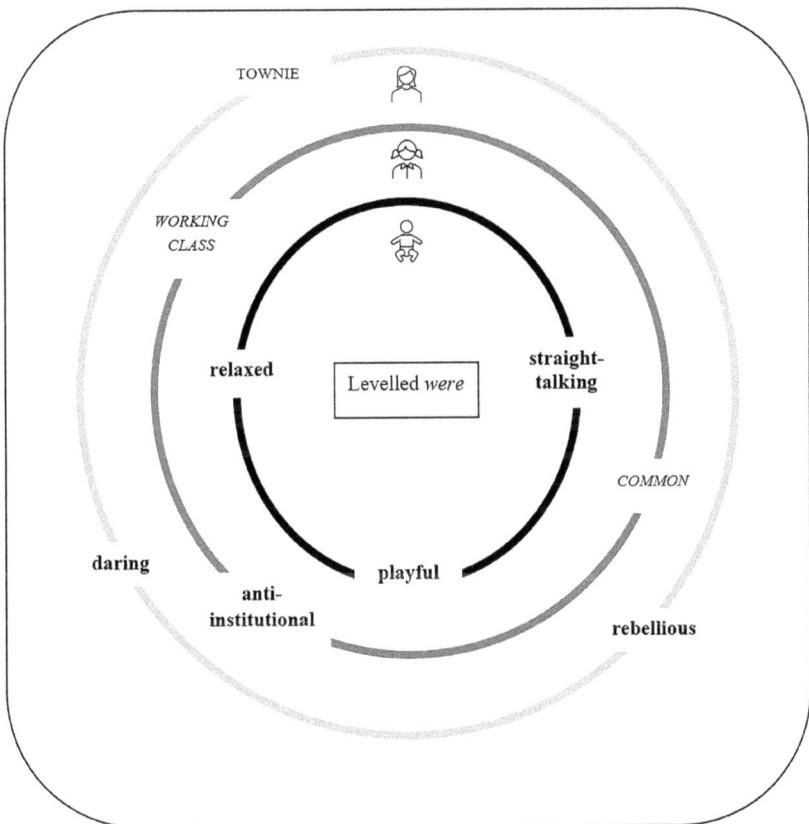

Figure 4.12 A hypothetical indexical field of levelled *were*, showing how social meaning may develop for an individual over time.

social types even if young children have yet to acquire this indexical link. The dark grey circle exemplifies the social meanings that children are likely to begin to encounter when they increase their social networks and encounter hegemonic discourse about the social order and associated meanings. Finally, the light grey circle exemplifies what young people can then do with this combination of social meanings as they develop personas in adolescence, using the Townies as a case in point.

What the indexical field in Figure 4.12 stresses is that all social meanings reflect a view from somewhere. Some of the previous literature on social meaning, with its focus on character-type social meanings, might be interpreted as being too narrowly focused on how localised variants recursively articulate quite pejorative class-based social meanings (like those in the dark grey circle in Figure 4.12). However, as noted in Chapter 3, working-class life is not something that is experienced negatively by all (or even most) of those categorised as working class. Positive experiences of working-class life are reflected in the attributes present in the inner black circle in Figure 4.12. Importantly, if an individual encounters these positive associations first, it is possible that these associations have some cognitive primacy in how that individual both processes and produces variants like levelled *were*. This has implications with regard to an individual's abilities to style shift and their motivation for doing so. These issues are explored in more depth in Chapter 8.

The analysis in this chapter has shown that language is not a simple reflex of social class, but that it is in a complex dialogue with it. Our language use is constrained by what we have access to, but when we have access to language variability, we can use it. However, we will only use a given linguistic resource if it works to represent who we want to be or how we want to appear in any given moment. In the next chapter, we consider how linguistic practice related to the use of a linguistic variant is further complicated when a variant has a more complex grammatical structure than levelled *were*.

5 How Do We Use Grammar to Design Our Talk?

Extract 5.1

1	EM	How do you think you've changed?
2	L	I don't know.
3	B	I've gone taller (LAUGHS).
4	EM	(LAUGHS)
5	L	Since I've been hanging around with you, my voice has got more common.
6	B	Aw, thanks!
7	EM	(LAUGHS)
8		
9	B	[That's nice!]
10	L	[Well, I don't just –] (LAUGHS)].
11		
12	L	No, I don't mean it nasty, but it has. (SNIFFS) **I don't talk proper no more**
13		(LAUGHS).
14	EM	(LAUGHS)
15	B	'Proper'.
16		
17	L	Properly.

(Beverley and Lindsey, Populars, 41A: 48–64)

Extract 5.1 comes from a recording I made with Populars, Beverley and Lindsey, when they were in Year 10. It was the first time that I had recorded them since I had last seen them at the end of Year 9. In response to a question about how they had changed since I last saw them, Lindsey observes that her 'voice has got more common' in l. 5. She goes on to say 'I don't talk proper no more' in l. 12. This is an instance of negative concord: the marking of negation by using both a negative particle and an indeterminate (*n't* and *no*, respectively, in this example) where standard English would use just one negative marker to relate the same referential meaning.

Lindsey's evaluation of her own speech is accurate if we take use of negative concord as an indicator of 'talking properly'. Lindsey, who is from the highest socioeconomic group, uses no negative concord at all in Year 9 (0/8 tokens), but she uses it 37.5 per cent of the time in Year 10 (3/8 tokens). Why has her use of negative concord changed? She clearly knows how to talk 'proper' as her correction on l. 17 indicates. She is also a high-achieving

Popular who is doing well in her school work. Her use of negative concord is not about ignorance of societal norms. Quite the opposite, it reflects explicit awareness of these norms and their social meanings.

Negative concord has been described as 'arguably the most common stigmatized variable in the English language' (Eckert 2000: 216). To a large extent, its general social stigma is inescapable. To use the terminology introduced in Chapter 3, its status as a shibboleth suggests it is *iconic*: an instance of negative concord is interpreted as depicting inherent social qualities of those who are believed to use it most frequently (Gal & Irvine 2019: 39). Negative concord is more frequently found in the speech of the lower social classes (Labov 1972a; Cheshire 1982; Eckert 2000; Smith 2001; Anderwald 2005; Childs 2017) and in social groups characterised as 'delinquent' or 'anti-school' (Cheshire 1982; Eckert 2000). Consequently, its dominant social meanings derive from how these kinds of groups are perceived: as tough, rebellious and anti-authority. As one of the Populars who maintained networks with some of the Townie girls, Lindsey's practice is somewhat aligned with these stances and social positions.

However, is the social meaning of negative concord that simple? As noted in Chapter 3, iconisation involves another ideological process, *erasure* (Gal & Irvine 2019: 20–21). It is not the case that all members of the lower social classes are tough, rebellious or anti-authority (and, even if they were, we might choose to depict these kinds of qualities more positively as resilience, independence, and being straight-talking). Rather, it is that these qualities have been ideologically linked to lower-class status whilst other qualities have been rendered invisible. This happens when a social group is depicted relative to the most powerful dominant group in society and found to be lacking, or – at best – 'other'. Members of lower social classes are 'tough' because the upper classes are 'refined'. They are 'rebellious' because they don't necessarily follow the rules as defined by the upper classes. And they are 'anti-authority' because they are outside the 'authority' making the rules.

The stigmatised status of negative concord is a consequence of its evaluation as a marked variant when contrasted with a standard norm. But how is negative concord viewed in communities where its use is not marked, as it is in wider society? In their work on the small fishing community of Buckie in Scotland (see Chapter 4), Smith and Holmes-Elliott (2022) find high use of negative concord in the forty-nine adults analysed – overall rates of use are at 49 per cent, with forty-three variable speakers, two categorical negative concord users, and four categorical standard negation speakers. They find little variation by age or gender. It is unusual to find no gender variation for negative concord (see the studies cited above) – leading Smith and Holmes-Elliott (2022: 71) to conclude that negative concord is 'a community norm for the vast majority of speakers in this sample'. The only significant social factor affecting use of negative concord in multivariate mixed effects logistic regression is whether or not the speaker is talking to a community insider or a community outsider: lower rates of negative concord are used with the community outsider. Overall, these findings suggest that negative concord is not stigmatised *within* the community; its status as stigmatised is only relevant when community members interact with outsiders and exocentric norms are interactionally salient.

Smith and Holmes-Elliott's work suggests that an emphasis on the stigma of negative concord has resulted in inadequate understandings of how this variant functions in communities where its use is more normative. Rather than framing negative concord as a stigmatised icon, it might be better to think of negative concord as a *rheme*: a sign 'that could be conjectured as iconic by some guesses, yet taken by others to be indexical, depending on the presuppositions and knowledge of those who make the guesses' (Gal & Irvine 2019: 106). Consider Extract 5.2.

Extract 5.2

It's lunchtime, and Townies, Ellie and Meg, are telling me and Kim (a Popular girl) about a fight they had with older girls at the weekend. The interaction is being recorded. As Ellie is talking, two dinnerladies come into the classroom and interrupt her.

1	E	And then, even though she'd bottled me and I saw everyone starting on her, I legged it
2		down and I pushed everyone away, and I stood in front of her like the little hero I am..
3		
4		(DINNERLADIES DL1 AND DL2 OPEN DOOR)
5		
6	E	D'you mind? We're recording in here .. Ey! Shut the door, we're recording in here.
7		(DL CAN BE HEARD TALKING TO SOMEONE ELSE) We're recording! .. (UNDER
8		BREATH) Shut the fecking door!
9	DL2	D'you want me to close the door?
10	E	Yeah.
11	EM	Thanks.
12		
13		DL1 COMES IN
14		
15	E	We're recording, [Miss!]
16	K	[We're recording] here.
17		
18	E	We're recording.
19	DL1	You don't say it like that. Just a nice explanation would–
20		
21	E	[Sorry, we're recording. Please,] please will you bog off.
22	K	[(POLITELY) We're recording, Miss.]
23		
24	K	Yes.
25	DL1	Aw, come on.
26	E	Miss, you know **it won't get no nicer than that**.

(Ellie, Townie, and Kim, Popular, 19B: 491–516)

Before the dinnerladies entered the classroom in which we were recording, Ellie had been recounting her heroic efforts to protect her friend, Meg, from older girls who had come over to punish her for throwing a bottle at Ellie ('bottling' her). Ellie is stressing the importance of Townie solidarity with Meg which endures despite Meg drunkenly throwing a bottle at her. The story is exciting and highlights the Townie's involvement in violence, drama and illicit activity. Ellie is visibly and audibly exhilarated as she relates the evening's events. She embodies Townieness as she relates the story, and this persona is also articulated in her response to the dinnerlady who refuses to leave us alone in the classroom. Ellie becomes more and more frustrated, and she articulates what she wants with increasing levels of intensity. She begins by simply informing the dinnerlady that we are recording on l. 15 and this is accompanied by the negatively polite marker 'Miss'. When the dinnerlady reprimands her for her tone (Ellie is shouting and markedly irritated), Ellie replies with politeness markers 'Sorry' and 'please' on l. 21, but then immediately follows this with a face threatening demand that the dinnerlady 'bog off'. As the dinnerlady persists in ignoring Ellie's implicit and explicit requests to leave, instead coaxing Ellie to amend her tone, Ellie explicitly rejects the dinnerlady's requests with the assertion that her manner of speaking 'won't get no nicer than that' (l. 26). This is uttered as a token of negative concord.

There are several things going on in this interaction. The girls had greeted me that day, excited about the story they wanted to tell. As mentioned in Chapter 2, the girls often treated our recording sessions like opportunities to set down events and occurrences that were important to them. It was clear that the story was something they wanted to be a permanent record of their activities. Its importance stemmed from its ability to represent the Townies through their actions – it showcased their strength, their toughness, and the durability of their friendship to one another. The telling of it was a performance of Townieness. However, there are other things going on in this interaction too – Ellie is frustrated with the dinnerlady and she expresses this frustration with increasing intensity. The instance of negative concord occurs at the nexus of these stances and states, and is embodied by Ellie's Townie persona.

This chapter will explore the extent to which negative concord serves to express different types of social meaning which are variably linked to the expression of stance and the embodiment of personae and social types. This builds on the analysis in Chapter 4 by more thoroughly exploring the relationship between stance and social meaning, and the extent to which individuals are able to flexibly employ a range of indexical meanings in the design of their talk. In moving from a morpholexical variant to a more firmly morphosyntactic one, the analysis in this chapter will begin to consider the extent to which the grammatical structure of a variable affects its pragmatic function, which, in turn, makes it more or less easy to use that construction to articulate certain stances in interaction. Are there differing in-group and out-group social meanings associated with negative concord and, if so, are there differences in the roots of these social meanings? Heightened metalinguistic awareness of negative concord suggests the stigmatised social meanings of negative concord operate via the character type (Type CT) trajectory described in Chapter 3 – i.e., its meanings are rooted in an association with social types or personas. But the possibility of grammatical structure affecting pragmatic structure might also result in social meanings rooted in semantics i.e., via a Type SM trajectory, particularly if negative concord has normative status in a community's linguistic repertoire. This leaves us with the following question: Does the pragmatics of the repetition of negative particles have any role to play in the development of in-group social meanings, or does the hegemonic presence of social stigma bleach out this pragmatic function? This chapter will attempt to explore the balance between social association and pragmatics for this highly stigmatised linguistic variable.

In the next section, we turn to consider the semantic inferences of negative concord in order to better understand its social distribution at Midlan High.

5.1 The Semantics of Negative Concord

There are two ways to read a sentence like *I didn't do nothing*. As Beltrama and Staum Casasanto (2021: 87) note, '[w]e normally interpret the semantic meaning of sentences by assembling the semantic meaning of their parts'. In standard English, each negation (*n't* and *nothing*) contributes independently to the sentence meaning, creating a reading that is logically equivalent to an affirmative (where *I didn't do nothing* = 'I did something'). However, with negative concord, the two negative particles yield only one semantic negation (such that *I didn't do nothing* = 'I didn't do anything'). It is not possible to infer the meaning of the sentence by deconstructing its individual parts – instead the negative markers work together to signal one semantic negation. This violation of the 'compositionality principle' has led to generative grammarians treating negative concord as an agreement phenomena (Blanchette 2015: 50); the indeterminate does not express negation, rather it serves to license the constructional expression of negation (Ladusaw 1992: 252).

Because the standard English reading of *I didn't do nothing* differs from the nonstandard English one, predominant syntactic theories have tended to assume that the two readings of this construction belong to separate grammars (Blanchette *et al.* 2018: 2). In this view, a variety either exhibits syntactic negation (as in negative concord) or semantic negation (as in standard English) but not both (Zeijlstra 2004: 8). However, Blanchette *et al.* (2018) provide evidence that standard English speakers who do not report use of negative concord still display grammatical knowledge of it. Experimental data (from gradient acceptability studies) shows that standard English speakers not only discriminate between negative concord and standard English readings, they prefer negative concord readings under certain syntactic and pragmatic conditions. This leads Blanchette *et al.* (2018: 13) to conclude that negative concord 'is grammatical but un- or under-realized in the usage of Standard English speakers'. They hypothesise that this is because of the heavily socially stigmatized nature of negative concord in contemporary English-speaking societies.

If negative concord (e.g., *I didn't do nothing*) and its standard variant (e.g., *I didn't do anything*) have the same semantic referential meaning within a single speaker's grammar then we must assume that differences in use are not driven by encoded semantics but by what each variant can infer pragmatically. That is to say, we must assume that they fulfil different roles in the system of negation in English. Negative concord is clearly the marked variant – both by its lower frequency in the general population and according to universally recognised prescriptive norms – although the salience of this markedness may vary significantly from community to community, as noted above. Perhaps more pertinently, negative concord is also marked by what could be construed as the semantic redundancy of additional negative markers. From the perspective of decoding, if extra steps are required to interpret the meaning of a construction then it is likely to become more salient.

Eckert (2019a: 754) notes that the social meanings of a linguistic variant can be intensified by repetition (compare *This is so interesting* with *This is so so interesting*). This point has been made with specific reference to the multiple negative markers of negative concord (Labov 1984; Eckert & Labov 2017: 469). Others have noted that negative concord is emphatic (Cheshire 1987: 270, citing Edwards *et al.* 1984; Palacios 2017: 174). More specifically, Labov (1972a: 803–804) observes that the cumulative nature of negative concord (i.e., the multiple negative markers) and the postposing of the negative indeterminate (i.e., its postverbal positioning) serves to place focus on the negation itself. He also notes that negative concord is an optional variant in almost all varieties that use it. Even in the Buckie example noted above, where negative concord is accepted as a community norm, only two of forty-nine speakers are invariant in their use of it, and the average use is 49 per cent. This variance leads Labov (1972a: 804) to conclude that '[w]hen the pattern typical of careful speech gives way to the vernacular, NEGCONCORD is used by speakers to make their strongest points stronger' – something evident in Ellie's use of negative concord in Extract 5.2. Given these observations, we might consider the syntactic structure of negative concord to predispose this form to the articulation of emphasis and/or intensity – at least in those varieties where its use varies with standard negation (i.e., negative concord is not categorical). That is to say, variable negative concord may have pragmatic utility, allowing speakers to position themselves in discourse via the emphatic projection of the particular stances articulated in their interactions.

This leaves us with a dilemma about the sources of social meaning for negative concord. The same dilemma was acknowledged by Levinson (1988: 166) in his work on another nonstandard negative marker, *ain't*. Are forms like negative concord and *ain't* more frequent in the speech of certain social groups because of their ability to index group identity? Or does their increased frequencies in some styles reflect their ability to convey certain states and stances that are more frequently articulated by certain social groups?

In order to answer this question, we now turn to an analysis of negative concord at Midlan High. We begin by examining how negative concord is distributed in the community. This provides clues about its relationship to social types and personas. We then turn to a more nuanced analysis of how this variant enters into the discourse of Midlan High girls. This analysis shows a correlation between negative concord and certain topics but, more specifically, a link between negative concord and the articulation of certain stances and states.

5.2 Negative Concord at Midlan High

Negative concord occurs much less frequently than levelled *were*, and it is also used by a much smaller subset of Midlan High girls than levelled *were*. Only ten of twenty-seven Midlan High girls (or 37 per cent) use negative concord, whereas twenty of twenty-seven Midlan High girls (or 74.1 per cent) used levelled *were*. This in itself indicates something about the function of negative concord, which we will explore further below.

The variable examined here is negation with postverbal indeterminates. The term 'indeterminate' is used following Labov (1972a: 775) who states that 'the label "indeterminate" was first applied by Klima (1964) to distinguish *any, ever* and *either* from other indefinites like *some*, primarily on the basis of their co-occurrence with negative and question features'. The variants are negative concord and standard negation. Five-hundred-and-eighty-four tokens of negation with postverbal indeterminates were found in the Midlan High corpus, but only fifty-seven (or 9.8 per cent) of these were realised as instances of negative concord. These low data counts make regression modelling unfeasible. Consequently, the following sections will present the raw data and some basic statistic hypothesis tests. Whilst readers are advised to interpret the data cautiously due to small data counts, there are good reasons to think the patterns in the data are meaningful. The key social patterns relating to social class, community of practice and parental place of birth largely replicate those found for levelled *were* (where it was possible to do more robust statistical modelling). Furthermore, in addition to the social analysis, each token of negation was coded for a number of linguistic factors, namely, the form of the indeterminate, the verb, the form of the negative element, the position of the indeterminate, the total number of indeterminates in the negated sentence, and the clause type. Any linguistic context that was categorical was removed from the analysis, ensuring that the analysis was undertaken on truly variable contexts. This left 547 tokens of negation with postverbal indeterminates; 10.4 per cent of these tokens were realised as negative concord.

The following sections provide information on how negative concord was distributed across linguistic and social factors at Midlan High. Predictors were tested for significance using either a chi-square test or a Fisher's Exact test. Post-hoc tests were subsequently used to evaluate which of the individual factors within a predictor group had a significant association with the use of negative concord. These tests were conducted in R using the function *chisq.posthoc.test (x, method = "bonferroni", round = 6)*, and by undertaking post hoc pairwise comparisons, also employing a Bonferroni correction.

5.2.1 The Distribution of Negative Concord by Linguistic Factors

Tables 5.1–5.3 show the linguistic factors significantly associated with postverbal negation with indeterminates according to either a chi-square test or a Fisher's Exact test. One asterisk indicates a factor that is positively associated with negative concord, and two asterisks indicate a factor that is positively associated with standard negation, according to post hoc testing.

Linguistic factors positively associated with negative concord include determiner *any/no*, nonstandard contracted negative elements (including *ain't, dint, wunt* etc.), and indeterminates positioned in the main clause. Given the focus of this chapter and space constraints, I will say no more about the distribution of these linguistic factors, other than to comment that the linguistic effects in

Table 5.1 *Results indicating the effect of indefinite type on the occurrence of negative concord (Fisher's Exact, two-sided, p = 0.004)*

Factor	Example	N	% neg concord
any/no (det)*	Rick dint give no water	59	22.0
anybody/nobody	Her mum doesn't talk horrible to anybody	28	17.9
any/none (pron)	Don't tell any of t'teachers	20	15.0
anyone/no one	Don't tell anyone I told you	66	12.1
anymore/no more	They don't have it anymore	120	10.8
anything/nothing☐	Zoe dint put **nothing** in your bag	254	5.9

5.2 Negative Concord at Midlan High

Table 5.2 *Results indicating the effect of negative element on the occurrence of negative concord (Chi-square, $\chi^2(3) = 8.36$, $p = 0.004$)*

Factor	Example	N	% neg concord
Nonstandard contracted form*	He **ain't** going out with that girl no more	86	18.6
n't	**Don't** tell no-one	282	9.9
not	Did she **not** have anything on?	126	7.9
never	She'd **never** do anything to hurt you	53	5.7

Table 5.3 *Results indicating the effect of position of the indeterminate on the occurrence of negative concord (Chi-square, $\chi^2(1) = 5.64$, $p = 0.018$)*

Factor	Example	N	% neg concord
within main clause*	I dint do nothing	439	12.1
elsewhere☐	They never call her a swot or anything	108	3.7

this dataset were comparable with those found in previous studies (such as Labov 1972a; Smith 2001; Anderwald 2005).

5.2.2 The Distribution of Negative Concord by Community of Practice

Community of practice is significantly associated with use of negative concord (Chi-square, $\chi^2(3) = 134.54$, $p < 0.000$). The raw data for each group is given in Table 5.4. It shows that Eden Village girls never use negative concord. Figure 5.2 shows that only two Geek girls (Susan and Jennifer) use negative concord. Susan uses it once out of sixteen possible occurrences, Jennifer uses it three times out of three possible occurrences. Both Susan and Jennifer only use negative concord in Year 10, as shown in Figure 5.1. Post hoc testing suggested that the Eden Villagers and the Geeks are not significantly different in their use of negative concord (Fisher's Exact, $p = 0.578$): both of these communities of practice are positively associated with the use of standard negation.

Roughly half of the Populars use negative concord (note that in Figure 5.2, it is not possible to see every individual speaker's circle where data counts overlap). Girls in this group tend to use it relatively frequently or not at all, with percentage use ranging from 0 per cent to 33 per cent. Although Figure 5.1 shows an overall decline in Popular use from Years 9 to 10, those

120   How Do We Use Grammar to Design Our Talk?

Table 5.4 *Use of negative concord by community of practice*

	Actual frequency of negative concord	Possible frequency of negative concord	% use of negative concord
Eden Village	0	75	0.0
Geek	4	250	1.6
Popular	15	169	8.9
Townie	38	90	42.2

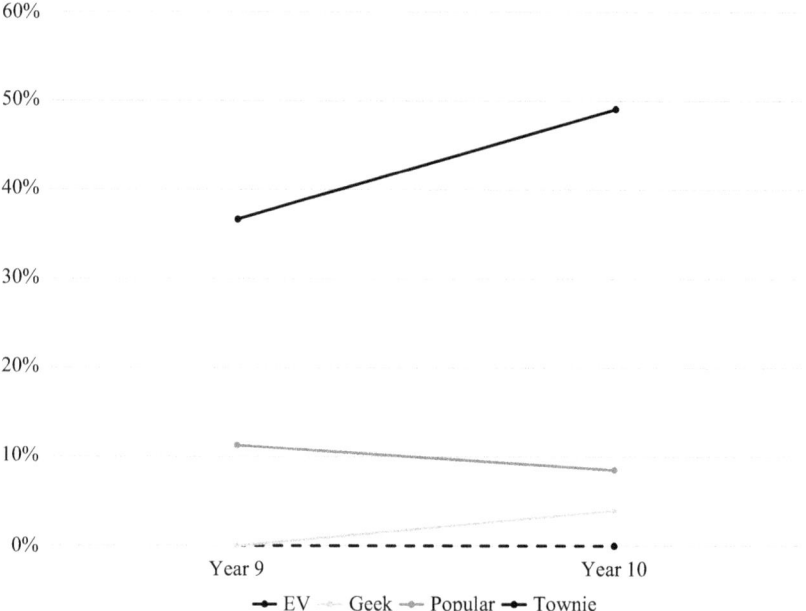

Figure 5.1 Mean use of negative concord over time, by community of practice.

Popular girls who use negative concord frequently tend to increase their use from Years 9 to 10. Post hoc testing suggested that the Populars were not significantly associated with standard negation nor were they significantly associated with negative concord. This is not surprising, given that the Popular group is split into those who use negative concord frequently and those who don't use it at all. Nonetheless, the Populars are significantly different from both the Eden Villagers (Fisher's Exact, *p = 0.006*), and the

5.2 Negative Concord at Midlan High

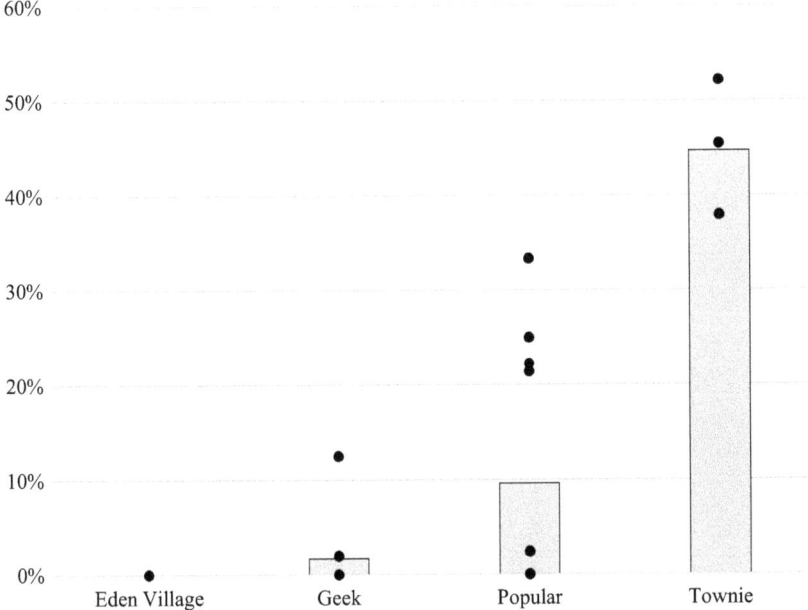

Figure 5.2 Distribution of negative concord according to community of practice. Bars show group means; circles show individual speakers.

Geeks in their use of negative concord (Chi-square with Yates' continuity correction, $\chi^2(1) = 11.185, p = 0.001$).

All of the Townies use negative concord frequently and their use of negative concord increases from Years 9 to 10, as shown in Figures 5.1–5.2. They are the only community of practice where all members behave consistently in their use of negative concord (with use ranging from 38 per cent to 55 per cent). Post hoc testing showed that the Townies are positively associated with negative concord and that they are significantly different from all other communities of practice in their use of negative concord (Eden Village/Townie: Chi-square with Yates' continuity correction, $\chi^2(1) = 38.582, p < 0.000$; Geek/Townie: Chi-square with Yates' continuity correction, $\chi^2(1) = 98.317, p < 0.000$; Popular/Townie: Chi-square with Yates' continuity correction, $\chi^2(1) = 37.473, p < 0.000$).

5.2.3 The Distribution of Negative Concord by Social Class

The raw social class data is given in Table 5.5. Statistical association tests suggest that social class is significantly associated with use of negative concord (Fisher's Exact, two-sided, $p = 0.005$). However, post hoc testing revealed that the significance of social class is a consequence of a positive association between

Table 5.5 *Use of negative concord by social class*

	Actual frequency negative concord	Possible frequency of negative concord	% use of negative concord
High	4	118	3.4
Mid-high	28	303	9.2
Mid-low	18	127	14.2
Low	7	36	19.4

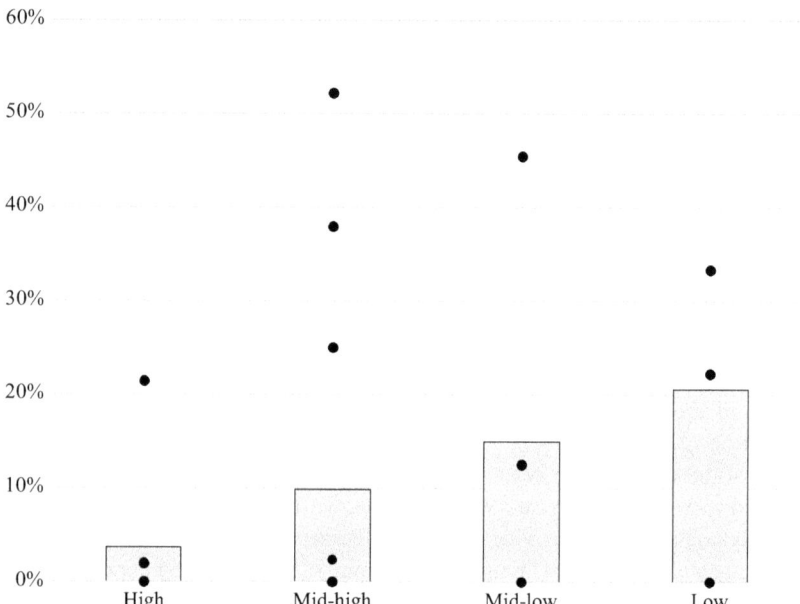

Figure 5.3 Distribution of negative concord by social class membership. Bars show group means; circles show individual speakers.

the highest social class group and standard negation. This association makes the High social class group significantly different from the Mid-low social class group (Chi-square with Yates' continuity correction, $\chi^2(1) = 7.0747, p < 0.008$) and the Low social class group (Fisher's Exact, $p = 0.004$), but none of the other social class groups are significantly different from one another.

Figure 5.3 appears to show a general negative correlation with class and mean use of negative concord (as class status decreases, mean use of negative concord increases). However, there is a good deal of intragroup diversity in the use of negative concord. There is a little more consistency in the highest social group. There are six girls in this group and four of the circles are overlapping: these girls do not use negative concord at all. The fifth girl uses negative concord 2 per cent of the time, and the sixth individual is anomalous with a reasonably high use of 21 per cent. The other social class groups are distributed across the scale of use with less homogeneous patterning in use of negative concord.

5.2.4 The Distribution of Negative Concord by Parental Place of Birth

In Chapter 4, linear regression modelling of the levelled *were* data failed to find a statistically significant effect for place of birth, suggesting that apparent patterns in the raw data were a consequence of place of birth interacting with more significant social factors such as social class. These collinearity effects are all the more acute in the negative concord data given the much smaller data counts for this variant. Table 5.6 shows the raw data for use of negative concord by parental place of birth. Whilst having one parent from Bolton appears to increase the frequency with which negative concord is used, recall that all the Townies have at least one parent from Bolton. As Table 5.6 shows, there are forty-three tokens of negative concord from girls who have at least one parent from Bolton. Thirty-eight of these (or 88.4 per cent) are from the Townie girls. Given the clear significance of Townie membership on use of negative concord, this suggests that an apparent correlation between use of negative concord and having at least one parent from Bolton arises from an interaction with community of practice membership and parental place of birth.

There are other good reasons to discount parental place of birth as having an effect on use of negative concord. Unlike levelled *were*, which patterns uniquely in Bolton and nearby Lancashire (when compared with other English regions), negative concord has been considered a 'vernacular universal' (Nevalainen 2006). It is found in localised varieties of English across the UK and beyond. For this reason, we would expect social class to have a more significant effect on use of this form, irrespective of what variety a person acquired in childhood (or any factor, like parental place of birth, that is serving as a proxy for childhood input). For this reason, the remaining

Table 5.6 *Use of negative concord by parental place of birth*

	Actual frequency negative concord	Possible frequency of negative concord	% use of negative concord
Bolton	43	297	14.5
Local	5	143	3.5
Elsewhere	9	144	6.3

discussion focuses on the association between the social meanings of negative concord and their relationship to social practice and social class.

5.2.5 Summary of the Social Distribution of Negative Concord

The Midlan High data show that use of negative concord correlates with social class but, as with levelled *were*, there seems to be a more substantial correlation with community of practice membership. The significance of social class is limited to a significant difference between the High social class group (which is positively associated with standard negation) and the Mid-low and Low social class groups. None of the other social class groups are significantly different from one another. This suggests that being in the highest social class group inhibits the use of negative concord, but being in another social class group is not significantly associated with use of negative concord. On the other hand, whilst the Eden Villagers and the Geeks do not differ significantly from one another in their use of negative concord, these two groups differ significantly from the Populars and from the Townies (who also differ significantly from one another). This suggests that the use of negative concord increases across the communities of practice in-line with their placement on a continuum of rebelliousness: Eden Village girls use no negative concord; Geeks largely also use none, with the exception of two girls; Populars split between those who have no use and those who have a moderate use; and Townies have the highest use of negative concord across the sample.

These findings accord with what previous studies have told us about negative concord. It has been suggested that negative concord is used less frequently by those in higher social classes, and more frequently by those in lower social class groups (Labov 1972b; Smith 2001; Anderwald 2005; Childs 2017). It has also been noted that negative concord tends to be used more by young people who have 'delinquent' personas (Cheshire 1982; Eckert 2000). The Midlan High data finds an association between use of standard negation and high social status, although, notably, not between negative concord and lower social class status. This suggests that high social class serves to inhibit use of negative concord, but lower social class does not predict use of negative concord. That is to say, use of negative concord is not simply a consequence of one's social background. Rather, at Midlan High, community of practice seems to be a more reliable predictor of negative concord use. This variant is used most frequently by the community of practice who embody the most 'delinquent' personas – the Townies – irrespective of individual Townies' social class statuses. Does this mean that negative concord is symbolic of the Townie persona?

If negative concord is a symbol of 'Townieness', why do people other than the Townies use negative concord? What does it mean when the Populars and Geeks use negative concord? To understand why we see these patterns

5.3 The Discourse Context of Negative Concord

amongst these speakers, we need to think about how negative concord functions in discourse. For this reason, the next section considers the kind of things people talk about when they use negative concord.

5.3 The Discourse Context of Negative Concord

One way to consider the social meanings of negative concord is to consider the nature of the talk it occurs within. Does it occur more frequently in some kinds of talk than others and, if so, what does this mean about its ability to communicate social meaning? The finding that Townies use more negative concord than anyone else, and that they engage in more risqué social practices than others, offers a potential association between use of negative concord and engagement with rebellious practices and/or rebellious discourses.

To examine the possibility that use of a linguistic form correlates with what people talk about, Figure 5.4 shows how topics are distributed within the talk of each community of practice for all instances of postverbal negation with indeterminates (i.e., negative concord and standard negation combined). This data is from the ten speakers who show variable use of negative concord and comprises 256 tokens. Tokens of negation with postverbal indeterminates most

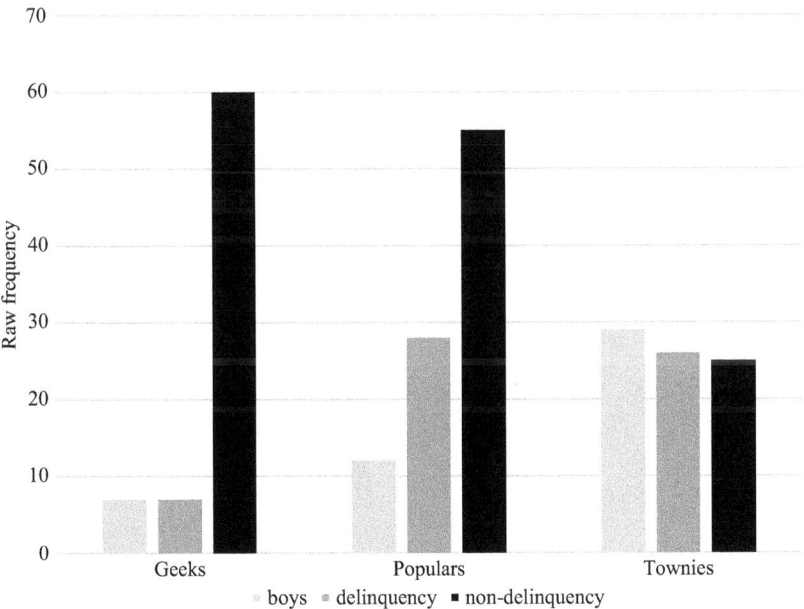

Figure 5.4 Raw frequencies of topics discussed in the instances of postverbal negation with indeterminates, by community of practice.

126   How Do We Use Grammar to Design Our Talk?

typically occur in narratives, in explicit accounts of incidents, or in evaluations of other people and their actions. Overall, when using this variable, girls talked about boys, delinquent behaviour (this included illegal activities such as drinking and taking drugs, as well as more mundane activities like being insolent to teachers), and behaviour which wasn't delinquent (for instance, going shopping or engaging in a hobby). Most talk referred to in-group activities as communities of practice tended to talk more about their own groups than out-groups. There were also seven tokens of the variable which were occasioned by the circumstances of the recording situation itself (for instance, arguing with a peer about where to sit during the recording). These instances were difficult to categorise, given their occurrence outside a larger narrative or explanatory chunk of discourse, so were excluded from the topic analyses described in this chapter.

Figure 5.4 shows that Geeks rarely talk about boys and delinquency, whereas Townies talk about boys and delinquency much more frequently than non-delinquent topics. The Populars are somewhere in between.

Figure 5.4 shows use of topic overall, but is there any evidence of a correlation between topic and use of a particular variant of postverbal negation with indeterminates? Figures 5.5 and 5.6 separate out topic

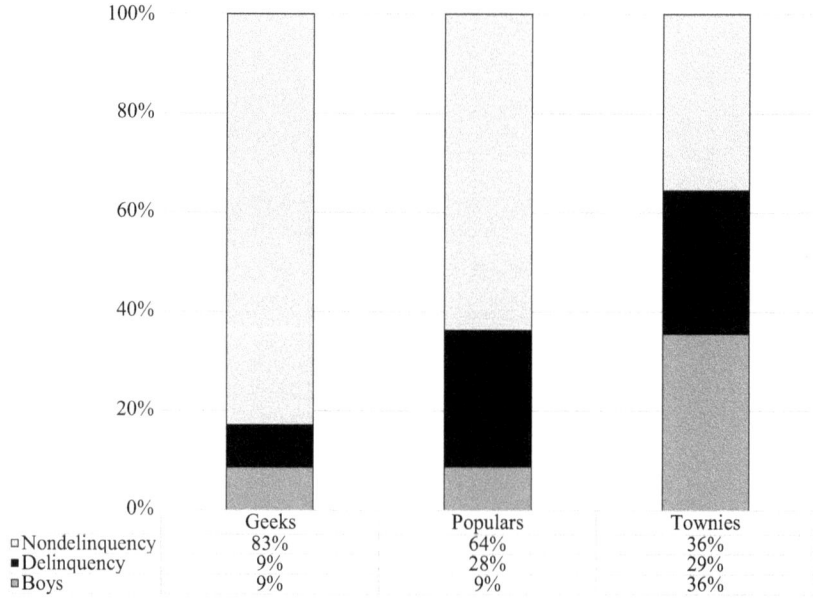

Figure 5.5 Percentage distribution of topic for instances of standard negation (e.g., *I don't like anything*), by community of practice.

distribution in standard negation and negative concord, respectively. When interpreting Figure 5.6, it is important to remember that instances of negative concord are much lower than instances of standard negation, as indicated in Table 5.4.

Notwithstanding the issues of low data counts, the differences in how topics are distributed between Figures 5.5 and 5.6 suggest that the topics of boys and delinquency are proportionally more frequent with negative concord than with standard negation for all communities of practice. The difference in use of standard negation and negative concord by topic was statistically significant (Chi-square, $\chi^2(2) = 23.402$, $p < 0.000$). Post hoc testing indicated a positive association between non-delinquency and standard negation, and a positive association between boys and negative concord, and delinquency and negative concord.

The topic of boys is worthy of further comment. Talk about boys typically involved some kind of illicit undertone – either because girls were describing emerging engagement with what Thorne (1993) calls 'the heterosexual market', or because they were describing sexual encounters with older boys. In this sense, whilst not necessarily entailing rebellion, engagement with

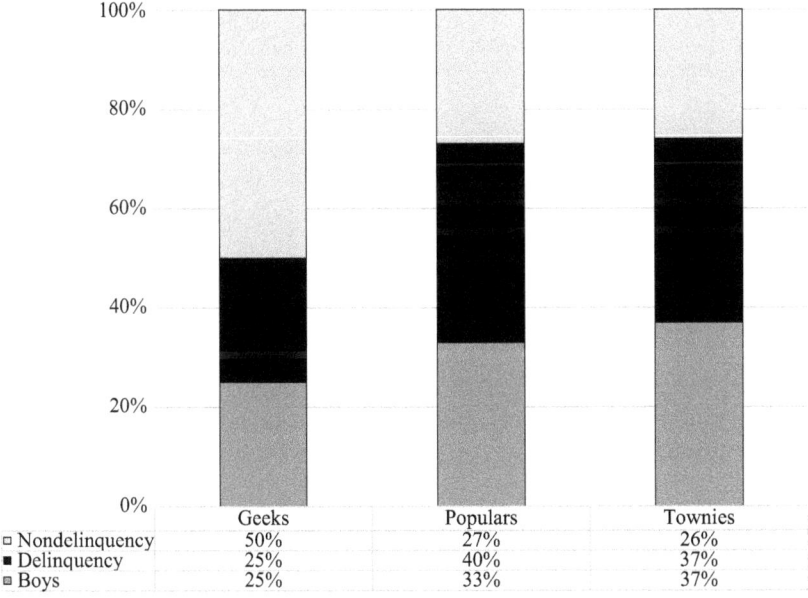

Figure 5.6 Percentage distribution of topic for instances of negative concord (e.g., *I don't like nothing*), by community of practice.

boys was frequently presented as both daring and thrilling. This can be seen in Extract 5.3 in which two Popular girls, Lindsey and Beverley, are talking about boys they met at the cinema. The instance of negative concord occurs on l. 54.

Extract 5.3

```
 1  B    And, er, we were just sat down at the cinema – just sat there¹ – cos we weren't – we
 2       just sat there for a bit and then we were going over and we were gonna try and get
 3       into this pub, which we got into – this – The Horseshoe. You know, just down there.
 4  EM   Yeah.
 5  B    We met Angie there. We were just sat at the cinema and he started shouting stuff to
 6       us, 'Oi you. D'you wanna have dinner with my mate?' (LAUGHS)
 7
 8  L    He's like our age, right, and his friend were [just there,]
 9  B                                                 [No, he's 16.]
10
11  L    scoffing fucking burgers and chips and he went, 'My mate wants to know if you'll go
12       and have summat to eat with him.'
13  EM   (LAUGHS)
14  L    Like that. I was like, 'You cheesy fuck-up,' right (LAUGHS).
15
16  (EM and B LAUGH)
17
18  L    So we sat down and his mate were just there fucking scoffing his food. And there
19       were about six of them or summat. And he were just sat harassing us for ages, right.
20  B    Um.
21  L    So we said, 'No, we're going.' He went, 'Right, I'll come out then. I bet you don't
22       go. I bet you don't go.' And we did. And then we seen him a couple of week ago.
23       And, erm..
24
25  B    He's got ...
26  L    He's sat there [harassing us again. He had – he has] a ring on each finger,
27  B                   [many rings. He's got pure² rings.]
28
29  L    like big knock-off sovereigns and shit like that. His nose goes like that. And
30       [his face is] just.. a spot
31  B    [Aw, it doesn't].
32
33  B    It's not (LAUGHS). It's not.
34  EM   (LAUGHS)
35
36  B    It's not, I swear, huh. He's really fit. And then he started harassing us again to go and
37       watch, erm, *The Fast and the Furious* with him. And we went, 'No, it's right,'
38       (LAUGHS). But he's proper fit. Don't you be – you even said [he were.]
39  L                                                               [I did!] But then I
40       fucking..
41
```

---

[1] This is an instance of irregular progressive SIT, discussed in Chapter 4 – meaning 'we were just sitting down'.

[2] *Pure* is a local lexical term used to refer to 'a large amount of' something.

5.4 The Social Meaning of Negative Concord

42	L	He sits right next to me and he talks down my ear even if he's not talking to me. So I
43		turned round like that and his face was just really, really – it's really, really spotty.
44		And all you could see of his nose was like that (INDICATES BENT NOSE).
45	B	(LAUGHS)
46	L	(LAUGHS) It goes like that. And like.. (LAUGHS) Well, huh.
47		
48	(EM and B LAUGH)	
49		
50	B	Aw.
51	EM	So did you just meet him at the cinema?
52	B	Yeah, but we don't really know him or anything. We know – I know he lives on Mill
53		Street.
54	L	And then, fucking Henry. **She dunt fancy him no more apparently**.
55	EM	(LAUGHS)
56		
57	B	[Henry, awww.]
58	L	[She knows] all the times he works.

(Beverley and Lindsey, Populars, 41A: 480–544)

In addition to providing an analysis of the boys' attractiveness (ll. 29–46), the conversation in Extract 5.3 indexes delinquency in some notable ways: it includes talk of sneaking into pubs (l. 3) and extensive swearing (l. 11, l. 14, l. 18, l. 29, l. 40, l. 54).

This analysis has suggested that negative concord is proportionally more frequent in talk about boys and rebellious topics irrespective of the speaker's community of practice membership. However, as Figure 5.4 showed, topics were not equally distributed across communities of practice – with Geeks rarely talking about boys and delinquency, and Townies talking about boys and delinquency much more frequently than non-delinquent topics. In determining the social meanings of negative concord, we need to account for the association between use of negative concord and three potential indexes: (1) rebellious discourses, (2) rebellious practices and (3) rebellious personas. These factors suggest that the increased frequency with which the Townies use negative concord may be a consequence of its correlation with rebellious and illicit topics, their tendency to engage in and, thus, talk about these topics more than most, and the potential knock-on effect of this: that negative concord itself is then iconically linked to Townieness. In the next section, we continue to build up understanding of the social meaning of negative concord by combining observations about its role in sociolinguistic practice, with understandings about the semantics of negative concord itself.

5.4 The Social Meaning of Negative Concord

The semantics of negative concord suggested that the construction itself, and the presence of two negative particles, might make negative concord a useful way to communicate that a speaker is intensifying or emphasising an element of their discourse. We have also seen that negative concord is used most frequently by the most rebellious and anti-school community of practice, the Townies, and that it is never used by the Eden Villagers, who comprise an elite and pro-school community of practice. It is also largely avoided by members of the highest social class group. Finally, we have observed that negative concord seems to occur more frequently in talk about delinquent or illicit social practices. How are all of these observations connected?

Let's start by thinking about how the semantics of negative concord might facilitate its association with rebellious social practices. Its ability to express emphasis makes negative concord a particularly useful way to express that something is surprising. Furthermore, expressing something remarkable might happen more frequently when a person is trying to be subversive or rebellious. This can be seen in Extract 5.4, which is taken from an interaction involving Townie girl, Amanda. She is discussing how teachers treat young people who are in the group considered to have the weakest academic abilities. Notice the two instances of negative concord, on ll. 3–4 and ll. 6–7. Both instances of negative concord emphasise surprising information – that teachers don't punish disobedient students, and that Amanda did not learn anything in a situation intended for learning. Amanda is talking about delinquency in Extract 5.4 (underage smoking [ll. 5–6], ignoring the teachers [l. 2]) and her use of negative concord indicates how intensifying linguistic strategies might be useful in this context. After all, talking about delinquency usually means we are communicating something surprising or remarkable – given that being delinquent involves going against what is usually expected in polite society.

Extract 5.4
1 I was in bottom set and I was with all them. It was everyone, like Ellie, Will, Sam, Paul –
2 everyone. And they'd all be there and we'd just talk all the way through. And because we
3 were in bottom set, they expect us to be like that. And **they don't give you DTs or nothing**
4 **like that.** They just go, 'Alright, quiet. You've had your laugh,' and everything. And they
5 know what we're doing. They talk to us, the teacher, going, 'Oh yeah. Go on, you can go for
6 a fag,' stuff like that. And they don't really care and you don't – **I dint learn nothing last**
7 **year.**

(Amanda, Townie, 40A: 1209–1216)

It is not just the Townies who exploit language in this way. Extract 5.5 provides another example, this time from the only occasion in which Geek girl, Susan, uses negative concord. At the time this was recorded, I hadn't been in school for a while and I had asked Susan if people had changed in my absence. Susan is telling me about how her friend, Kara, has changed.

Extract 5.5
1 S   Just like – everyone's grown up and stopped being so pathetic and everything about
2   falling out with people. Just..
3 EM Yeah.

5.4 The Social Meaning of Negative Concord

4	S	Yeah. Matured a lot and everything. Especially Kara and everything. She was all
5		sweet and innocent and stuff. **She's not no more**.
6	EM	(LAUGHS)
7	S	As you know. She's just going to <a night club> and everything and drugging and
8		stuff, but..

(Susan, Geek, 49A: 8–15)

Susan is talking about delinquent forms of behaviour in Extract 5.5 (going to night clubs underage and taking drugs [ll. 7–8]). Susan knew that it would be surprising to me that Kara was engaging in these activities because, as Susan notes, she had been quite a shy and quiet person when I'd last seen her (ll. 4–5).

Both of these examples suggest that high levels of negative concord occur in talk about delinquency because such talk requires linguistic strategies that permit the emphasis of unexpected information. But, of course, saying or doing something remarkable may happen more frequently when people are trying to project a particularly marked identity. At Midlan High, the people who most frequently expressed many of the stances noted here are the Townies. This suggests that the use of negative concord might also signal 'Townie' at Midlan High, and its use might be linked to any social behaviours seen to be typical of Townies.

This link to certain social behaviours can be seen in how another Geek girl, Jennifer, uses negative concord. All Jennifer's instances of negative concord occur in an interview with Georgia, a Popular girl. Their friendship developed in Year 10, when they were recorded together. Although there were only three places in this recording where she could have used negative concord, she uses negative concord every time she could have. In contrast, she never uses negative concord in Year 9, despite there being twenty-one places where it could have been used. What changed between Years 9 and 10 for Jennifer?

Jennifer and Georgia were the only girls in my dataset to attend St. Mary's primary school. Subsequent to their arrival at secondary school, they were placed in the same form group, but their involvement in a serious argument about the bullying of another girl resulted in Jennifer being moved into another form group. Between Years 7 and 8, Jennifer and Georgia stopped hanging out together – accounting for the divergence in their social practice at the outset of the study and their different group membership. However, in the course of Year 9, the girls found themselves once again sharing classes. With the disagreement long behind them, the girls rediscovered their liking for and connection to one another, which had been generated by shared elements of their personal history (they not only shared the same primary school, but lived in the same area until Jennifer moved at age thirteen). This reconciliatory process was expedited by the fact that Jennifer's previous best friend moved to another secondary school in Year 9, leaving her in a position to develop new friendships.

Jennifer started to hang out with Georgia on Friday nights. The Popular girls with whom Georgia associated gradually stopped referring to Jennifer as 'a Geek' as she worked hard to contribute to their social practice (smoking and drinking being the obvious practices she had earlier shunned). Jennifer developed an extreme visual style (heavy eye make-up, jewellery and wearing of branded sports jumpers over her school uniform). However, she remained on the margins of the group as I completed my fieldwork.

As noted above, all of Jennifer's instances of negative concord occur in a recording with Georgia. One example, shown in Extract 5.6, occurs when Jennifer is trying to dispute Georgia's description of her as a Geek. Rather than evoking different social groups, Jennifer argues that 'everyone hung around with everyone' (l. 4) at primary school, but then recalls an occasion when she was ostracised by her peers (ll. 4–5). Jennifer notes how unpleasant this was with the token of negative concord on l. 11.

Extract 5.6

```
1   G   No, we didn't really hang around with each other at primary, did we?
2   J   No.
3   G   I was a Popular, she was a Geek.
4   J   I weren't! Everyone hung around with everyone! Oh, except for the time that Mr.
5       Jones – that thing about Mr. Jones.
6
7   G   [What?]
8   J   [Where Katy] Parkinson spreaded round that I tried't get [[him sacked]].
9   G                                                          [[(LAUGHS)]]
10
11  J   It weren't funny at all. I dint have no friends for two weeks.
```

(Georgia, Popular and Jennifer, Geek 48A: 726–736)

Another instance of negative concord follows Jennifer introducing a story about Georgia having sex in a car. Georgia initially tells Jennifer to shut up, and Jennifer replies, 'No, **I won't say nothing**' (48A: 642). Georgia then quickly tells me the story herself before encouraging Jennifer to talk about her own sexual experiences.

The final instance of negative concord used by Jennifer occurs when I ask her if it is better now that she is in Year 10 and she replies 'No, they don't – **teachers don't treat you no different** ... teachers treat – still treat you like kids, dunt they? Like shit' (48A: 1050–1054).

The idea that Jennifer is a Geek who is less rebellious and delinquent than Georgia resounds throughout the entire interaction containing these instances of negative concord. Jennifer is constantly on the back foot, trying to prove that she is tough and subversive, that she is knowledgeable about and has experience of sex, and that she disrespects teachers and their authority. This is evident in the topics that she introduces but also through the linguistic

5.4 The Social Meaning of Negative Concord

resources she exploits: this includes her use of swearing and, of course, her use of negative concord.

So far, we have seen that negative concord has a core pragmatic function via its ability to express emphasis. This function makes it effective at expressing surprising or remarkable information, which often conveys an anti-authority or rebellious stance. In turn, we have seen that these stances are most frequently articulated by a particular social group, the Townies. This association may also facilitate links between the use of negative concord and other aspects of the Townie's persona, including being tough and subversive, being worldly-wise (e.g., by being sexually experienced) and being independent of adults.

Figure 5.7 schematises a hypothetical indexical field for negative concord at Midlan High. Like the hypothetical indexical field for levelled *were*

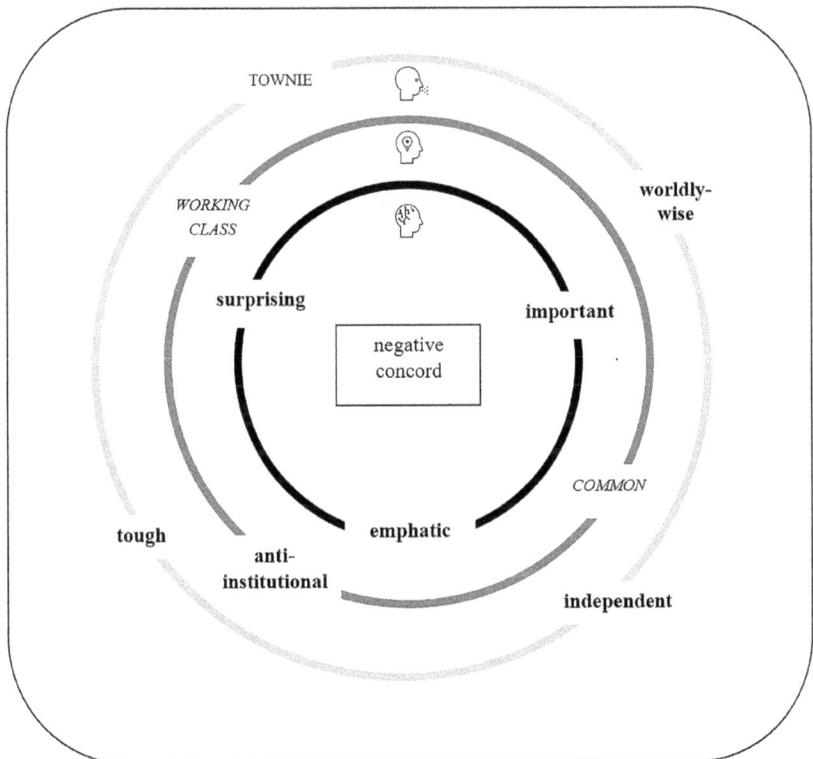

Figure 5.7 A hypothetical indexical field of negative concord, showing how social meaning may be rooted in semantics (black circle), association with character types (dark grey circle), and embodiment of character types in local space.

(Chapter 4, Figure 4.12), there are three circles, representing the different ways in which individuals might encounter or interact with the social meanings of this linguistic variant. However, in this indexical field (as opposed to the one in the previous chapter), the circles represent where meaning is rooted, rather than when and how it is acquired. The inner black circle shows social meanings rooted in semantics. These meanings all stem from the grammatical structure of negative concord and what can be inferred about its meaning when this structure is used variably alongside standard negation. Negative concord has multiple negative markers, one of which is postposed. Compared to standard negation, this serves to emphasise the negation encoded in the negatively concorded structure. It is important to stress that negative concord will only become routinised as an interactional resource to the extent that a speaker has variable usage of negative concord and standard negation. This is because this meaning relies upon systematic variation between (and comparison of) these two forms. If a speaker is truly invariant (as some speakers in Buckie seem to be, for instance – see earlier discussion of Smith and Holmes-Elliott 2022), then negative concord cannot be emphatic (or at least emphatic in the same way), as it is the only means of expressing negation with postverbal indeterminates. All meanings in this inner circle relate to pragmatic inferences (e.g., that information is 'surprising' or 'important', for instance), based on comparison with a standard variant. They describe stances by virtue of their ability to describe how speaker's orient themselves to the content of their talk.

The dark grey circle shows meanings that arise from character-type associations. They arise from negative concord being evaluated as a (pejoratively) marked variant when contrasted with the standard norm used by those with social and cultural power. They are the consequence of appraisal of character types considered to use negative concord and their related indexes. As noted earlier, it is not the case that everyone views members of lower social classes as 'common' or 'anti-institutional' but these social meanings result from value-laden comparison with the most powerful and dominant groups in society. The dominance of these powerful groups means that these social meanings are culturally pervasive. They are not how everyone experiences negative concord on the ground, but everyone is aware of them, given that we all come to interact with dominant discourses of power to some degree. (As the Buckie study shows, even habitual users of negative concord reduce their use of this form when interacting with individuals who represent this wider cultural space). The degree to which we interact with these discourses increases as we approach adulthood. This likely explains why, despite studies showing clear class stratification of negative concord in adults, young people do not show regular class stratification of this form (see for instance, Wolfram (1969) and Eckert (1988: 186) and, of course, the analysis above).

5.4 The Social Meaning of Negative Concord

In Chapter 4, it was noted how school-related discourse enables children to acquire associations between distinct varieties of language and different places in the social order. It was also observed that adolescence provides a life stage in which young people are especially motivated to utilise all the linguistic variability at their disposal as they reconfigure their relationships with adults and their place in relation to the other young people around them. The patterns of negative concord at Midlan High (and particularly the changes from Years 9 to 10) demonstrate the girls' increasing awareness of the more general social stigma of negative concord. Their use of it does not necessarily reflect their place in the social order, but it does reflect an understanding that its indexical field includes class-linked and anti-institutional social meanings. The increase in negative concord for some reflects how these girls expand their use of negative concord to more fully exploit its indexical potential. But, importantly, there is not a unidirectional shift in use of this linguistic variant: some girls never use negative concord (irrespective of their place in the social order – four girls in the Mid-low/Low social class groups never use negative concord) whereas others, like Popular girl, Annabel, reduce their use between Years 9 and 10. How girls use negative concord depends upon how they want to position themselves vis-à-vis the school as institution, and vis-à-vis the other girls in their school. Evidence that girls are increasingly aware of the more general societal stigma around negative concord can be seen in Extract 5.1, which opened this chapter.

The light grey circle in Figure 5.7 shows the consequences of this emerging awareness. It shows how the dominant character-type meanings of the dark grey circle are embodied and repackaged on the ground during everyday interaction. The frequency with which a particular social group co-produces certain stances (e.g., 'being tough' or 'subversive'), which derive from the character-type association in the dark grey circle, may cause an 'ideological crystallization' of meaning (Moore & Podesva 2009: 478), such that the stances accrete into the group categorisation itself (on the notion of 'stance accretion' see the discussion in Chapter 1). The frequency with which Townies produce negative concord suggests that 'Townieness' itself may be indexically linked to negative concord at Midlan High. In this way, the group's persona, and any stances associated with that group, such as being 'independent' and 'worldly-wise', may also become associated with the use of negative concord

At the beginning of this chapter, I suggested that we might consider negative concord to be a *rheme*. This variant can be iconically linked to character types and their indexical associations, e.g., 'working class', 'common', 'anti-institutional', 'Townie', 'tough'). These meanings are encoded in the two outer circles of the indexical field in Figure 5.7. However, negative concord may also index social meanings that are less iconic. These would include any social meanings which are more closely tied to its pragmatic function (i.e., those encoded in the inner circle of the indexical field in Figure 5.7), or to its more local embodiment (i.e., its associations with being 'independent' and 'worldly-wise', which are linked to the contextually specific Townie persona in the outer circle, rather than class *per se*). Negative concord will only ever be heard as 'working class' and/or 'common' by some. However, others, for whom negative concord has a more expansive social life, will hear negative concord in all its socioindexical glory. Their decoding of this linguistic variant will rely upon its interactional context and its stylistic embedding. Negative concord is a rheme because it may be iconic in some interpretations and indexical in others, depending on the presuppositions of the person doing the interpreting (Peirce & Welby-Gregory 1977, as discussed in Gal & Irvine 2019: 106).

5.5 Highly Stigmatised Grammar, Pragmatics and Social Association

Negative concord's status as a rheme (i.e., that it can be both index and icon) explains why some girls at Midlan High never use negative concord despite its apparent pragmatic utility as a way to articulate emphasis. For these girls, negative concord's status as an icon is strong enough to stop them using the form completely – even if it is available in their input and even if they might want to express some of the semantically based inferences that the syntax of the form enables it to portray. For these girls, the strength of the association with lower social class social types and the more general stigma around lower social class status is sufficient to inhibit use of negative concord in all but the most heightened stylised performances.

This chapter has explored the many ways in which we might infer social meaning about a grammatical variable like negative concord. Firstly, its precise syntactic configuration may convey some pragmatic meaning. Consequently, someone's use of negative concord, as opposed to another linguistic alternative, might suggest something about their stance towards what they are saying – for instance, that it is surprising or remarkable. However, the highly stigmatised nature of negative concord in general society is pervasive and the analysis of its use at Midlan High has shown how this perception of negative concord increasingly influences how it is employed in the localised environment of this school. The fact that negative concord is so strongly associated with lower social classes might mean that any time it is used, by any kind of speaker, these social associations are inescapable. This plays out in different ways for different speakers. For most of the girls at Midlan High, these social associations are antithetical to their persona style and this inhibits their use of negative concord in any circumstances. However, for other girls, in particular, the Townies, these social associations align with (and help to construct) their rebellious, anti-institutional style.

5.5 Grammar, Pragmatics and Social Association

The iconic nature of negative concord goes some way to explaining why we see it used much less frequently then other localised forms like levelled *were*. The stakes are much higher in its use because it is so strongly associated with rebelliousness and anti-authority practices. What differs for non-users and users of negative concord is how these associations are evaluated. For instance, for the Eden Villagers, negative concord's association with lower social class groups indexes the negative characteristics of lack of refinement, aggression, and institutional failure. For the Townies, it indexes the positive characteristics of toughness, independence and being worldly-wise. It is vital that we understand all of these perspectives to understand the complete indexical field of negative concord.

This chapter has attempted to highlight the interface between pragmatics and social correlation for a highly stigmatised grammatical variant. The distinct roots of meaning may work independently (i.e., some people may perceive emphasis over other social meanings; others may only perceive that a speaker is 'common'). However, it is also possible (indeed, probable) that character type and semantically rooted inferences may work synergistically, such that the pragmatic force of negative concord, which produces 'an intensification effect' (Palacios 2017: 176), heightens the social meanings generated by ideologies about 'typical' negative concord users. That is to say, the pragmatic function generated by a variant's syntactic configuration may significantly enrich the expressiveness of the social meanings generated by ideologies about the societal distribution of a linguistic form.

This chapter has also shown the importance of observing how linguistic variants feature in a specific system of distinction. We have seen how negative concord can develop more specific, locally conditioned, meanings – such as those generated when negative concord is vivified within a specific group's sociolinguistic practice. Nonetheless, it is important to reiterate that negative concord is a highly stigmatised grammatical variant. If a grammatical variant is less socially stigmatised are its social meanings less tightly constrained, and/or more strongly determined by pragmatics? Furthermore, are there any factors other than degree of iconicity which can intensify or attenuate the pragmatic function of a grammatical variant? To explore these questions further, in the next chapter, we consider a more purely syntactic variant which does not easily conform to notions of stigma and nonstandardness.

6 Does Everyone Use Grammar to Make Social Meaning?

Extract 6.1

Emma is talking to Townies, Amanda and Meg, about the differences between how people talk in the school.

```
1   M     ... all the little gothicky people, they all talk proper posh.
2
3   A     Use big words, [don't they]?
4   M                   [That Shona] girl, who's in X class, she were going, 'And, erm, well,
5         ohh – and talking like that.' And I thought, 'Oh my God, [[(INAUDIBLE)]].'
6   A                                                         [[Oh, that were it]] – it were
7         in Art. Right, I sit on a table. And on a different table, though, but next to me, is this
8         girl. She's a goth. I was sat there. I thought, 'Oh God, you dint let us into your
9         party, you.' [So] I was sat there, and she went –
10  M                  [(LAUGHS)]
11
12  A     we were looking at these pictures and Sir went, 'What d'you think – erm, d'you like
13        these?' I went, 'Oh, they're top, them.' And then she went, 'Wow, they're amazing.'
14        [And I thought, 'God you're so different.]
15  M     [(LAUGHS)]
16  EM    [(LAUGHS)]
17
18  A     Why can't you just say, 'They're top, them.' 'They're amazing.' 'Look at the
19        colours. It's a lovely collage.' I'm like going, 'Nice colours,' [(LAUGHS)].
20  M                                                                    [(LAUGHS)]
21        Yeah, they do – they pronounce their words .. correctly.
22
23  A     Yeah. [But –]
24  M           [I can't] even talk proper anymore.
25
26  A     I never could!
```

(Amanda and Meg, Townies, 55A: 97–130)

Chapters 4 and 5 considered the social meaning of grammatical variants that are highly stigmatised because of their relationship with the codified written standard. Levelled *were* and negative concord are nonstandard forms which have obvious standard alternatives in writing. But what about syntactic features that occur only, or at least predominantly, in spoken discourse? As Cheshire (1987, 1999, 2005b) has pointed out numerous times, we simply do not know enough about the social meaning and the social functions of this type of grammatical variant.

One example of a variant that occurs exclusively in spoken interaction in British English is right dislocation. In Extract 6.1, Amanda uses right dislocation on ll. 8–9, l. 13 and l. 18. Right dislocation refers to the occurrence of a clause followed by a noun phrase or pronoun tag which is co-referential with the preceding subject or object pronoun; for instance, *She's lovely, her mum* or *They're top, them*. Right dislocation – also known as 'postponed identification' and 'tails' – is described as common in colloquial British English speech (Huddleston & Pullum 2002: 1408; Wales 1996: 43; Shorrocks 1998: 85; Huddleston & Pullum 2002: 1408), but it has no obvious 'alternate' form in writing.

Nonetheless, Amanda clearly juxtaposes her use of right dislocation (and her speech more generally) with what she describes as a 'different' way of speaking, that uses 'big words'. This alternative way of speaking is identified as belonging to a 'goth'. As mentioned in Chapter 3, some of the Geek girls started to constitute a 'goth' persona at the end of Year 9. 'Goth' is a recognised subculture (Hodkinson 2002) which involves listening to particular styles of rock music and wearing black clothing and make-up. At Midlan High, the goth style was embodied by high achievers – for instance, both the Head Boy and the Head Girl were described as goths. As well as being associated with the goth subculture, this 'different' way of speaking is also described by Amanda's friend Meg as 'posh' (l. 1) and a way of 'pronounc[ing] ... words... correctly' (l. 21). By juxtaposing right dislocation with 'difference', 'poshness' and 'correctness', Amanda and Meg suggest that right dislocation has social meaning: it may symbolise certain social personas (e.g., 'Townie'), which are negatively evaluated (as being 'not correct' and/or the opposite of 'posh', i.e., 'common') in the dominant societal system of value. Note, however, that whilst Amanda and Meg acknowledge this value system, they do not align with it. For instance, Amanda doesn't wonder why she cannot sound more like the goth girl, she wonders why the goth girl cannot sound more like her.

Despite the earlier observation that right dislocation does not have a codified standard alternative, Amanda's commentary indicates that the goth girl's differing word choice expresses the same referential meaning as right dislocation. In Extract 6.1, both girls are admiring the artwork, but Amanda's 'They're top, them' is contrasted with the goth girl's 'Wow, they're amazing' (l. 13). Furthermore, Amanda doesn't just highlight different lexical choices ('top' versus 'amazing', the interjection 'wow'), she also adapts her pronunciation to illustrate how the goth girl's evaluation is delivered in a more standardised style [ameɪzɪŋ] (this differs from how Amanda might more commonly utter this word, e.g., as [əmeːzɪn]). This suggests that use of right dislocation – at least examples of the type given in Extract 6.1 – are not just associated with particular personas, but with certain styles of speaking.

Amanda and Meg's discussion of right dislocation situates its social meaning within the local economy of Midlan High. But to what extent does right dislocation index social information at the level of social type beyond Midlan High? Dines (1980: 19) notes that the association between working-class identity and use of clause-terminal tags (like *or anything* or *and stuff*) causes these tags to be stigmatised as vague or inexplicit. Similarly, Mendoza-Denton (2008: 285) observes that discourse markers more generally can be the subject of prescriptive criticism. Previous research on right dislocation has found correlations with social categories. Right dislocation has been found to occur more frequently in the speech of Northern English and Scottish individuals who are either categorised as working-class (Macaulay 2005: 94; Snell 2008, 2018), or are in communities of practice which orient towards working-class practice (Moore & Snell 2011). Durham (2011), the only other variationist study available on right dislocation, does not include class in the analysis, but finds some ambiguous gender and age differences in how right-dislocated forms are distributed.

As we will see below, the Midlan High data shows that there are social class and community of practice differences in the use of right dislocation, but these differences are not as marked as those found for levelled *were* and negative concord. However, differences in distribution are much more apparent when the *type* of right dislocation is examined – particularly as it relates to the clause subject and, more particularly, the semantic roles encoded in right-dislocated utterances. This suggests that speakers use right dislocation to communicate specific interactional meanings. That is to say, variability in right dislocation seems to be driven by pragmatics, and its social distribution is determined by the need for different groups to express difference types of stances and states. Put another way, right dislocation seems to show a Type SM trajectory: its social meaning seems to be rooted in semantics.

In order to examine this variation, we first consider the possible types of right dislocation before examining their pragmatic function. This discussion is then followed by an analysis of the social and linguistic distribution of right dislocation. The analysis not only suggests that different groups use right dislocation at differing frequencies, but also that different groups use different formulations of right dislocation. It would seem that this is not necessarily a consequence of variability in input, but because different formulations enable different inferences, with frequency of use less firmly tied to character-type associations.

6.1   What Types of Right Dislocation Are Possible?

As noted above, right dislocation is common in colloquial British English, but not all of the possible formulations shown in Table 6.1 are equally common. At Midlan High, the right-dislocated tag can be:

6.1 What Types of Right Dislocation Are Possible?

Example 6.1 a full noun phrase (Example 6.1i) or a proper name (Example 6.1ii);

Example 6.2 a demonstrative pronoun, which can be co-referential with either a demonstrative pronoun subject (Example 6.2i) or a third-person subject (Examples 6.2ii, 6.2iii);

Example 6.3 a personal pronoun in the first- (Examples 6.3i, 6.3ii), second- (Example 6.3iii) or third person (Examples 6.3iv, 6.3v);

Example 6.4 a non-finite verb phrase (Examples 6.4i, 6.4ii) or a relative clause (Example 6.4iii).

The tag can also be co-referential with the subject or – much less frequently – with the object of the main clause. In the Midlan High data, tags that were co-referential with the subject were much more common than those co-referential with the object (96.6 per cent versus 3.4 per cent). Furthermore, only noun phrase (Example 6.1ii) and non-finite verb phrase tags (Example 6.4ii) were co-referential with objects.

Descriptive accounts of right dislocation have tended to focus on a reduced set of right-dislocated tags, suggesting that only some of the types in Table 6.1 are widespread. Biber *et al.* (1999: 956–958) only discuss noun-phrase tags and demonstrative tags, whereas Quirk *et al.* (1985: 1310, 1417) and Huddleston and Pullum (2002: 1408–1414) only mention noun-phrase tags and nonfinite verb phrase tags. Beyond British English, Toma (2018: 11)

Table 6.1 *Types of right dislocation found in British English*

Example 6.1 Full noun phrases	i. *They had a massive fight, her mum and dad* (Faye, Geek, 46B: 217) ii. *That's his name now, Cob.* (Melanie, Geek, 42B: 368)
Example 6.2 Demonstrative pronouns	i. *That were bad, that* (Kim, Popular, 45B: 282) ii. *And it's nice, that, but, I mean.* (Suzanne, Geek, 39B: 401) iii. *I think they were awful, those.* (Annabel, Popular 2B: 480)
Example 6.3 Personal pronouns	i. *I hate her nanna, me.* (Tanya, Geek, 47A: 965) ii. *We sound like slags, us.* (Amanda, Townie, 45A: 383) iii. *You well pissed me off, you.* (Ellie, Townie, 36A: 208) iv. *Oh! That's where she lives, her.* (Georgia, Popular, 48B: 433) v. *They're horrible, them.* (Meg, Popular, 19B: 282)
Example 6.4 Nonfinite verb phrases/ relative clauses	i. *It was quite good fun, being at a different school* (Alex, EV, 43A: 144) ii. *No I – I wunt do that, get bullied, cos everyone is scared of me* (Georgia, Popular, 17B: 485) iii. *And she went, 'That's cheating, what you're doing.'* (Beverley, Popular, 30B: 765)

hypothesises that, in general, right dislocation occurs less frequently in US English than British English, and accounts of right dislocation by North American scholars (Ziv 1994; Ziv & Grosz 1994; Ward & Birner 1996) indicate that personal pronoun tags do not occur in North American English.

However, accounts of right dislocation in the wider north of England (Beal 1993; Fyne 2005; Snell 2008, 2018; Durham 2011; Mycock 2019), and in Bolton specifically (Shorrocks 1982; Timmis 2009), suggest that the girls of Midlan High are not anomalous in their use of personal pronoun tags. Timmis (2009) does not provide frequency counts of different types of right dislocation but his examples indicate the presence of second- and third-person pronoun tags. Shorrocks (1980: 547–548) focuses on noun-phrase and demonstrative pronoun tags in his discussion, but he lists a first-person pronoun tag in a list of examples from audio recordings he collected in south Bolton.

Interestingly, all of the examples cited by Timmis, and some given by Shorrocks, seem to be a form of right dislocation that Durham (2011) refers to as 'expanded right dislocation', where the tag includes an auxiliary. There is only one example of this type in the Midlan High data (*She was like calling me, Catherine was.* Helen, EV, 51A: 382). There is also one instance of the form of right dislocation referred to by Durham (2011) as 'reverse right dislocation' (*She loves me, does Amanda.* Annabel, Popular, 7A: 269).

It is worth noting that Timmis' data is unusual as it comes from the UK's Mass Observation archives. This was an anthropological study of the British working class that was founded in 1937. A team of observers were sent to Bolton to record aspects of working-class behaviour, including speech.[1] The records of speech, which are real-time transcriptions of 'overheards' or question and answer sessions, rather than audio recordings, include eighty examples of right dislocation in approximately 50,000 words of transcription. Although Timmis' data is unconventional, it is useful because it demonstrates the salience of right dislocation. The observers in the Mass Observation study were neither local to Bolton nor working class themselves (Timmis 2009: 326). The anthropological nature of the project meant that the observers were tasked with recording remarkable aspects of working-class life. The inclusion of right dislocation in their records hints at the markedness of this syntactic construction to the non-local observer.

The absence of personal pronoun tags from descriptive grammars of English leads Snell (2008: 172) to propose that the personal pronoun variant is dialectal whereas the noun-phrase tag is more widespread and part of informal spoken English. It is clearly the case that different dialects have different types of right dislocation (for instance, whilst York English favours reverse right dislocation, Bolton English does not) but, as explored further below, use of personal pronoun tags varies even within the same dialect.

---

[1] The artwork on the cover of this book was produced by Julian Trevelyan, who, as an artist, contributed to the Mass Observation project.

Before turning to the patterns of variation found at Midlan High, the next section considers the syntactic formulation of right dislocation and the interaction between its syntax and its semantics. In doing so, this section seeks to explore how the grammar of right dislocation affects the types of meanings it can express.

6.2 What Are the Functions of Right Dislocation?

Rightward moving constructions with postverbal noun phrases tend to present information that is new to the hearer, or, at the very least, they present information that serves to remind hearers of information they could feasibly have forgotten (Horn 1986; Birner 1994; Ward & Birner 1996). For instance, in Extract 6.2, Faye's use of a rightward moving construction, existential *there*, on l. 3 – *there was like .. a fight* – serves to introduce the new information to me that her friend, Scarlet, has been involved in a fight with Popular girl, Nina.

Extract 6.2

1 EM Oh. Is Scarlet still hanging around with Lara?
2 C Well, she got really popular at one time, dint she?
3 F Yeah, and then **there was like.. a fight** between her and Nina – like they fell out, dint
4 they?

(Caroline and Faye, Geeks, 46A: 908–912)

Like existential *there*, right dislocation also occurs with a postverbal noun phrase. However, Ward and Birner (1996) argue that they are pragmatically different. This can be seen in Extract 6.3. Suzanne is talking about her preference for the north of England over the south of England. The existential *there* construction on l. 2, *there's no hills*, introduces the discourse new information about the lack of hills in the south of the country. This is elaborated on ll. 4–5 with a second existential *there* construction, *there's no hills blocking out the sky*. This second existential *there* construction reiterates the first one, but elaborates on it (making it an example of Ward and Birner's type III postverbal noun phrase, which marks a discourse-old entity in a new instantiation). However, the right-dislocated expression on l. 5, *it's nice, that,* unquestionably presents discourse old information, with no further referential elaboration. It is not news to the listeners that Suzanne thinks the big skies in the south of England are nice; she has already stated this in the immediately prior discourse with her utterance *the only thing that's nice about down there is that they have bigger skies* (ll. 1–2).

Extract 6.3

1 S It's just nicer here. The – the only thing that's nice about down there is that they have
2 bigger skies. You know, because **there's no hills**.
3 EM Yeah.
4 S The sky kind of goes all the way, you know, like **there's no hills blocking out the**
5 **sky**. And **it's nice, that**, but, I mean..

(Suzanne, Geek, 39B: 499–504)

Ward and Birner (1996) use this difference in information status to argue that right dislocation is only superficially similar to rightward moving postverbal noun phrase constructions like existential *there*. Whereas rightward moving postverbal noun phrase constructions use syntactic movement to postpose unfamiliar or new information, the postverbal noun phrase in the right-dislocated tag is 'base generated in the postverbal position' and constitutes 'familiar, discourse old information in context' (Ward & Birner 1996). Given the established given-before-new constraint on discourse structure (Biber *et al.* 1999: 896–897), this leaves the question of why speakers would place familiar, given, information at the end of an utterance.

Many accounts of right dislocation have argued that the right-dislocated tag is clarificatory and indicates real-time utterance processing (Givon 1976; Tomlin 1986; Geluykens 1987; Huddleston & Pullum 2002: 1411). In this sense, it represents a repair mechanism or 'afterthought'. However, this view has been disputed, with researchers pointing out that afterthoughts are marked by pauses and distinct intonational contours, making them structurally distinct from genuine instances of right dislocation (Aijmer 1989: 148; Ziv 1994: 639). This can be seen if we compare a rightward moving construction in Extract 6.3 with the right-dislocated construction in Extract 6.4.

Extract 6.4

```
1   J    There's like [really, really] popular ones who think they know everything
2   P                 [Faye -]
3
4   J    [and they're so horrible to everyone else]
5   P    [And there's some middle ones who ... Yeah.]
6
7   J    like you saw Ellie saying, 'This is the swotty people that we told you bout.' Erm..
8
9   J    [There's those and then there's like the medium people]
10  P    [There's.. Faye and them lot..]
11
12  J    [and then there's like real swots -]
13  P    [who like really good at work]
14
15  J    really, really swots, [int there?]
16  P                          [The medium] people, like, they're like good at work and **they**
17       **always hang around each other, don't they – like that's ...**
18
19  J    They all like- They're all like [the girls, the popular girls, are those type]
20  P                                    [**Faye and Kara.**]
21
22  J    that link arms in a big long row.
```

(Jennifer and Pippa, Geeks, 3A: 79–88)

In Extract 6.4, Jennifer and Pippa are telling me about the groups in the school. The interaction is full of overlap, and Jennifer tends to talk over Pippa. Pippa starts talking about 'the middle [people]' on l. 5, and Jennifer takes this

6.2 What Are the Functions of Right Dislocation?

up but relabels them as 'the medium people' on l. 16. Pippa identifies these people as 'Faye and them lot' on l. 10, but Jennifer continues to talk over Pippa throughout this part of the discussion. Pippa finally gets the floor on l. 16, where she elaborates on what the label 'the medium people' means. She uses the pronoun 'they' (ll. 16–17) before clarifying precisely who she is referring to as a 'medium person' in l. 20 where she reiterates Faye's name and adds in the name of another Geek girl, Kara. Note that the clarification of who 'they' refers to comes after a pause (indicated by the '...' on l. 17). When she utters 'Faye and Kara' on l. 20, their names are spoken with falling intonation. Arguably, this utterance could be considered discourse new as her first attempt to utter it was masked by Jennifer's overlap. In contrast, the right-dislocated utterance in Extract 6.3 gives discourse old information, there is no pause before the tag, and the tag is part of the same Intonational Phrase as the preceding clause.

Nonetheless, some right-dislocated tags, namely those that are full noun phrases, do appear to function – at least superficially – to clarify references. The example, 'we caught the train, me and Tanya' on ll. 1–2 of Extract 6.5 seems to be one such case.

Extract 6.5

```
1   s   Aw, yeah, d'you know yesterday, I caught the bus? The 105, yeah, cos we caught the
2       train, me and Tanya, and then, like, we catch the bus home, then. Right. So I walked
3       to the bus stop and everyone's banging on the bus, going, 'Scarlet, get on the bus! Get
4       on the bus!' I'm like, 'No, I'm waiting for my-, I'm waiting for Tanya to get on hers.'
5       And there's like, 'No, come on! Come on! Get on!' – like that. And Tanya's, like,
6       'God, you're popular.' Like, like that and th-, then I got on the bus and I'm talking to
7       all my friends and I just think – and she's there, like, on her s-, by herself, on her tod –
8       I felt well mean. And she's got no friends on her bus and she's been catching it for
9       years and I've got like millions of friends on mine. And there's – It's well good. I
10      love it (LAUGHS). I love that – Sorry.
```
(Scarlet, Geek, 12A: 579–589)

In this extract, Scarlet is talking to me and her friend, Faye, about the difference between her and another Geek girl, Tanya. Faye knows full well that both Scarlet and Tanya live on the other side of town and share part of a journey home. Whilst I also knew this (Tanya was one of the girls I had known the longest as she was in the youth theatre group that led to my focus on Midlan High), I hadn't known Scarlet for very long when this interview took place. This makes it feasible that she is unsure about what I know. In this sense, the tag may serve to clarify a referent that she subsequently realised was opaque to me. Further evidence that this is the case comes from Scarlet's switch from talking about a specific event in the past tense ('we caught the train') to talking about a habitual event in the present tense ('we catch the bus'). This serves to provide me with the contextual information that she and Tanya do the same journey home every day.

Related to the function of clarification, it has also been argued that right-dislocated tags may be 'amplificatory', in that they function to mark emphasis (Quirk *et al.* 1985: 1310). Biber *et al.* (1999: 956) argue that this is why we find them in speech rather than writing, given the prevalence of emotive expressions in the former. Of course, the simple fact that right-dislocated constructions involve the repetition of content (due to the co-referential nature of the tag and the subject or object of the preceding clause) could be read as a marking of emphasis. In Extract 6.5, a clarificatory reading of Scarlet's tag does not preclude a emphatic reading of it, in the sense that her story serves to emphasise the difference between Scarlet and Tanya.

However, some scholars have disputed the claim that emphasis is one of the – or indeed *the* – main functions of right dislocation. For instance, when writing about right dislocation in Bolton English, Shorrocks (1980: 548) notes that right-dislocated tags may express emphasis, but they also occur 'on some occasions when no emphasis would seem to be required'. Furthermore, Mycock (2019: 258) notes that pronoun tags are often unstressed – with forms like *her* being reduced to [ə]. This has led scholars to look beyond functions related to clarification and emphasis, to explore the function of right-dislocated tags as discourse organisers. Ziv (1994: 641) argues that right-dislocated tags may function to retrieve and reintroduce entities which occurred earlier in the discourse. In this way, they 'seem to constitute instructions to the addressees to search their surroundings for the appropriate situationally evoked entities and to attend to them' (Ziv 1994: 640). This theory is also in line with the principle of end-focus: that items of importance are placed at the end of an utterance to mark topic and get the speaker to focus upon what will come next (Quirk *et al.* 1985: 1356; Biber *et al.* 1999: 897–898).

This interpretation works well in the context of Extract 6.5. Tanya was actually first mentioned in the conversation three minutes before being referenced in Extract 6.5. Furthermore, Tanya has an important role to play in Scarlet's story: Scarlet juxtaposes her position with that of Tanya's and uses it to highlight her own popularity. This is important in the context of the evolving conversation: immediately before the story about Tanya and the bus, Scarlet was trying to persuade Faye how she was friends with one of the Popular girls, who she described as being 'really nice' to her. Not long after this recording, Scarlet started to drift away from the other Geek girls who began to criticise her for what they perceived to be immoral behaviour around boys. So, her claim to being popular in this conversation may reflect an attempt to focus attention on a long-term goal to assume status as a Popular girl. The focus on Tanya (and her difference from Scarlet) provides a vehicle for Scarlet to foreground the notion of popularity.

The focusing function of right-dislocated tags requires that they feature given or discourse old information but that the information is not *so*

6.2 What Are the Functions of Right Dislocation?

discourse-old that it lacks relevance in the unfolding conversation (Huddleston & Pullum 2002: 1411–1412). However, Ziv (1994: 641) suggests that there is a kind of sweet spot where a tag's referent is sufficiently distal but not too distal. She gives the example of an immediately prior referent in (Example 6.5) and argues that it is infelicitous. This is because the proximity of 'Jack' in A's utterance means that 'Jack' is already on the floor as the current topic and it is not necessary for B to utter a right-dislocated tag to establish topicality.

Example 6.5   A: Did you see Jack yesterday?
              B: Yes. He is going to Europe, Jack.

(Example (20) in Ziv 1994: 641)

However, we have already seen that right-dislocated tags can occur immediately following a prior referent: this occurs with the right-dislocated tag in Extract 6.3. Here Suzanne's tag ('it's nice, that') reiterates something she has already articulated in the directly proximate discourse, namely, that a big sky is a nice thing. However, it is notable that Suzanne's tag is a pronoun and not a full noun phrase. If we reframe Ziv's example, as in (Example 6.6), so that the tag is a pronoun, B's response no longer seems infelicitous – at least to me as a speaker of Northern English.

Example 6.6   A: Did you see Jack yesterday?
              B: Yes. He is going to Europe, him.

In work with Grosz, Ziv acknowledges that these violations of the 'distal but not too distal' constraint can occur, stating that if tags include referents which are in the immediately preceding discourse, then they tend to express additional descriptive or emotive content (Ziv & Grosz 1994: 1990). In Example 6.6, to me at least, the tag has an evaluative flavour. Macaulay (2005: 174) notes that 'evaluation' is a difficult notion to define, but cites the following definition from Hunston and Thompson (2000: 5): 'Evaluation is the broad cover term for the expression of the speaker or writer's attitude or stance towards, viewpoint on, or feelings about the entities or propositions that he or she is talking about'. To me, it sounds like B is marking Jack's trip as remarkable, or unexpected – particularly in relation to what A and B might jointly understand about Jack's normal character or behaviours.

The idea that right-dislocated tags have affective functions has also been suggested by Aijmer (1989: 151), who claims that it is the 'typical function of [right dislocation] in spoken English'. This is so much the case that she considers right dislocation to be 'a grammaticalized device ... [which] emphasises the phatic character of the utterance and contributes to the intimacy between speaker and hearer' (Aijmer 1989: 150–151). The idea that right dislocation has grammaticalised interpersonal functions is also supported by Snell (2008: 191). Building on Biber *et al.*'s (1999: 969–970) discussion of grammatical devices used to express stance, she proposes that right dislocation may entail the 'grammaticalization of evaluation'. Biber *et al.* (1999: 698) state that grammatical stance devices include two distinct components, 'one expressing the stance, and the other presenting a proposition that is framed by that stance'. Right dislocation would seem to fit this description. Returning to the right dislocation found in Extract 6.3, 'it's nice, that', it is possible to see this two-part structure: 'it's nice' is the proposition, and the 'that' tag grammatically marks Suzanne's evaluation of the proposition. However, it is less clear that this explanation works for the right dislocation in Extract 6.5, 'we caught the train, Tanya and me'.

The distinction between NP tags like 'we caught the train, Tanya and me' and pronoun tags like 'it's nice, that' leads Mycock (2019) to propose that right-dislocated pronoun tags (which she terms 'ProTags') be distinguished from other forms of right dislocation. She argues that, unlike other types of tag, pronoun tags function as adjuncts and can occur with object referents, adverbs, tag questions and discourse markers (a phenomenon she refers to as 'tag stacking'); compare:

Example 6.7 a. *It's nice, that, though, isn't it?*
             b. *?We caught the train, Tanya and me, though, didn't we?*

Mycock (2019: 264–265) argues that utterances like Example 6.7b are ungrammatical because, unlike pronoun tags, NPs like the one in Example 6.7b do not function as adjuncts that express stance. However, 22.4 per cent of NP tags (34/152) occur as 'stacked tags' in the Midlan High dataset. Examples are given in Examples 6.8–6.12 below.

Example 6.8 *She's quite rough, my mum, as well* (Helen, Eden Village, 17A: 380)

Example 6.9 *She rang Kara's house, you know, her nanna* (Faye, Geek, 3B: 753)

Example 6.10 *It's like – they do look stupid, though, some of them, don't they?* (Cindy, Popular, 37B: 336)

Example 6.11 *They're so bitchy, though, girls, aren't they?* (Marie, Popular, 53A: 1214)

Example 6.12 *They've got no sense, these teachers, at all* (Ellie, Townie, 36A: 257)

The discussion in this section indicates that previous research on right dislocation has suggested a number of possible functions for this construction. These function are real-time utterance processing (clarification), information management (emphasis, topic focusing) and interpersonal functions (alignment, evaluation). However, we have also seen evidence to suggest that not all of these functions are equally distributed across different types of tag. Whilst clarification may be a valid function for noun-phrase tags ('we caught the train, me and Tanya'), it cannot be a valid function for pronoun tags ('it's nice, that') where the tag adds no additional referential content to the utterance. On the other hand, where right-dislocated tags might mark grammaticalisation of evaluation for pronoun tags, this function may be less valid for noun-phrase tags which may provide additional descriptive detail that is not always framed as an expression of affect. However, given the discussion above, these differences are gradable rather than absolute.

Nonetheless, there are clear differences in NP tags and pronoun tags – not least in their distribution. Whilst all right-dislocated tags may have the potential to fulfil information management functions as a consequence of their syntactic shape, it may be that pronoun tags are *more likely* to function to fulfil interpersonal functions. The comparatively small amount of work on pronoun tags thus far has made it difficult to interrogate how the various functions of right dislocation are distributed, and how their distribution relates to the articulation of social meaning in interaction. To address this, the remainder of this chapter provides a comprehensive analysis of the distribution of the various types of right dislocation and how they relate to social class, community of practice, interactional content and interactional stance.

6.3 How Were Right-dislocated Tags Analysed?

This chapter presents an analysis of the 347 tokens of right dislocation that were extracted from the Midlan High recordings. The distribution of right dislocation across different social classes and communities of practice is analysed, followed by an analysis of the way different tag types patterned across each community of practice. The frequency of right dislocation cannot be calculated as a percentage of application versus non-application. As noted earlier, unlike nonstandard *were* and negative concord, there is no obvious 'alternate' form for right dislocation. Consequently, use of right dislocation is reported according to the number of right-dislocated tags per 1,000 words, following methods used in corpus linguistics. This ensures that the data is normalised to enable comparison across speakers who produced variable amounts of talk during the recordings.

In order to further probe differences in the frequency of personal pronoun tags across communities of practices, tokens containing personal pronouns (n = 97) were analysed for their interactional content and interactional stance. The purpose of this analysis was to test for correlations between use of personal pronouns and certain discourse functions. Interactional content was evaluated by coding for the verb process of the verb contained in the main clause of the right-dislocated construction, following Halliday (1985). Although Halliday's verb processes have been critiqued for being somewhat superficial (see, e.g., Levin 1993 for a more comprehensive account of verb typology), they are

150   Does Everyone Use Grammar to Make Social Meaning?

utilised here because they offer a window on the semantics of the verb phrase, enabling (a somewhat imprecise, but nonetheless instructive) consideration of the types of states, actions or experiences expressed through the use of right dislocation. The verb process types used in the analysis are shown in Table 6.2.

Evaluative stance was considered in order to examine how speakers orient to the content of the token of right dislocation. As noted in Chapter 3, 'stance' refers to inferences that can be made about the speaker's alignment with the content of their talk or to their interlocutors. The analysis in this chapter considers what can be inferred about a speaker's alignment with the person referenced by the main clause's subject pronoun. This was determined qualitatively by close listening to the data and consideration of the context in which the token was uttered. Evaluative stance was coded in a simplified way as positive, negative and neutral; examples are given in Table 6.3. It is important to note that the stance represents how the speaker orients to the subject of the main clause, not how a syntactic proposition is framed. For example, in the

Table 6.2 *Verb process types used in the analysis of personal pronoun tags according to Halliday (1985)*

Verb type	Processes	Example from dataset
Material	'doing'	*I couldn't **run** away, me* (Michelle, Geek, 47A: 831)
Mental	'sensing'	*I **hate** her nanna, me* (Tanya, Geek, 47A: 815)
Relational	'being'	*She's a bitch, her* (Lindsey, Popular, 29B: 210)
Verbal	'saying'	*I **talk** dead high, me* (Georgia, Popular 48A: 350)
Behavioural	'sensing represented as external behaviour'	*You **take** everything I say too serious, you* (Meg, Townie, 40B: 274)

Table 6.3 *Evaluative stances expressed in the context of right dislocation use*

Evaluative stance to subject	Example from dataset	Context
Positive	*I've never had a detention, me* (Michelle, Geek)	Michelle is contrasting her own behaviour to a peer's, who is portrayed negatively for being expelled from school.
Negative	*You well pissed me off, you* (Ellie, Townie, 36A: 208)	Ellie is talking about how she speaks to friends who annoy her.
Neutral	*I live in Holstead, me.* (Beverley, Popular, 41A: 897)	Beverley is gently correcting Emma for inaccurately identifying where she lives.

example of a positive stance in Table 6.3, the clause is negated, but Michelle is expressing a positive evaluation of herself in this context (she is the 'good girl' who has never had a detention).

In sum, to assess the patterns of socio-pragmatic variation associated with right dislocation, the following are analysed in subsequent sections:

- the general social distribution of right dislocation;
- the subject type of the right-dislocated tags;
- the correlation between verb process types and personal pronoun type tags;
- the correlation between evaluative stance and personal pronoun type tags.

These patterns are described in the next section.

6.4 How Are Right-dislocated Tags Distributed at Midlan High?

6.4.1 General Patterns of Use

Figure 6.1 shows the frequency of right-dislocation by social class at Midlan High. The bars in the figure show mean use of right dislocation for each social class group, whereas the individual dots in the graph indicate the use by each individual in that social-class group.

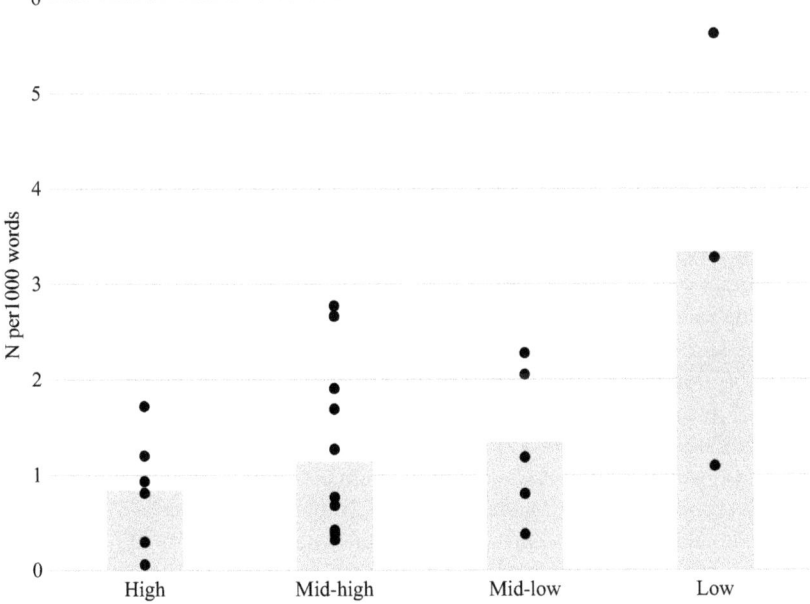

Figure 6.1 Frequency of right dislocation by social class. Each dot represents one individual. Bars represent group averages.

Table 6.4 *Log likelihood comparisons for social class groups*

Social groups			
High	Mid	$\chi^2(1) = 9.41$	$p < 0.01$
Mid	Low	$\chi^2(1) = 41.19$	$p < 0.0001$
High	Low	$\chi^2(1) = 57.24$	$p < 0.0001$

Figure 6.1 suggests that there are differences in how frequently social class groups use right dislocation: on average, use of right dislocation increases as social class status lowers, although there are overlaps in individual frequencies across social class groups. A log likelihood comparison confirmed that differences across social groups were statistically significant ($\chi^2(3) = 60.81$, $p < 0.0001$). However, a pairwise comparison across the different social groups showed that the Mid-high and Mid-low groups were not statistically different from one another. Consequently, further pairwise comparison combined the two Mid- social class groups. As shown in Table 6.4, log likelihood comparisons revealed that the High group was statistically different from both the Mid and Low groups, and the combined Mid group was statistically different from the Low group.

Figure 6.2 shows right dislocation patterns by community of practice at Midlan High. As with Figure 6.1, the bars in the figure show mean use of right dislocation for each community of practice, whereas the individual dots in the graph indicate the precise use by each individual in that community of practice.

Log likelihood comparisons found statistically significant differences between the communities of practice (CofPs) ($\chi^2(3) = 111.64$, $p < 0.0001$). Further testing showed that the Eden Village CofP was not statistically different from Geeks; and the Popular CofP was not statistically different from the Townies. However, a pairwise comparison of the Eden Village/Geeks and the Populars/Townies was statistically significant ($\chi^2(1) = 111.17$, $p < 0.0001$). This suggests a difference in the frequencies of right dislocation, with the Eden Village and Geek groups using significantly fewer tokens of right dislocation than the Popular and Townie groups. Note, however, that there are some outliers in the community of practice data, namely Michelle (who uses right dislocation 2.28 times per 1,000 words, compared to the Geek mean of 0.63 per 1,000 words) and Georgia (who uses right dislocation 5.62 times per 1,000 words, compared to the Popular mean of 2.16 per 1,000 words). We return to Michelle and Georgia towards the end of this chapter.

This data suggests that both social class and community of practice have a significant effect on the use of right dislocation. However, the larger log likelihood for community of practice ($\chi^2(3) = 111.64$, $p < 0.0001$) suggests that the community of practice model is a better model of the data than the

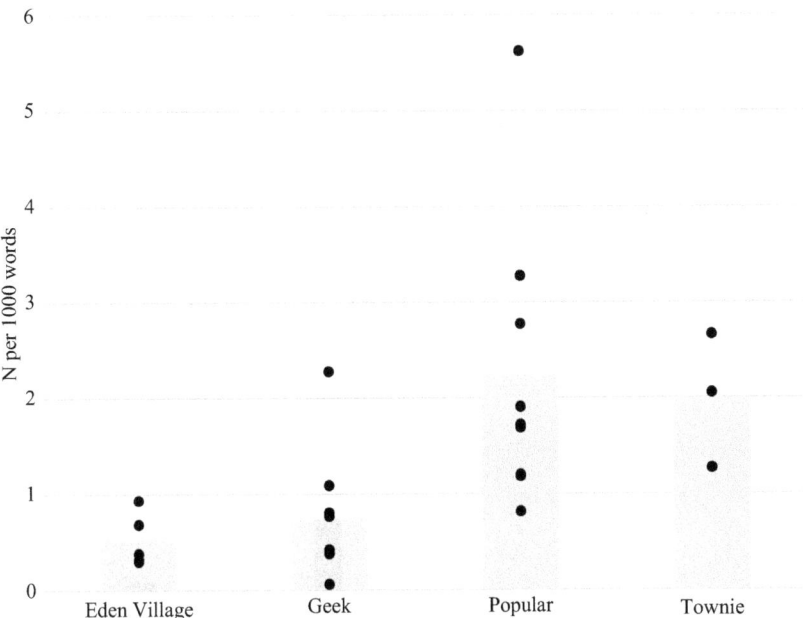

Figure 6.2 Frequency of right dislocation by community of practice. Each dot represents one individual. Bars represent group averages.

social class model ($\chi^2(3) = 60.81$, $p < 0.0001$). This can be seen by visual inspection of Figures 6.1 and 6.2: with the exception of the two outliers, the data in the community of practice figure is more tightly distributed around the mean than is the data in the social class figure.

6.4.2 Breakdown of Right Dislocation Tag Types

Table 6.5 shows how right dislocation is distributed by type of tag. It shows that the majority of tags are noun phrases and only a small minority of tags are non-finite or relative clauses. Demonstrative and personal pronoun tags are used robustly, with slightly more personal pronoun tags than demonstrative tags. The high frequency of noun phrase tags matches the pattern noted by Durham (2011: 274) in her study of York English.

However, Figure 6.3 reveals that right-dislocated tag types are not homogeneously distributed across different communities of practice. Whereas the Eden Villagers, Geeks and Populars use noun phrase tags more than any other kind of tag, the Townies use personal pronoun tags most frequently. Infact, the frequency with which personal pronoun tags are used follows a cline reflecting

154 Does Everyone Use Grammar to Make Social Meaning?

Table 6.5 *Distribution of right dislocation at Midlan High by tag type*

Tag Type	Number of tags	% of tag type
Noun phrase	152	43.8
Personal pronoun	97	28.0
Demonstrative	83	23.9
Non-finite clause/relative clause	15	4.3

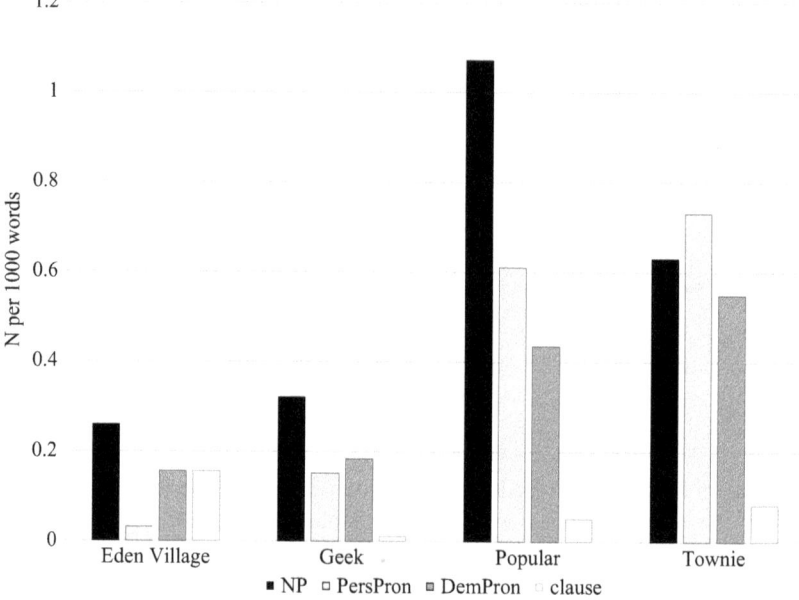

Figure 6.3 Use of right dislocation by tag type for each community of practice.

how communities of practice orient towards the school as institution, with Townies using them most, then Populars, then Geeks and, finally, Eden Villagers (who use just one personal pronoun tag). Furthermore, whereas demonstrative tags are used most frequently after noun phrase tags for the Eden Villagers and the Geeks, both the Populars and the Townies use more personal pronoun tags than demonstrative tags.

The difference in use of right-dislocated tag types across communities of practice was found to be statistically significant (Chi-square, $\chi^2(6) = 15.491$, $p = 0.017$). In this testing, noun phrase and clause tags were combined, given that both serve to provide further descriptive referential information about the subject of the main clause (whereas demonstrative tags and personal pronoun tags do not). Post hoc testing did not reveal which precise patterns underpinned this result (most likely because of low data counts in some cells), although the finding that the Townies used fewer noun phrase tags than expected was close to significance ($z = -2.84$).

A further comparison considered whether the Eden Villagers and the Geeks, on the one hand, and the Populars and the Townies, on the other, were significantly different from one another. They were: Chi-square, $\chi^2(2) = 6.247, p = 0.044$. Again, post hoc testing did not find significant differences in the residuals, but the personal pronoun results were close to significance, with the Eden Villagers/Geeks using fewer personal pronoun tags than expected ($z = -2.50$) and the Populars/Townies using more ($z = 2.50$).

Given this difference in the use of personal pronoun tags, and the hypothesis that pronoun tags function differently from noun phrase tags, the next section looks more closely at the type of personal pronoun tags found in the Midlan High data.

6.4.3 The Distribution of Personal Pronoun Tags

Figure 6.4 shows how first-, second- and third-person personal pronoun tags are distributed. The Eden Villagers only use one third-person tag, but looking at the groups who use right dislocation consistently with personal pronoun tags, it is possible to see that both the Geeks and the Populars use first-person tags more frequently than other person types. On the other hand, the Townies use of personal pronoun types is more evenly distributed across all three personal pronoun types. Perhaps more strikingly, the Populars and the Townies are the only groups to use second-person pronoun tags, although the Populars only use one of these tags.

The difference in how the Geeks, Populars and Townies use personal pronoun tags is statistically significant (Fisher Exact, two-sided, $p = 0.000$). Post hoc testing confirmed that the Populars use more first-person pronouns than expected ($z = 3.32$), and the Townies use fewer first-person pronouns than expected ($z = -4.01$) and more second-person pronouns than expected ($z = 3.66$).

6.4.4 Summary of Preliminary Distributions

Summing up the findings in the previous sections, it is possible to see that social class seems to interact with use of right dislocation, with average use of right dislocation increasing as social class status lowers. Put simply, those lower down the social hierarchy seem to use right dislocation more.

Furthermore, the communities of practice who less readily orient to the school as institution – the Populars and the Townies – use almost twice as much right dislocation as the communities of practice who orient to the school as institution – the Eden Villagers and the Geeks. The type of right-dislocated tag also differed across communities of practice. Whilst all groups have reasonably high rates of noun phrase and demonstrative pronoun tags, the Townies use fewer noun phrase tags than expected, and both the Populars and the Townies use more personal pronoun tags than other communities of practice.

The personal pronoun tag analysis revealed further statistically significant differences in how groups use types of personal pronoun tag. Most notably, the Populars used more first-person pronoun tags than expected and, whilst both Populars and Townies use second-person pronoun tags, the Townies use them statistically more significantly than the Populars. This leaves us with the question of why numbers of personal pronoun tags differ. What do speakers do with personal pronoun tags? In the next section, we attempt to answer this question by considering how frequency differences in the use of personal pronoun tags correspond with how right dislocation functions interactionally.

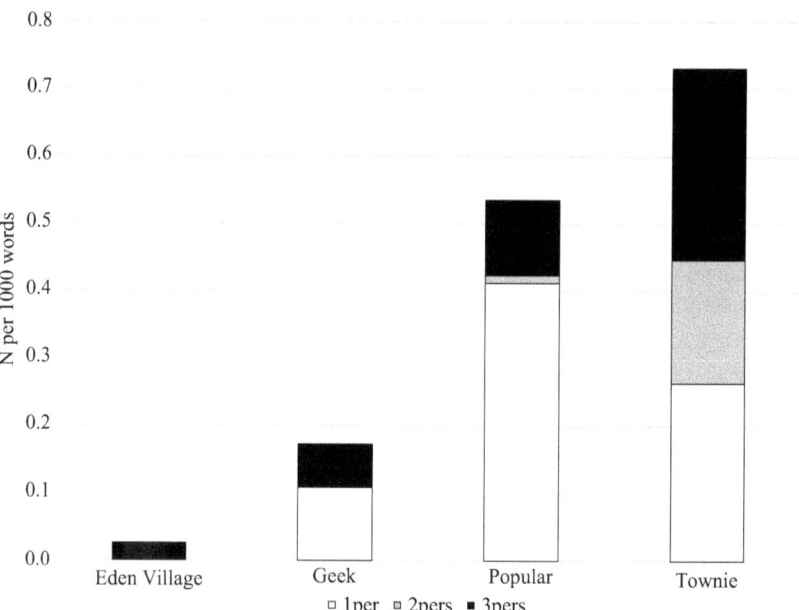

Figure 6.4 Use of right-dislocated personal pronoun tags by community of practice.

6.5 How Are Personal Pronoun Tags Distributed at Midlan High?

6.5.1 Personal Pronoun Tags and Verb Process Types

As noted earlier, verb process types were analysed to offer insight into the types of states, actions or experiences expressed through the use of right-dislocated personal pronouns. Figure 6.5 indicates that there are differences in which verb processes co-occur with certain personal pronoun types. Whereas first-person pronoun tags occur with all verb processes, third-person tags, and especially second-person tags, occur with a more highly restricted set. Furthermore, first-person tags most frequently occur with mental verb processes, whereas both second- and third-person tags occur most frequently with relational verb processes.

Put simply, it seems that first-person pronoun tags are used most frequently in constructions which portray the thoughts, perceptions, desires and affective states of the speakers themselves (for instance, *I dint like it, me,* Lindsey, Popular, 41A: 641); whereas second- and third-person tags seem to most frequently occur in statements which comment on the attributes and identities of others (for instance, *You're scary, you,* Meg, Townie, 23A: 617; or *She's a cow, her,* Beverley, Popular, 41B: 584).

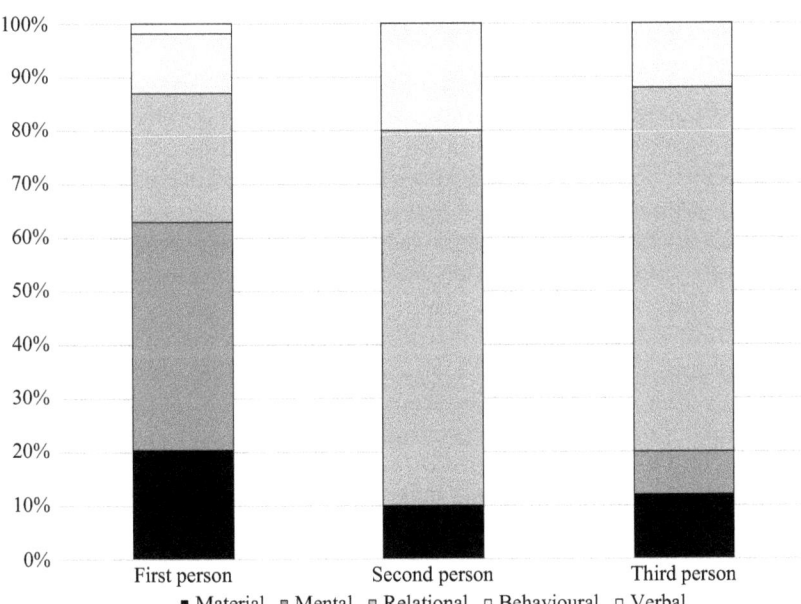

Figure 6.5 Distribution of verb processes by personal pronoun type.

The difference in how verb processes are distributed across personal pronoun type is statistically significant (Fisher's Exact, two-sided, $p = 0.000$) (note that the analysis excluded the single token of a verbal process). In line with the observations above, post hoc testing showed that first-person tags occur more frequently with mental processes than expected ($z = 3.99$), and less frequently with relational processes than expected ($z = -4.41$). Conversely, third-person tags occurred more frequently with relational processes than expected ($z = 3.56$), and less frequently with mental processes than expected ($z = 2.98$). Small data counts might explain why the relationship between second-person pronoun types and relational processes did not reach statistical significance in post hoc testing.

Importantly, further statistical testing on first- and third-person pronouns (the ones used robustly by the Geeks, Populars and Townies) suggests that all communities of practice follow this same distributional pattern. That is to say, there is no statistically significant difference in how the Geeks, Populars or Townies combine personal pronoun types and verb processes. This means that speakers do not differ in how they combine verb processes and personal pronoun tags; some groups of speakers simply use more personal pronoun tags than others – presumably because they more frequently have cause to exploit the pragmatics of certain personal pronoun tags in their day-to-day interactions.

6.5.2 *Personal Pronoun Tags and Stance*

As noted earlier, stance was examined to consider how speakers orient to the person identified as the subject in the token of right dislocation. Figure 6.6 suggests that there are clear differences in the stances articulated by different personal pronoun types. Whereas first-person pronoun tags occur predominantly with positive stances, second- and third-person tags occur overwhelmingly with negative stances. The difference between stance and personal pronoun type was statistically significant (Fisher's Exact, two-sided, $p < 0.000$). Post hoc testing shows that first-person tags occur more frequently than expected with positive ($z = 3.04$) and neutral ($z = 2.86$) stances, and less frequently than expected with negative stances ($z = -5.15$). Both second-person tags ($z = 3.08$) and third-person tags ($z = 3.48$) occur more frequently than expected with negative stances.

As with the verb process type data, there are no statistically significant differences in how different groups project stances with first-person or third-person pronoun types. That is to say, speakers do not differ in how they combine stance and personal pronoun tags; negative stances are just more likely to occur when anyone uses a second- or third-person pronoun tag to evaluate someone else.

6.5 Personal Pronoun Tags Distributed at Midlan High

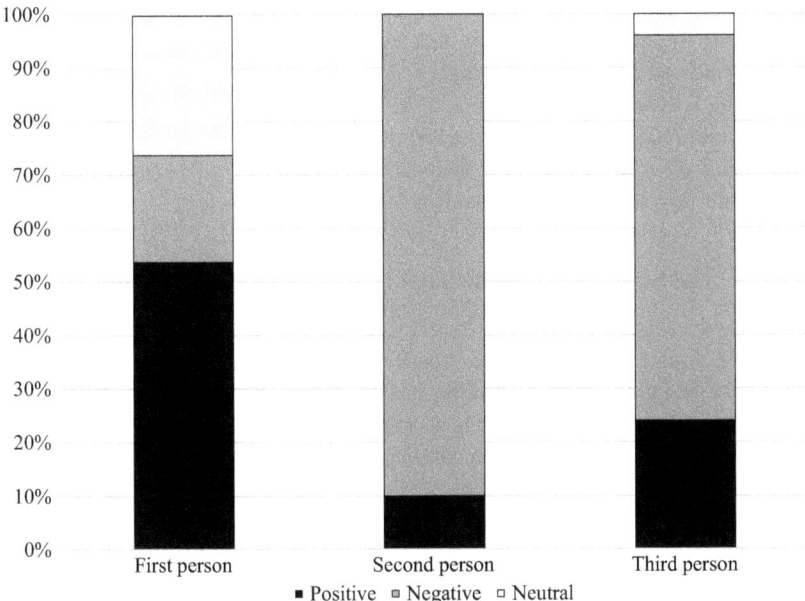

Figure 6.6 Distribution of stance according to personal pronoun types.

6.5.3 Summary of Personal Pronoun Analysis

The verb processes and stances identified for first-person tags suggest that individuals use these tags to comment on and evaluate their own states and experiences. Comments are predominantly framed positively, but not exclusively so – individuals may evaluate themselves positively, negatively or neutrally. It is notable that Geeks, Populars and Townies all use first-person pronoun tags.

The verb processes and stances identified for third-person tags suggest that individuals primarily use these tags to comment on and negatively evaluate other people's attributes and identities. In this way, third-person pronoun tags are implicated in critical and potentially face-threatening interactional moves. Geeks, Populars and Townies all use third-person tags, although the Townies use these at a much higher frequency than any other group.

The verb processes and stances identified for second-person tags suggest that individuals use these tags to directly comment on and negatively evaluate other people's attributes and identities. In this way, second-person pronoun tags are used in potentially aggressive and directly face-threatening ways. This observation echoes comments in previous work on right dislocation; Timmis (2009: 336–337) suggests that second-person tags are 'sarcastic and/or derogatory' and that their 'emotional colour or attitudinal overlay threatens face.' One Popular girl, Beverley, use a second-person pronoun tag and all of the Townies use these types of tag.

Having focused on the specifics of how personal pronoun tags are socially and interactionally distributed, we next consider all aspects of the interactional and social distribution of right dislocation to arrive at a full account of the social and interactional functions of this variable.

6.6   The Social and Interactional Functions of Right Dislocation

Not only does the total use of right dislocation differ in frequency across social class and community of practice groupings, but the types of right dislocation used by social groups differs too. Both of these facts provide clues about what a listener might infer when they hear an instance of right dislocation. Starting with frequency differences, what can these tell us about the social meaning of right dislocation?

In the introductory sections of this chapter, right dislocation was reported to occur more frequently in the speech of working-class groups. This finding was corroborated by the Midlan High data, although – notably – community of practice membership seemed to better explain the distribution of right dislocation in this dataset. In addition to right dislocation occurring more frequently in the speech of lower social classes and anti-school social groups, we also observed that right dislocation was explicitly identified as marking differences between types of speakers. Amanda and Meg's comparison of ways of expressing evaluation in Extract 6.1 suggested that right dislocation is associated with the opposite of 'poshness' – namely, being 'common'. Whilst its restriction to spoken interactions means that right dislocation is clearly not at the same level of salience as levelled *were* and negative concord, the overt commentary on right dislocation suggests that speakers are able to associate this linguistic form with specific social groups and, importantly, the social meanings indexically linked to these social groups.

The discussion in the book so far suggests that there are differing factors which govern the extent to which different types of people engage with certain grammatical variables. One factor is the extent to which speakers are exposed to a variant and another is the extent to which that variant has established social meanings. A child living in a working-class neighbourhood is much more likely to hear forms more frequently found in working-class discourse than one living in a middle-class neighbourhood. But of course, as the discussion in preceding chapters has shown, not all working-class young people will align themselves with the social meanings of these forms, and some middle-class young people will be motivated to acquire them if they are exposed to them, for instance, via their school peers. Hence, the better correlation between

6.6 Social and Interactional Functions of Right Dislocation

right dislocation and community of practice than between right dislocation and social class.

Whilst right dislocation is used by all social groups at Midlan High, the significant frequency differences across social classes and communities of practice suggest that its social associations may be powerful enough to inhibit how some individuals and groups utilise this linguistic form. Importantly, though, differences in the frequencies with which certain social groups use different types of right-dislocated tag indicate that these social associations may be intensified or reduced, dependent upon the precise grammatical formulation of the right-dislocated tag. So, what does variability in function and frequency of right-dislocated tag type add to our understanding of the social meanings of right dislocation?

It was noted earlier that right dislocation can have the following functions: real-time utterance processing (clarification), information management (emphasis, topic focusing) and interpersonal purposes (alignment, evaluation). It was also proposed that, by virtue of introducing new referential information, noun phrase tags predominantly function to clarify, emphasise and focus topic. On the other hand, the lack of additional referential information in pronoun tags indicates that pronoun tags predominantly have focusing and interpersonal functions. Given these differences, it is unsurprising that we find all social groups using noun phrase tags reasonably frequently, irrespective of the specific forms of practice in which they engage. The ability to clarify utterances, combined with the need to undertake forms of information management, such as topic focusing, is useful to all speakers.

Of the interpersonal functions facilitated by the use of pronoun tags, evaluation has been found to be particularly notable – both in this study and in previous work (Aijmer 1989: 150; Snell 2008: 191). To evaluate something or someone else is a powerful move: it implies that the speaker has the authority to pass judgement. If right-dislocated tags can serve to be both evaluative and emphatic (given their information structure) then, as Snell (2008: 190) has observed, an act of evaluation that uses a right-dislocated tag may be an especially powerful social move. But do different types of pronoun tags carry the same interactional force?

If we consider demonstrative pronoun tags, these typically reference events or artefacts. In Example 6.13, Kara is commenting on a falling out between Leah (an Eden Villager) and another girl. Notably, although Kara evaluates the occurrence negatively, she does not evaluate Leah directly. In this way, her negative evaluation is directed at something abstract, which only indirectly implicates a person. This may explain why we see relatively frequent use of demonstrative pronoun tags across all communities of practice. They are useful ways to structure discourse information and, whilst they are potentially powerful evaluative speech acts, they are not directly face-threatening to interlocutors or others.

Example 6.13 *That was so pathetic, that* (Kara, Geek, 44A: 621)

This is not necessarily the case with personal pronoun tags, which typically directly reference (and potentially evaluate) people. However, who is referenced, and how direct that reference is, depends upon the precise person of the pronoun used in the tag. This means that different personal pronoun types can potentially correlate with different levels of face-threat. Consider Examples 6.14 to 6.16 below.

Example 6.14 *I hate her nanna, me* (Tanya, Geek, 47A: 815; about a friend's grandmother)

Example 6.15 *You're scary, you* (Meg, Townie, 23A: 617; to an older boy)

Example 6.16 *She's a bitch, her* (Lindsey, Popular, 29B: 210; about Geek, Melanie)

All of these examples express negative feelings about another person, but in subtly different ways. In Example 6.14, Tanya expresses her dislike of her friend's grandmother, but she doesn't say what it is about the grandmother that has caused her to arrive at this judgement. Instead, the structure of her utterance places focus on her viewpoint, not on the grandmother's attributes. In this way, the right-dislocated tag emphasises how Tanya feels, not how the grandmother is.

This can be directly compared with Example 6.16, in which Lindsey directly identifies Melanie in an aggressively negative way. Lindsey articulates this view as fact, not as her opinion. Similarly, in Example 6.15, Meg assigns a negative attribute directly to the older boy she is talking to. Comparing Examples 6.15 and 6.16, the former is the most face-threatening because evaluating someone directly to their face potentially attacks both agency and sense of solidarity. Third-person tags are also face threatening, but if the person is not present, the severity of the face-threat is reduced.

This hierarchy of face-threat reflects the way in which tag types are distributed, with the most directly face-threatening types only used by groups who pay less attention to interactional norms around politeness. First-person tags, which only ever evaluate the speaker themself, are used widely by Geeks, Populars and Townies. Third-person tags, which tend to evaluate other people's identities and attributes negatively, are only robustly used by the Populars and the Townies. Finally, second-person pronoun tags, which are the most face threatening by virtue of their potential to evaluate other people's identities and attributes directly to their face, are only robustly used by the most extreme rebellious group, the Townies, who are known for their physically and verbally aggressive behaviour.

Further evidence for links between tag type, interactional moves and persona types is provided by the way in which tag types are used by social group

6.6.1 Further Evidence of the Social Meaning of Right Dislocation

Starting with how outliers use tag types, Figure 6.7 shows data from Michelle (who uses right dislocation 2.28 times per 1,000 words, compared to the Geek mean of 0.63 per 1,000 words) and Georgia (who uses right dislocation 5.62 times per 1,000 words, compared to the Popular mean of 2.16 per 1,000 words). It is important to note that both of these girls are situated at the lower end of the socioeconomic hierarchy: Michelle is in the Mid-low social class group and Georgia is in the lowest social class group. Consequently, we might hypothesise that their high use is a consequence of ample opportunities to acquire and practice the use of right dislocation. However, the types of tags that they use suggest that there are other constraints on how they employ right dislocation in interaction.

Figure 6.7 shows that despite using more right dislocation than their Geek and Popular peers, both Michelle and Georgia still employ the same general proportional patterns of tag types as their respective communities of practice.

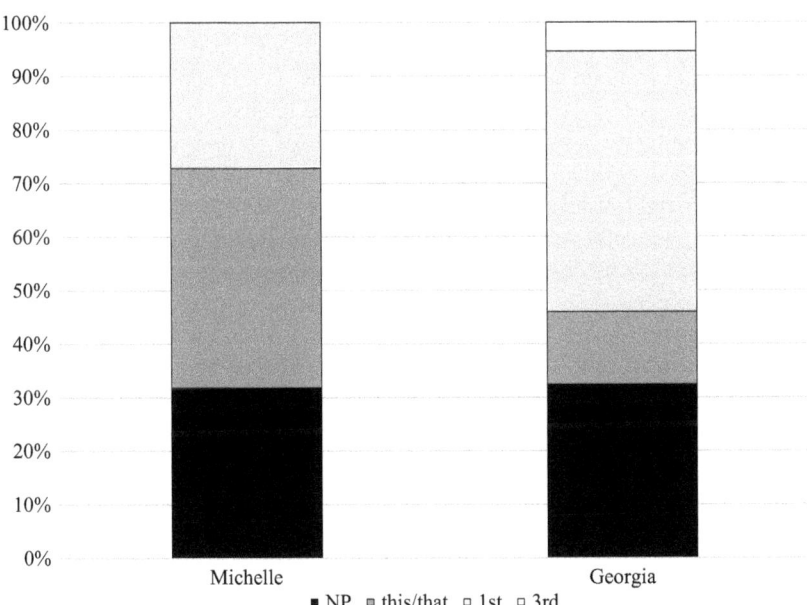

Figure 6.7 Distribution of right-dislocated tag types for the two outliers in the analysis (Michelle, Geek and Georgia, Popular).

All of Michelle's (6/6), and 90 per cent (18/20) of Georgia's personal pronoun tags are first-person ones. Additionally, in line with her status as a Popular girl, Georgia also uses a small number – two – of the potentially more face-threatening third-person pronoun tags. Importantly, Figure 6.7 shows that Michelle and Georgia are clearly able to use a range of right-dislocated tags (noun phrases, demonstrative pronouns, personal pronouns), but by only exploiting a limited range of personal pronoun types (first-person ones and, in Georgia's case, a small number of third-person ones), they restrict the inferences drawn about their speech. In so doing, they construct personas that are appropriate to their status as a Geek and a Popular girl, respectively.

But why do they use so many more first-person right-dislocated tags than their peers? This may be down to individual personality. If right-dislocated tags are organisational in that they make previously evoked references the most salient for subsequent discussion, it is possible that high *me* users may use these tags as a way of controlling the conversational floor or as an attempt to make themselves the centre of the discussion. In this way, Michelle and Georgia's anomalously high use of first-person tags allows them to express their individual personalities, without violating what may be inferred about their community of practice personas.

How use of tag types changes over time provides further evidence that communities of practice exploit the links between tag type, interactional moves and persona types. Figures 6.8 and 6.9 respectively show use of first- and third-personal pronoun tags over time. The figures clearly show that, whilst the Geeks, Populars and Townies increase their use of first-person pronoun tags over time, only the Townies increase their use of second- and third-person pronoun tags over time. What is more, the Townies' increase in second- and third-person right-dislocated tags is dramatic between Years 9 and 10. This corresponds perfectly with the timeframe in which they separated themselves from the Populars by engaging in more risky, aggressive and rebellious forms of social practice.

The discussion in this section suggests that the precise grammatical environment in which right dislocation occurs may intensify or attenuate both its pragmatic and its social effect, such that – despite its universality – different social groups interact with right dislocation and types of right-dislocated tags in socially meaningful and socially nuanced ways. Given that Geeks and Populars use first-person pronoun tags, there is no reason to think they are not equally capable of using second- and third-person ones. That the latter tag types seem to be off-limits to the Geeks and restricted for the Populars suggests that speakers are actively designing their syntax to facilitate certain inferences about the kind of people they are. Likewise, the fact that second- and third-person tags are not restricted in Townie discourse indicates the extent to which the Townies exploit their interactional functions to construct

6.6 Social and Interactional Functions of Right Dislocation

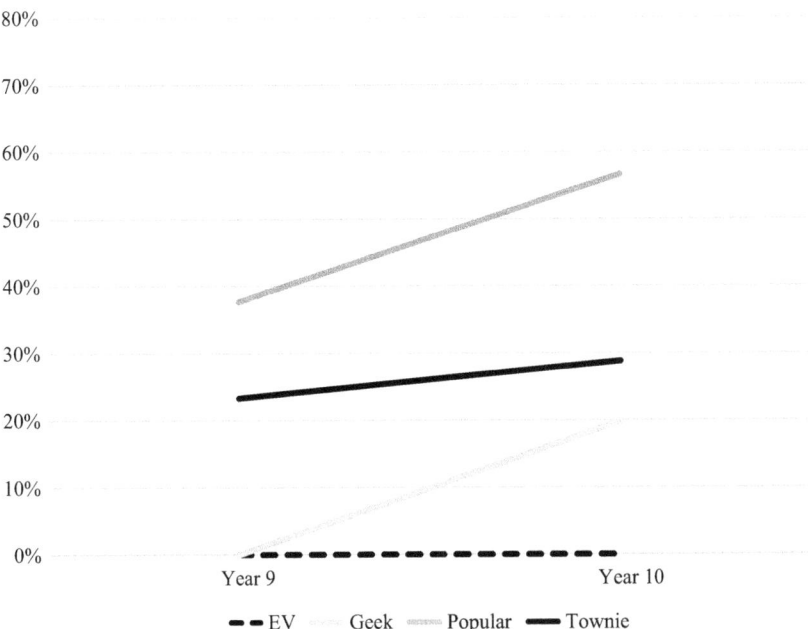

Figure 6.8 Use of first-person pronoun tags as a proportion of all personal pronoun tags, over time.

their rebellious and aggressive personas. Taken together, this data indicates that people do not avoid or employ certain grammatical constructions purely because of probabilistic variability in language input. The pragmatic utility of a syntactic form, rather than simply being exposed to it, plays a key role in usage.

This last point is important. Historically, sociolinguists have tended to treat social effects as orthogonal to linguistic effects, treating each as exerting independent constraints on language variation. However, if certain syntactic configurations (i.e., linguistic constraints) result in certain inferences, then different types of speakers may favour or disfavour certain linguistic environments because of the social value associated with an utterance – rather than because a particular linguistic constraint has not been acquired. So, whilst second-person pronoun environments are disfavoured overall in the use of right dislocation, the way they are employed by Townies indicates that this may be a result of their social value. As Bender (2001: 258) observes, 'if the speaker [goes] out of his/her way to use a variant disfavoured by the environment, then s/he must be particularly interested in conveying the social value associated with that variant'. In this way, the social and linguistic constraints on the use of grammatical

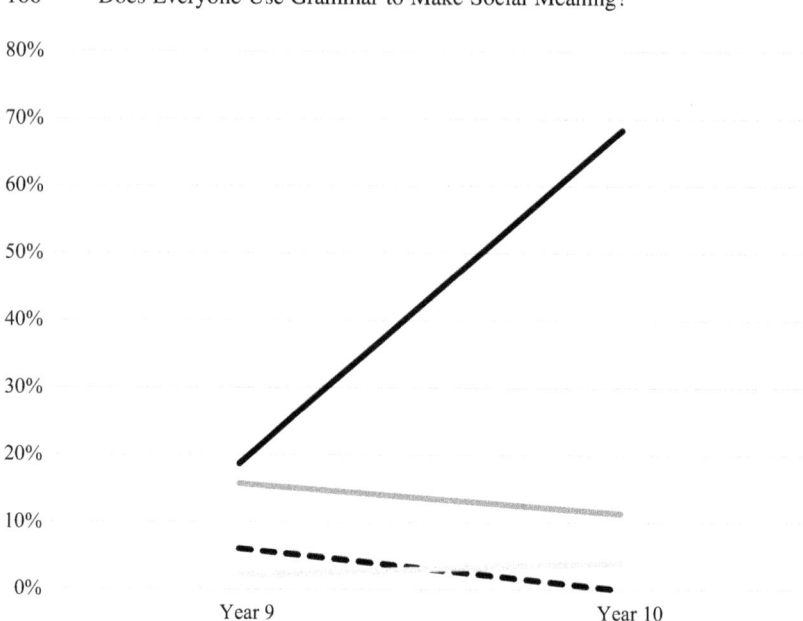

Figure 6.9 Use of second- and third-person pronoun tags as a proportion of all personal pronoun tags, over time.

variables are intertwined – something suggested by Bender (2001: 258), and further evidenced in the Midlan High data.

This chapter has shown correlations between the underlying semantic referential meaning of right-dislocated tags, their precise grammatical formulation (i.e., the type of tag) and specific pragmatic effects (linked to the articulation of states, experiences and stances). The frequencies with which certain social groups use these tags seems to be a direct consequence of situated persona level variability in the need or willingness to express the pragmatic outcomes of the relationship between the semantics and grammatical formulation of right-dislocated tags.

Although we have shown a relationship between right dislocation and pragmatic function, questions still remain about how speakers express interpersonal functions relating to evaluation if they don't use right dislocation. Does the fact that the Eden Villagers and the Geeks produce far fewer tokens of right dislocation mean that they don't engage in evaluative linguistic behaviours, or do they use 'variants' that are alternative forms? In the next section, we attempt to answer these questions by considering the interactions between type of grammatical construction and expressions of pragmatic meaning.

6.7 What Is the Relationship between Form, Frequency and Function?

As noted earlier, Snell (2008: 191) notes that right dislocation may be a way to grammaticalise evaluation. Her observation draws upon Biber *et al.*'s (1999: 969–970) research into the grammaticalisation of stance. As shown in the following examples, constructions such as stance adverbials (Example 6.17), complement clause constructions (Example 6.18), and right dislocation (Example 6.19) all have two distinct parts – one expressing the stance [a] and the other expressing the proposition evaluated by the stance [b]. Biber *et al.* suggest that the grammatical encoding of these constructions means that they more explicitly express stance than lexical stance expressions like the adjective in Example 6.20 or the verb in Example 6.21.

Example 6.17 [*To be frank*,]$_a$ [*I can't see it working*] $_b$

Example 6.18 [*I'm thrilled*] $_a$ [*that we're going on holiday*] $_b$

Example 6.19 [*I'm daft,*] $_a$ [*me*] $_b$

Example 6.20 *They're amazing*.

Example 6.21 *I love those pictures*.

Whilst stance is grammatically marked in Examples 6.17–6.19, there is nothing in the grammatical structure of Example 6.20 and Example 6.21 to indicate that they mark stance. Instead, 'they are simple declarative structures that give the appearance of presenting stanceless "facts"' (Biber *et al.* 1999: 968).

Macaulay (2005) finds that these distinctive ways of marking stances correlate with the different strategies used by working-class and middle-class speakers to mark evaluation. Whereas his working-class speakers use more instances of dislocated syntax (a group which includes right dislocation) to mark evaluation, his middle-class speakers use more adjectives and adverbs (so lexical stance expressions). We have also seen evidence of social group differences at Midlan High too. In Extract 6.1, Amanda shows her goth peer articulating her stance towards the pictures using an adjective ('amazing') and an interjection ('wow') – that is, Amanda directly contrasts her evaluative use of right dislocation with a more implicit expression of evaluation using lexical expressions of stance. Furthermore, she marks one as 'posh' and, by comparison, the other as 'common'.

This discussion suggests rather than perceiving the Eden Villagers' and Geeks' infrequent use of right dislocation to indicate that they use fewer evaluative speech acts, it is more likely that they simply express evaluation in different (potentially less explicit and less stigmatised) ways. Of course, this may include the use of adjectives and verbs as in Example 6.20 and Example 6.21, but it may also extend to the use of nonlinguistic (body shape or gesture) or paralinguistic (volume, pitch or duration) means. Precisely how the variable strategies used to express evaluation are interactionally and socially distributed is an open question, but it is one worth answering. For variables like levelled *were*, two different variants of the verb are compared. For negative concord, the use of two (or more) negative particles are contrasted with the use of one. In both of these cases there are clear variants contained within otherwise similar grammatical frames, and one variant is clearly marked as standard and the other as nonstandard. This chapter has shown that by shifting focus from grammatical variation around standard and nonstandard versions of the same structurally similar forms to examining variation that is perceived as 'colloquial' rather than 'nonstandard', we can get a clearer sense of speakers' linguistic dexterity. Importantly, this helps to avoid further entrenching the view that linguistic variation is predominantly about the marking of prestige and stigma, rather than about effective communication in everyday interaction.

In shifting our focus on the type of syntactic item considered, we have demonstrated that understanding the social meaning of syntax requires that we think about information structure; our starting point should be 'the function of a specific syntactic construction rather than the form' (Cheshire 2005a: 500). Only by understanding how a form is used can we appreciate the alternatives ways in which speakers use language to fulfil the same functions. This has far-reaching implications, as discussed further in Chapter 8. If we cannot fully appreciate how different speakers use different forms of language to do the same kinds of social work, we will continue to underestimate the linguistic skill of some speakers – namely, those who use forms that are undervalued purely because of their perceived social value, not their functionality. But, of course, it is not the case every syntactic variation has social value. How this meaning is established is addressed in the final section.

6.8   Syntactic Variables, Semantics and Social Meaning

It is important to note that not all variably used syntactic constructions will index social group or social category. For instance, Cheshire's (2005a) work on bare noun phrases (discussed in Chapter 1) showed that working-class girls used more bare noun phrases in discourse-new contexts than any other social group, and middle-class boys used them less frequently than any other social group. However, Cheshire argues that this is a consequence of the types of discourse that certain social groups tend to engage in, not because bare noun phrases index gender and/or social class. Drawing on how interactional styles are reported in second wave language and gender research, she argues that

6.8 Syntactic Variables, Semantics and Social Meaning   169

working-class girls are more likely to use styles which seek to convey intimacy and solidarity, whereas middle-class boys are more likely to use referential, information-focused styles of speech. The ability to communicate in these distinctive ways drives the use of bare noun phrases, but there is no metalinguistic awareness linking bare noun phrases to gender and/or social class. That is to say, bare noun phrases do not have meaning at the characterological level (Agha 2003) – they do not signal conventionalised personas or social types.

The analysis of right dislocation in this chapter has revealed what it takes for a syntactic variable to gain characterological meaning. Eckert (2019a: 756) argues that syntactic constructions only gain social meanings when they occur more frequently in styles that themselves have reached conventionalised social meanings. Extract 6.1 showed Amanda associating the use of right dislocation with her status as a Townie. We might conclude that right dislocation is associated with Townies for two main reasons. Firstly, it occurs very frequently in their discourse, most likely because they are comfortable explicitly marking their attitudes and stances in interaction (whereas other girls might prefer to mark opinions in ways which are less likely to be perceived as 'subjective'). Secondly, when Townies use right dislocation, they use more marked instantiations of the variable (more personal pronouns, and more second-person pronouns in particular). Put another way, an expression like *You're scary, you* (Meg, Townie, 23A: 617) might not just signal that a speaker is a Townie, but that she is a Townie who is directly and aggressively evaluating someone else. Consequently, Townies exploit the general interpersonal functions of right dislocation (such as evaluation) for specific persona-level social work (to position themselves not just as evaluators, but as frank, aggressive and direct). In this way, their marked use of right dislocation both reflects and constructs their social characters in quite overt ways. Importantly, their particular use of right dislocation is entirely compatible with (and, in part, interpreted through) their wider sociolinguistic style. Townies exploit the semantic meaning of right dislocation to express their social persona in interaction. In this way, the meaning of right dislocation is rooted in semantics, but how Townies' use it enables a further link to character type. It suggests that, for this variable, a Type SM trajectory (rooted in semantics) is a prerequisite for a Type CT one (rooted in character type).

That syntactic constructions like right dislocation have discourse functions (so interpersonal, topic and focusing functions) as well as propositional meanings (Cheshire 2005a: 479) means that a full understanding of their social meaning requires them to be viewed in relation to their stylistic framing. In isolation, their meaning is restricted to their semantics but, in context, their meaning is elaborated by their social context, but also 'components of language besides syntax' (Cheshire 2005a: 480). These other components include discourse placement (topic and content), in addition to segmental (use of vowels and consonants) and suprasegmental (prosody) features, paralinguistic (volume, pitch or duration), or nonlinguistic (body shape or gesture) features. In the next chapter, the analysis turns from considering the relationship between syntactic variation and pragmatics to thinking about how syntax might work alongside discourse and segmental variation to construct social meaning. As we have seen in this chapter, syntactic variants bring together pragmatics and structure, but – when used in speech – they also house phonetic variation. As discussed in Chapter 1, the search for social meaning has tended to focus on phonetic variation. But what are the effects of housing phonetic variants in certain syntactic frames? In the next chapter, we consider how the pragmatic functions of syntactic forms interact with the expressivity of phonetic form.

7 How Does Grammar Combine with Other Elements of Language?

Extract 7.1

Popular girls, Beverley and Lindsey, have been listening to some dialect recordings and looking at transcripts of conversations with people who have Bolton dialects.

1	EM	And what about, erm – like all these little questions that people ask at the end of stuff,
2		like, 'dunt she?' [and 'dint he?' and] 'innit?'
3	B	[Ah, yeah.]
4		
5	EM	'In(Ø) 'e?'
6	B	We do that.
7	L	Yeah.
8	B	When you – when you're slagging someone off. 'Int/?/ she?' Yeah (LAUGHS).

(Beverley and Lindsey, Populars, 56A: 15–62)

We have seen how grammatical variation can be socially stratified and embedded in practice, and how pragmatic function can determine the occurrence of grammatical items in the interactions of certain groups. We have also seen how the precise configuration of a syntactic item can be meaningful, such that the type of pronoun used within a right-dislocated construction can modulate the specific inferences it conveys. But there is another important way in which syntactic items can be modulated in speech: they can be shaped by the sound of their delivery. This is apparent in Extract 7.1. Populars, Beverley and Lindsey, are discussing tag questions. Tag questions are constructions where a statement is followed by a question tag, the subject of which is co-referential with the subject of the preceding main clause (e.g., *we went out on Friday night, didn't we?*). On l. 6, Beverley confirms that Populars like her and Lindsey use these grammatical items in their talk. But, in l. 8, she provides more information about the typical composition of their tags: they tend to be in the context of criticism (of someone who is usually female), and they vary in their phonetic make up. Whilst I offer 'In(Ø) 'e?' as a typical tag (l. 5), Beverley offers 'Int[?] she?' (l. 8) in return.

Work in variationist sociolinguistics has tended to focus on different levels of linguistic architecture in isolation. Whilst some studies have looked at the distribution of both phonological and morphosyntactic variants within one speech community (Wolfram 1969; Eckert 2000; Guy 2013; Smith & Durham 2019; Beaman 2021), few studies have considered the moment-by-moment co-occurrence of phonetic and grammatical detail. That is to say, studies have examined how phonological and morphosyntactic variants pattern, but they do not consider how social meanings may be derived from the interactional co-occurrence of phonetic and syntactic detail. As Eckert and Labov (2017: 485) note, 'the realization of a phonological variable is a short (and frequent) event in a syntactic series of events'. That is to say, speakers utter phonological features in the context of syntactic constructions, and listeners perceive them within syntactic frames. To explore the implications of this co-occurrence, this chapter will examine the discourse shape and phonetic realisation of the same syntactic form, the tag question.

In addition to providing an opportunity to look at how different levels of linguistic structure interact, an analysis of tag questions also provides the opportunity to more closely examine the relationship between pragmatics and social meaning. Tag questions have primarily been analysed in order to understand their form and function, as opposed to their frequency or social distribution. Lakoff's (1975) seminal work on 'women's language' cemented an association between tag questions and female speech, but this was based on her intuition rather than on quantitative data. It is a pattern that has been long disputed (Cameron *et al.* 1989). Tottie and Hoffmann (2006: 303–304) find a difference between men and women in corpora of British and American English, but the differences are small and not statistically verified. Tottie and Hoffmann (2006: 304–305) do, however, find a more robust difference by age: younger British speakers (aged twenty-five and under) use fewer tag questions than their older counterparts, and there is a general positive correlation between age and use of tag questions in American English data. They hypothesise that this is because younger people tend to use more lexical tags than older people (e.g., *yeah, right, OK*), replacing this use with more canonical tag questions as they age (Tottie & Hoffmann 2006: 306). The only other social factor mentioned in the literature on tag questions is social class. Algeo (1988: 182–188) surmises that tag questions which close off discourse by asking for confirmation of 'obvious' truths (e.g., 'We always tidy toys away, don't we?'), and aggressive tag questions (e.g., 'I'm not here for the fun of it, am I?'), are more typical of lower class discourse, but no quantitative data is provided to support this claim. So far, then, despite claims that tag questions have social type meanings linking them to women, and – for some types of tag – the lower classes, only the correlation between age and tag questions is clearly evidenced in the existing literature.

On the other hand, research has identified multiple pragmatic functions for tag questions, highlighting their ability to serve as requests for information, facilitate talk, increase an utterance's politeness, express concern for an addressee, and/or challenge an addressee (Lakoff 1975; Holmes 1984; Algeo

1988; Cameron *et al.* 1989; Tottie & Hoffmann 2006; Kimps 2007; Kimps *et al.* 2014). The ability for tags to convey these pragmatic functions is undoubtedly linked to their syntactic structure. Hudson (1975: 24) observes that tag questions carry the sincerity conditions of both a declarative (asserting something the speaker knows to be true) and a question (suggesting the speaker believes the hearer knows equally well whether the assertion is true). Consequently, tags tend to steer interlocutors to respond to talk in quite specific ways. In an earlier analysis of the Midlan High data, Moore and Podesva (2009) suggest that this 'conducive' function of tags is at the core of their social meaning, noting that speakers can be conducive for many reasons – both positive (e.g., facilitating talk) and negative (challenging an addressee). The precise way in which this conduciveness articulates more specific social meanings is determined by the discursive, grammatical and phonological elements of a tag question's design.

This chapter will draw upon the analysis in Moore and Podesva (2009), but it will further interrogate the extent to which character-type social meanings can attach to the tag question itself, as opposed to attaching to the internal components of the tag question. Moore and Podesva (2009) demonstrated that community of practice can correlate with frequency of tag questions and that different communities of practice design their tags in distinct ways. However, their analysis did not fully examine the extent to which correlation with a community of practice results in a character-type social meaning for tag questions. The re-analysis of the data in this chapter will suggest that, of all the variables studied in this book, tag questions are the most likely to have social meaning rooted in semantics (i.e., a Type SM trajectory), and the least likely to have character-type associations. That is to say, their social meaning is rooted in pragmatic function and extended through interactional use, however, their link to personas and social types is not well-evidenced. In examining why it is that tag questions have limited indexical meanings, the analysis will consider the nature of their distribution and their syntactic complexity. More so than any other grammatical feature studied in this book, tag questions are universally employed by all communities of practice. How does this universality impact upon the indexical meanings of tag questions? Moving beyond the analysis in Moore and Podesva (2009), this chapter benefits from the ability to compare tag questions with less syntactically complex grammatical items (like negative concord). This makes it possible to provide a clearer picture of where social meaning resides in more syntactically complex, and universally available, grammatical items.

The next section outlines the tag question data and the methods used to analyse it. As noted, the analysis draws upon Moore and Podesva (2009) but the data has been revisited for the purposes of this chapter, and new analyses are presented. Given that the pragmatic functions of tag questions are well-established, the analysis begins by considering the social distributions of tag questions at Midlan High. It then interrogates tag question variation above the utterance level (i.e., in relation to discourse patterns), before addressing variation below the utterance level (i.e., in relation to their internal phonetic and morpholexical composition). The results of these analyses are used to hypothesise about where the social meaning of tag questions resides and its potential indexical trajectory. These hypotheses are then tested by examining how tag questions were implicated in a specific moment of social change at Midlan High.

7.1   The Tag Questions Dataset

Seven-hundred-and-seventy-eight tag questions were extracted from the Midlan High corpus. As with right dislocation, the frequency of tag questions cannot be calculated as a percentage of application versus non-application. Consequently, use of tag questions is reported according to the number of tags per 1,000 words, enabling comparisons across speakers who produced variable amounts of talk during the recordings. Only tags consisting minimally of a verb and a subject were considered, so lexical tags (such as *eh, right*) were excluded. The corpus contained a single invariant *innit* tag ('Cos it depends what mood she's in, innit?', Amanda, Townie, 40A: 223), so this was excluded too. Most tags had negative polarity, with positive polarity in the anchor clause ('Everybody just grows up in their own time, though, don't they?', Tanya, Geek, 47B: 581), although tags with positive polarity were also found in the corpus ('She never usually comes, does she?', Helen, Eden Village, 16A: 254).

Tag questions were coded for social class and community of practice. In order to better understand the discourse function of tag questions, they were coded for whether tag questions occurred turn-finally or turn-medially, and the extent to which tag questions occurred in contexts of overlap (with overlap defined as two or more interlocutors speaking when a turn containing a tag question is uttered). The data was also coded for the responses elicited by tag questions (whether interlocutors responded positively by agreeing with the proposition in the tag, negatively by disagreeing, or by not responding to the tag at all). The topic of the tag was also recorded according to whether the talk referred to the speaker's own social group, another social group, or a generic topic that didn't reference other groups).

In order to evaluate the internal composition of tags, they were coded for grammatical subject (which could be a first-, second- or third-person singular or plural pronoun), and the degree to which the tag's negated verb was nonstandard or not (as evidenced through the use of forms like *int* and *ain't* for 'isn't'). At the phonological level, the realisation of two highly salient variables were considered: word-initial (h) and word-final (t). The nonstandard variant of word-initial (h), referred to as /h/-dropping, has been described as 'the single most powerful pronunciation shibboleth in England' (Wells 1982: 254). Nonstandard variants of word-final (t) have also indicated that these forms are stigmatised when contrasted with /t/-release. Accounts of variability in word-final (t) in British English have tended to focus on the occurrence of glottal variants, with studies reporting the spread of /t/-glottalling in urban centres (Milroy *et al.* 1994; Straw & Patrick 2007; Drummond 2011; Schleef 2013). Fabricius (2000) has argued that the frequency of /t/-glottalling has reduced the stigma once attached to this variant, but a large body of metalinguistic commentary (Kirkham & Moore 2016: 90) suggests that this variant is still subject to prescription. There is a smaller body of work on word-final /t/ deletion in British Englishes, and the social patterning of this variant suggests that this form is stigmatised – potentially more so than /t/-glottalling (Tagliamonte & Temple 2005; Baranowski & Turton 2020). Therefore, in addition to exploring how groups stylistically design their tags, the inclusion of these two phonetic variables allows us to consider how tag-question use correlates with known stigmatised phonetic forms.

More detail on all of these factors, and further justification for their inclusion, is provided when the patterns of variation are presented below. This discussion begins in the next section, which considers how tag questions are distributed at Midlan High.

7.2 How Are Tag Questions Distributed at Midlan High?

7.2.1 General Patterns of Use

There are 2.97 tag questions per 1,000 words in the Midlan High corpus. This is roughly in line with the frequency of tag questions that Tottie and Hoffmann (2006: 305) found for zero- to fourteen-year-olds (fewer than 3,000 per million words) in their study of tag questions found in the spoken demographic subpart of the British National Corpus.

Tag questions are more than twice as frequent as right dislocation (there were 1.32 instances of the latter per 1,000 words) at Midlan High. Also, whilst the mean and median use of tag questions is 3.06 and 2.46 per 1,000 words respectively, the mean and median use of right dislocation is 1.31 and 0.94 per 1,000 words respectively. The smaller difference ratio between the mean and the median for tag questions suggests that the dataset is more evenly distributed for tag questions than for right dislocation. That is to say – however tag questions function – their frequencies across speakers are more similar than those for right dislocation. What this means about their social meaning is explored further below.

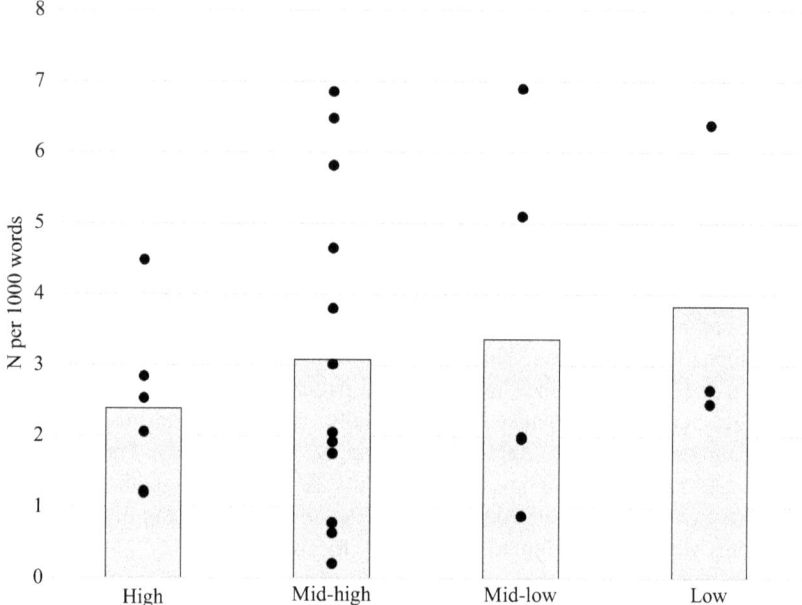

Figure 7.1 Frequency of tag questions by social class. Each dot represents one individual. Bars represent group means.

Figure 7.1 shows how tag questions pattern by social class at Midlan High. The bars in the figure show mean use of tag questions for each social class group, whereas the individual dots in the graph indicate the use by each individual in that social class group. It is difficult to tell whether there are significant differences across social class groupings from Figure 7.1 alone; mean differences are small and there is large variation within social class groups. A log likelihood comparison indicated that differences across social class groups were statistically significant ($\chi^2(3) = 20.16$, $p < 0.0001$). However, a pairwise comparison across the different social groups showed that only the High group was significantly different from the other groups (this is shown in Table 7.1). The frequencies of tag questions used by the Mid-high, Mid-low and Low class groups were not significantly differently from one another.

Figure 7.2 shows how tag questions pattern by community of practice at Midlan High. As with the previous figure, the bars in the figure show mean use of tag questions for each community of practice, whereas the individual dots in the graph indicate the precise use by each individual in that community of practice.

7.2 How Are Tag Questions Distributed?

Table 7.1 *Significant pairwise log likelihood comparisons with the High social class group*

Social groups			
High	Mid-high	$\chi^2(1) = 11.82$	$p < 0.001$
	Mid-low	$\chi^2(1) = 13.24$	$p < 0.001$
	Low	$\chi^2(1) = 14.16$	$p < 0.001$

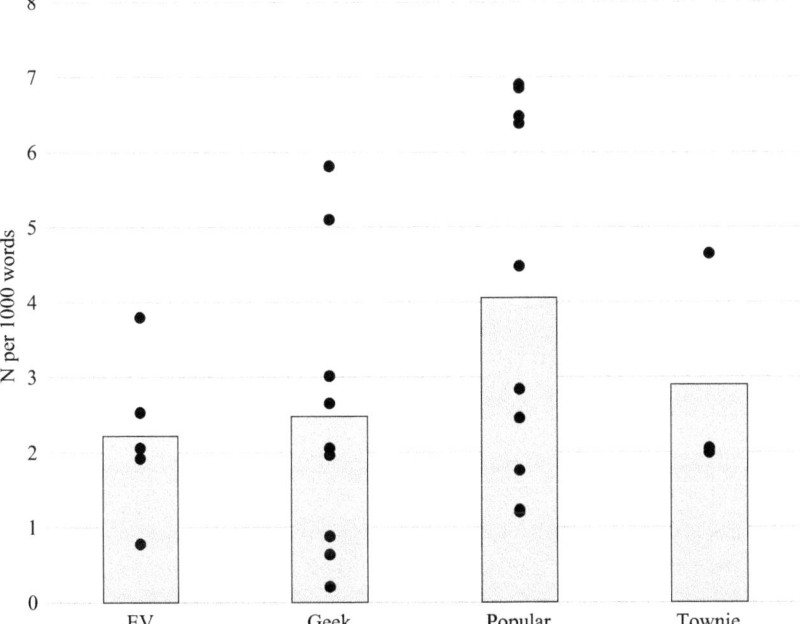

Figure 7.2 Frequency of tag questions by community of practice. Each dot represents one individual. Bars represent group means.

Log likelihood comparisons found statistically significant differences between the communities of practice ($\chi^2(3) = 58.68$, $p < 0.0001$). Further pairwise testing showed that the Popular community of practice was significantly different from all other communities of practice. The only other significant difference was between the Eden Villagers and the Townies, but this difference is less significant than the ones between the Populars and all the other groups. These results are shown in Table 7.2. Note, however, that there are a number of outliers in each of the communities of practices. So, whilst

Table 7.2 *Significant pairwise log likelihood comparisons for communities of practice*

Social groups			
Populars	Eden Village	$\chi^2(1) = 34.20$	$p < 0.0001$
	Geeks	$\chi^2(1) = 46.38$	$p < 0.0001$
	Townies	$\chi^2(1) = 15.03$	$p < 0.001$
Eden Village	Townies	$\chi^2(1) = 4.67$	$p < 0.05$

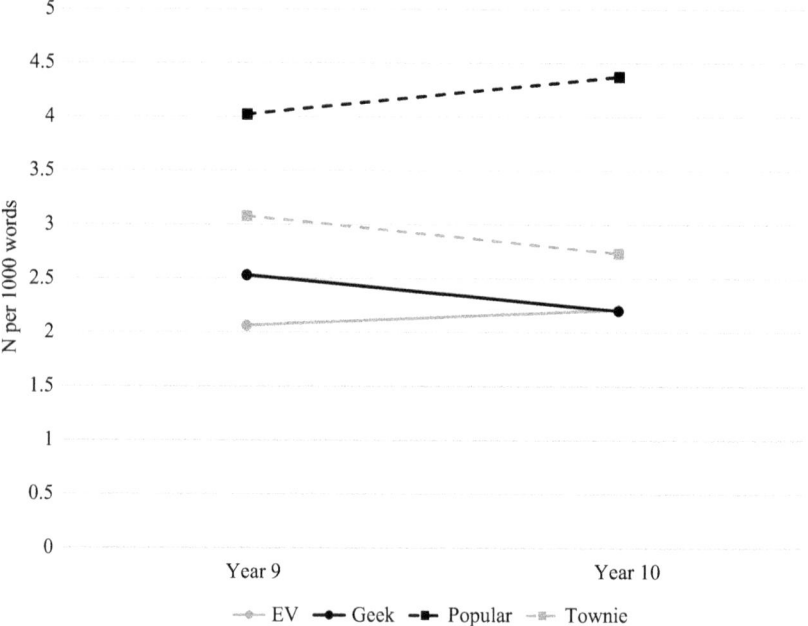

Figure 7.3 Use of tag questions over time, by community of practice.

there are far higher frequencies of tag questions in the Popular group – the distributions in each community of practice are generally fairly wide.

The difference between the Popular groups and the other social groups is more stark when we consider how use of tag questions changes over time. Figure 7.3 shows that, not only do the Populars generally use more tag questions than other social groups, they also show a marked increase in the use of tag questions from Years 9 to 10. The Eden Villagers use increases slightly from Years 9 to 10, but they continue to use markedly fewer tags than other girls at Midlan High. Both the Geeks and the Townies decrease their use of tag questions over time.

This data suggests that there are significant correlations between the use of tag questions and both social class and community of practice membership, although effects are driven by the means of certain social groups: more specifically, the High social class group (who use fewer tags than other groups) and the Populars community of practice (who use more tags than other groups). Importantly, frequency differences in the use of tag questions do not follow the patterns found for the variables studied in Chapters 4–6. We do not see an increase in tag questions in the order Townies ≥ Populars > Geeks ≥ Eden Villagers. Instead, the Populars use more tags than any other group, and the other groups do not really differ from one another.

This raises questions about the relationship between tag questions and Popular identity. Is there something about a tag question that constructs and reflects the Popular persona? If so, we might assume that tag questions have social meaning at the level of character type. However, given the more general spread of tag questions (when compared to right dislocation), it could also be the case that the discourse function of tag questions is particularly useful to the Populars, making them use these forms more than other communities of practice. In order to interrogate these questions further, the next section considers the discourse functions of tag questions at Midlan High.

7.3 How Do Tag Questions Vary at the Discourse Level?

7.3.1 Placement within a Turn

As noted at the beginning of the chapter, tag questions have a particular syntactic shape that makes them especially effective devices for conducing agreement and alignment; they carry the sincerity conditions of a declarative and a question (Hudson 1975: 24). Consider Example 7.1.

Example 7.1 *And then they <the Geeks> always have fights, don't they?* (Tina, Popular, 20A: 1051).

With the declarative, 'And then they always have fights', Tina indicates that she believes it is true that the Geeks frequently fall out (notably, she is not referring to physical fights). The addition of the tag question, 'don't they?', suggests that Tina believes her interlocutors, Kim and Meg, know at least as well as she does that her claim about Geeks is true. By attaching a question to a declarative, Tina's viewpoint is foregrounded, signalling what the expected response to her question is (a function of tag questions recognised by Kimps 2007: 272). It is easier for interlocutors to agree with an established proposition than it is to construct dissent against it, especially when the syntax of the utterance has already set up the speaker's viewpoint and the expected response.

The conduciveness of tag questions is evident in their typical discourse shape. Generally speaking, tag questions can occur turn-finally, as in Extract 7.2 and Extract 7.3, or turn-medially as in Extract 7.4. Tag questions are marked in bold in these extracts.

Extract 7.2

1	S	I don't like London that much. I mean, it's alright to go and visit and stuff like that. I
2		wouldn't wanna live down there.
3	L	Um.
4	S	It's too flat (LAUGHS).
5	EM	(LAUGHS)
6	L	**You get used to like where you live, though, don't you?**
7	S	Yeah.

(Louise and Suzanne, Geeks, 39B: 587–594)

Extract 7.3

1	K	Yeah, but you can still have kids when you're not married.
2	S	Yeah, but then **it'd make everything different, wunt it?**
3	K	I don't see – I don't think so.
4	S	I think it does.

(Kara and Susan, Geeks, 5B: 565–566)

Extract 7.4

1	L	In Year 8, we'd all just sit round that table in our form. We'd all just have this
2		massive table to sit round. And now, it's changed into all – we're all set – sat in like
3		the groups that we hang around with. There's like Meg, Ellie and Smithy sit next to
4		each other, and then we sit – cos.. **we're in between them all, aren't we?** [Like we'll
5		go out with Ellie and Meg] but then we'll go out with Tina and Paula as well.
6	B	[Um.
7		We're sat between the two groups.]
8		
9	L	So we're not either in one or the other. We're both. But, erm.. **Tina and that lot**
10		**don't go out with Ellie and that, do they?** And then last week it was so annoying,
11		right.

(Beverley and Lindsey, Populars, 41A: 375–384)

Tag questions occur more frequently turn-finally than turn-medially ($\chi^2(1) = 25.92$, $p < 0.0001$) irrespective of social group (there are no significant differences in frequency of turn-type across groups). This is in-line with previous work (e.g., Barron *et al.* 2015: 511). It suggests that tags may function as 'exit devices' (Sacks *et al.* 1974: 719) and, in doing so, they serve to solicit an on-topic response that aligns with the last proposition expressed by the speaker. Notably, the vast majority of tag questions (72 per cent) were produced in interactions where the speaker was in the same social group as their interlocutor(s), so we might consider them to most frequently elicit responses that indicate alignment with shared group norms or values.

7.3 How Do Tag Questions Vary?

7.3.2 Responses to Tag Questions

Tag questions can elicit three main responses. The interlocuter can

- explicitly agree with the proposition expressed in the tag (as in Extract 7.2, where Suzanne utters 'Yeah' on l. 7., and Extract 7.4 where Beverley utters 'Um' on l. 6);
- disagree with the proposition expressed in the tag (as in Extract 7.3, where Kara utters 'I don't think so' on l. 3 in response to Susan's tag question); or
- make no response to the proposition expressed in the tag (as in Extract 7.4, where Lindsey's tag on ll. 9–10 is not responded to by Beverley).

Figures 7.4 and 7.5 shows how interlocutors respond to turn-final and turn-medial tags, respectively. Figure 7.4 indicates that interlocutors most frequently explicitly agree with the propositions expressed in turn-final tags, as opposed to disagreeing or offering no response ($\chi^2(1) = 6.26$, $p < 0.01$). This is irrespective of social group. This provides support for the idea that tag questions are conducive: they encourage the interlocutor to explicitly agree with the last proposition expressed by the speaker of the tag question.

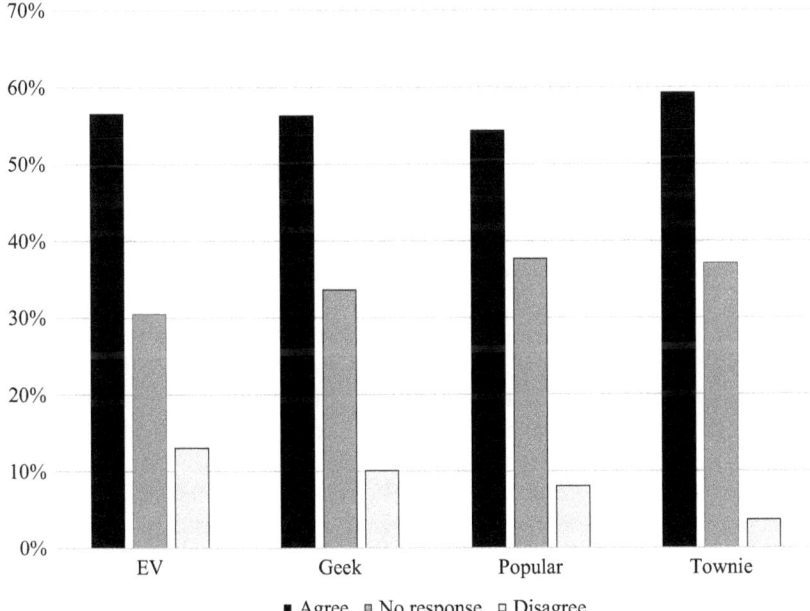

Figure 7.4 Proportional differences in the type of response to turn-final tags, by social group.

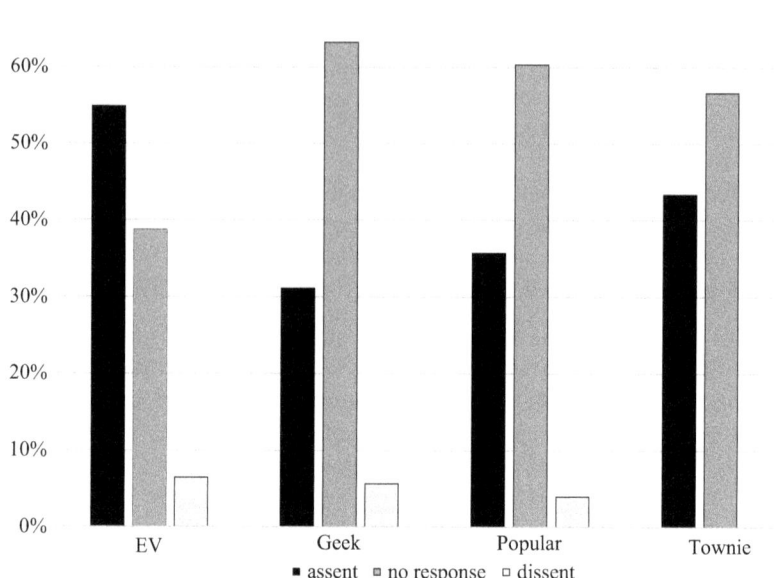

Figure 7.5 Proportional differences in the type of response to turn-medial tags, by social group.

However, as shown in Figure 7.5, the Geeks, Populars and Townies exhibit a different pattern for turn-medial tags: for these social groups, these turn-medial tags most often elicit no response. This means that Geek ($\chi^2(1) = 18.52, p < 0.000$), Popular ($\chi^2(1) = 14.63, p < 0.0001$) and Townie ($\chi^2(1) = 4.20, p < 0.04$) turn-final tags are more likely to elicit agreement than turn-medial tags. This is not very surprising – if the speaker continues to speak after the tag has been uttered, they have not relinquished the conversational floor. However, the Eden Villagers exhibit a different pattern. A comparison of Figures 7.4 and 7.5 shows that they most frequently respond with agreement to turn-final *and* turn-medial tags. Unlike the other social groups, the difference in responses to Eden Villagers' turn-final and turn-medial tags is not significant – their tags most frequently elicit agreement, irrespective of whether the tags are turn-final or turn-medial.

Given that Eden Villagers almost exclusively produce tags when interacting with their own social group, this suggests that the Eden Villagers collectively produce a somewhat more agreeable interactional style than other social groups.

7.3.3 Overlap and Tag Questions

The differences in the Eden Villagers' tagging style is also evident in how tag questions interact with overlap, as shown in Figure 7.6. Recall that overlap was

7.3 How Do Tag Questions Vary?

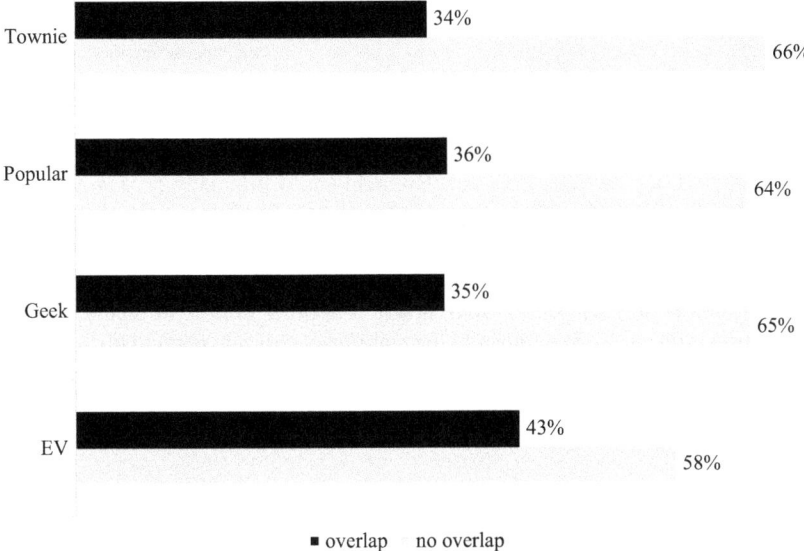

Figure 7.6. Proportional occurrence of overlap with tag question usage, by social group.

defined as two or more interlocutors speaking when a turn containing a tag question is uttered. Whereas the tag questions of the Geeks ($\chi^2(1) = 19.27, p < 0.000$), Populars ($\chi^2(1) = 19.77, p < 0.000$) and Townies ($\chi^2(1) = 14.57, p < 0.0001$) are significantly more likely to occur without overlap of any kind, the difference between the number of tags that co-occur with overlap and those that do not is insignificant for the Eden Villagers. Put another way, the Eden Villagers' tag questions are more likely to occur in the context of overlap than those of other social groups.

This suggests that Eden Villagers may not just be more agreeable, they also produce a more highly involved style. Taking account of the co-occurrence of agreement and overlap, we might characterise their overlap as co-operative and engaged. Extract 7.5 comes from an Eden Village interaction where the girls are discussing the time a classmate, Natalie, exposed herself to some boys during a school trip to France. Tag questions are marked in bold.

Extract 7.5

```
1  L    It was mainly Natalie,   [wasn't it?]
2  R                             [It] was Natalie [[was flashing.]]
3  H                                              [[You –
4
```

```
5        [me and]] Lucy] didn't, did we? [[We were]]   the good   [girls.]
6   L    [No.]
7   C                                 [[Natalie was flashing.]]
8   R                                                       [She] kept lifting her top
9        up .. in front of him.
```
                                    (Catherine, Helen, Lucy and Ruth, Eden Villagers, 32A: 317–326)

Both of the tag questions in this extract receive agreement. On l. 2, Ruth agrees with Lucy by reiterating her statement and overlapping her tag. On l. 6, Lucy then confirms the statement in Helen's tag that Helen and Lucy did not 'flash' at the boys. The discourse here works to differentiate Natalie from the girls speaking in this extract. The Eden Villagers collaborate on the negotiation of their comparatively conservative position in order to present themselves as 'the good girls' (l. 5). We return to the significance of this particular use of tag questions below when we consider the relationship between tag questions, their social functions and group identity.

7.3.4   Topic and Tag Questions

Group differences were not only found in overlap and agreement. Continuing with variation above the level of the utterance, significant differences were found in the topic of tag questions used by different social groups ($\chi^2(6) = 36.71$, $p < 0.000$). As illustrated below, Midlan High girls tend to use tag questions to talk about their own group (Example 7.2), another social group (Example 7.3), or about generic topics (Example 7.4, other examples include whether or not it is safe to use public transport, talk about pets, or the use of make-up).

Example 7.2 *Me and you were laughing our heads off, weren't we?* (Ellie, Townie, 27B: 117)

Example 7.3 *Ellie goes up to her and does all this stuff* (SHAKING FINGER IN FACE), *dunt she?* (Kim, Popular, 45A: 201)

Example 7.4 *And Physics is just Physics really, isn't it?* (Kara, Geek, 12B: 309)

Figure 7.7 shows that all groups talk about their own social group more than anything else, but there are some differences in the degree to which they talk about generic topics. Post hoc testing (allowing for a Bonferroni correction) found that Geeks were negatively associated with talk about their own group ($z = -3.45$) but positively associated with talk about generic topics ($z = 4.76$). On the other hand, Populars were negatively associated with talk about generic topics ($z = -3.81$). That is to say, relative to the other communities of practice, Geeks are less likely to talk about their own group and more likely to talk

7.3 How Do Tag Questions Vary?

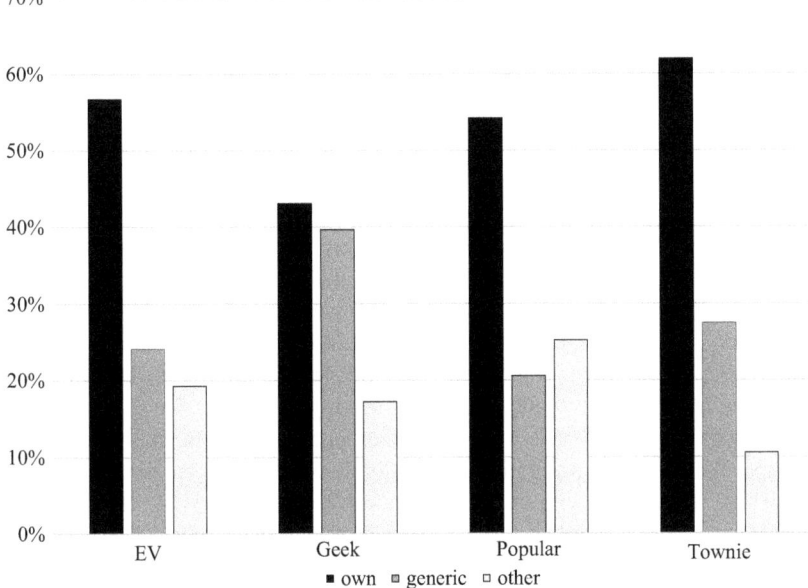

Figure 7.7 Topic of talk used in tag questions by social group.

about generic topics; whereas Populars are less likely to talk about generic topics than they are to talk about specific people (either within or outside their own social group). Neither the Eden Village group nor the Townies were specifically associated with particular topics of talk when compared with the other communities of practice.

The analysis of the discourse structure of tag questions has shown some clear patterns. Overall, tag questions tend to occur turn-finally more frequently than turn-medially. Disagreeing with a tag question is interactionally marked, with agreement the norm for turn-final tags and no response the most frequent response to a turn-medial tag question. This is true for all social groups except the Eden Villagers, who most typically agree with tags irrespective of their turn placement. There are further intergroup differences when it comes to patterns of overlap: Eden Villagers are more likely to overlap tag questions when compared to the other social groups. Finally, there are topic differences by social group: Geeks are more likely to talk about generic topics, whereas Populars are less likely to talk about generic topics than other social groups. Having established these general patterns above the level of the utterance, we now move to consider variation within the utterance.

186 How Does Grammar Combine with Elements of Language?

7.4 How Do Tag Questions Vary in Their Linguistic Content?

7.4.1 Subject Type

Just as the topic analysis provided clues about what different groups talk about when using tag questions, an analysis of subject type can give a very general indication of who or what individuals talk about when using tag questions (notwithstanding the distinction between syntax and semantics). Figure 7.8 shows how subject types are distributed across tag questions by social group.

Figure 7.8 shows a good deal of similarity in the proportions of subject types used by different communities of practice. However, it also indicates that there are a few differences in the subject types used by different social groups. Firstly, there are differences in how frequently groups use *she* and *he* subjects ($\chi^2(3) = 26.421$, $p < 0.000$). Post hoc testing (allowing for a Bonferroni correction) suggests that it is the Townies who differ from the other social groups. Townies have a negative association with *she* subjects (z = −4.22) and a positive association with *he* subjects (z = 4.22). That is to say, they use *she* less frequently and *he* more frequently than other social groups. The Populars pattern in the opposite direction: using *she* more frequently than *he*, but this tendency does not quite reach statistical significance when the Bonferroni

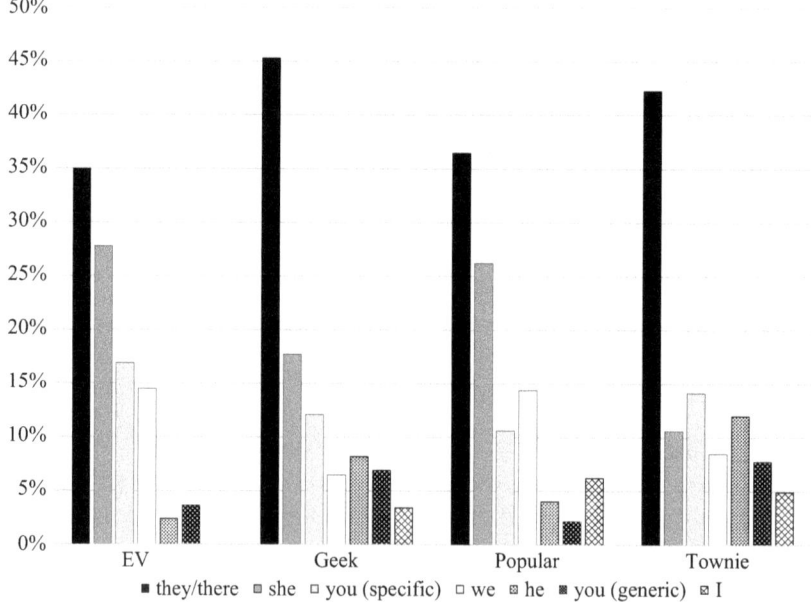

Figure 7.8 Use of personal pronouns in tag questions, by social group.

7.4 Linguistic Content

correction is applied (*she* subjects: $z = 3.26$; *he* subjects: $z = -3.26$). Finally, a log likelihood test reveals that there is a statistically significant difference in the use of *we* subjects across social groups ($\chi^2(3) = 26.94$, $p < 0.000$). Figure 7.8 suggests that both the Eden Villagers and the Populars use this subject type more than other social groups.

This use of subject types correlates with what we know about tag questions already. The tendency for Eden Villagers to engage in agreeable, collaborative talk correlates with their relatively high use of *we* subjects: part of the consensual nature of their talk involves collective and inclusive negotiation of shared norms. On the other hand, that the Geeks do not exhibit an association with any one particular subject type reflects their high use of generic topics. Conversely, the Populars' relatively high use of *she* and *we* subjects reflects their tendency to talk about girls in other groups and in their own group. Finally, the Townies' relatively high use of *he* subjects and their tendency to talk about their own group reflects their status as the only group who actively and intimately engage with older boys.

7.4.2 *Phonetic and Morpholexical Variation Within Tag Questions*

Another way in which spoken tag questions can exhibit variation below the level of the utterance is in their phonetic composition. Two well-known phonetic variables occur across tag questions: (h) – whether speaker's pronounce or 'drop' word-initial /h/ in words like *have* and *he*, and (t) – whether speakers fully release word-final /t/ in words like *don't* and *int*. One morpholexical variable also regularly occurs: whether speakers produce negated verbs in a standard (Example 7.5), reduced (Example 7.6) or nonstandard (Example 7.7) form, as shown below.

Example 7.5 It's usually Science, **isn't** it? (Leah EV, 38A: 270)

Example 7.6 Sasha is annoying, **int** she? (Tina, Popular, 20A: 1103)

Example 7.7 Most of them are, **ain't** they? (Georgia, Popular, 48B: 554)

Note that these three variables do not occur within every tag question: (h) occurs in 12 per cent of tag questions (n = 90) whereas (t) occurs in 79 per cent of tag questions (n = 614). Seventy-nine per cent of tag questions (n = 615) exhibit negative polarity. Nonetheless, they occur in sufficient numbers to indicate the co-occurrence of tag questions and certain well-known phonetic and morpholexical variables.

Figure 7.9 shows frequency of /h/-dropping in tag questions for each social group. It shows an increase in dropped /h/ across social groups in the expected direction, however, the extent to which different groups drop /h/ within tag

188   How Does Grammar Combine with Elements of Language?

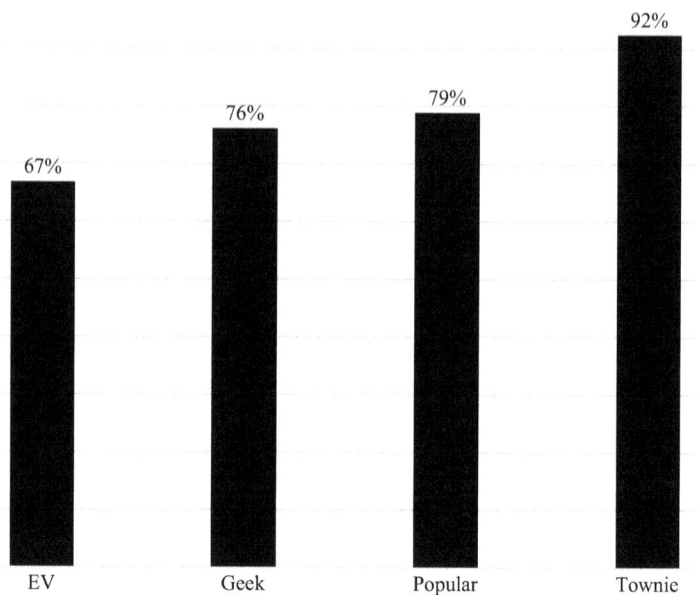

Figure 7.9 Proportion of /h/-dropping within tag questions, by social group.

questions is not statistically significant. That is to say, in the context of tag questions, all social groups more frequently drop /h/ than retain it, irrespective of the number of tag questions they use.

Moving to (t), three possible realisations of /t/ were considered: deleted, glottalised or fully released /t/. Figure 7.10 shows that all groups rank the variants of /t/ in the same order: glottals > deleted > released. However, the Townies never release /t/, and there are statistically significant differences across groups in the proportional distributions of variants ($\chi^2(6) = 28.089$, $p = 0.000$). Post hoc pairwise testing of glottal versus deleted /t/, accounting for a Bonferroni correction, suggests that Townies delete /t/ more than the other communities of practice ($\chi^2(1) = 7.866$, $p = 0.005$). Post hoc pairwise testing (also accounting for a Bonferroni correction) comparing use of released /t/ versus nonstandard articulations of /t/ suggests that the Geeks release /t/ more than other communities of practice ($\chi^2(1) = 10.149$, $p = 0.001$).

Finally, Figure 7.11 compares the morpholexical variants of negated verbs. As noted above, a three-way distinction was applied. Speakers could produce standard verb forms (e.g., *isn't, wasn't*), reduced verb forms (*int, wont*) or fully lexicalised nonstandard forms (*ain't, levelled weren't*). Figure 7.11 shows that, whilst all groups use reduced variants most frequently, there are differences in proportions of variants. These differences are statistically significant

7.4 Linguistic Content 189

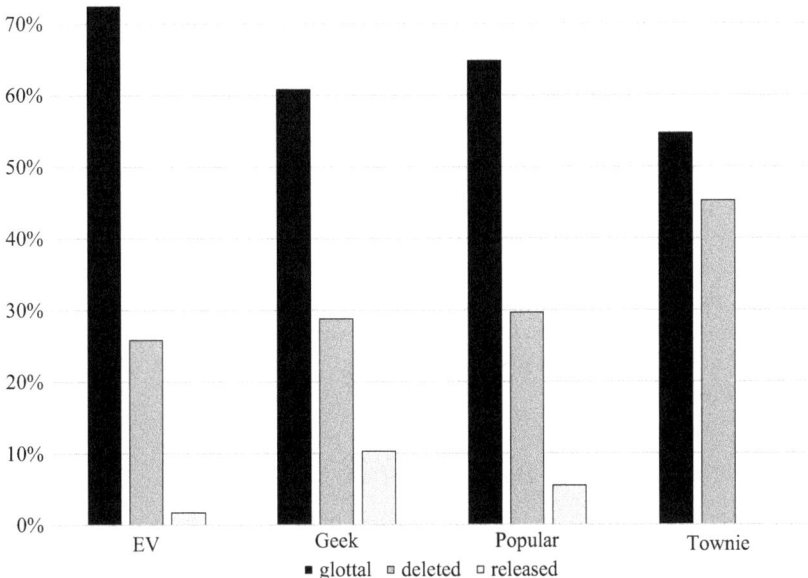

Figure 7.10 Proportion of /t/ variants, by social group.

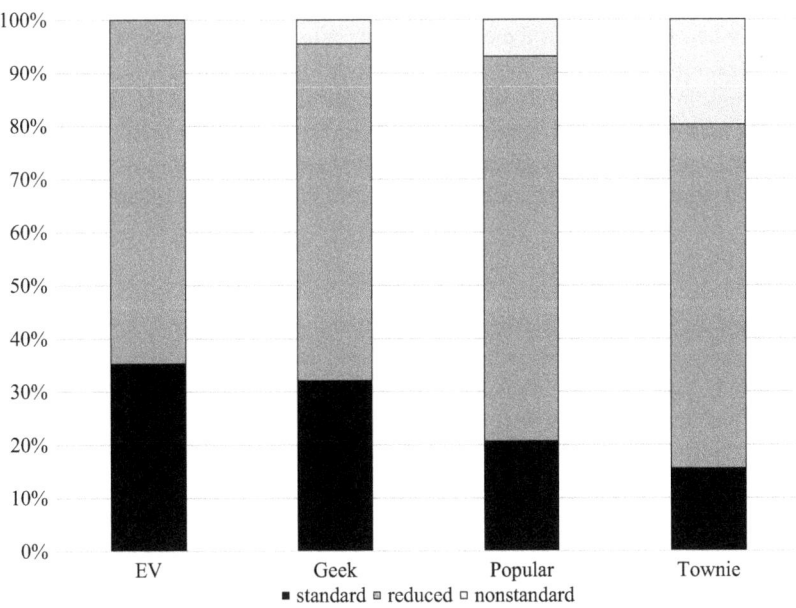

Figure 7.11 Use of morphosyntax within tag questions, by social group.

($\chi^2(4) = 33.044$, $p < 0.000$) in an analysis combining the Eden Villager and the Geeks (due to small data counts and similar proportions of use). Post hoc testing based on residuals of Pearson's Chi-squared Test for Count Data (using a Bonferroni correction) suggests that Eden Villagers/Geeks are positively associated with standard morphosyntax ($z = 3.46$) and the Townies are positively associated with nonstandard morphosyntax ($z = 4.72$). Further post hoc pairwise testing suggests that Populars and Townies use reduced and nonstandard forms significantly differently from each other ($\chi^2(1) = 10.149$, $p = 0.003$).

The results for the use of (h), (t) and verb morpholexis are unsurprising. Overall, they show a trend for increasing 'nonstandardness' in line with school orientation. In this way, the distribution of sociolinguistic variables within tag questions differs from the distribution of tag questions themselves – a point returned to below.

7.5 Summary: How Do Tag Questions Vary?

The frequency analysis showed use of tag questions to correlate with social class and community of practice, but the most marked correlation was between status as a Popular girl and use of tag questions. Put simply, Populars use more tags than any other group.

The analysis also supported previous research noting that tags are conducive by virtue of their syntactic shape. Data on turn type and agreement patterns revealed that tags tend to conduce alignment with speaker propositions, especially when tags occur at the end of a turn. Whilst the discourse functions of tag questions means that they are useful to all groups, different groups style their tags in subtly distinct ways. This is further evidenced by the way tag questions co-occur with topics and subject types, on the one hand, and phonetic and morpholexical variants, on the other. Precisely how each social group design their tag questions is outlined in the following sections.

7.5.1 The Typical Eden Village Tag Question

The tendency to elicit agreement with tag questions was more extreme for one community of practice; the Eden Village girls elicited tag question agreement more frequently than other communities of practice – doing so, even with turn-medial tags. They also engaged in more overlap when using tag questions, suggesting that they exploit the conducive function of tag questions to produce a more agreeable and consensual discourse style than that produced by other social groups.

As we saw in Extract 7.5, Eden Villagers tend to use tag questions to calibrate group norms, often around a particular type of conservative morality, and their utterances are articulated in a conservative linguistic style. This is shown in the co-occurrence of standard linguistic variants with tag questions, but also in what we already know about their linguistic style from the data in Chapters 4–6.

7.5.2 The Typical Geek Tag Question

Chapters 4–6 demonstrate some similarity in how Eden Villagers and Geeks utilise grammatical variants, nonetheless, these two groups stylise tag questions in slightly different ways. The Geeks do not share the 'cliqueness' of the Eden Villagers; in fact, their social networks are relatively loose, as discussed in Chapter 3. These weak(er) connections make it more difficult to build consensus, or even to share experiences of people and events. This may be reflected in the Geeks' focus on generic topics which tend to be more information-focused (as opposed to talk about people).

Extract 7.6 is from an interaction between Geek girls, Jennifer and Pippa (Pippa was not included in the quantitative analysis as she left Midlan High in the middle of Year 9). The girls are talking about Pippa's pet rat. The tag question on ll. 4–5 is articulated with a fully released /t/, and the tag question on l. 39 is uttered using standard morpholexis, and a glottal. Note, too, the way that Jennifer foregrounds her knowledge about Pippa's rats. She emphasises her connection to Butch the rat – even stating her knowledge of his variety ('badger white') on l. 28. In l. 36, she attempts to move the conversation to her own experience of looking after Pippa's rats ('I remember when I looked after them'). On failing to shift the direction of the conversation, she highlights her knowledge of Butch's habits and attempts to conduce Pippa's confirmation of this knowledge with the tag question on l. 39. This extract suggests that Geeks may well use tag questions to conduce agreement, but it is around knowledge, presented as objective fact. The precision of the Geeks' linguistic output (reflected in a higher frequency of released /t/s and a preponderance of standard morpholexis) may also give an authoritative tone to their discourse.

Extract 7.6

```
1   J     She's got a rat.
2
3   EM    Oh [no!]
4   J         [It's] gorgeous! And there's this big one, called Butch. And I love Butch,
5         don't/t/] I? And he runs around your neck and he's just a real, lazy..slob-, slobby
6         [[one.]]
7   P     [[Big]] fat one.
8
9   J     Big fat one - He's [absolutely gorg-]
10  P                        [But it's had its -] it's had its balls chopped off recently, as well.
11
12  (ALL LAUGH)
13
14  EM    Oh God [(LAUGHS)
15  P            [That's what] you always –
16
17  EM    [Has that made it nicer or worse?]
18  J     [(LAUGHS)]
19
```

20	P	Erm, [it stopped him -]
21	J	[No, he always pees on you.]
22		
23	M	It stopped him peeing a bit and it - and Lambkin is a girl, so he's.. stopped getting
24		frisky, cos he hates Lambkin.
25	EM	So you've got two?
26	P	Yeah, but.. if you leave them together - they fight.
27		And it's not very good [cos Lambkin chews him.]
28	J	[Cos they're different types] of rats. He's a badger white, and
29		she's a -
30		
31	P	But Butch snores. And he burps as well and he [farts.]
32	J	[And he] got - he gets hiccups.
33		
34	P	Yeah, and he g-, he- . . . But Lambkin, she's just - she's a wild thing
35		and [she ate my favourite] teddy. In the one night.
36	J	[I remember when I looked after them.]
37		
38	P	And she ate my carpet. . . [my whole carpet.]
39	J	[Aw, **you're always**] **getting done for that, aren't/?/ you**?
40		Chews up everything.

(Jennifer and Pippa, Geeks, 3A: 212–246)

7.5.3 The Typical Townie Tag Question

The Townie's tagging style seems to reflect confidence in their own status and their disinterest in other communities of practice. As Extract 7.7 shows, they talk about boys, and they tell stories about their exploits. Their distinctive linguistic style demonstrates disregard for school norms and their tags attempt to conduce agreement around engagement in illegal and violent behaviours. The rebellious activities the Townies engage in, and the way they talk about those activities, is reflected in their stylised use of tag questions. Ellie's tag question on l. 20 contains nonstandard morpholexis and a deleted /t/. Note that it is also swiftly followed up with an instance of negative concord on l. 23. Amanda's tag question on l. 28 also contains nonstandard morpholexis and a deleted /t/. Note, too, the profane language: 'twat' on l. 28 (this refers to hitting someone but it is also a term used for female genitalia); and 'piss' on l. 33. The design of the Townies' tags seems to reflect how their interests go beyond high-school dynamics, extending into an older cohort of young males and the excitement to be had engaging beyond their school peers.

Extract 7.7

1	E	And I really like Karl. He's phwoar-gorgeous.
2	A	Who? [Who's that?]
3	T	[He's not.]
4		
5	E	[Karl.]

7.5 Summary: How Do Tag Questions Vary?

```
 6  EM  [(LAUGHS)]
 7
 8  T   Oo. He's horrible.
 9
10  E   [He's not.]
11  M   [Acne.]
12
13  E   It's not acne, right. [His face] is [[messed up [because he's – because he's on]]
14      smack and that.]
15  T                         [No-]
16  M                                   [[OK, so it's pill spots (LAUGHS)]].
17  T                                                       [If he were- He's got a good
18      personality.]
19
20  E   [**Well, he was on smack,**] **weren't(Ø)'e?**
21  T   [Except he's like..]
22
23  E   [[But he's]] not on smack no more.
24  T   [[No.]]
25
26  ...
27
28  A   Oh – **that was night** [**when Lee twatted that lad, weren't(Ø) it?** Lee and Jay.]
29  T                           (INTAKE OF BREATH) Have you told her about –
30      have you [[told her about]] glass bottle and]
31  E                [[Oh yeah.]]
32
33  T   [piss?]
34  A   [The boys.]
35  M   [Jay hit-]
36
37  T   [Oh no, that were bad.]
38  M   [Jay hit him with his left hand.]
```
(Amanda, Ellie, Meg, Tracy, Townies 21A: 174–203, 806–811)

7.5.4 The Typical Popular Tag Question

We have seen that Populars are the tag question users *par excellence*. They use tags more frequently than any other group and have a tendency to use them to talk about people – in their own group and in other groups. As can be seen in Extract 7.8, the tags often serve a regulatory function, conducing agreement on the current social status quo. In the tag question on l. 1, Beverley seeks to establish the social group that she shares with her interlocutor, Lindsey. Here the 'we' pronoun reinforces the collaborative flavour of her discourse. The two following tags on l. 17 and ll. 41–42 both seek to address how Popular, Georgia, fits in with Beverley and Lindsey. All three tags are moderately nonstandard but not extremely so: they use glottals, but not a deleted /t/ which is more typical of the Townies; reduced morpholexical forms are used, but not the fully lexicalised nonstandard forms. The content of their tags indicates that these Popular girls are not afraid to evaluate and position other people, but the moderate nonstandardness of the variants within them suggests that they may be aware of how they themselves are judged by others. Popular tag design helps to conduce the creation of a blunt, straight-talking persona but one that is measured in comparison with the Townies.

Extract 7.8

```
 1  B    It's like me, Lindsey and Emily are like a tight group, aren't/?/ we?
 2
 3  L    [And then we] go out with like –
 4  B    [And then, so..]
 5
 6  L    Like they've – them four go out and then mix with people like in different years or
 7       people who don't come to school no more. And, erm, if we go out – oh, we always go
 8       to the cinema. And it's so boring (LAUGHS).
 9
10  (ALL LAUGH)
11
12  L    And, erm, we see like.. [Tina and Paula come.]
13  B                            [There's a fair on tonight.]
14
15  L    Georgia.. Rachel.
16
17  B    Georgia is kind of separated from us now, though, ant/?/ she? [Georgia –]
18  L                                                                  [It's ever since]
19       that time at the cinema.
20
21  B    Yeah. Ever [since –]
22  L               [Ellie] and Georgia fell out about a year ago, so – no.. less than a year ago.
23
24  B    Yeah, about [at the beginning of this year.]
25  L               [They fell out ages – ]
26
27  L    Bo, it were bef-, it were in Year 9.
28
29  B    [Yeah. At the] beginning of this year.
30  L    [Oh –]
31
32  L    Oh right. I thought you meant school year.
33  EM   (LAUGHS)
34  L    And erm.. And they fell out, cos we went to the cinemas, and then.. Ellie and that lot
35       dint come so they f-, Georgia and E-, erm, Ellie fell out about that. And then Georgia
36       stopped hanging around with us and all that.
37
38  B    And started [going off with other] people.
39  L               [And then went off..]
40
41  L    So she hangs around – she – she dint hang around with us much then. **Now she's**
42       **started to come back, ant/?/ she?**
43  B    Yeah, she's come back a bit more, but, like on Friday nights, she'll go out with.. like
44       Abbie Hughes and – Abbie Hughes and –
```

(Beverley and Lindsey, Populars, 41A: 134–178)

7.6 Tag Questions and Social Meaning

By examining how each social group use tag questions, it has been possible to observe what is shared in tag question usage and what differs. What is the significance of these similarities and differences? In the next section, we start to build a clearer understanding of the social meaning of tag questions.

7.6 Tag Questions and Social Meaning

In analysing the syntactic and discoursal shape of tag questions, it has been possible to identify an underlying interactional function: They are effective devices for conducing agreement around the propositions they express. We might assume, then, that the extent to which they are utilised depends upon the extent to which speakers need to elicit agreement around concepts, propositions, ideas and evaluations. This need is not restricted to certain social groups – at some point in interaction, we may expect all speakers to make attempts to elicit agreement. However, tag questions are not the only way to conduce agreement. Consider Extract 7.9 in which two Eden Village girls are discussing their friendship group.

Extract 7.9

```
1   H   We might not sh-, show it, cos we b-, we're not the sort of people [to have a]
2       confrontation.
3   L                                                                      [Yeah, w-, we're all
4       like] really different. And so, like sometimes our personalities clash and..
5
6   H   Yeah. Definitely, cos we all like different things. I mean, some of us are quite alike, I
7       suppose.
8   L   Yeah. We all like doing the same things.
9
10  H   Yeah, our habits [are] quite the same, so..
11  L                    [Um.]
12
13  H   And we have – we're like – we like m-, the same music.
14  L   Yeah.
15
16  H   But we do sometimes get fed up with each other, [but] we don't go on.
17  L                                                   [Um.]
```
(Helen and Lucy, Eden Village, 51A: 314–328)

Although not as explicit as a tag question, there are certain linguistic strategies used in this extract which help to conduce (or at least give the impression of) agreement around the propositions each speaker expresses. To begin with, the high number of first-person plural pronouns (*we, us, our*) in this short extract indicates how the two girls are working collaboratively to construct a shared depiction of their friendship group: although each girl speaks in turn, they individually speak as the same collective. Secondly, there are turn-final features which help to shape the following speaker's turn. For instance, in l. 4, Lucy finishes her turn with a conjunction, *and*. There is a clear pause of 0.68 milliseconds after Lucy's turn, serving as an invitation for Helen to complete the utterance. Helen responds with two agreement markers, *yeah* and *definitely*, and a partial reiteration of Lucy's proposal. Similarly, on ll. 6–7, Helen finishes her turn with *I suppose*. This not only hedges her claim that some of her friends are quite alike, but provides Lucy with an opportunity to further support or contest this claim. Lucy supports the claim in l. 8.

Although more research is necessary to explore precisely how speakers conduce agreement in discourse, Extract 7.9 indicates that there may be a number of potential strategies. This raises the possibility that some individuals or groups may favour certain strategies over others, perhaps explaining why the high social class group (of which Helen is a member) uses significantly fewer tag questions than other social class groups. Tag questions are syntactic constructions, but they share the properties of other more typical discourse markers (such as more general tags, e.g., *yeah* or *you know*), which have been described as 'stylistically deplored' (Brinton 1990: 46) and 'stigmatised' – especially when perceived to represent the inarticulacy of youth (Mendoza-Denton 2008: 288–290). It may be that this view bleeds into the perception of tag questions, which have certainly faced heavy critique when perceived to be a feature of 'women's language' (Lakoff 1975: 15). Again more research is required here, but the significant difference between the frequency with which members of the highest social class use tag questions compared to the other social class groups suggests that there is something which inhibits this social class group from using tag questions. It raises the possibility that tag questions have some social meaning by virtue of an association with other types of tag which are more explicitly stigmatised as indexing 'inarticulate youth'.

Nonetheless, tag questions do still get used, to some degree, by all individuals at Midlan High, indicating that they are available to all speakers, irrespective of their place in the social order. Furthermore, we have seen that, when they are used, they can be adapted to more precisely reflect and construct a speaker's social persona – this makes tags a useful construction for communicating both general and specific interactional alignments. That is to say, they are generally conducive whoever uses them, but they may be more likely to contribute to an agreeable, collaborative persona when designed by an Eden Villager, for example. On the other hand, when articulated in a prototypical Townie style, they may be more likely to conduce agreement around what constitutes an independent, rebellious persona. The thematic and linguistic content of the tag clearly helps constitute these personas, but does the act of using the tag itself contribute to persona construction?

Moore and Podesva (2009) suggested that tag questions are characterologically meaningful because of their association with Populars. That is to say, tag questions may index the Popular persona. We rely on two criteria to make this claim: the frequency with which Populars use tag questions, and metalinguistic commentary about this use. Frequency in and of itself is not necessarily an

7.6 Tag Questions and Social Meaning

indicator of social meaning, although very high use of a particular variant often does entail increased association between the form and its typical users as we have seen in previous chapters. However, comparing tag questions with other grammatical variables has shown that tag questions are not like other grammatical variables: they are more evenly spread across the Midlan High population and they are not linearly distributed by class or community of practice. This raises some doubt over the extent to which tag questions can be associated with a single social group.

In their utilisation of metalinguistic commentary, Moore and Podesva (2009: 468) give the example of Populars, Beverley and Lindsey, confirming their use of tag questions when critiquing another person. This is reproduced with additional context in Extract 7.1 which begins this chapter. This extract comes from the language interviews which took place at the end of the fieldwork and the girls had just been asked to listen to some people using Bolton accents. In ll. 6–7 of Extract 7.1, Beverley and Lindsey confirm that they do use tag questions and, furthermore, that they use these forms when criticising other girls as the topic analysis suggested. This indicates that they have metalinguistic awareness about their use of tag questions. However, note that what they seem to focus on is not the tag question itself but its linguistic composition. On l. 5, I suggest that they typically use tags composed of 'int' with a deleted /t/ and with a *he* pronoun, but Beverley reframes this on l. 8: she pronounces (t) with a glottal, and gives her subject a feminine pronoun. Notably, whilst Beverley confirms that she uses tag questions in this extract, she focuses on what is distinct about her tag questions, rather than the simple fact of using them.

Beverley and Lindsey's response to being asked whether they use tag questions can be compared with how Townies, Meg and Amanda, respond to the same question (in the same context) in Extract 7.10.

Extract 7.10

```
1   A   Yeah, we'll say summat like – I don't know – we'll say a question, we'll go,
2       'innit/?/?' [like that.]
3   M                           [Yeah.]
4
5   A   And it'll just be like that. We won't know we're doing [[it.]]
6   M                                                          [['He's]] fit, him, in(Ø) 'e?'
7
8   A   [Yeah]
9   M   [We've] already asked the question and say 'in(Ø) 'e?' on the [[end.]]
10  A                                                                  [[Yeah]] (LAUGHS).
                                              (Amanda and Meg, Townies, 55: 405–415)
```

On ll. 1–2, Amanda confirms that Townies use tag questions, giving *innit* (with a glottal /t/) as her initial example. However, in the reverse to what happens in Extract 7.1, when Meg gives a more contextualised example of how the Townies might use tag questions, she uses a deleted /t/ and has *he* as the subject pronoun (l. 6). She then reiterates this format of tag question in l. 9. As with the Popular example, Meg's observations on tag questions match the outcome of the analysis above but, notably, they focus on what is distinct about Townie tag questions, not the act of using a tag question itself.

Although these are just two examples of talk about tag questions, they suggest that what Midlan High girls see as significant in their use of tag questions is their composition, rather than use of the tag itself. This provides further evidence that it is the content of talk (i.e., the topic) and the linguistic characteristics below the level of the utterance (phonetics, morpholexis) that provides a basis for persona presentation, not the tag itself. But this doesn't explain why Populars use so many more tag questions than other girls. Why are tag questions used so much by Populars and why does their use of them increase from Years 9 to 10? To answer this question, we must rely on ethnographic observation.

7.6.1 Tag Questions As a Resource During Social Change: The Smoothies

Chapter 3 detailed how the Townies emerged from the Popular group towards the end of Year 9. In distinguishing themselves from their Popular peers, the Townies engaged in new social practices (for instance, drug-taking and hanging around with older boys), as well as rejecting the more tame activities of their Popular peers (going to the cinema, participating in talent shows). How did the Populars respond to this shifting social landscape?

The splitting off of the Townies resulted in the negotiation of alliances and oppositions. While some Populars (Beverley and Lindsey, for instance) would still occasionally hang out with the Townie girls, as time passed, it became apparent that other Populars were starting to create more explicit forms of opposition to the Townie identity. Towards the end of Year 10, I started hearing people talk about a new social group, the Smoothies. In Extract 7.11, some Popular girls discuss the initial Popular–Townie split and the subsequent emergence of the new Smoothie group. In the following example, the term 'scally' is used as a synonym for 'Townie'. This term was favoured when providing a negative evaluation of the type of person who engages in practices associated with Townies. Tag questions are shown in bold.

Extract 7.11

```
1  T    It was because we all – we all used to hang around together, dint we? ..
2
3  M    [Yeah.]
4  T    [Like] one big gang and it was really good. It was like – it was really fun actually. It –
5       like we'd go out and we'd probably go out on the street, but we'd go to a field. And –
6       cos you can't go when there's like a hundred of you, anywhere, can you?
7  M    Yeah, I know.
8  T    So we'd just sit on a field or something. And then, they all – like Meg and all Ellie
9       and that lot started going out with Mark Turner.
```

7.6 Tag Questions and Social Meaning

```
10  M   Oh yeah.
11
12  T   And he was like .. minging. And he's really [rough and..]
13  M                                              [He's a sc-,] yeah.
14
15  C   Um.
16  T   And then – then we just all drifted apart and they were like, 'Yo, well, we're really
17      hard,' and everything.
18
19  C   I'm glad that we drifted apart, cos it's better like it [is now, I think.]
20  T                                                           [I know.]
21  M                                                           [Um.]
22
23  C   It's well better. That's what I think.
24  EM  Yeah.
25
26  M   I – I can't – I'm looking forward like to going to uni and like going to Sixth Form
27      where there's like just – where all the sc-, like the people who don't give a toss really
28      just.. [go away.]
29  P          [Um.. and trendy boys.]
30
31  M   Yeah.
32  C   Um... Smoothies.
33
34  M   [Um, yeah.]
35  EM  [(LAUGHS)]
36
37  T   [I know]
38  C   [Those that wear] [[nice clothes]]
39  P                     [[I'd rather -]]
40
41  M   [I know!]
42  P   [I'd rather] be a Smoothie any day.. than a scally.
43
44  C   We've not got a single – well, we have, but **they're not very nice, are they?**
45  EM  So what's the difference between a Smoothie and a scally?
46
47  T   [Well –]
48  M   [Smoothies] dress nicely and [[scallies just have like.. Rockports.. and.. stripey
49      Henry Lloyd jumpers.]]
50  T                                [[Yeah. Smoothies are just nicer people, to be honest.]]
51
52  P   [(LAUGHS) And] CAT trackie bottoms.
53  T   [And..]
54
55  M   [[Yeah.]]
56  T   [[With –]] with like the scallies, they always go – criticising everyone and go, 'Oh,
57      fucking Smoothies. Fucking..' [you know.]
58  M                                 [It's just because] like the Smoothies are nicer than
59      [[them. And they dress nicer. They act –]]
60  T   [[Yeah. And the Smoothies are]] always better looking than the scallies. Oh, you could
61      put your money on that (laughs). And, **they just dress nicer, don't they?** They're
62      nicer people. They don't do [drugs.]
63  C                                [And they're funny.]
64
```

65	T	They go and do normal things like go to the cinema and.. Like, they're really nice to
66		girls and stuff.
67	EM	So how do they speak like?
68	T	Normal. Just like us. Just..
69	EM	Yeah.
70	T	And they just take the mickey out of scallies as well.
71	EM	Yeah.
72	M	Um.
73	T	Yeah.
74	EM	Yeah.
75	T	Cos all – and like the scallies (INAUDIBLE) all they do is pop pills, do weed and stuff like
76		that. 'I'm going having a bucket.. of mix.' And – I don't even know what a bucket of mix is..
77		me. (LAUGHS) I don't have a clue what they are.

(Cindy, Marie, Paula and Tina, Populars, 58A: 388–448)

The discussion in Extract 7.11 starts with Tina describing how the once harmonious shared activity of hanging out changed when the Townie girls started to hang out with an older boy, Mark (ll. 8–9). Mark is described as 'minging' ('unpleasant') and 'rough' (l. 12) and, in turn, the Townies are described as attempting to present themselves as 'hard' ('tough') (l. 17). Cindy states that the split led to an improvement, making things better than they had been previously, and Tina and Marie explicitly agree (ll. 19–21). Marie then imagines a future entirely free of Townies, when the girls will go to college and encounter Smoothie boys. Whilst the girls don't label themselves as Smoothies, Paula clearly states that she would rather be a Smoothie than a scally (l. 42) and this viewpoint is implicitly shared by the other girls in the remainder of the extract which focuses on juxtaposing Smoothies and scallies. As far as these Popular girls are concerned, Smoothies are 'trendy' (l. 29), 'nicer people' (l. 50, l. 58, l. 65), they 'wear nice clothes' (l. 38, l. 48), are 'better looking' (l. 60), 'act nicer', 'don't do drugs' (ll. 61–62) and 'are funny' (l. 63). They also do 'normal' activities, like going to the cinema (l. 65), they treat girls well (ll. 65–66), and they poke fun at ('take the mickey out of') scallies (l. 70). Cindy, Marie, Paula and Tina clearly align themselves with the Smoothie group, whilst distancing themselves from the scallies. Scallies are not very nice (l. 44), they don't care ('give a toss') about school (ll. 27–28), criticise people (ll. 56–57), and take drugs (ll. 75–76).

The emergence of the Smoothies did not go unnoticed by the Townies, who describe them in Extract 7.12.

Extract 7.12

1	A	[Smoothies are the.. poofs.]
2	M	[Smoothies. They're the ones..] who have the stripey jumper – even though Mark
3		wears a stripey jumper, it's not a Henry Lloyd and Fred Perry one, [[like that.]]
4	A	[[And the jeans.]]
5		And the clean Rockies.
6		
7	M	You – you know that they st-, they look after themselves.
8	EM	Right.
9		

7.6 Tag Questions and Social Meaning   201

10 M   [Yeah.]
11 A   [They come] like – you know if you're [[going out for a meal, but you dress – you
12   dress up a bit?]]
13 M   [[They're not Geeks or nothing, but they're
14   not Townies.]]
15
16 A   They come out on a Friday night like that, [you know.]
17 M   [No,] they don't really. They're not Geeks and..
18   all, but they're not Townie kind of people. They're just like..
19   [[I don't know.]]
20 A   [[(US ACCENT) And they don't do drugs.]]
21
22   (ALL LAUGH)
23
24 A   And they rarely smoke and you see them with like a can of Stella or summat (LAUGHS).
25   Oh, just drinking [one of them.]
26 M   [Like, we might laugh at them but they're like the good
27   (INAUDIBLE) people.

(Amanda and Meg, Townies, 40B: 1020–1042)

Much of what Amanda and Meg say about the Smoothies aligns with the Populars' description of this group: Smoothies look after themselves (l. 7), they dress well (ll. 11–12), and they don't do drugs (l. 20). It's also clear that the Townies do criticise Smoothies (as claimed by Tina in Extract 7.11, ll. 56–57) – for instance, by 'laugh[ing] at them' (l. 26), and calling them 'poofs' (l. 1: a derogatory term historically used to refer to gay people and subsequently to depict people as lacking 'toughness'). However, Meg notes that Smoothies are not Geeks (l. 13, l. 17). Although they are described as not being Townies either, they are depicted as somewhat 'diluted' Townies, who 'clean up' Townie style. For instance, both groups wear the same styles of clothing, but the Smoothies' versions are branded and clean (ll. 2–7); they both go out on a Friday night, but Smoothies only drink rather than smoke or do drugs (ll. 24–25).

Although, initially, Smoothies were identified as people in older year groups at the school, towards the very end of Year 10, people started to identify certain Popular girls as Smoothies. Ellie describes Kim (a Popular girl who had a longstanding, if somewhat strained friendship with Townie girl, Amanda) as being 'more bothered about the Smoothie crew' and as having a Smoothie boyfriend (Ellie, Townie, 59A: 226–240). Meg relates a story in which Popular girl Annabel refers to Cindy, Paula and Tina as 'the little, erm, Smoothie crew of our year' (Meg, Townie, 55: 907). Beverley and Lindsey identify Cindy, Kim, Marie, Paula and Tina as Smoothies in a conversation about social groups (Beverley and Lindsey, Populars, 55: 814–818).

Figure 7.12 shows the distribution of tag questions within the Popular community of practice over Years 9 and 10. Four of the girls identified as Smoothies (Kim, Cindy, Marie and Tina) are shown in black (Paula is not included in the Midlan High dataset as I was unable to collect data from her

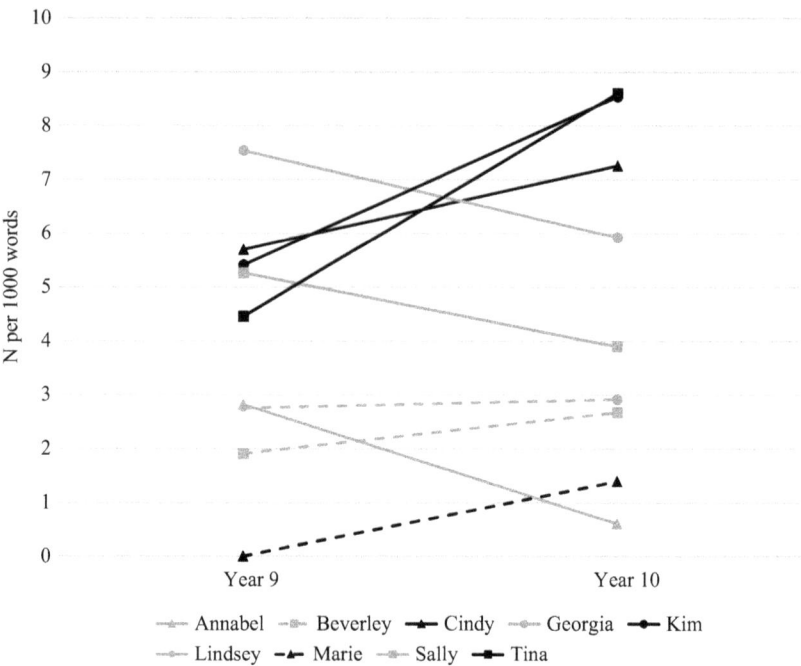

Figure 7.12 Populars' use of tag questions over time. Smoothies are shown in black.

across both years of the study). The remaining Popular girls are shown in grey. Figure 7.12 shows that, in Year 10, the three highest users of tag questions are girls identified as Smoothies: Cindy, Kim and Tina. The fourth Smoothie, Marie, does not have a high use of tag questions but, like the other Smoothie girls, she increases her use of tag questions from Years 9 to 10. The remaining Popular girls decrease their use of tag questions from Years 9 to 10, or show only a very slight increase, keeping their overall use at a moderate level (i.e., Beverley and Lindsey).

There are other differences in how Smoothies employ tag questions. Smoothies are significantly more likely to elicit agreement to tag questions than the remaining Populars ($\chi^2(1) = 5.33$, $p = 0.02$). Figures 7.13 and 7.14 show the responses elicited by Smoothies, on the one hand, and the remaining non-Smoothie Populars, on the other, to turn-final and turn-medial tags, respectively. Whilst Smoothies are more likely to agree with turn-final tags than turn-medial tags ($\chi^2(1) = 6.16$, $p = 0.01$), there is no significant difference between how the remaining Populars respond to tags by turn type: non-Smoothie Populars are most likely to offer no response to tag questions irrespective of turn type.

7.6 Tag Questions and Social Meaning 203

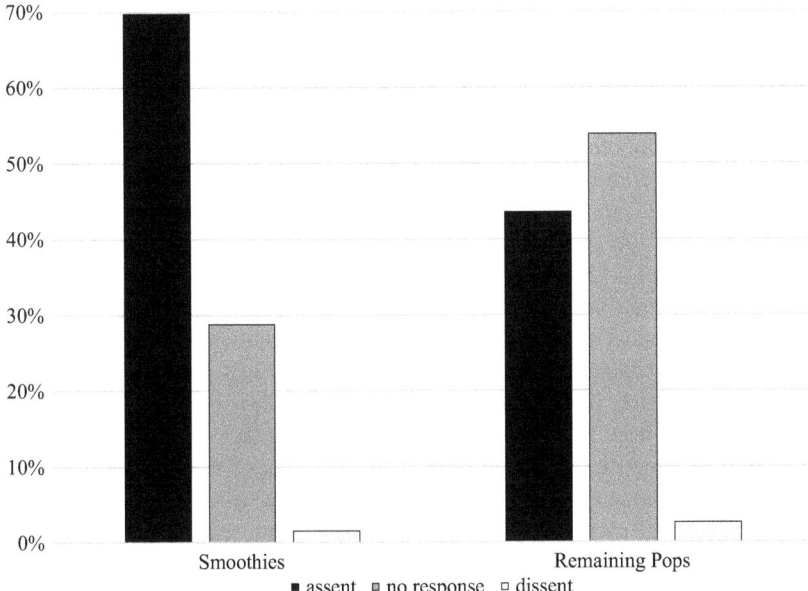

Figure 7.13 Responses to turn-final tags in Year 10.

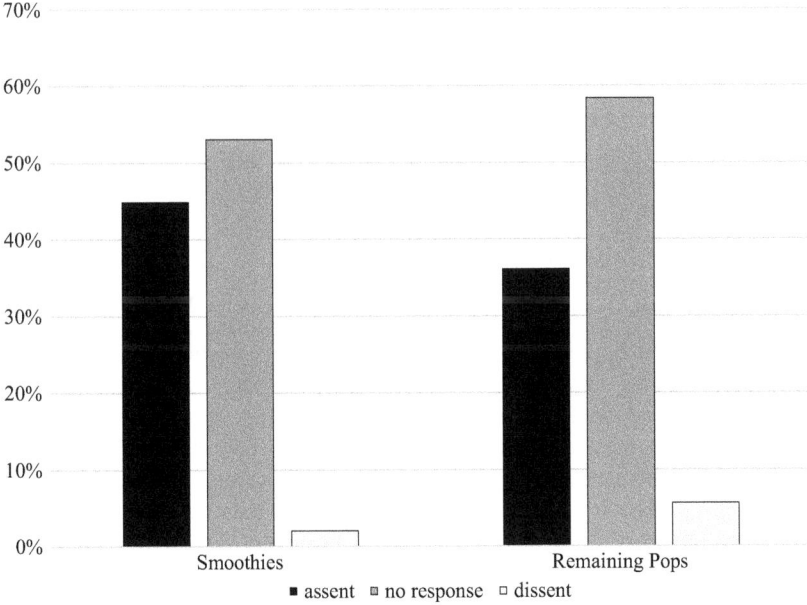

Figure 7.14 Responses to turn-medial tags in Year 10.

Interestingly, though, whilst Smoothies and the remaining Populars differ in tag question use across time, and in agreement patterns, there are no significant differences between the Smoothies and the remaining Populars in the topics and subject types which co-occur with tag questions, or in use of (h), (t), and morpholexis. Smoothies may use more tag questions, but they do not style these questions in a way that is distinct from more general Popular practices. This is reflected in Lindsey view of Smoothies' language: she told me that Smoothies can be 'quite common' and 'just seem[s] normal' (Lindsey, Popular, 56B: 851–857).

To explain what is going on with Smoothies' use of tag questions, it is necessary to reflect on the function of tag questions and the sociocultural environment in which the Smoothies use of tag questions increases over time. The Smoothie girls were engaged in a new enterprise – one which sought to distance them from the Townies. Such a task requires consensus on how groups and identities are defined. Essentially, the Smoothies girls were engaged in conducing agreement about their status as a collective and its relationship with particular practices and norms. This can be seen in Extract 7.11. Four tag questions occur in this short extract. Two of the four elicit explicit agreement (l. 1; l. 6), and a third elicits an elaboration which adds weight to the observation made in the tag question (l. 61). This data suggest that Smoothies use lots of tag questions – not necessarily because they represent some essence of Smoothieness – but because they are an excellent resource for building consensus at precisely the moment that consensus is required.

The case of the emerging Smoothies provides yet more data to support the assertion that the social meaning of tag questions is rooted in pragmatics, not in any character type association. In the final section, we consider the implications of the findings about tag questions and what these findings suggest about the social meaning of grammar more generally.

7.7 Do Tag Questions Have Character-type Social Meanings?

This chapter has highlighted differences in how tag questions compare with other grammatical variants. We explore these differences, and their implications, in the next chapter. However, for the time being, it is worth reiterating that this chapter has suggested that a group's increased use of a grammatical feature does not necessarily result in that feature acquiring social meaning linked to a particular persona or social type (i.e., at the character-type level). For those grammatical features which are universally deployed, changes in frequency may reflect the extent to which certain groups engage in particular interactional tasks. The need to exploit the interactional functions of syntactic

7.7 Character-type Social Meanings

configurations may be dependent on specific and time-sensitive social circumstances, not social identity *per se*.

This is not to say that syntactic forms are not involved in sociolinguistic variation; rather it is to note that some syntactic forms may link to patterns of sociolinguistic variation indirectly (Cheshire 2005a: 480). For instance, if a group tends to engage in regulatory behaviour (perhaps because – like the Populars – they are concerned with establishing agreement around social norms and boundaries), members of that group will tend to use linguistic devices that facilitate agreement about what is acceptable. At Midlan High, the high frequency of tag questions (and the attitudinal meaning they encode) reflects and constructs the Populars' distinctive interactive style. The sociolinguistic variation is at the level of pragmatics, not at the level of identity. That is to say, tag questions are a component of Popular style, but they are not enregistered as 'Popular'. For tag questions to be enregistered, the process of rhematisation would need to have occurred. Recall from Chapter 5 that rhematisation occurs when a linguistic feature is interpreted as depicting 'inherent' social qualities of those who use them most frequently (Gal & Irvine 2019: 39). Although the Populars are not as extreme in their behaviours as the Townies, the social qualities associated with them include a degree of rebelliousness: they are drawn to trouble and excitement and are willing to challenge adult authority. They also use a good number of stigmatised non-standard features, irrespective of their social class background, and the use of these also helps to construct the social meaning of their style. If tag questions were rhematised, we would expect them to be associated with the Popular social qualities of rebellion, excitement, and anti-authoritarianism. The fact that tag questions are used robustly by groups which do not embody these attributes suggest that the tag itself is not carrying this social meaning. Instead, the attitudes and alignments observed for tag questions (e.g., regulatory, critical, collaborative, knowledgeable) are shared across communities of practice. This provides evidence that tag questions do not carry character-type meaning.

Nonetheless, tag questions do constitute a heightened discourse frame. Consequently, they may highlight the linguistic features they contain. If the phonetic and morpholexical features tag questions contain are themselves linked to persona or social types, the marked syntactic configuration of the tag question may serve to frame the style of an interaction and draw attention to that style in a heightened discourse moment. In this way, tag questions and syntactic configurations like them, may enable a speaker to 'pack a multiple punch' (Mendoza-Denton 2008: 286) by simultaneously marking persona or social type, orientation to language norms and interactional alignment.

Analysing how syntactic configurations co-occur with other linguistic variables will help us to better understand the interaction between language and social meaning. If well-known phonetic variants do not have a linear correlation with a particular syntactic variant then that may be a cue to the scope of that specific syntactic configuration's social meaning. Similarly, if we know that a syntactic configuration has a specific pragmatic function, we can use that knowledge to nuance the social meaning of the linguistic variables it contains. The analysis of (h) demonstrated that /h/-dropping occurs at a high frequency in tag questions – even in the speech of otherwise linguistically conservative groups like the Eden Villagers and the Geeks. What does this mean? Given that we know that tag questions are conducing, it suggests compatibility between conducement and /h/-dropping. Could this be because when we are trying to conduce a particular interactional outcome, we aim to position ourselves as personable and laid-back as opposed to fastidious and authoritarian? This requires further research but it points at the potential to use syntactic configuration as a way to access the extent of a linguistic variant's indexical field.

Finally, this chapter has demonstrated that understanding how grammatical items function socially requires a specific analytical approach. To fully understand how language functions socially, it may be necessary to centre analysis on a particular pragmatic act (e.g., conducement, intensification, evaluation) in order to work out the totality of the linguistic features recruited to communicate that meaning (Hall-Lew *et al.* 2021: 19). As noted earlier, Eden Villagers use fewer tag questions than other groups but it is unlikely that they do not engage in conducive pragmatic acts; it is more likely that they are conducive in a different way. In focusing on how different groups of speakers engage in pragmatic acts, we avoid presenting the linguistic behaviours of certain groups (typically low-status ones) as marked when the behaviour of their peers (typically of high status) goes unmarked.

This chapter has investigated how a universally utilised grammatical feature is distributed. It has also considered the extent to which this kind of feature interacts with pragmatics and social meaning. We have now examined a range of grammatical items and observed differences in their distributions, their ideological embedding, and their functional utility. The final chapter considers what these individual analyses mean for our understanding of the social life of grammar more generally.

8 What Does It Mean to View Grammar as a Fluid, Flexible Social Resource?

Extract 8.1

1	M	Will this be published, this book?
2		
3	EM	Oh (EXHALES). I'd like it to be. What – what happens is, erm – what I'm doing's called
4		a PhD and you have to write – I think it's something like 80,000 words, [which is like
5		about this much (INDICATES BOOK WIDTH).]
6	M	[(MAKES
7		SCARED NOISE)]
8		
9	EM	Erm, and then that's like your exam. So you – that gets sent to the tutors [and they]
10		read it [[and then you pass or fail.]]
11	M	[Yeah.]
12	C	[[God, that must take a long]] time to read.
13		
14	EM	Yeah, and then, erm, if it's good, then you can take it to a publisher and say,
15		['This is what] I did.' And..
16	M	[Wow.]
17		
18	...	
19		
20	EM	The hardest – the hardest thing at the moment is I wanna write something that
21		everybody could read [here – everybody] at this school could read.
22	M	[Um, yeah.]
23		
24	EM	But I've gotta be really careful how I do it because, erm..
25		
26	T	Because you don't want people [to know..]
27	EM	[I don't want] people to know.
28		
29		And cos I'm talking about different groups as well [and] sometimes I'm saying stuff
30		like, erm, certain people don't quite fit into the group, or, erm..
31	M	[Yeah.]
32		
33		People might think that [you –]
34	EM	[other] people don't get on so well [[with them and..]]
35	T	[[Yeah, cos]] like there's
36		no names then people'll think, 'Oh, she means me.'
37		

```
38   EM   Yeah, exactly. And then I don't want people to feel bad or like, you know.
39
40   T    But then on the other hand you can't put names in [cos −]
41   EM                                                    [No.]
42
43   T    Well, then you'll just make it worse [on some people.]
44   EM                                        [That's it.]
45
46   EM   So I've gotta be really care-, I mean, it's taking me a long time to write because I have
47        to be really careful how I write it.
```

(Cindy, Marie, Paula, Tina, Populars, 58A:2175-2233)

It was never easy to talk to the young people about what I was doing in their school. Extract 8.1 documents my bumbling attempt to walk them through the intricacies of the PhD process that resulted in the data I have analysed in this book. Extract 8.1 comes from the penultimate interview I did for the project. I had been coming into the school for over two years when it was recorded and I had begun writing up my PhD. The PhD dissertation was submitted and passed a year or so later but, as I noted in Chapter 2, it has taken me much, much longer to write the 'book'.

It took so long for three reasons. Firstly, as I note in l. 24 of Extract 8.1, I wanted to be careful about how I wrote it. I wasn't just dealing with data and a corpus. I was dealing with people. It was, of course, important to protect their privacy and their well-being, but I also wanted to make the data count in terms of its potential impact on young people like the ones I had met (and, significantly, on young people like the one I had been). Like most ethnographers, I had sleepless nights worrying about how their data might be interpreted by others and how I could represent my participants as complicated, fascinating and three-dimensional. I also wanted to justify the hours of time they had spent with me, laying out the detail of their everyday interactions. Sadly, I don't believe that I've achieved the goal of writing something that everyone could – or rather would – want to read (ll. 20–21). When I first submitted the proposal for this book I had intended to make it accessible to multiple audiences, but a more experienced and wiser reviewer pointed out that I needed to decide whether I was writing something that would move forward thinking in sociolinguistics, or whether I was providing a more generic account of high school life. I hope that there are elements of the book that are accessible to all (especially the ethnography that is detailed in Chapter 2), but I was forced to concede that my ultimate goal was to provide the first comprehensive account of the social meaning of grammar. To do that, it was necessary to engage with the latest research on semiotics, social meaning, indexicality and ideology: the cornerstones of what has now become known as the third-wave of variationist sociolinguistics (Eckert 2018). As with all approaches, third-wave variationism is constantly evolving, but recently there has been increased clarity around the extent of its scope, and the definition of social meaning itself (Hall-Lew *et al.* 2021) – in part as a consequence of the kind of cross-engagement with pragmatics (Acton

2021) shown in this book. The second reason this book took so long was because of the thinking and theoretical development that was required between the data collection and now.

The final reason this book took so long to write is because it took me nearly twenty years to feel confident enough to write it. As academics, we are taught to detach ourselves from our personalities as we write, in order to present our research as objective. But research is not objective, it is deeply personal. We tend to research things that matter to us (and, when we don't, it tends not to be our best work). If we don't fit the mould of a traditional academic (to be explicit: if we aren't brought up in a middle-class household, if we didn't go to private school, if we are the first generation in our family to go to university, if we have to work our way through higher education), it is an even bigger task to resist the voice that comes most unthinkingly to us. When I had my PhD viva, one of my examiners told me that the thesis had been easy and enjoyable to read because it wasn't written in the 'usual style'. At the time, I didn't really know what to do with that – especially coming from someone who was very much a traditional academic. I wondered if it meant they thought it was light-weight, and I pondered this for a long time afterwards, even though I had passed with no corrections. I subsequently published in academic journals and I learnt to suppress my voice in my writing in order to do so. Being an academic is a lifetime of being told you haven't got it quite right. Not just for those of us who don't fit the mould – for all of us. We are constantly evaluated and found lacking. We submit excellent funding bids but the shortage of funding means that only a minuscule proportion make it through (yes, these are often the 'best', but they may be the best because they happen to hit a current hot-topic, or they reach a broader audience, or they are lucky enough to get the reviewers who are sympathetic to your approach); and we write publications that are reviewed by our competitors who might have alternative research priorities. It is easier to learn to play the game, than to resist it. I'm writing about this because this book and its contents have been shaped by *my* life experience – just like every bit of academic work is. I'm a case study of what happens when someone feels that their sociolinguistic style isn't the right one. The third reason this book took so long is because it took time for me to feel like I could say what I wanted to say, in the way I wanted to say it, without worrying about the consequences.

Being able to say what you want to say, in the way you want to say it, is extraordinarily liberating. This final chapter explores the consequences of giving more young people this opportunity. In addition to reviewing the key findings of the study (as they pertain to sociolinguistic theory), this chapter will also consider the wider implications of the research as they relate to the education of young people who have diverse linguistic repertoires. Educational linguists have pointed out the benefits of teaching grammar explicitly to school pupils, but have noted that this teaching is most effective when grammar is presented as a semiotic resource for meaning-making (Myhill *et al.* 2012;

Myhill 2018). However, it has been argued that current educational policy not only shapes how teachers conceptualise grammar (as rigid and inflexible), it also encourages negative and potentially damaging responses to any deviations from standard English and to the children who make them (Cushing 2019a, 2019b, 2020; Hudson 2016). This is despite there being no significant evidence that speaking in a local dialect affects literacy (Snell & Andrews 2017), or that children's literacy improves by decontextualised grammar teaching (Elley 1994; Hudson 2001; Wyse 2001; Andrews *et al.* 2004). Consequently, in addressing the wider implications of the research, this final chapter will suggest ways to better model components of language variation in order to understand which elements of grammar can vary, precisely when they vary, and why. In doing so, it will propose a framework for analysing the indexical and cognitive embedding of grammatical variation, and consider what such an approach could mean for young people's well-being and development.

8.1 What Are the Key Findings of This Study?

The main goal of this book was to understand how people adapt their use of grammatical variables to communicate social detail. In particular, this study has explored how and why the social meaning of grammar differs from social meanings assigned to phonetic or phonological variants. It has also examined different types of grammatical construction in order to determine how their social and regional distribution, and their precise configuration, affects the types of social meanings associated with them. In relation to these goals, the key findings of this study are the following, which are further detailed in the following subsections.

- The social meaning of grammatical variants has a number of roots;
- The precise configuration of a grammatical item determines the possible social meanings associated with it;
- The social distribution of a grammatical variant strongly interacts with the type of social meaning it can index.

8.1.1 The Social Meaning of Grammatical Variants Has a Number of Roots

In Chapter 3, I proposed that social meaning can develop from three roots:

(1) the semantics of a variant (Type SM),
(2) an indexical association between a variant and character type(s) (Type CT),
(3) sound symbolism (Type SS).

The discussion in previous chapters has focused more on Type SM and Type CT roots than Type SS roots. This is a consequence of the architecture of

8.1 What Are the Key Findings of This Study?

grammatical variation. For phonetic variants, sound symbolism may operate via assumptions about the relationship between phonetic items and sounds in the natural world. For instance, as noted in Chapter 2, size of a body may be associated with pitch due to an association between length of the vocal tract and acoustic frequency. This leads to certain pitches indexing certain body sizes and, in turn, all the affects and qualities ideologically associated with that body size (Eckert 2019a; Drager *et al.* 2021). Importantly, for phonetic items, social meaning that derives from sound symbolism might (at least initially) index affect rather than character type. For instance, studies of /s/ fronting and backing find correlations between /s/-fronting and straight women (Fuchs & Toda 2010), higher social classes (Stuart-Smith 2007), gay men (Munson, Ryherd & Kemper 2017; Pharao & Maegaard 2017), sporty personas (Cuddy 2019), and genderqueer personas (Zimman 2017). The social categories here are diverse, but what might unite them is their reliance on /s/-fronting to index certain stances and affects in the course of discourse management (Holmes-Elliott & Levon 2017). These stances and affects may be possible because of the ideological association between /s/-fronting and smaller body sizes, which, in turn, mediates articulatory habits irrespective of a person's actual body or its size (Zimman 2017: 994).

As this discussion suggests, sound symbolism is a consequence of phonetic items having embodied as well as acoustic properties (Eckert 2019a: 765). For instance, Podesva (2021) shows the relationship between variants of the California Vowel Shift, and expression of affect (e.g., smiling) and facial postures (such as an open jaw setting). He argues that how people use their bodies is a form of social practice which can have acoustic consequences. Because grammatical items are more structurally complex than phonetic items, it is tricky to think of them as embodied in the same way. It is not the case that iconic associations lead to different body types being variably perceived as capable of articulating particular grammatical variants. While /s/-fronting might be associated with smaller bodies, a further ideological move is required to generate a character-type association (i.e., that smaller bodies index women, or the middle classes). The ability to perceive a grammatical variant as more typical of one body than another is dependent on character type being a first level indexical order. That is to say, the use of *ain't* to mark negative BE will only be associated with larger bodies if *ain't* has first indexed a working class character type and the working classes are associated with larger bodies.

This means that, while we might see the social meaning of a phonetic item as rooted in an embodied articulatory move, it is difficult to decouple character type (Type CT) and and sound symbolic (Type SS) roots for grammatical variants. This is demonstrated in Chapter 3, using the example of possessive *me* (Snell 2010). Its status as a morphophonemic variant perhaps makes it more amenable to a Type SS root, however it is still unclear as to whether the social meaning of possessive *me* comes from its status as a variant that occurs in unstressed contexts (facilitating a perception that it is a 'laid-back' or 'lazy' articulation – a Type SS root) or whether it is a consequence of its increased frequency in working class speech which is often, in turn, associated with social meanings like 'laid-back' or 'lazy' – a Type CT root which leads to a Type SS association).

There are, of course, some other important differences between phonetic and grammatical variants that interact with the roots of their social meanings. We have a written code for grammar, but not for pronunciation. This percept of fixedness means that grammatical variants tend to be more easily identified as standard or not – simply because there is a written codified standard to compare them to. Of course, the systems of speech and writing are very different but, in the everyday, young people are often told to 'talk in full sentences' as if this were a thing that people consistently do. The presence of codified grammar raises awareness about grammatical items above that of phonetic ones, making them 'the focus of standard ideology and educational attention' and more likely to be 'highly enregistered, functioning as shibboleths, with quite fixed social meanings associated with class and ethnicity' (Eckert 2019a: 758). Localised grammatical variants are clearly associated with hegemonically stigmatised groups, consequently, their social meanings are inextricably linked to how those social groups are perceived. In turn, via the process of indexicality, the linguistic item will be assumed to share the perceived qualities of its users. This is precisely the process we saw in operation with levelled *were* in Chapter 4. Levelled *were* is associated with the lower classes; people of lower class status are often portrayed as unrefined; so levelled *were* itself is heard as 'unrefined', even in the absence of cues which mark the speaker as lower class. Any sound symbolic meaning is dependent upon the local variant being perceived as missing a standard articulatory target. In actuality, this is nonsense – people do not produce levelled *were* because they are trying for standard *was* and 'miss' through lack of effort. But this doesn't change how levelled *were* is perceived by those without linguistic training who are susceptible to dominant ideologies about class and typical class attributes. Levelled *were* is stigmatised in dominant discourse, via comparison with standard *was*. When compared to its standard alternative, the type of social meanings identified for it in Chapter 4 ('common', 'anti-institutional', 'daring', 'rebellious') are a direct consequence of this ideological interplay.

The other reason that grammatical items are different from phonetic ones is their segmental size and the way in which they are processed cognitively. The Interface Principle (Labov 1993) proposes that more complex syntactic structures cannot easily take on social meanings because they constitute deep structure. The concept 'deep structure' is taken from generative syntactic theory. It refers to the claim that syntax has phrase structure rules (deep

8.1 What Are the Key Findings of This Study?

structure) which are the output of underlying structural properties. These are transformed to produce the grammatical form that is articulated (surface structure). In this theory, an utterance in the passive voice like 'The Geeks were teased by the Townies' would be considered to be a transformed version of the underlying active voice construction 'The Townies teased the Geeks' (i.e., the deep structure). If underlying structural properties are innate and shared by all language varieties – as in the theory of Universal Grammar (Chomsky 2017: 2) – then complex syntactic structures are less likely to carry social meaning – simply because their deep structure doesn't vary across language varieties.

However, there are a number of problems with the Interface Principle which have yet to be adequately addressed in the sociolinguistic literature. Firstly, the Principle itself is based upon a generative syntactic theory which has continued to be revised in the field in which it developed. In current work in generative syntax, the distinction between deep and surface structure has been interrogated and is no longer assumed to be unproblematic (Cipriani 2019). Furthermore, there are other theories of syntax (e.g., Head-driven Phrase Structure Grammar (HPSG), Lexical Functional Grammar (LFG)) which view syntax as having constraint-based parallel architecture, rather than serial, transformational derivations (Pollard & Sag 1994; Bresnan *et al.* 2016). The intricacies of these competing syntactic theories is beyond the purview of this book, but their very existence indicates that claims about the social meaning of syntax based on the notion of 'deep structure' alone inadequately represent current understandings of syntactic structure and its relation to meaning (be that referential or social).

There is a less controversial argument for why the social meaning of grammar (and the roots of that social meaning) differs from that of phonetic items: the clear differences in the structure, frequency, and distribution of syntactic variants compared to lexical or phonetic variants (Levon & Buchstaller 2015: 319–321). These differences may, of course, be the consequence of the specific role of syntax in language, but they can be observed and measured irrespective of one's theory of syntax. The issues of (a) structure and (b) frequency and distribution are taken up in the next two sections, respectively.

8.1.2 The Precise Configuration of a Grammatical Item Determines the Possible Social Meanings Associated With It

In Chapter 1, it was noted that the concept of the 'grammatical variant' incorporates a number of diverse linguistic structures including ones that are morphophonemic, morpholexical, morphosyntactic and syntactic. However, when the social meaning of grammar is discussed, these differing structures are frequently treated as being the same. Chapters 4–7 have confirmed the hypothesis suggested in Chapter 2: the precise configuration of a grammatical item matters with respect to the types of social meaning it can potentially index.

A variant like levelled *were* has a very simple morphological structure, making it akin to a lexical variant. Furthermore, as Smith and Durham (2019: 192) have noted, agreement with the verb BE involves selection between morphologically simple variants (*was* and *were*, in the Midlan High dataset), rather than involving potentially more complex syntactic phenomena, such as deletion or transformation (in a generative account) or constraint-based architecture (in a HPSG or a LFG account). To be clear, this isn't to claim that the use of levelled *were* is not linguistically constrained; Chapter 4 clearly shows the effect of polarity, subject type and clause type. Rather, my claim is that the meaning potential of a grammatical item is not just governed by the social and linguistic distribution of the item itself, but also by the semantic implications of what goes on within the structure of the item.

In Chapter 5, evidence was provided from a slightly more complex syntactic item: negative concord. In this case, the variation is not restricted to morpheme alternation but to a broader alternation in syntax which affects at least two aspects of the variant's structure: the negative particle *and* the polarity of the corresponding indeterminate (e.g., I'm *not* going *nowhere*). The alternation is still essentially lexicalised (it involves alternation between forms of *not*, some of which involve the preceding verb, and whether the indeterminate has positive or negative polarity). Nonetheless, it goes across a clause, rather than being contained in one morpheme of that clause. This opens up the possibility that listeners can interpret the variability as related to information structure (Lambrecht 1994), whereby the selection of one variant over another is construed as a way of focusing on information and/or influencing how that information is interpreted.

In Chapter 5, it was suggested that, by involving two negative particles, rather than the one found in standard English, negative concord may be construed as emphatic (by virtue of the general effects of repetition cross-linguistically). In this way, negative concord is not just linked to particular styles of speech, but also to particular types of expression which may be utilised to articulate particular alignments in interaction. In this way, negative concord may have a semantically rooted (Type SM) social meaning. In this case, social meaning is generated from pragmatic inference which is, in turn, derived from the structure's underlying semantics, as follows:

I'm not going nowhere
Semantic meaning:	*not* = negative polarity;
	<u>*nowhere*</u> = negative polarity
Pragmatic meaning:	two negative polarity items = 'emphasis'
Social meaning:	people who tend towards emphasis are 'forceful, assertive…'

8.1 What Are the Key Findings of This Study? 215

Whereas the semantic meaning is based upon truth conditional indexes in English, the pragmatic meaning is based on commonalities in information structure in English. The social meaning is ideological: it is based upon what English society believes about the qualities of individuals who markedly use emphasis in speech. I have given the social meanings 'forceful' and 'assertive' here but, of course, this reflects my own ideological biases. Other interpretations are, of course, possible.

I argue in Chapter 5 that meaning can exist in this way in communities where negative concord is productively variable. It relies upon there being a functional contrast between standard negation and negative concord. In communities like Buckie (see Smith & Durham 2019, and Chapter 5, this volume), where negative concord is acknowledged as part of the local dialect, then the syntactic variability may be used for pragmatic ends. However, in communities which lack Buckie's close-knit social structure, there is less insulation from the standard ideology which enregisters variants like negative concord as unequivocally stigmatised. So, whilst its pragmatic meaning potential remains, it is more likely to be secondary to character-type (Type CT) social meanings, i.e., those which follow from negative concord's association with lower social class speech. This Type CT meaning is culturally pervasive. As noted in Chapter 5, it does not reflect how everyone experiences negative concord on the ground, but everyone is aware of it, given dominant discourses about class relations and values.

The example of negative concord demonstrates that grammatical variants above the level of the morpheme have the potential to develop social meaning rooted in their semantics. However, the hegemonic presence of social stigma may bleach out the meaning derived from this root, such that their social distribution (and the social situation of the speaker and their interlocutor) more strongly influences their meaning potential. The role that social distribution plays in social meaning is interrogated in the next section, but, in the current section, one other important way in which grammatical configuration affects social meaning needs to be addressed.

In Chapter 6, we saw that, like negative concord, right dislocation is meaningful by virtue of its grammatical configuration and the implication of this structure on its pragmatic function. This could be schematised as follows:

They're great, them
Semantic meaning: a referent, 'they', is assigned the quality 'great' in present time
Pragmatic meaning: the entity that is assigned the quality 'great' is given end-focus via a anaphoric pronoun tag, emphasising the speaker's viewpoint or interpersonal stance towards the referent 'they'.
Social meaning: people who emphasise viewpoint or interpersonal stance are 'evaluative'.

As with the negative concord example, the semantic meaning is truth referential, the pragmatic meaning is depends on how information is structured, and the social meaning is the consequence of an ideological construal of those who engage in emphasising their own viewpoint in interaction.

With negative concord, the referent in the variable components of the clause never directly indexes a specific person or entity: *not* simply marks negative polarity and, whilst the indeterminate might point to an entity (e.g., *nothing*) or a person (e.g., *nobody, no one*), it does so generically. In right dislocation, on the other hand, the referent in the clause and the associated tag is always a specific person or entity when personal pronouns are used. So, whilst both negative concord and right dislocation gain meaning from their syntactic configuration, they differ semantically in what is referenced by that configuration. This was shown in Chapter 6: right-dislocated constructions can be variably face-threatening, dependent upon the nature of the subject referent and the semantics of the verb. Whether the referent is in the first, second or third person affects who is the focus of the speaker's evaluation. In the case of second- and third-person referents, someone other than the speaker is evaluated, with most face-threat apparent when the evaluation is directly addressed to another person who is present in the interaction. Verbs may also reference a range of processes, with relational verbs ascribing identities and attributes to the subject of the right-dislocated clause. Consequently, the most face-threatening right-dislocated constructions are likely to be those in the second person which include a relational verb, as shown below:

You're tight, **you**   >   *She's a cow,* **her**   >   *I'm so soft,* **me**
(Meg, Townie)   (Georgia, Popular)   (Michelle, Geek)

Chapter 6 revealed that the syntactic configuration of these tags (and their ability to be variably face-threatening) mapped onto their distribution by social group, with only Townies and one Popular girl using second-person pronoun tags, only Townie and Populars consistently using third-person pronoun tags, and Townies, Populars and Geeks all using first-person tags.

In the example of right-dislocated tags, there is a direct correlation between the semantics of a grammatical construction and its social distribution. In sociolinguistics, the linguistic and social constraints on variation are normally treated as separate and distinct. However, in the case of right dislocation, we see that a linguistic factor (syntactic formulation, i.e., subject type, verb) has pragmatic consequences (markedness as reflected in level of face-threat). This then constrains the social meaning a specific right-dislocated configuration can communicate and, ultimately, its social distribution. Rather than linguistic factors being distinct from social ones, they are tightly interwoven: the use of a second-person pronoun right-dislocated tag is not simply determined by an abstract algorithm of how frequently second-person pronouns are

8.1 What Are the Key Findings of This Study?

used in a language, but by speakers' desires to express different kinds of pragmatic meaning. As Bender (2001: 258) has noted, speakers have to go out of their way to use constructions that are disfavoured in a particular linguistic environment – and this reflects what can be communicated socially via pragmatic inference.

Right-dislocated tags are much more widely distributed amongst the population than constructions like negative concord or levelled *were* are. Whereas some English speakers will never use negative concord or levelled *were*, right dislocation is found across all English-speaking communities. However, one kind of right-dislocated tag *is* restricted (personal pronoun tags), as discussed in Chapter 6. In the next section, the implications of restricted social distribution on social meaning is explored more fully.

8.1.3 The Social Distribution of a Grammatical Variant Strongly Interacts with the Type of Social Meaning It Can Index

Research on grammatical variation in sociolinguistics has tended to focus on a handful of highly stigmatised localised forms such as deletion of plural markers, negated forms like *ain't*, subject–verb agreement and negative concord. These variants tend to be socially restricted – in the UK, this is most typically by class, but also by race, ethnicity and region (and the intersection of all of these). Any form of social restriction generates the conditions in which character type (Type CT) social meanings can emerge. However, whether a Type CT meaning emerges or not is contingent on the noticing of that distribution and the attribution of social meaning to it. Of course, the nature of the social meaning attributed (and its general circulation) depends upon who has done the noticing and how they ideologically construe what they have noticed.

As we have seen above, grammatical variants like negative concord and right dislocation can have social meaning rooted in semantics (Type SM meanings) as a consequence of their syntactic configuration. In the case of negative concord, the social restriction on this form may bleach out any meaning derived in this way, such that its social distribution more strongly influences its meaning potential. The case of right dislocation is a little more tricky: this form is more widely used, across different social and regional groups – so much so that it features in general descriptive grammars of English (Quirk *et al.* 1985; Biber *et al.* 1999; Huddleston & Pullum 2002) which typically codify standard and colloquial grammar. However, Chapter 6 demonstrated that right dislocation generally occurs more frequently in the speech of lower social class groups and that certain types of right dislocation are restricted further still, only occurring in the speech of certain communities of practice. The situation with tag questions is even more complicated: these forms show *some* social restriction at Midlan High (they are used significantly less frequently by members of the highest social group compared to all other groups); and they are also used more frequently by one community of practice: the Populars. Unlike the right dislocation patterns, the correlations between tag questions and social groups do not suggest an easily interpretable pattern of social distribution in relation to typical power or prestige norms in communities.

Starting with the case of right dislocation, it is possible that the pragmatics of this construction have led to its restricted distribution by virtue of the politeness norms of different social groups. As noted in Chapter 3, plain-speaking (which can variably be described as being blunt, honest, or rude) is often highly valued in working-class communities. Whilst being able to evaluate something or someone is useful to everyone, doing this in a direct way is distasteful to some. Consequently, whilst all speakers make use of right dislocation to perform evaluative speech acts, only those who value plain-speaking will use it when the construction can be decoded as potentially blunt or face-threatening. In this case, the social distribution of right dislocation is contingent upon its pragmatic function *and* its precise formulation.

We could hypothesise that, over time, the social restriction of some kinds of right dislocation (resulting from the consequences of pragmatic inference) has led to the entire construction becoming rhematised (see Chapter 3) as indexing lower social class status, irrespective of the type of right dislocation used. Evidence to support this hypothesis can be found in metapragmatic commentary presented in Chapter 6 (Extract 6.1), where Amanda (Townie) was observed juxtaposing the use of right dislocation with other forms of evaluation that are less direct. Notably, the alternative expressions of evaluation are associated with speakers who have prestige according to dominant hierarchical norms, whereas right dislocation is associated with those who do not orientate to these dominant hierarchical norms. In this way, the social meaning of right dislocation is originally rooted in semantics (a Type SM meaning), but it has developed a character type (Type CT) meaning over time as certain of its configurations are socially restricted. This Type CT meaning is much less well enregistered (see Chapter 3, Section 3.1) than that of negative concord, but it is nonetheless discernible in the sociolinguistic practice observed at Midlan High.

Like right dislocation, tag questions are also widely distributed across populations of speakers, but there is much less evidence for this linguistic construction having become rhematised, such that it indexes a dominant character type. Its general pragmatic utility as a conducive device conflicts to some degree with its ability to convey face-threat or directness: its categorisation as an indirect speech act has long seen linguists associate it with the speech of women (Lakoff 1975), although it remains unclear whether the general public share this perception. Whilst the extensive discussion in Chapter 7 reveals that the link between tag questions and indirectness is an oversimplification (see especially the category of 'challenging' tag questions identified by Holmes 1984), it nonetheless speaks to how the pragmatic inferences of tag questions are ideologically construed.

Although tag questions are used less frequently by those in the highest social class at Midlan High, and more frequently by the Populars, they do not exhibit the orderly heterogeneity that we see for the other variables examined in this book. In Chapter 7, we saw that the Populars' increased use of tag questions corresponded with an increasing need to renegotiate group boundaries in the context of the changing high-school landscape. That is to say, the increased use by the Populars was motivated by a particular need – at a particular point in time – to deploy the pragmatic inferences facilitated by the information structure of tag questions. The specifics of this use are important. When discussing the social meaning of right dislocation, I suggested that its evaluative function may have resulted in its social distribution. The sustained nature of this distribution (see, for instance, Timmis 2009, who notes a correlation between lower socioeconomic status and right dislocation in Bolton data from the 1950s) points to the enregisterment of right dislocation's character type meaning. On the other hand, the correlation between the Populars and the use of tag questions seems to be more ephemeral – coinciding as it does with flux in social categorisations at Midlan High, as detailed in Chapter 7.

When Rob Podesva and I discussed tag questions at Midlan High in our (2009) paper, we suggested that the form had become enregistered as 'Popular' based on metalinguistic commentary at Midlan High. However, reflecting further on this analysis, the discussion in Chapter 7 concluded that what appears to be enregistered at Midlan High is not the social meaning of tag questions themselves, but the social meanings of phonetic and morphological features which occur within tag questions. That is to say, as a marked discourse frame, a tag question may serve to highlight the features it contains, rather than carrying character-type social meaning *per se.*

One indication that the social meaning of tag questions is not enregistered at Midlan High is the breadth of their social distribution. This reach may be because their pragmatic functions (such as being regulatory, critical, collaborative, and knowledgeable) are more socially benign than the directly evaluative function of right dislocation. Consequently, tag questions can be called upon at specific moments irrespective of a speaker's more general persona type or style. Their ability to gain character type social meaning is determined by the extent to which their pragmatic function(s) become associated with a particular social group. We have already seen that tag questions have been associated with women, and also – like other discourse markers – with the perception of youthful inarticulacy (see Chapter 7). These are potential routes for character type meanings. However, the consistent and persistent use of these forms across all social groups suggests that this enregisterment may be more localised or ephemeral than that seen for the other linguistic variables studied in this book.

The discussion in this and the preceding section supports the conclusion that both the type of grammatical item and its social distribution affect the social meaning assigned to that grammatical item. In the next section, this knowledge is used to make some general hypotheses about the trajectories of social meaning for different grammatical forms.

8.1.4 Trajectories of Social Meaning for Grammatical Items

Table 3.1 in Chapter 3 categorised grammatical variables by their type (morpholexical, morphosyntactic, syntactic) and their distribution (socially restricted versus widespread). Drawing upon the findings of Chapters 4–7, Table 8.1 below supplements this original table by hypothesising about the likely trajectory of social meaning for each grammatical type.

The social meaning of socially restricted, and grammatically simple, morpholexical features, like levelled *were*, is likely to be rooted in character type (Type CT) meanings. Their Type CT meaning may lead to a sound symbolic

Table 8.1 *Types of grammatical variation and their likely trajectories of social meaning*

	Grammatical type	Example	Likely trajectory
Socially restricted	morpholexical	levelled *were* e.g., *It weren't great* ('I wasn't great').	Type CT => Type SS
	morphosyntactic	negative concord e.g., *I didn't do nothing* ('I didn't do anything').	Type CT => Type SS > Type SM => Type SS
	syntactic	right dislocation e.g., *I'm daft, me.*	Type SM => Type SS => Type CT
Widespread	morpholexical	intensifier *totally* e.g., *the bag was totally full*	Type SM => Type SS => Type CT
	morphosyntactic	historic present e.g., [*He looked at me,*] *so, I give him the book*	Type SM => Type SS => ?Type CT
	syntactic	tag questions e.g., *It's good, isn't it?*	Type SM => Type SS => ?Type CT

8.1 What Are the Key Findings of This Study?

(Type SS meaning) if the character-type association serves to bestow embodied qualities onto the variant (such that, for instance, levelled *were* is perceived to be the consequence of a 'lazy' articulation of *was* by those who embody working-class identities; that is to say, the form itself is perceived to 'sound lazy'). Variables like levelled *were* are unlikely to have any social meaning rooted in their semantics (a Type SM meaning) because the simplicity of their structure does not provide much scope for their semantics (i.e., the reference to 'existence' encoded by the verb BE) to influence the pragmatic interpretation of their use.

The more complex syntactic configuration of morphosyntactic variables raises the possibility of there being competing roots of social meaning. Importantly, how social meaning is attributed to variables like negative concord will depend upon where the interpreter is standing in the social landscape and on their own linguistic repertoire. Those who have not acquired negative concord as part of the normal language acquisition process are likely to draw on character-type associations to interpret the social meaning of negative concord. They may then use these character type meanings to infer other qualities that they perceive as being embodied by the social groups who most frequently use these forms: hence the subsequent generation of sound symbolic (Type SS) meanings. The nature of the Type SS meanings generated will depend upon the qualities believed to be embodied by the character types. In Figure 8.1, negative concord is shown to be embodied by the Townie persona and/or a working-class social type. The subsequent Type SS associations of 'aggressive' or 'resilient' depend upon negative and positive interpretations of character type respectively.

In addition to being readily associated with particular types of speakers, for morphosyntactic forms, speakers may also exploit semantically grounded pragmatic inferences to make social meaning – especially when a speaker has command of a localised form (like negative concord) *and* its standard alternative. This root is shown in Figure 8.2. Here, the information structure of negative concord facilitates a pragmatic function: the expression of emphasis.

Figure 8.1 Type CT: Trajectory of social meaning derived from a character-type index.

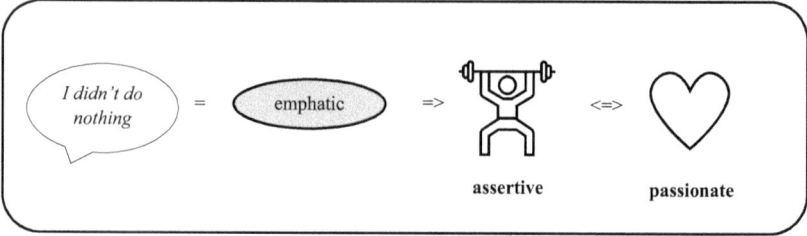

Figure 8.2 Type SM: Trajectory of social meaning rooted in semantics.

People who tend towards the use of emphasis can, in turn, be perceived to embody qualities such as 'assertiveness' or 'passion'. These sound symbolic (Type SS) meanings result from how the use of emphasis is believed to make a body 'sound'.

Whilst morphosyntactic variants that are socially restricted have the potential to develop social meanings from Type SM and Type CT sources, where their use is strongly associated with certain social groups (due to their restricted distribution), character type social meanings are likely to be especially prevalent – to the extent that these social meanings may reduce, or interact with the semantically derived pragmatic specificity of these forms. For this reason, Table 8.1 suggests that the social meaning of socially restricted morphosyntactic items may be more strongly influenced by character type indexes, despite both Type CT and Type SM roots being possible sources of social meaning.

Like morphosyntactic variables, the social meanings of socially restricted syntactic variables, like right dislocation, can also be rooted in character type or semantics. However, the referential meaning of these items is more deeply embedded in the grammatical complexity of their configuration, increasing their semantically derived pragmatic specificity. This makes it difficult for any character type (Type CT) meanings to arise separately from the social meanings derived from their semantics, or for these Type CT meanings to entirely bleach out pragmatic function derived from semantics. The character-type indexes they have are a consequence of ideological associations between the types of speakers who are considered to embody qualities associated with their pragmatics. Hence, social meaning is rooted in semantics (a Type SM root), which results in the grammatical construction being perceived to make speakers sound a particular way (i.e., sound symbolic or Type SS meanings are generated). These Type SS meanings are then ideologically associated with character types who are believed to embody the qualities entailed by pragmatic inference. In this way, Type CT meanings are more directly contingent on Type SM meanings than is the case for morphosyntactic variants like negative concord (where the two meanings can be relatively independent to the extent that Type CT meanings may arise in a separate ideological process).

The extent to which social meanings can be linked to a character type index for grammatical items that are even more widespread than right dislocation, depends upon any real or perceived reduction in social distribution. Beltrama and Staum Casasanto's (2017, 2021) research suggests that this can happen for morpholexical variants like *totally*, given that they present evidence indicating that *totally* has come to index 'youthful' character types. This character type association is a consequence of the changing semantics of *totally* from denoting reaching the top of a concrete gradable scale, to denoting reaching the top of an attitudinal scale. The move from a concrete scale to a more abstract attitudinal referent intimately connects the semantic meaning of *totally* to an embodied state or set of qualities (a Type SS meaning) which, in turn, facilitates indexical links to personas or social types who are perceived to more typically embody those attitudinal alignments (a Type CT meaning).

The extent to which more syntactically complex variants can acquire meaning in this way is questionable. Whilst widespread morphosyntactic variants were not studied in this book, widespread syntactic variants were, in the analysis of tag questions. This discussion suggested that the semantically derived pragmatic specificity of these forms, alongside their widespread distribution, inhibits their ability to acquire character-type social meanings. That is to say, their social meanings seem to remain at the level of stance, where they are perceived to make speakers sound as if they embody certain qualities, positions or alignments (Type SS meanings). Of course, we cannot rule out that character type meanings may arise for these variables should their distribution be affected by normal processes of language change (this would effectively give tag questions the same status as right dislocation). At this moment in time, though, there is little evidence to suggest that tag questions have been enregistered in this way. Furthermore, the general cross-linguistic utility of structures like tag questions is also likely to inhibit any strong character type indexes.

8.2 What Are the Wider Implications of Foregrounding the Social Meanings of Grammar?

In the preceding sections, I have proposed an account which models the diversity of social meaning trajectories and explores how social meaning develops in line with the type of grammatical item considered and its social distribution. Reflecting on previous sociolinguistic work on grammatical variants, this proposal challenges the tendency to generalise about the fixity of the social meaning of grammar. These generalisations come from a focus on a narrow range of grammatical types and a reliance upon the Interface Principle (a principle which draws on a relatively outdated notion of Universal Grammar). This is not to say that cognitive factors have no role to play in how social meaning attaches to linguistic variants (see Sharma 2018, 2021, 2022; and Mansfield 2022 for recent work that addresses social meaning and cognition), rather that we need to think about the relationship between cognition, pragmatics, information structure and social indexes in more sophisticated ways. In part, this requires that our data be more representative of language in use so that we can more readily access the breadth and depth of social contexts in which it is employed in interaction.

The analysis in this book has also pointed to the importance of considering how different levels of linguistic architecture interact. For instance, to understand the social meaning of tag questions, it was necessary to reflect on the components of a tag question (i.e., its information structure, its phonological composition, its syntactic configuration) and consider what these components contribute to its ability to communicate information about the speaker's stance, persona or social type. Work on the social meaning of phonological variation is more advanced than that on grammatical variation, but to advance understanding of the social meaning of language more generally, it is now necessary to start analysing spoken language holistically. As noted above, lexical and phonological items occur in syntactic frames when they occur in spoken discourse, and the nature of the syntactic framing may restrict or enhance which social meanings can be articulated. Furthermore, we have seen that linguistic effects are not necessarily orthogonal to social effects because information structure matters to social meaning. The importance of this was demonstrated in the analysis of levelled *were* (which is more frequent in tag questions) and in the discussion of right dislocation (where certain personal pronoun types are infrequent and highly socially restricted due to pragmatic inference), but it also has implications for how we think about the social meaning of phonological variation too. For instance, we saw that tag questions served as a salient discourse frame in which Midlan High girls were able to highlight the social correlates of different variants of word-final /t/. This has implications for how we identify and characterise salient community variables. It may also have implications for our understanding of language variation and change. We are used to thinking about linguistic constraints on language change, but to what extent are these linguistic constraints determined by the pragmatics of different discourse structures and their social significance? This book suggests a strong interaction between pragmatics and linguistic constraints but much more data is required to fully understand this relationship and its consequences for language variation and change. Promising studies, that combine insights from semantics, syntax and sociolinguistics are beginning to emerge (Bajona 2022; Wilson 2022), but more work is needed.

The content of this book also has implications for how we think about, and talk about, the diversity of linguistic repertoires. We have seen that grammatical variants are capable of articulating a wide range of social meanings, at the level of stance, persona and subject type. In the penultimate section of this chapter, the implications of this on how we conceptualise 'grammar', particularly in educational contexts, is considered.

8.3 The Educational Consequence of Recognising the Social Meaning of Grammar

I'm not very good at remembering things that happened to me in childhood, despite being a very happy child. I loved learning and went to a progressive and supportive primary school – the kind where every child felt seen. I especially loved my Year 2 teacher who always knew which book I'd enjoy and encouraged me to write creatively. I have a very clear memory of being around the age of seven and standing at her desk. She had been marking some of my writing. I had a habit of missing 's' of plurals and would write things like 'a packet of crisp' and 'two pound of sugar'. I remember her telling me that she was going to write an 's' on my nose so that I would see it every time I looked in the mirror. I was embarrassed and I didn't understand what I was doing wrong. I now know that I was probably using forms of unmarked plurality which are very common in regional English dialects (Hughes *et al.* 2005: 33).

This anecdote is around forty years old and some people have questioned whether language policing in classrooms really happens any more. Hudson (2020: 457) queries the extent to which teachers hold prescriptive views about language, critiquing Cushing (2020) for overstating the problem of language policing in schools. Sarah Spencer and I raised the issue of 'dialect correction' in a recent article on young people's use of grammar (Moore & Spencer 2021) and one of our anonymous reviewers also questioned whether significant dialect stigma continues to exist. Recent research in what has become known as 'raciolinguistics' argues that this type of discrimination is alive and well: it continues in both overt and covert ways to position less socially powerful speakers 'as linguistically deficient unrelated to any objective linguistic practice' (Flores & Rosa 2015: 150). Drawing on inspection reports, Cushing and Snell (2022) provide a strong body of evidence to show raciolinguistic ideologies are embedded in the sociopolitical culture of Ofsted, England's schools' inspectorate. Further, Snell and Cushing (2022) use data collected in primary schools to show that many teachers conceptualise spoken local dialect as a 'problem' in the classroom. Significantly, classroom data has revealed that teachers sometimes focus on the style of speech used over a child's ability and willingness to engage in the kind of dialogue that is known to enhance learning and cognitive development (Lefstein & Snell 2013; Resnick, Asterhan & Clarke 2015).

Snell and Cushing (2022) suggest that misconceptions about the relationship between speech and writing serve to justify the policing of local dialect. Few would argue with the necessity of teaching children to write using standard English and, if writing is viewed as a simple rendering of speech, then there is motivation to reduce local dialect in speech to facilitate acquisition of standard written English. However, as linguists have long documented (Carter & McCarthy 1995, 2017), speech and writing are distinct linguistic modes which differ by acquisition, levels of structure, retrievability, and standardisation, amongst other things (Bright nd). The anecdote above suggests that children do sometimes use spoken dialect features in their writing but the evidence suggests that this decreases rapidly as children age and the appearance of local dialect grammar is much less significant than issues with spelling, punctuation and structure (Williamson & Hardman 1997). Furthermore, the only dialect forms that occur with any frequency are those related to verbal agreement and tense (Constantinou & Chambers 2020); Snell and Cushing (2022) found the most frequent of these in their Leeds and London datasets (levelled *was* and *were*) occurred only 1.3 and 1.6 times per pupil respectively.

Nonetheless, policy and practice continues to insist upon the modelling of spoken standard English to children in schools: Cushing and Snell (2022: 14–15) cite Ofsted reports critiquing teachers for not being 'careful enough about grammar and spoken English' (2001), for not correcting 'oral use of spoken English' (2003); and for modelling 'incorrect grammar in their spoken English' (2018). Other reports praise 'grammar policing' when local dialect features are identified and made the butt of classroom jokes (2014; Cushing and Snell 2022: 16). Researchers have now argued that this persistent focus on spoken standard English reflects ideological opposition to local dialects, rather than a genuine concern for children's abilities to learn written standard English (Flores & Rosa 2015; Rosa & Flores 2017; Cushing & Snell 2022).

Sociolinguists have long tried to address negative views about local dialects via the 'principle of error correction' (Labov 1982) which requires that sociolinguists advocate for those who speak local dialects and take up opportunities to educate the general public about the systematicity and grammaticality of these dialects. However, as Cushing and Snell (2022) observe, little has changed in nearly 200 years of there being a schools' inspectorate in England. Lewis (2018) argues that the principle of error correction has had limited success in changing perceptions of stigmatised dialects because it does not focus on changing perceptions of people who are viewed as having lower status in society. As Snell (forthcoming) notes, 'even when working class children are willing and able to change the way they speak or write in order to adhere to rules of "correctness" or "appropriateness", this may do little to alter the way they are perceived by others.' This makes sense, of course, when we view language as just one component of stylistic practice: if we change how we speak, but not the way we dress, walk, appear and act, then our use of a particular linguistic resource is afforded a different social meaning from when that same linguistic resource appears within an alternative, more legitimate style. This has been apparent in the analyses presented in this book. Populars and Townies use many of the same linguistic features – indeed some Populars, like Beverley and Lindsey, use features like levelled *were* within the same range as the Townies. But Beverley and Lindsey's use occurs within the context of a range of social practices that collectively constitute Popular, not Townie. It is this unique bricolage of resources that distinguishes them from Townie girls, not the use of one linguistic resource in isolation.

As Eckert (2019a: 752) notes, style 'is inherent in every utterance and binds the utterer to the social world.' However, the current dominant model of grammar in our education system significantly underestimates the social meaning of grammatical variation. Educational discourse continues to juxtapose 'standard' and 'nonstandard' English, reinforcing the idea that if children learn standard grammar and are taught to recognise the relative formality of a situation, they will be able to switch between standard English and other varieties, and no longer experience societal discrimination.[1] But using a linguistic resource from one or the other type of English is not enough to position us socially. Furthermore, as this book has made clear, there are social and cognitive constraints which affect the extent to which children are able to acquire and use standard English in the first place.

The discussion of Smith *et al.*'s work (2013) in Chapter 4 demonstrated that children can style shift between standard and local variants if there is variation in their input. In Buckie, Smith and Durham (2019) show that negation does vary by context but agreement patterns do not. Consequently, on going to school, a child from Buckie is likely to find it easier to adapt their use of negation in-line with educational expectations, than to adapt the agreement patterns they use. Indeed, in the discussion above, it was noted that verbal agreement was the main local dialect variant that occurs in children's writing. As Levey (2012) has eloquently argued, we need to learn much more about what varies in children's grammatical input (and the extent to which it varies) and what doesn't. It is difficult to argue with the goal of ensuring that all children are able to write in standard English, but we can't help children to acquire written standard English if we don't understand the cognitive processes that govern how and why we use language variably in context. The Key Stage 1 and 2 guidance (for children aged between five and eleven) states that

---

[1] As this book went to press, my eight-year-old daughter, Lara, came home from school, telling me how she had been taught the difference between formal and informal speech. This was exemplified by a comparison between 'Isn't it a lovely day today?' and 'Innit a nice day today?' Notably, she didn't just alter her grammar when she uttered these two variant phrases.

'[p]upils should be taught to control their speaking and writing consciously and to use Standard English' (Department of Education 2014: 5), but we are a long way from understanding the extent to which children (or any of us, for that matter) can control our spoken language 'consciously' – never mind whether this is a desirable goal when it comes to creativity and sophistication of expression.

The discussion in Chapter 4 also highlighted that, when linguistic forms do vary, children learn to vary them on the basis of stance and alignment in the first instance, not according to societal norms of prestige and stigma. Consequently, the acquisition process itself ties these forms to their interactional function – they are vehicles through which children express variability in what they want, how they want it, and how they feel. This suggests that asking children to use standard English irrespective of these constraints is not just requiring that they learn an alternative language form, it is asking them to reconfigure their cognitive schemas for the expression of evaluation, positioning, and alignment. The extent to which this is a form of additional and significant labour (Young 2009; Flores & Rosa 2015; Baker-Bell 2020; Snell forthcoming) is currently being investigated in innovative research which measures cognitive processing demands on the use of different varieties of English (Mansfield 2022). Nonetheless, this book has made clear that the setting in which children acquire language imbues that language with social meaning which conditions the contexts in which it is used. The data from Midlan High suggests that this process continues into adolescence, where children learn to design their language to fit their developing personas as they transition from child to adult. It is undoubtedly the case that some children's use of standard English is limited because of restricted pre-school input, but it is equally possible that some (even most) children use standard English selectively, not through ignorance of it, but because the social values it indexes for them differ from those proposed in schooling. This book has suggested that the intertwined nature of language and persona is perhaps the most powerful constraint on language use in the high school years, yet the power of this constraint is almost completely ignored in educational policy.

Ultimately, better understanding the social and cognitive embedding of grammatical variation allows us to better advocate for alternative models of linguistic variability in educational discourse. When standard English is presented as a simple alternative to local dialect forms, educational policy offers a version of language use that is at odds with how children experience language. We have seen that some grammatical variants are more available for adaptation than others (in part due to the nature of their acquisition) and that certain variants occupy a broader continuum of social meaning than others. If our goal is to facilitate the use of standard English in specific educational tasks, then we need to build on how children already employ their linguistic repertoires in

8.3 Educational Consequences

relation to interactional positioning and alignment. By allowing them to understand the constraints on this variation, and encouraging them to identify and value the skills already at their disposal, we situate fluidity and flexibility at the heart of all linguistic practice, rather than situating deviations from standard English as an indicator of linguistic deficiency.

Reconceptualising the ability to use grammatical variation to do interactional work so that it is considered a linguistic skill could be transformative. It is rarely acknowledged that the child with significant local dialect input has a broader linguistic tool box than the child who only (or at least predominantly) learns standard English. Instead, the focus of much debate in disciplines as diverse as psychology (Hoff 2013), anthropology (Avineri *et al.* 2015), and speech and language therapy (Law *et al.* 2011) has focused on children's inability to master one abstract dialect (standard English), rather than on their impressive mastery of a complex sociolinguistic repertoire. Of course, much of this debate is driven by a commendable desire to help children with recognised language disorders succeed linguistically. However, some speech and language therapists have pushed the boundaries of their field by pointing out that language assessments do not measure children's expertise at constructing style, alignment and social distance (Spencer *et al.* 2017; Spencer 2017). Consequently, we do not know whether these stylistic skills are orthogonal to the conservative definition of 'language ability' that speech and language therapists typically test (e.g., receptive and expressive vocabulary, grammar and narrative) or whether children's sociolinguistic adaptation interacts with more general language abilities. Do the strengths and relative difficulties children have across language areas also extend to their ability to use language stylistically? If we could answer this question, we might take an alternative view of why working-class children (i.e., those most likely to have local dialect input) are at a disadvantage at all levels of the education system in the UK (Fergusson, Horwood & Boden 2008; Andrews, Robinson & Hutchinson 2017; Reay 2017). Multidisciplinary approaches to understanding the processes by which language influences educational outcomes have provided evidence that children may experience a variety of 'linguistic hurdles' resulting from a mismatch between the language and literacy practices of home versus school (Charity Hudley & Mallinson 2011). In addition, teachers' linguistic attitudes and ideologies towards nonstandard forms may contribute to the role of the educational system itself in producing unequal outcomes, for example, through differentiated practices in classrooms and systematic bias in curriculum and assessment (Bourdieu 1973; Willis 1977; Lucas 1999; Godley, Carpenter & Werner 2007; Bowles & Gintis 2011). Addressing the persistent idea in much research (Hoff 2013), policy (Gross 2010; Department of Education 2017), and public discourse (Sheppard 2012; Curtis 2016; Reitemeier 2018) that the problem lies in working-class children's use of language requires more data showing the sophisticated ways in which working-class children manipulate the pragmatic function and social meaning of grammar to communicate in creative ways.

Snell and Cushing (2022) demonstrate how Ofsted characterises linguistic creativity solely in relation to vocabulary and lexical expression, rendering localised grammar as a hinderance to creativity. However, Myhill (2018, 2021) has been instrumental in re-imagining how grammar might be taught in schools as a series of choices that language users make. 'Choice' is perhaps the wrong word here, given that the complex cognitive and linguistic forces which act on our language output cause us to use language unthinkingly most of the time. Nonetheless, grammatical variability is certainly a resource that can be used creatively (if unthinkingly) to reflect one's sociolinguistic experience and project one's social desires. This view of grammar has been endorsed by influential and high-profile public figures, such as one-time children's laureate, Michael Rosen (2021). This suggests that there is an appetite for such a step change. Sociolinguists need to provide more data on language in use to provide a stronger evidence base for alternative modes of grammar teaching.

Historically, linguists have supported modelling 'appropriateness' of different language varieties to children in an attempt to give local dialects a place in everyday life (Trudgill 1975; Cheshire 1982; Stubbs 1984: 234; Cheshire & Trudgill 1989). However, it is now generally acknowledged that this way of depicting stylistic variation is problematic because what is appropriate is 'continually up for negotiation and contestation, depending on the exigencies of the interactional moments as well as speakers' relative position in the local social order' (Snell forthcoming). Instead, Snell (2019) reframes 'appropriateness' by arguing for a distinction to be made between *talk for performance* (to include speeches, debates, presentations) and *talk for learning* (to include all evolving dialogue in the classroom). She argues that the use of standard English should only be required for the former, implying that it is a style of speech one might adopt in much the same way as an actor might use a particular mode of speaking to portray a particular role. In this way, the use of standard English is marked as a style with particular and specific functions, whereas the use of other modes of speech is unmarked: they are the default expectation in the classroom.

In addition to encouraging language variety in the classroom, linguists have always supported there being increased knowledge about language in schools (Carter 1991, 1994; Giovanelli & Clayton 2016). Making language a topic of discussion in classrooms increases metalinguistic awareness of the social and contextual value of language and encourages reflection on language as a mode of social action and, indeed, social resistance. When I didn't understand why my Year 2 teacher had an issue with my use of plural 's', I was embarrassed because I thought it was my own individual failing. If my use of this dialect form had been addressed in the context of a discussion about the differences between speech and writing, the functions of language to communicate referential *and* social detail, and the relationship between power and the value of language variants, I might not have developed the feeling that I'm inarticulate; I remain far more confident in my written communicative skills than I do in my spoken ones. It's empowering to know that what you are experiencing is unfair and a form of discrimination. Children need to experience an alternative viewpoint: there is nothing wrong with language variation, but there is something wrong with how society views it. This isn't a hard lesson to teach. Extract 8.2 comes from a discussion with the Eden Village girls about different forms of language used in the school. The girls immediately acknowledge that language variation is tied to persona (ll. 1–6). They also observe that language can change over time, in-line with shifts in linguistic practice (ll. 7–27). Most significantly, they recognise that the characterisation of what is 'normal' depends upon where one is standing in the social landscape; 'everyone has a uniform' (l. 31). This discussion shows that young people are capable of reaching the conclusion that language variation is meaningful and functional – if only they are given the space to reflect on their own and others' use of language.

Extract 8.2

```
1   EM    D'you think it makes a difference who you hang around with how you speak?
2   R     Yeah.
3   LE    Yeah.
4   LU    Yeah.
5
6   R     [Definitely.]
7   C     [Cos] there's, er, people in Year 7 that were like – weren't Townies. They got to Year
8         9 and they were just.. all Townies (LAUGHS).
9
10  EM    Yeah.
11  L     Like, they'd say things more to try and make them look good. Like they'd do the put-
12        on cockiness.
13  EM    Where d'you think they pick it up from?
14  LU    Dunno.
15
16  (PAUSE)
17
18  R     Each other (LAUGHS).
19
20  C     [Their friends.]
21  R     [I don't know.]
22
23  C     Cos a lot of them have friends outside school, I think. They're a lot older, like 18 year
24        old, that are Townies -
```

25	R	Yeah, well, it's like the clothes, so you have to –
26	C	They pick it up off them.
27	R	You have to fit in, don't you? But.. I don't think that's – that's not just Townies. Cos
28		like, if I came out wearing some-, you have to fit in with your own group, don't you?
29	LE	Uh-huh.
30		
31	R	Everyone has like a uniform [whether you – whether you] realise it or not.
32	LE	[If you wore a catsuit, we'd just disown you
33		(LAUGHS)].
34		
35	EM	[(LAUGHS)]
36	R	[Like] if I started speaking really differently, then everyone'd pick up on it – my
37		friends would.
38		
39	R	So it's not just like, 'Oh Townies all try and speak the same way,' or – that's just what
40		they – they speak like because..
41		
42	C	They probably don't see it as though they've [changed].
43	R	[No,] they don't see it.
44		
45	C	We just – oh – er – [if you stand back and – if you stand back.]
46	R	[But they probably think that we talk] in a certain way.
47		
48	LE	Yeah.
49	C	If you stand back and look, then we'll see a difference, but they'll just think that it's
50		normal.

(Catherine, Leah, Lucy and Ruth, Eden Villagers, 54A: 361–406)

8.4 Final Words

> ... *it's stupid the way you're judged because of the way you speak*
> (Beverley, Popular, 56A)

I started this book by talking about social class, and the extent to which non-linguists think about the language that they use and its role in their own self-presentation. I suggested that people don't think much about how they use language, but I've concluded by proposing that all of us should think about it more. This has both academic and real-world benefits. Understanding the social meaning of grammar opens up new avenues of research in language variation and change, language and cognition, and language and education. Additionally, the impact of this research on everyday perceptions of language in use could be transformative for educational attainment and in addressing systemic inequality. It's an ambitious goal, but some of us have had a lifetime of feeling like we don't fit in with established practice. The benefit of not fitting in is that you have the opportunity to carve out a new and different path.

References

Abbas, Tahir. 2007. British South Asians and pathways into selective schooling: Social class, culture and ethnicity. *British Educational Research Journal* 33(1). 75–90. https://doi.org/10.1080/01411920601104474.

Acton, Eric K. 2019. Pragmatics and the social life of the English definite article. *Language* 95(1). 37–65.

    2021. Pragmatics and the third wave: The social meaning of definites. In Lauren Hall-Lew, Emma Moore & Robert J. Podesva (eds.), *Social Meaning and Linguistic Variation: Theorizing the Third Wave*, 105–126. Cambridge: Cambridge University Press.

Acton, Eric K. & Christopher Potts. 2014. That straight talk: Sarah Palin and the sociolinguistics of demonstratives. *Journal of Sociolinguistics* 18(1). 3–31. https://doi.org/10.1111/josl.12062.

Agha, Asif. 2003. The social life of cultural value. *Language & Communication* 23 (3–4). 231–273. https://doi.org/10.1016/S0271-5309(03)00012-0.

    2005. Voice, footing, enregisterment. *Journal of Linguistic Anthropology* 15(1). 38–59. https://doi.org/10.1525/jlin.2005.15.1.38.

Aijmer, Karin. 1989. Themes and tails: The discourse functions of dislocated elements. *Nordic Journal of Linguistics* 12. 137–154.

Alam, Farhana. 2015. *"Glaswasian"? A Sociophonetic Analysis of Glasgow-Asian Accent and Identity*. Glasgow, UK: University of Glasgow.

Algeo, John. 1988. The Tag Question in British English: It's Different, I'N'It? *English World-Wide* 9(2). 171–191. https://doi.org/10.1075/eww.9.2.03alg.

Anderwald, Lieselotte. 2001. Was/were variation in non-standard British English today. *English Today* 22(1). 1–22.

    2002. *Negation in Non-standard British English: Gaps, Regularizations and Asymmetrics*. London: Routledge.

    2005. Negative concord in British English dialects. In Yoko Iyeiri (ed.), *Aspects of English Negation*, 113–137. Amsterdam: John Benjamins Publishing Company.

Andrews, Jon, David Robinson & Jo Hutchinson. 2017. Closing the gap? Trends in educational attainment and disadvantage. London: Education Policy Institute. Available from: https://epi.org.uk/wp-content/uploads/2017/08/Closing-the-Gap_EPI.pdf [last accessed 13 June 2023].

Andrews, Richard, Sue Beverton, Terry Locke, Graham Low, Alison Robinson, Carole Togerson & Die Zhu. 2004. *The effect of grammar teaching (syntax) in English on 5 to 16 year olds' accuracy and quality in written composition*. Review. University of London: EPPI-Centre, Institute of Education.

Ash, Sharon. 2013. Social class. In J. K. Chambers & Natalie Schilling (eds.), *Handbook of Language Variation and Change*, second edition, 350–367. Oxford: Wiley-Blackwell. Available from: https://onlinelibrary.wiley.com/doi/abs/10.1002/9781118335598.ch16 [last accessed 2 June 2023].

Avineri, N., E. Johnson, S. Brice-Heath, T. McCarty, E. Ochs, T. Kremer-Sadlik & H. S. Alim. 2015. Invited forum: Bridging the "language gap." *Journal of Linguistic Anthropology* 25(1). 66–86.

Bajona, Giulio. 2022. *Mandative subjunctives in present-day British English*. Leeds: University of Leeds PhD dissertation.

Baker-Bell, April. 2020. Dismantling anti-black linguistic racism in English language arts classrooms: Toward an anti-racist black language pedagogy. *Theory Into Practice* 59(1). 8–21. https://doi.org/10.1080/00405841.2019.1665415.

Ball, Stephen J. 1981. *Beachside Comprehensive: A Case-Study of Secondary Schooling*. Cambridge: Cambridge University Press.

Baranowski, Maciej & Danielle Turton. 2020. TD-deletion in British English: New evidence for the long-lost morphological effect. *Language Variation and Change* 32. 1–23.

Barbu, Stéphanie, Aurélie Nardy, Jean-Pierre Chevrot & Jacques Juhel. 2013. Language evaluation and use during early childhood: Adhesion to social norms or integration of environmental regularities? *Linguistics* 51(2). 381–411. https://doi.org/10.1515/ling-2013-0015.

Barron, Anne, Irina Pandarova & Karoline Muderack. 2015. Tag questions across Irish English and British English: A corpus analysis of form and function. *Multilingua* 34(4). 495–525. https://doi.org/10.1515/multi-2014-0099.

Bates, Douglas, Martin Maechler, Ben Bolker, Stephen Walker, Rune Haubo Bojesen Christensen, Henrik Singmann, Bin Dai, Fabian Scheipl & Gabor Grothendieck. 2019. Linear Mixed-Effects Models using "Eigen" and S4, R Package, Version 1.1-19. https://cran.r-project.org/web/packages/lme4/lme4.pdf [last accessed 2 June 2023].

Beal, Joan C. 1993. The grammar of Tyneside and Northumbrian English. In James Milroy & Lesley Milroy (eds.), *Real English: The Grammar of English Dialects in the British Isles*, 187–213. London: Longman.

  2004. The phonology of English dialects in the north of England. In Bernd Kortmann (ed.), *A Handbook of Varieties of English*, 113–133. Berlin: Mouton de Gruyter.

  2010. *An Introduction to Regional Englishes*. Edinburgh: Edinburgh University Press.

Beaman, Karen V. 2021. *Coherence in real- and apparent-time: A sociolinguistic variationist investigation of language change in Swabia*. London: Queen Mary, University of London PhD dissertation.

Bell, Allan. 2001. Back in style: Reworking audience design. In Penelope Eckert & John Rickford (eds.), *Style and Sociolinguistic Variation*, 139–169. Cambridge: Cambridge University Press.

Bellinger, Charles K. 2020. *Othering: The Original Sin of Humanity*. Eugene, OR: Wipf and Stock Publishers.

Beltrama, Andrea & Laura Staum Casasanto. 2017. Totally tall sounds totally younger: Intensification at the socio-semantics interface. *Journal of Sociolinguistics* 21(2). 154–182. https://doi.org/10.1111/josl.12230.

2021. The social meaning of semantic properties. In Lauren Hall-Lew, Emma Moore & Robert J. Podesva (eds.), *Social Meaning and Linguistic Variation: Theorizing the Third Wave*, 80–104. Cambridge: Cambridge University Press.

Bender, Emily M. 2001. *Syntactic Variation and Linguistic Competence: The Case of AAVE Copula Absence*. California, CA: Stanford University.

Bennett, Joe. 2012. 'And what comes out may be a kind of screeching': The stylisation of chavspeak in contemporary Britain. *Journal of Sociolinguistics* 16(1). 5–27. https://doi.org/10.1111/j.1467-9841.2011.00521.x.

Biber, Douglas, S. Johansson, G. Leech & E. Finegan. 1999. *Longman Grammar of Spoken and Written English*. Harlow: Longman.

Birner, Betty. 1994. Information status and word order: An analysis of English inversion. *Language* 70. 233–259.

Blanchette, Frances. 2015. *English negative concord, negative polarity, and double negation*. New York, NY: City University of New York PhD dissertation.

Blanchette, Frances, Marianna Nadeu, Jeremy Yeaton & Viviane Déprez. 2018. English negative concord and double negation: The division of labor between syntax and pragmatics. *Proceedings of the Linguistic Society of America* 3(53). 1–15.

Block, David. 2014. *Social Class in Applied Linguistics*. London: Routledge.

2018. *Political Economy and Sociolinguistics*. London: Bloomsbury Academic.

Bourdieu, Pierre. 1973. Cultural reproduction and social reproduction. In R. Brown (ed.), *Knowledge, Education and Cultural Change: Papers in the Sociology of Education*, 71–112. London: Tavistock.

1977. The economics of linguistic exchanges. *Social Science Information* 16(6). 645–668.

1990. *In Other Words: Essays towards a Reflexive Sociology*. Stanford, CA: Stanford University Press.

Bourdieu, Pierre & Jean-Claude Passeron. 1990. *Reproduction in Education, Society and Culture, second edition*. London: SAGE Publications.

Bowles, Samuel & Herbert Gintis. 2011. *Schooling in Capitalist America: Educational Reform and the Contradictions of Economic Life*. Revised edition. Chicago, IL: Haymarket.

Brechwald, Whitney A. & Mitchell J. Prinstein. 2011. Beyond homophily: A decade of advances in understanding peer influence processes. *Journal of Research on Adolescence* 21(1). 116–179.

Bresnan, Joan, Ash Asudeh, Ada Toivonen & Stephen Wechsler. 2016. *Lexical-Functional Syntax*. Second edition. Oxford: Wiley Blackwell.

Bright, William. Nd. What's the difference between speech and writing? Resource Hub. Linguistic Society of America.

Brinton, Laurel. 1990. The development of discourse markers in English. In Jacek Fisiak (ed.), *Historical Linguistics and Philology*, 45–76. Berlin: Walter de Gruyter.

Britain, David. 2002. Diffusion, levelling, simplification and reallocation in past tense BE in the English Fens. *Journal of Sociolinguistics* 6(1). 16–43.

Britain, David & Sudbury, Andrea. 2002. There's sheep and there's penguins: "Drift," "slant" and singular verb forms following existentials in New Zealand and Falkland Island English. In M. Jones & E. Esch (eds.), *Language Change: The Interplay of Internal, External and Extralinguistic Factors*, 209–242. Berlin: Mouton de Gruyter.

Brook, Marisa, Bridget L. Jankowski, Lex Konnelly & Sali A. Tagliamonte. 2018. 'I don't come off as timid anymore': Real-time change in early adulthood against the backdrop of the community. *Journal of Sociolinguistics* 22(4). 351–374. https://doi.org/10.1111/josl.12310.

Brownstein, Michael & Jennifer Saul. 2016. *Implicit Bias and Philosophy, Volume 1: Metaphysics and Epistemology*. Oxford: Oxford University Press.

Bucholtz, Mary. 1996. Geek the girl: Language, femininity, and female nerds. In Jocelyn Ahlers, Leela Bilmes, Melinda Chen, Monica Oliver, Natasha Warner & Suzanne Wertheim (eds.), *Gender and Belief Systems: Proceedings of the Third Berkeley Women and Language Conference*, 119–132. Berkeley, CA: Berkeley Women and Language Group.

2002. Youth and cultural practice. *Annual Review of Anthropology* 31. 525–552.

2011. *White Kids: Language, Race, and Styles of Youth Identity*. Cambridge: Cambridge University Press.

Bucholtz, Mary & Kira Hall. 2008. All of the above: New coalitions in sociocultural linguistics. *Journal of Sociolinguistics* 12(4). 401–431.

Buchstaller, Isabelle. 2004. *The sociolinguistic constraints on the quotative system – British English and U.S. English compared*. PhD dissertation, University of Edinburgh.

2013. *Quotatives: New Trends and Sociolinguistic Implications*. Chichester, West Sussex and Malden, MA: John Wiley & Sons.

2016. Investigating the effect of socio-cognitive salience and speaker-based factors in morpho-syntactic life-span change. *Journal of English Linguistics* 44(3). 199–229. https://doi.org/10.1177/0075424216639645.

Burnett, Heather, Hilda Koopman & Sali A. Tagliamonte. 2018. Structural explanations in syntactic variation: The evolution of English negative and polarity indefinites. *Language Variation and Change* 30(1). 83–107.

Buson, Laurence & Jacqueline Billiez. 2013. Representations of stylistic variation in 9- to 11-year-olds: Cognitive processes and salience. *Linguistics* 51(2). 325–354.

Cameron, Deborah, Fiona McAlinden & Kathy O'Leary. 1989. Lakoff in context: The social and linguistic functions of tag questions. In Jennifer Coates & Deborah Cameron (eds.), *Women in Their Speech Communities: New Perspectives on Language and Sex*, 74–93. London: Longman.

Cameron, Richard & Scott Schwenter. 2013. Pragmatics and variationist sociolinguistics. In Robert Bayley, Richard Cameron, & Ceil Lucas (eds.), *The Oxford Handbook of Sociolinguistics*, 464–483. Oxford: Oxford University Press.

Campbell-Kibler, Kathryn. 2011. The sociolinguistic variant as a carrier of social meaning. *Language Variation and Change* 22. 423–441.

Carter, Ronald (ed.). 1991. *Knowledge About Language and the Curriculum: The Linc Reader*. Reprint edition. London: Hodder & Arnold.

1994. Knowledge about language in the curriculum. In Susan Brindley (ed.), *Teaching English*, 246–259. Hove, UK: Psychology Press.

Carter, Ronald & Michael McCarthy. 1995. Grammar and the spoken language. *Applied Linguistics* 16(2). 141–158.

2017. Spoken grammar: Where are we and where are we going? *Applied Linguistics* 38(1). 1–20.

Chambers, J. K. 1995. *Sociolinguistic Theory: Linguistic Variation and Its Social Significance*. Oxford: Blackwell.

Charity Hudley, Anne H. & Christine Mallinson. 2011. *Understanding English Language Variation in U.S. Schools*. New York, NY: Teachers College Press.

Cheshire, Jenny. 1982. *Variation in an English Dialect: A Sociolinguistic Study*. Cambridge: Cambridge University Press.

   1987. Syntactic variation, the linguistic variable, and sociolinguistic theory. *Linguistics* 25(2). 257–282.

   1999. Taming the vernacular: Some repercussions for the study of syntactic variation and spoken grammar. *Cuadernos de Filologia Inglesa* 8. 59–80.

   2005a. Syntactic variation and beyond: Gender and social class variation in the use of discourse-new markers. *Journal of Sociolinguistics* 9(4). 479–508.

   2005b. Syntactic variation and spoken language. In L. Cornips & Karen P. Corrigan (eds.), *Syntax and Variation: Reconciling the Biological and the Social*, 81–106. Amsterdam: John Benjamins.

Cheshire, Jenny, Viv Edwards & Pamela Whittle. 1993. Non-standard English and dialect levelling. In James Milroy & Lesley Milroy (eds.), *Real English: The Grammar of English Dialects in the British Isles*, 53–96. London: Routledge.

Cheshire, Jenny & Sue Fox. 2009. New perspectives on was/were variation in London. *Language Variation and Change* 21(1). 1–38.

Cheshire, Jenny & Peter Trudgill. 1989. Dialect and education in the United Kingdom. In Jenny Cheshire, Viv Edwards, Henk Munstermann & Bert Weltens (eds.), *Dialect and Education: Some European Perspectives*, 94–110. Clevedon, UK: Multilingual Matters.

Chevrot, Jean-Pierre & Paul Foulkes. 2013. Introduction: Language acquisition and sociolinguistic variation. *Linguistics* 51(2). 251–254. https://doi.org/10.1515/ling-2013-0010.

Childs, Claire. 2017. *Variation and change in negation: A cross-dialectal perspective. Unpublished PhD dissertation*. University of Newcastle, ms.

Chomsky, Noam. 2017. The Galilean challenge: Architecture and evolution of language. *Journal of Physics*: Conference Series. IOP Publishing 880. 012015. https://doi.org/10.1088/1742-6596/880/1/012015.

Chun, Christian W. 2019. Language, discourse, and class: What's next for sociolinguistics? *Journal of Sociolinguistics* 23. 332–345.

Cipriani, Enrico. 2019. Semantics in generative grammar: A critical survey. *Lingvisticae Investigationes* 42(2). 134–185. https://doi.org/10.1075/li.00033.cip.

Constantinou, Filio & Lucy Chambers. 2020. Non-standard English in UK students' writing over time. *Language and Education* 34(1). 22–35.

Coupland, Nikolas. 2007. *Style: Language Variation and Identity*. Cambridge: Cambridge University Press.

   2010. The authentic speaker and the speech community. In Carmen Llamas & Dominic Watt (eds.), *Language and Identities*, 99–112. Edinburgh: Edinburgh University Press.

Crosnoe, Robert & Monica Kirkpatrick Johnson. 2011. Research on adolescence in the twenty-first century. *Annual Review of Sociology* 27. 439–460.

Cuddy, Salina. 2019. *Can women "sound gay"? A sociophonetic study of /s/ and pitch of gay and straight British-English speaking women*. York, UK: University of York PhD dissertation.

Curtis, J. 2016. Shut up! Geezer who runs Essex school is like 'pupils must stop speaking as if they were in TOWIE.' The Mail Online. Available from: www.dailymail.co.uk/news/article-3565133/Shut-Geezer-runs-Essex-school-like-pupils-stop-speaking-Towie.html [last accessed 13 June 2023].

Cushing, Ian. 2019a. Resources not rulebooks. *Metaphor and the Social World* 9(2). 155–176.

  2019b. Grammar policy and pedagogy from primary to secondary school. *Literacy* 53(3). 170–179.

  2020. The policy and policing of language in schools. *Language in Society* 49(3). 425–450.

Cushing, Ian & Julia Snell. 2022. The (white) ears of Ofsted: A raciolinguistic perspective on the listening practices of the schools inspectorate. *Language in Society* 52(3). 1–24.

Dann, Holly Rebeka. 2019. *Productions and perceptions of BATH and TRAP vowels in cornish English*. Sheffield: University of Sheffield PhD dissertation.

D'Onofrio, Annette. 2015. Persona-based information shapes linguistic perception: Valley Girls and California vowels. *Journal of Sociolinguistics* 19(2). 241–256. https://doi.org/10.1111/josl.12115.

D'Onofrio, Annette & Penelope Eckert. 2021. Affect and iconicity in phonological variation. *Language in Society* 50(1). 29–51. https://doi.org/10.1017/S0047404520000871.

Department of Education. 2014. English programmes of study: Key Stages 1 and 2: National curriculum in England. London, ms.

  2017. Unlocking talent, fulfilling potential: A plan for improving social mobility through education. London: Department of Education. Available from: https://assets.publishing.service.gov.uk/government/uploads/system/uploads/attachment_data/file/667690/Social_Mobility_Action_Plan_-_for_printing.pdf [last accessed 13 June 2023].

Dines, Elizabeth R. 1980. Variation in discourse - "and stuff like that." *Language in Society* 9(1). 13–31.

Drager, Katie, Kate Hardeman Guthrie, Rachel Schutz & Ivan Chik. 2021. Perceptions of style: A focus on fundamental frequency and perceived social characteristics. In Lauren Hall-Lew, Emma Moore & Robert J. Podesva (eds.), *Social Variation and Linguistic Meaning: Theorizing the Third Wave*, 176–202. Cambridge, UK and New York, NY: Cambridge University Press.

Drummond, Rob. 2011. Glottal variation in /t/ in non-native English speech: Patterns of acquisition. *English World-Wide* 32(3). 280–308. https://doi.org/10.1075/eww.32.3.02dru.

  2018a. Maybe it's a grime [t]ing: th-stopping among urban British youth. *Language in Society* 47(02). 171–196. https://doi.org/10.1017/S0047404517000999.

  2018b. *Researching Urban Youth Language and Identity*. London: Palgrave Macmillan.

Du Bois, John W. 2002. Stance and consequence. Conference paper presented at the American Anthropological Association, New Orleans, USA.

  2007. The stance triangle. In R. Englebretson (ed.), *Stancetaking in Discourse: Subjectivity, Evaluation, Interaction*, 139–177. Amsterdam, NL & Philadelphia, PA: John Benjamins Publishing Company.

Durham, Mercedes. 2011. Right dislocation in Northern England: Frequency and use – perception meets reality. *English World-Wide* 32(3). 257–279. https://doi.org/10.1075/eww.32.3.01dur.

Eckert, Penelope. 1988. Adolescent social structure and the spread of linguistic change. *Language in Society* 17(2). 183–207. https://doi.org/10.1017/S0047404500012756.

1989. *Jocks and Burnouts: Social Categories and Identity in the High School*. New York, NY: Teachers College Press.

1998. Gender and sociolinguistic variation. In Jennifer Coates (ed.), *Language and Gender: A Reader*, 64–75. Oxford: Blackwell.

2000. *Linguistic Variation as Social Practice: The Linguistic Construction of Identity at Belten High*. Oxford: Blackwell.

2003. Language and adolescent peer groups. *Journal of Language and Social Psychology* 22(1). 112–118. https://doi.org/10.1177/0261927X02250063.

2006. Communities of practice. In *Encyclopedia of Language and Linguistics*, second edition, 683–685. Amsterdam: Elsevier.

2008. Variation and the indexical field. *Journal of Sociolinguistics* 12(4). 453–476.

2011. Language and power in the preadolescent heterosexual market. *American Speech* 86(1). 85–97. https://doi.org/10.1215/00031283-1277528.

2014. Language and gender in adolescence. In Susan Ehrlich, Miriam Meyerhoff & Janet Holmes (eds.), *The Handbook of Language, Gender, and Sexuality*, 529–545. Malden, MA: John Wiley & Sons, Ltd. https://doi.org/10.1002/9781118584248.ch27.

2017. Comment: The most perfect of signs: Iconicity in variation. *Linguistics* 55(5). 1197–1207. https://doi.org/10.1515/ling-2017-0025.

2018. *Meaning and Linguistic Variation: The Third Wave in Sociolinguistics*. Cambridge and New York, NY: Cambridge University Press.

2019a. The limits of meaning: Social indexicality, variation, and the cline of interiority. *Language* 95(4). 751–776. https://doi.org/10.1353/lan.2019.0072.

2019b. The individual in the semiotic landscape. *Glossa* 4(1). 14. https://doi.org/10.5334/gjgl.640.

Eckert, Penelope & Sally McConnell-Ginet. 1992. Think practically and look locally: Language and gender as community-based practice. *Annual Review of Anthropology* 21. 461–490.

Eckert, Penelope & Etienne Wenger. 1993. *Seven Principles of Learning*. Palo Alto, CA: Institute for Research on Learning.

Eckert, Penelope & John Rickford. 2001. *Style and Sociolinguistic Variation*. Cambridge: Cambridge University Press.

Eckert, Penelope & William Labov. 2017. Phonetic, phonology and social meaning. *Journal of Sociolinguistics* 21(4). 467–496.

Edwards, Viv, Peter Trudgill & Bert Weltens. 1984. *The Grammar of English Dialect*. London: Economic and Social Research Council.

Edwards, Viv & Bert Weltens. 1985. Research on non-standard dialects of British English: Progress and prospects. In W. Viereck (ed.), *Focus on: England and Wales*, 97–139. Amsterdam: John Benjamins.

Eisikovits, Edina. 1991. Variation in subject-verb agreement in Inner Sydney English. In Jenny Cheshire (ed.), *English Around the World: Sociolinguistic Perspectives*, 235–255. Cambridge: Cambridge University Press.

Elley, W. 1994. Grammar teaching and language skill. In R. E. Asher (ed.), *Encyclopedia of Language and Linguistics*, 1468–1471. Oxford: Pergamon.

Ellis, Alexander J. 1869. *On Early English Pronunciation*. 5 volumes. London: Trubner & Co.

Fabricius, Anne H. 2000. *T-glottalling between stigma and prestige: a sociolinguistic study of modern RP*. Copenhagen: Copenhagen University PhD dissertation.

Fergusson, D. M., L. John Horwood & Joseph M. Boden. 2008. The transmission of social inequality: Examination of the linkages between family socioeconomic status in childhood and educational achievement in young adulthood. *Research in Social Stratification and Mobility* 26(3). 277–295.

Flores, Nelson & Jonathan Rosa. 2015. Undoing appropriateness: Raciolinguistic ideologies and language diversity in education. *Harvard Educational Review* 85(2). 149–171.

Foulkes, Paul, Gerald. J. Docherty & Dominic Watt. 1999. Tracking the emergence of sociophonetic variation in 2- to 4-year-olds. *ICPhS-14*, 1625–1628.

Fox, S. 2015. *The New Cockney: New Ethnicities and Adolescent Speech in the Traditional East End of London*. London: Palgrave Macmillan. https://doi.org/10.1057/9781137318251.

Fuchs, Susanne & Martine Toda. 2010. Do differences in male versus female /s/ reflect biological or sociophonetic factors? In Susanne Fuchs, Martine Toda & Marzena Zygis (eds.), *Turbulent Sounds*, 281–302. Berlin and New York, NY: Mouton de Gruyter.

Fyne, John. 2005. *The dialect of New Mills: Linguistic change in a north-west Derbyshire community*. Sheffield, UK: University of Sheffield PhD dissertation.

Gal, Susan. 2013. Tastes of talk: Qualia and the moral flavor of signs. *Anthropological Theory* 13(1–2). 31–48. https://doi.org/10.1177/1463499613483396.

Gal, Susan & Judith T. Irvine. 1995. The boundaries of languages and disciplines: How ideologies construct difference. *Social Research* 62(4). 967–1001.

 2019. *Signs of Difference: Language and Ideology in Social Life*. Cambridge: Cambridge University Press. https://doi.org/10.1017/9781108649209.

Gates, Shivonne. 2019. *Language variation and ethnicity in a multicultural East London secondary school*. PhD dissertation. Queen Mary, University of London, ms.

Geluykens, Ronald. 1987. Tails (right dislocations) as a repair mechanism in English conversations. In Jan Nuyts & George de Schutter (eds.), *Getting One's Words into Line: On word Order and Functional Grammar*, 119–130. Dordrecht: Foris.

Ghimenton, Anna, Jean-Pierre Chevrot & Jacqueline Billiez. 2013. Language choice adjustments in child production during dyadic and multiparty interactions: A quantitative approach to multilingual interactions. *Linguistics* 51(2). 413–438. https://doi.org/10.1515/ling-2013-0016.

Giovanelli, Marcello & Dan Clayton (eds.). 2016. *Knowing About Language: Linguistics and the Secondary English Classroom*. London: Routledge. https://doi.org/10.4324/9781315719818.

Givon, Talmy. 1976. Topic, pronoun, and grammatical agreement. In Charles N. Li (ed.), *Subject and Topic*, 149–158. New York, NY: Academic Press.

Glass, Lelia. 2015. Strong necessity modals: Four socio-pragmatic corpus studies. *Penn Working Papers in Linguistics* 21(2). 77–88.

Godley, Amanda J., Brian D. Carpenter & Cynthia A. Werner. 2007. "I'll speak in proper slang": Language ideologies in a daily editing activity. *Reading Research Quarterly* 42(1). 100–131.

Gray, Bethany & Douglas Biber. 2012. Current conceptions of stance. In Ken Hyland & Carmen Sancho Guinda (eds.), *Stance and Voice in Written Academic Genres*, 15–33. London: Palgrave Macmillan. https://doi.org/10.1057/9781137030825_2.

Gross, Miriam. 2010. *So Why Can't They Read?* London: Centre for Policy Studies.

Guasti, Maria Teresa. 2002. *Language Acquisition: The Growth of Grammar*. Cambridge, MA: MIT Press.

Guy, Gregory R. 1988. Advanced Varbrul analysis. In *Linguistic Change and Contact: Proceedings of the Sixteenth Annual Conference on New Ways of Analyzing Variation*, 124–136. Austin, TX: Department of Linguistics, University of Texas.

2013. The cognitive coherence of sociolects: How do speakers handle multiple sociolinguistic variables? *Journal of Pragmatics* 52. 63–71. https://doi.org/10.1016/j.pragma.2012.12.019.

Halliday, Michael A. K. 1985. *An Introduction to Functional Grammar*. London: Edward Arnold.

Hall-Lew, Lauren, Emma Moore & Robert J. Podesva (eds.). 2021. *Social Meaning and Linguistic Variation: Theorizing the Third Wave*. Cambridge: Cambridge University Press.

Hargreaves, David H. 1967. *Social Relations in a Secondary School*. London: Routledge and Kegan Paul.

Hay, Jennifer & Daniel Schreier. 2004. Reversing the trajectory of language change: Subject–verb agreement with be in New Zealand English. *Language Variation and Change* 16(3). 209–235. https://doi.org/10.1017/S0954394504163047

Hebdige, Dick. 1979. *Subculture: The Meaning of Style*. London: Routledge.

Henley, Nancy M., Michelle Miller & Jo Anne Beazley. 1995. Syntax, semantics, and sexual violence: Agency and the passive voice. *Journal of Language and Social Psychology* 14(1–2). 60–84. https://doi.org/10.1177/0261927X95141004.

Henry, Alison. 2016. Acquiring language from variable input: Subject-verb agreement and negative concord in Belfast English. *Linguistic Variation* 16(1). 131–150.

Hodkinson, Paul. 2002. *Goth: Identity, Style and Subculture*. Bloomsbury. Available from: www.bloomsbury.com/uk/goth-9781859736050/ [last accessed 2 June 2023].

Hoff, E. 2013. Interpreting the early language trajectories of children from low-SES and language minority homes: Implications for closing achievement gaps. *Developmental Psychology* 49(1). 4–14.

Holmes, Janet. 1984. Hedging your bets and sitting on the fence: Some evidence for hedges as support structures. *Te Reo* 27. 47–62.

Holmes-Elliott, Sophie & Erez Levon. 2017. The substance of style: Gender, social class and interactional stance in /s/-fronting in southeast England. *Linguistics* 55(5). 1045–1072. https://doi.org/10.1515/ling-2017-0020.

Horn, Laurence R. 1986. Presupposition, theme and variations. In *Papers from the Parasession on Pragmatics and Grammatical Theory, Chicago Linguistic Society*, 168–192. University of Chicago, IL: Chicago Linguistic Society.

2004. Implicature. In Laurence R. Horn & Gregory Ward (eds.), *Handbook of Pragmatics*, 3–28. Oxford: Blackwell.

Huddleston, R. & Geoffrey. K. Pullum. 2002. *The Cambridge Grammar of the English Language*. Cambridge: Cambridge University Press.
Hudson, Richard A. 1975. The meaning of questions. *Language* 51. 1–31.
  2001. Grammar teaching and writing skills: The research evidence. *Syntax in the Schools* 17. 1–6.
  2016. The impact of policy on language teaching in UK schools. In Marco Giovanelli & Dan Clayton (eds.), *Knowing About Language: Linguistics and the Secondary English Classroom*, 25–35. London: Routledge.
  2020. Comment on 'The policy and policing of language in schools' by Ian Cushing. *Language in Society* 49(3). 451–460. https://doi.org/10.1017/S0047404520000366.
Hughes, Arthur, Peter Trudgill & Dominic Watt. 2005. *English Accents and Dialects: An Introduction to Social and Regional Varieties of English in the British Isles*, fourth edition. London: Hodder Education.
Hunston, Susan & Geoffrey Thompson. 2000. *Evaluation in Text: Authorial Stance and the Construction of Discourse*. Oxford: Oxford University Press.
Ilbury, Christian. 2019. *"Beyond the offline": Social media and the social meaning of variation in East London*. London: Queen Mary, University of London PhD dissertation.
Irvine, Judith T. 2001. "Style" as distinctiveness: The culture and ideology of linguistic differentiation. In Penelope Eckert & John R. Rickford (eds.), *Style and Sociolinguistic Variation*, 21–43. Cambridge: Cambridge University Press.
Irvine, Judith T. & Susan Gal. 2000. Language ideology and linguistic differentiation. In Paul Kroskrity (ed.), *Regimes of Language*, 35–83. Santa Fe, New Mexico: School of American Research Press.
Jaffe, Alexandra (ed.). 2009. *Stance: Sociolinguistic Perspectives*. Oxford: Oxford University Press.
Jeffries, Ella. 2019. Preschool children's categorization of speakers by regional accent. *Language Variation and Change* 31(3). 329–352. https://doi.org/10.1017/S0954394519000176.
Johnson, Daniel Ezra. 2009. Getting off the GoldVarb Standard: Introducing Rbrul for mixed-effects variable rule analysis. *Language and Linguistics Compass* 3(1). 359–383. https://doi.org/10.1111/j.1749-818X.2008.00108.x.
Johnstone, Barbara. 2004. Place, globalization and linguistic variation. In Carmen Fought (ed.), *Sociolinguistic Variation: Critical Reflections*, 65–83. Cambridge: Cambridge University Press.
  2016. Enregisterment: How linguistic items become linked with ways of speaking. *Language and Linguistics Compass* 10(11). 632–643. https://doi.org/10.1111/lnc3.12210.
  2017. Characterological figures and expressive style in the enregisterment of linguistic variety. In Chris Montgomery & Emma Moore (eds.), *Language and a Sense of Place: Studies in Language and Region*, 283–300. Cambridge: Cambridge University Press. https://doi.org/10.1017/9781316162477.015.
Kearsley, Greg P. 1976. Questions and question asking in verbal discourse: A cross-disciplinary review. *Journal of Psycholinguistic Research* 5. 355–375.
Kefalas, Maria. 2003. *Working-Class Heroes: Protecting Home, Community, and Nation in a Chicago Neighborhood*. California, CA: University of California Press.

Kerswill, Paul. 1996. Children, adolescents and language change. *Language Variation and Change* 8. 177–202.

Kerswill, Paul & Ann Williams. 2000. Creating a New Town koine: Children and language change in Milton Keynes. *Language in Society* 29. 65–115.

Khan, Arfaan. 2006. *A sociolinguistic study of Birmingham English: Language variation and change in a multi-ethnic British community.* Lancaster, UK: Lancaster University Unpublished PhD dissertation.

Khattab, Ghada. 2013. Phonetic convergence and divergence strategies in English-Arabic bilingual children. *Linguistics* 51(2). 439–472.

Kiesling, Scott F. 2004. Dude. *American Speech* 79(3). 281–305. https://doi.org/10.1215/00031283-79-3-281.

  2009. Style as stance. In Alexandra Jaffe (ed.), *Stance: Sociolinguistic Perspectives*, 171–195. Oxford: Oxford University Press.

Kimps, Ditte. 2007. Declarative constant polarity tag questions: A data-driven analysis of their form, meaning, and attitudinal uses. *Journal of Pragmatics* 39. 270–291.

Kimps, Ditte, Kristin Davidse & Bert Cornillie. 2014. A speech function analysis of tag questions in British English spontaneous dialogue. *Journal of Pragmatics* 66. 64–85. https://doi.org/10.1016/j.pragma.2014.02.013.

Kirkham, Sam. 2013. *Ethnicity, social practice and phonetic variation in a Sheffield secondary school.* Sheffield: University of Sheffield PhD dissertation.

Kirkham, Sam & Emma Moore. 2016. Constructing social meaning in political discourse: Phonetic variation and verb processes in Ed Miliband's speeches. *Language in Society* 45(1). 87–111. https://doi.org/10.1017/S0047404515000755.

Klima, Edward S. 1964. Negation in English. In J. A. Fodor & J. J. Katz (eds.), *The Structure of Language*, 246–323. Englewood Cliffs, NJ: Prentice-Hall.

Kloe, Donald R. 1977. *A Dictionary of Onomatopoeic Sounds, Tones, and Noises in English and Spanish, Including Those of Animals, Man, Nature, Machinery and Musical Instruments, Together with Some That Are Not Imitative or Echoic.* S Leonard, OK: B. Ethridge.

Labov, William. 1964. Stages in the acquisition of Standard English. In Roger Shuy, Alva Davis & Robert Hogan (eds.), *Social Dialects and Language Learning*, 77–103. Champaign, IL: National Council of Teachers of English.

  1966. *The Social Stratification of English in New York City.* Washington, DC: Center for Applied Linguistics.

  1972a. Negative attraction and negative concord in English grammar. *Language* 48(4). 773–818. https://doi.org/10.2307/411989.

  1972b. The logic of nonstandard English. In William Labov (ed.), *Language in the Inner City: Studies in the Black English Vernacular*, 201–240. Philadelphia, PA: University of Pennsylvania Press.

  1978. Where does the sociolinguistic variable stop: A response to Beatriz R. Lavandera. *Working Papers in Sociolinguistics* 44. 1–16.

  1982. Objectivity and commitment in Linguistic Science: The case of the Black English trial in Ann Arbor. *Language in Society* 11. 165–201.

  1984. Intensity. In Deborah Schriffrin (ed.), *Meaning, Form, and Use in Context: Linguistic Applications. Georgetown Roundtable in Linguistics*, 43–70. Washington, DC: Georgetown University Press.

1993. The unobservability of structure and its linguistic consequences. *Paper presented at the 22nd New Ways in Analyzing Variation conference*, University of Ottawa.
2001. *Principles of Linguistic Change*. Vol. II: Social Factors. Malden, MA: Wiley-Blackwell.
2013. *The Language of Life and Death: The Transformation of Experience in Oral Narrative*. Cambridge: Cambridge University Press.
Labov, William, Sharon Ash, Maya Ravindranath, Tracey Weldon, Maciej Baranowski & Naomi Nagy. 2011. Properties of the sociolinguistic monitor. *Journal of Sociolinguistics* 15(4). 431–463.
Lacey, Colin. 1970. *Hightown Grammar: The School as a Social System*. Manchester: Manchester University Press.
Ladusaw, William A. 1992. Expressing negation. *Ohio State Working Papers in Linguistics* 40. 237–260.
Lakoff, Robin. 1974. Remarks on 'this' and 'that.' *Proceedings of the Chicago Linguistics Society* 10. 345–356.
1975. *Language and Woman's Place*. New York, NY: Harper and Row.
Lambrecht, Knud. 1994. *Information Structure and Sentence Form: Topic, Focus, and the Mental Representations of Discourse Referents* (Cambridge Studies in Linguistics). Cambridge: Cambridge University Press. https://doi.org/10.1017/CBO9780511620607.
Lavandera, Beatriz R. 1978. Where does the sociolinguistic variable stop? *Language in Society* 7(2). 171–182.
Lave, Jean & Etienne Wenger. 1991. *Situated Learning: Legitimate Peripheral Participation*. Cambridge: Cambridge University Press.
Law, James, Kirsty McBean & Robert Rush. 2011. Communication skills in a population of primary school-aged children raised in an area of pronounced social disadvantage. *International Journal of Language & Communication Disorders* 46 (6). 657–664. https://doi.org/10.1111/j.1460-6984.2011.00036.x.
Lawson, Robert. 2009. *Sociolinguistic constructions of identity in a Glasgow high school*. Unpublished PhD dissertation. University of Glasgow, ms.
Lefstein, Adam & Julia Snell. 2013. *Better than Best Practice: Developing Teaching and Learning through Dialogue*. London and New York, NY: Routledge.
Leith, Dick. 1995. Tense variation as a performance feature in a Scottish folktale. *Language in Society* 24(1). 53–77. https://doi.org/10.1017/S0047404500018406.
Levey, Stephen. 2007. *The next generation: Aspects of grammatical variation in the speech of some London preadolescents*. Queen Mary, University of London.
Levin, Beth. 1993. *English Verb Classes and Alternations: A Preliminary Investigation*. Chicago, IL: University of Chicago Press.
Levinson, Stephen C. 1988. Conceptual problems in the study of regional and cultural style. In Norbert Dittmar & Peter Schlobinski (eds.), *The Sociolinguistics of Urban Vernaculars*, 161–190. Berlin: Walter de Gruyter.
Levon, Erez & Sue Fox. 2014. Social salience and the sociolinguistic monitor: A case study of ING and TH-fronting in Britain. *Journal of English Linguistics* 42(3). 185–217. https://doi.org/10.1177/0075424214531487.
Levon, Erez & Isabelle Buchstaller. 2015. Perception, cognition, and linguistic structure: The effect of linguistic modularity and cognitive style on sociolinguistic processing. *Language Variation and Change* 27(3). 319–348.

2012. Understanding children's non-standard spoken English: A perspective from variationist sociolinguistics. *Language and Education* 26(5). 405–421. https://doi.org/10.1080/09500782.2011.651144.

Lewis, Mark C. 2018. A critique of the principle of error correction as a theory of social change. *Language in Society* 47. 325–346.

Lucas, Samuel. 1999. *Tracking Inequality: Stratification and Mobility in American High Schools*. New York, NY: Teachers College Press.

Macaulay, Ronald K. S. 2005. *Talk That Counts: Age, Gender, and Social Class Differences in Discourse*. Illustrated edition. Oxford and New York, NY: Oxford University Press.

Mansfield, Katie. 2022. Is Style Control a Potential Factor in Working-Class Educational Underachievement? Paper presented at NWAV 50, Stanford University, October 2022.

Maybin, J. 2006. *Children's Voices: Talk, Knowledge and Identity*. London: Palgrave Macmillan. https://doi.org/10.1057/9780230511958.

McRobbie, Angela. 2000. *Feminism and Youth Culture*, second edition. Houndmills, Basingstoke, Hampshire, London: Palgrave.

Medhurst, A. 2000. If anywhere: Class identifications and cultural studies academics. In S. Munt (ed.), *Cultural Studies and the Working Class: Subject to Change*, 19–35. London: Cassell.

Meecham, Marjory & Michele Foley. 1994. On resolving disagreement: Linguistic theory and variation – There's bridges. *Language Variation and Change* 6. 63–85.

Mendoza-Denton, Norma. 2008. *Homegirls: Language and Cultural Practice Among Latina Youth Gangs*. Oxford: Wiley-Blackwell.

2011. The semiotic Hitchhiker's Guide to creaky voice: Circulation and gendered hardcore in a chicana/o gang persona. *Journal of Linguistic Anthropology* 21. 261–280.

Meyerhoff, Miriam & James A. Walker. 2007. The persistence of variation in individual grammars: Copula absence in 'urban sojourners' and their stay-at-home peers, Bequia (St Vincent and the Grenadines)1. *Journal of Sociolinguistics* 11(3). 346–366. https://doi.org/10.1111/j.1467-9841.2007.00327.x.

2013. An existential problem: The sociolinguistic monitor and variation in existential constructions on Bequia (St. Vincent and the Grenadines). *Language in Society* 42 (4). 407–428. https://doi.org/10.1017/S0047404513000456.

Milroy, James, Lesley Milroy, Sue Hartley & David Walshaw. 1994. Glottal stops and Tyneside glottalization: Competing patterns of variation and change in British English. *Language Variation and Change* 6. 327–357.

Montgomery, Chris & Emma Moore (eds.). 2017. *Language and a Sense of Place: Studies in Language and Region*. Cambridge: Cambridge University Press. https://doi.org/10.1017/9781316162477.

Moore, Emma. 2010. The interaction between social category and social practice: Explaining was/were variation. *Language Variation and Change* 22. 347–371.

Moore, Emma & Robert P. Podesva. 2009. Style, indexicality, and the social meaning of tag questions. *Language in Society* 38. 447–485.

Moore, Emma & Julia Snell. 2011. "Oh, they're top, them": Right dislocated tags and interactional stance. In Frans Gregersen, Jeffrey K. Parrott & Pia Quist (eds.),

Language Variation – European Perspectives III, 97–110. Amsterdam: John Benjamins.

Moore, Emma & Sarah Spencer. 2021. "It just sounds proper common": Exploring the social meanings expressed by nonstandard grammar. *Linguistics and Education* 63. 2–14.

Munson, Benjamin, Kayleigh Ryherd & Sara Kemper. 2017. Implicit and explicit gender priming in English lingual sibilant fricative perception. *Linguistics* 55(5). 1073–1107. https://doi.org/10.1515/ling-2017-0021.

Mycock, Louise. 2019. Right-dislocated pronouns in British English: The form and functions of ProTag constructions. *English Language & Linguistics*. 23(2). 253–275. https://doi.org/10.1017/S1360674317000399.

Myhill, Debra A. 2018. Grammar as a meaning-making resource for improving writing. *L1-Educational Studies in Language and Literature* 18. 1–21.

2021. Grammar re-imagined: Foregrounding understanding of language choice in writing. *English in Education* 55(3). 265–278. https://doi.org/10.1080/04250494.2021.1885975.

Myhill, Debra A., Susan M. Jones, Helen Lines & Annabel Watson. 2012. Re-thinking grammar: The impact of embedded grammar teaching on students' writing and students' metalinguistic understanding. *Research Papers in Education* 27(2). 139–166. https://doi.org/10.1080/02671522.2011.637640.

Nardy, Aurélie, Jean-Pierre Chevrot & Stéphanie Barbu. 2014. Sociolinguistic convergence and social interactions within a group of preschoolers: A longitudinal study. *Language Variation and Change* 26(3). 273–301. https://doi.org/10.1017/S0954394514000131.

Nevalainen, Terttu. 2006. Negative concord as an English "vernacular universal": Social history and linguistic typology. *Journal of English Linguistics* 34(3). 257–278.

Ochs, Elinor. 1992. Indexing gender. In Alessandro Duranti & Charles Goodwin (eds.), *Language as Interactive Phenomenon*, 335–358. Cambridge: Cambridge University Press.

Office of Population Censuses and Surveys. 1980. Classification of Occupations and Coding Index. London: Her Majesty's Stationery Office.

Ohala, John. 1994. The frequency code underlies the sound-symbolic use of voice pitch. In Leanne Hinton, Johanna Nichols & John Ohala (eds.), *Sound Symbolism*, 325–347. Cambridge: Cambridge University Press.

Pabst, Katharina. 2022. *Putting 'the other Maine' on the map: Language variation, local affiliation, and co-occurrence in Aroostook County English*. Toronto, Canada: University of Toronto PhD dissertation.

Palacios, Ignacio M. 2017. Negative concord in the language of British adults and teenagers. *English World-Wide* 38(2). 153–180. https://doi.org/10.1075/eww.38.2.02pal.

Pea, Roy D. 1980. The development of negation in early child language. In David R. Olson (ed.), *The Social Foundations of Language and Thought*, 597–626. New York, NY: Norton.

Peirce, Charles S. 1895. Of reasoning in general. In N. Houser, A. De Tienne, J. R. Eller, A. C. Lewis, C. L. Clark & D. Bront Davis (eds.), *The Essential Peirce: Selected Philosophical Writings (1893–1913)*, 11–26. Bloomington, IN: Indiana University Press.

Peirce, Charles S. & Victoria Welby-Gregory. 1977. In C. S. Hardwick & J. Cook (eds.), *Semiotic and Significs: The Correspondence between Charles S. Peirce and Victoria Lady Welby*. Bloomington, IN: Indiana University Press.

Peirce Edition Project, Peirce Edition. 1998. *The Essential Peirce, Volume 2: Selected Philosophical Writings (1893–1913)*. Bloomington, IN: Indiana University Press.

Pharao, Nicolai & Marie Maegaard. 2017. On the influence of coronal sibilants and stops on the perception of social meanings in Copenhagen Danish. *Linguistics* 55(5). 1141–1167. https://doi.org/10.1515/ling-2017-0023.

Pharao, Nicolai, Marie Maegaard, Janus Spindler Møller & Tore Kristiansen. 2014. Indexical meanings of [s+] among Copenhagen youth: Social perception of a phonetic variant in different prosodic contexts. *Language in Society* 43(1). 1–31.

Podesva, Robert P. 2008. Three sources of stylistic meaning. *Texas Linguistic Forum* 51. 134–143.

Podesva, Robert J. 2021. The role of the body in language change. In Lauren Hall-Lew, Emma Moore & Robert J. Podesva (eds.), *Social Meaning and Linguistic Variation: Theorizing the Third Wave*, 363–381. Cambridge, UK and New York, NY: Cambridge University Press.

Pollard, Carl & Ivan A. Sag. 1994. *Head-Driven Phrase Structure Grammar*. Chicago, IL: University of Chicago Press.

Pratt, Teresa. 2018. *Affective Sociolinguistic Style: An Ethnography of Embodied Linguistic Variation in an Arts High School*. California, CA: Stanford University Press.

Quirk, R., S. Greenbaum, G. Leech & J. Svartvik. 1985. *A Comprehensive Grammar of the English Language*. London: Longman.

Quist, Pia. 2021. Multiethnolect and dialect in and across communities. In Lauren Hall-Lew, Emma Moore & Robert J. Podesva (eds.), *Social Meaning and Linguistic Variation: Theorizing the Third Wave*, 292–314. Cambridge: Cambridge University Press.

Rampton, Ben. 2010. Social class and sociolinguistics. *Applied Linguistics Review* 1. 1–22. https://doi.org/10.1515/9783110222654.1.

Rathje, Marianne. 2009. Quotation and quotatives in the speech of three Danish generations. Paper presented at ICLAVE 5, University of Copenhagen. 25–27 June, 2009.

Rauniomaa, Mirka. 2003. Stance accretion. Conference paper presented at the Language, Interaction, and Social Organization Research Focus Group, University of California, Santa Barbara.

Reay, Diane. 2004. 'Mostly roughs and toughs': Social class, race and representation in inner city schooling. *Sociology* 38(5). 1005–1023. https://doi.org/10.1177/0038038504047183.

2007. 'Unruly places' : Inner-city comprehensives, middle-class imaginaries and working-class children. *Urban Studies* 44(7). 1191–1201. https://doi.org/10.1080/00420980701302965.

2017. *Miseducation: Inequality, Education and the Working Classes*. Bristol: Policy Press.

Reitemeier, Bob. 2018. The key to social mobility lies in language. *Times Education Supplement*. 11 July 2018.

Resnick, Lauren, Christa Asterhan, & Sherice Clarke (eds.). 2015. *Socializing Intelligence Through Academic Talk and Dialogue*. Washington, DC: American Educational Research Association.

Rickford, John, Thomas Wasow, Arnold Zwicky, & Isabelle Buchstaller. 2007. Intensive and quotative all: Something old, something new. *American Speech* 82. 3–31.

Roberts, Julie. 1997. The acquisition of sociolinguistic variation: A study of (-t, d) deletion in preschool children. *Journal of Child Language* 24. 351–372.

Robinson, Mary. 2021. Negative concord as a window into the social perception of (morpho-) syntactic variables. Research talk presented at the Linguistics Seminar Series, University of Newcastle. Available from: https://drive.google.com/file/d/1FjEPd2535VZtAakn7PRsqKy_K1SxheiA/view [last accessed 2 June 2023].

Romaine, Suzanne. 1984. On the problem of syntactic variation and pragmatic meaning in sociolinguistic theory. *Folia Linguistica* 18(3–4). 409–438.

Rosa, Jonathan & Nelson Flores. 2017. Unsettling race and language: Toward a raciolinguistic perspective. *Language in Society* 46(5). 621–647. https://doi.org/10.1017/S0047404517000562.

Rosen, Michael. 2021. Dear Gavin Williamson, could you tell parents what a fronted adverbial is? The Guardian, sec. Education. Available from: www.theguardian.com/education/2021/jan/23/dear-gavin-williamson-could-you-tell-parents-what-a-fronted-adverbial-is [last accessed 13 June 2023].

Sacks, Harvey, Emanuel Schegloff & Gail Jefferson. 1974. A simplest systematics for the organization of turn-taking for conversation. *Language* 50. 696–735.

Schilling, Natalie. 2013. Investigating stylistic variation. In J. K. Chambers & Natalie Schilling (eds.), *The Handbook of Language Variation and Change*, second edition, 325–349. Hoboken, NJ: Wiley-Blackwell.

Schilling-Estes, Natalie & Walt Wolfram. 1994. Convergent explanation and alternative regularization patterns: _Were/weren't_ levelling in a vernacular English variety. *Language Variation and Change* 6. 273–302.

Schleef, Erik. 2013. Glottal replacement of /t/ in two British capitals: Effects of word frequency and morphological compositionality. *Language Variation and Change* 25. 201–223.

Sharma, Devyani. 2018. Style dominance: Attention, audience, and the 'real me.' *Language in Society* 47(1). 1–31. https://doi.org/10.1017/S0047404517000835.

2021. Biographical indexicality. In Lauren Hall-Lew, Emma Moore & Robert J. Podesva (eds.), *Social Meaning and Linguistic Variation: Theorizing the Third Wave*, 243–264. Cambridge: Cambridge University Press.

2022. False oppositions in the study of coherence. In Karen V. Beaman & Gregory R. Guy (eds.), *The Coherence of Linguistic Communities: Orderly Heterogeneity and Social Meaning*. London and New York, NY: Routledge.

Sheppard, J. 2012. Hiya pupils, please avoid slang, ta. The Guardian. Available from: www.theguardian.com/education/2012/feb/14/hiya-pupils-avoid-slang-sheffield [last accessed 13 June 2023].

Shin, Naomi & Karen Miller. 2021. Children's acquisition of morphosyntactic variation. *Language Learning and Development* 18(2). 1–26.

Shorrocks, Graham. 1980. *A grammar of the dialect of Farnworth and district (Greater Manchester County, formerly Lancashire)*. Sheffield: Thesis, University of Sheffield.

1982. Relative pronouns and relative clauses in the dialect of Farnworth and district (Greater Manchester County, formerly Lancashire). *Zeitschrift für Dialektologie und Linguistik* 49(3). 334–343.

1998. *A Grammar of the Dialect of the Bolton Area: Introduction, phonology.* Amsterdam: Peter Lang.

1999. *A Grammar of the Dialect of the Bolton Area: Morphology and syntax.* Amsterdam: Peter Lang.

Silverstein, Michael. 1976. Shifters, linguistic categories, and cultural description. In Keith Basso & H. A. Selby (eds.), *Meaning in Anthropology*, 11–56. Albuquerque, NM: University of Mexico Press.

1985. Language and the culture of gender: At the intersection of structure, usage and ideology. In Elizabeth Mertz & Richard J. Parmentier (eds.), *Semiotic Mediation*, 219–259. Orlando, FL: Academic Press.

2003. Indexical order and the dialectics of sociolinguistic life. *Language and Communication* 23. 193–229.

Skeggs, Beverley. 1997. *Formations of Class & Gender: Becoming Respectable.* London: SAGE Publications.

Smith, Jennifer. 2001. Negative concord in the Old and New World: Evidence from Scotland. *Language Variation and Change* 13(2). 109–134. https://doi.org/10.1017/S0954394501132011.

Smith, Jennifer, Mercedes Durham & Liane Fortune. 2007. "Mam, my trousers is fa'in doon!": Community, caregiver, and child in the acquisition of variation in a Scottish dialect. *Language Variation and Change* 19(1). 63–99. https://doi.org/10.1017/S0954394507070044.

2009. Universal and dialect-specific pathways of acquisition: Caregivers, children, and t/d deletion. *Language Variation and Change* 21. 69–95.

Smith, Jennifer, Mercedes Durham & Hazel Richards. 2013. The social and linguistic in the acquisition of sociolinguistic norms: Caregivers, children, and variation. *Linguistics* 51(2). 285–324.

Smith, Jennifer & Mercedes Durham. 2019. *Sociolinguistic Variation in Children's Language.* Cambridge: Cambridge University Press. https://doi.org/10.1017/9781316779248.

Smith, Jennifer & Sophie Holmes-Elliott. 2022. Mapping syntax and the sociolinguistic monitor. In Tanya Karoli Christensen & Torben Juel Jensen (eds.), *Explanations in Sociosyntactic Variation*, 58–89. Cambridge and New York, NY: Cambridge University Press.

Snell, Julia. 2008. *Pronouns, dialect and discourse: A socio-pragmatic account of children's language in Teeside.* Unpublished PhD dissertation. University of Leeds, ms.

2010. From sociolinguistic variation to socially strategic stylisation. *Journal of Sociolinguistics* 14(5). 630–656.

2013. Dialect, interaction and class positioning at school: From deficit to difference to repertoire. *Language and Education* 27(2). 110–128. https://doi.org/10.1080/09500782.2012.760584.

2014. Social class and language. In Jan-Ola Östman & Jef Verschueren (eds.), *Handbook of Pragmatics: 2014 Installment.* Amsterdam: John Benjamins. Available from: https://benjamins.com/catalog/hop.18.soc6/details [last accessed 2 June 2023].

    2018. Solidarity, stance, and class identities. *Language in Society* 47(5). 665–691. https://doi.org/10.1017/S0047404518000970.

    2019. Evidence submitted to the Oracy APPG "Speak for Change" Inquiry. Available from: www.snell.me.uk/wp-content/uploads/JSnell_Speaking_for_Change.pdf [last accessed 13 June 2023].

    Forthcoming. Social class and educational inequalities. In Chris Montgomery & Emma Moore (eds.), *The Handbook of British Englishes*. Oxford and New York, NY: Oxford University Press.

Snell, Julia & Richard Andrews. 2017. To what extent does a regional dialect and accent impact on the development of reading and writing skills? *Cambridge Journal of Education* 47(3). 297–313. https://doi.org/10.1080/0305764X.2016.1159660.

Snell, Julia & Ian Cushing. 2022. "A lot of them write how they speak": Policy, pedagogy and the policing of 'nonstandard' English. *Literacy* 56(3). 199–211. https://doi.org/10.1111/lit.12298.

Spencer, Sarah. 2017. Research as working-class resistance: Lessons learned from getting by. *Pedagogy, Culture & Society* 25(3). 481–486. https://doi.org/10.1080/14681366.2016.1173962.

Spencer, Sarah, Judy Clegg, Joy Stackhouse & Robert Rush. 2017. Contribution of spoken language and socio-economic background to adolescents' educational achievement at age 16 years. *International Journal of Language & Communication Disorders* 52(2). 184–196. https://doi.org/10.1111/1460-6984.12264.

Squires, Lauren. 2013. It don't go both ways: Limited bidirectionality in sociolinguistic perception. *Journal of Sociolinguistics* 17(2). 200–237. https://doi.org/10.1111/josl.12025.

    2014. Processing, evaluation, knowledge: Testing the perception of English subject–verb agreement variation. *Journal of English Linguistics* 42(2). 144–172. https://doi.org/10.1177/0075424214526057.

    2016. Processing grammatical differences: Perceiving v. noticing. In Anna M. Babel (ed.), *Awareness and Control in Sociolinguistic Research*, 80–103. Cambridge: Cambridge University Press.

Starr, Rebecca L. 2021. Changing language, changing character types. In Lauren Hall-Lew, Emma Moore & Robert J. Podesva (eds.), *Social Meaning and Linguistic Variation: Theorizing the Third Wave*, 315–337. Cambridge and New York, NY: Cambridge University Press.

Stein, Ellen. 1990. I'm sitting there: Another new quotative? *American Speech* 65. 303.

Straw, Michelle & Peter L. Patrick. 2007. Dialect acquisition of glottal variation in /t/: Barbadians in Ipswich. *Language Sciences* 29. 385–407.

Stuart-Smith, Jane, Claire Timmins & Fiona Tweedie. 2007. 'Talkin' Jockney'? Variation and change in Glaswegian accent. *Journal of Sociolinguistics* 11(2). 221–260. https://doi.org/10.1111/j.1467-9841.2007.00319.x.

Stubbs, Michael. 1984. Applied discourse analysis and educational linguistics. In Peter Trudgill (ed.), *Applied Sociolinguistics*, 203–244. London: Academic Press.

Tagliamonte, Sali. 1998. Was/were variation across the generations: View from the city of York. *Language Variation and Change* 10. 153–191.

2006. *Analysing Sociolinguistic Variation*. Cambridge: Cambridge University Press.

2011. *Variationist Sociolinguistics: Change, Observation, Interpretation*. Oxford: Wiley-Blackwell.

2012. *Variationist Sociolinguistics: Change, Observation, Interpretation*. John Wiley & Sons.

Tagliamonte, Sali A. & Rosalind Temple. 2005. New perspectives on an ol' variable: (t,d) in British English. *Language Variation and Change* 17. 281–302.

Tagliamonte, Sali A. & Rebecca V. Roeder. 2009. Variation in the English definite article: Socio-historical linguistics in t'speech community. *Journal of Sociolinguistics* 13(4). 435–471. https://doi.org/10.1111/j.1467-9841.2009.00418.x.

Thorne, Barrie. 1993. *Gender Play*. Buckingham, UK: McGraw-Hill Education.

Timmis, Ivor. 2009. "Tails" of linguistic survival. *Applied Linguistics* 31(3). 325–345.

Toma, Bethany E. 2018. *The semantics and pragmatics of right dislocation: Odd thing, that*. Undergraduate Research Thesis. Ohio State University, ms.

Tomlin, Russell. 1986. *Basic Word Order: Functional Principles*. London: Croom Helm.

Tottie, Gunnel & Sebastian Hoffmann. 2006. Tag questions in British and American English. *Journal of English Linguistics* 34(4). 283–311. https://doi.org/10.1177/0075424206294369.

Trudgill, Peter. 1975. *Accent, Dialect and the School*. London: Edward Arnold & Co.

Vincent, Carol, Stephen Ball, Nicola Rollock & David Gillborn. 2013. Three generations of racism: Black middle-class children and schooling. *British Journal of Sociology of Education* 34(5/6). 929–946.

Wales, Katie. 1996. *Personal Pronouns in Present-day English*. Cambridge: Cambridge University Press.

Ward, Gregory & Betty Birner. 1996. On the discourse function of rightward movement in English. In Adele Goldberg (ed.), *Conceptual Structure, Discourse and Language*, 463–479. Stanford University, CA: CSLI Publications.

Watt, Paul. 2006. Respectability, roughness and 'race': Neighbourhood place images and the making of working-class social distinctions in London. *International Journal of Urban and Regional Research* 30(4). 776–797. https://doi.org/10.1111/j.1468-2427.2006.00688.x.

Weiner, E. Judith & William Labov. 1983. Constraints on the agentless passive. *Journal of Linguistics* 19(1). 29–53.

Wells, John Christopher. 1982. *Accents of English: The British Isles*. Cambridge: Cambridge University Press.

Wenger, Etienne. 1998. *Communities of Practice: Learning, Meaning and Identity*. Cambridge: Cambridge University Press.

Williamson, J. & F. Hardman. 1997. Those terrible marks of the beast: Nonstandard dialect in children's writing. *Language and Education* 23. 157–168.

Willis, Paul. 1977. *Learning to Labour: How Working Class Kids Get Working Class Jobs*. New York, NY: Colombia University Press.

Wilson, Brianna. 2022. The social meaning of unbound reflexives. Paper presented at NWAV 50, University of Stanford, October 2022.

Winford, Donald. 1984. The linguistic variable and syntactic variation in creole continua. *Lingua* 62. 267–288.

Winter, Bodo. 2013. Linear models and linear mixed effects models in R with linguistic applications. arXiv preprint arXiv:1308.5499 [cs].
Wolfram, Walt. 1969. *A Sociolinguistic Description of Detroit Negro Speech*. Washington, DC: Center for Applied Linguistics.
Wolfram, Walt & Jason Sellers. 1999. Ethnolinguistic marking of past be in Lumbee vernacular English. *Journal of English Linguistics* 27. 94–114.
Wolfram, Walt & Natalie Schilling-Estes. 2003. Parallel development and alternative restructuring: The case of weren't regularization. In David Britain & Jenny Cheshire (eds.), *Social Dialectology: In Honour of Peter Trudgill*, 131–154. Amsterdam: John Benjamins.
Wolfson, Nessa. 1979. The conversational historic present alternation. *Language* 55. 168–182.
Wright, Joseph. 1905. *The English Dialect Grammar*. Oxford: Frowde.
Wyse, Dominic. 2001. Grammar for writing? A critical review of empirical evidence. *British Journal of Educational Studies* 49. 411–427.
Yakin, Halina Sendera Mohd & Andreas Totu. 2014. The semiotic perspectives of Peirce and Saussure: A brief comparative study. *Procedia - Social and Behavioral Sciences* 155. 4–8. https://doi.org/10.1016/j.sbspro.2014.10.247.
Young, Vershawn Ashanti. 2009. "Nah, we straight": An argument against code switching. *Journal of Advanced Composition* 29(1/2). 49–76.
Zeijlstra, H. 2004. *Sentential negation and negative concord*. PhD dissertation. University of Amsterdam, ms.
Zhang, Qing. 2008. Rhotacization and the "Beijing Smooth Operator": The social meaning of a linguistic variable. *Journal of Sociolinguistics* 12(2). 201–222.
  2021. Emergence of social meaning in sociolinguistic change. In Lauren Hall-Lew, Emma Moore & Robert J. Podesva (eds.), *Social Meaning and Linguistic Variation: Theorizing the Third Wave*, 265–291. Cambridge: Cambridge University Press.
Zimman, Lal. 2017. Variability in /s/ among transgender speakers: Evidence for a socially grounded account of gender and sibilants. *Linguistics* 55(5). 993–1019. https://doi.org/10.1515/ling-2017-0018.
Ziv, Yael. 1994. Left and right dislocations: Discourse functions and anaphora. *Journal of Pragmatics* 22(6). 629–645. https://doi.org/10.1016/0378-2166(94)90033-7.
Ziv, Yael & Barbara Grosz. 1994. Right dislocation and attentional state. In *Proceedings of the Ninth Annual Conference and of the Workshop on Discourse*, 184–199. The Israeli Association for Theoretical Linguistics.

Index

(th)-fronting, 71
/h/-dropping, 175, 187, 206
/s/ fronting, 211
   character type, 211
/t/-glottalling. *See* word-final (t)
/t/-release. *See* word-final (t)

adolescence
   life stage, 80–81, 135
   persona development, 110, 228
   social class, 105
affect, 73
   /s/ fronting, 211
   California Vowel Shift, 211
   possessive *me*, 66
   right dislocation, 149, 157
agentless passive, 69
ain't, 54, 83, 117, 118, 174, 211, 217
axis of differentiation, 59

BE, past-tense, 81–83
Birmingham English, 83
Bolton
   description of, 18
   Survey of English Dialects, 84
Bourdieu, Pierre, 2, 3, 86–87

California Vowel Shift, 211
capital
   cultural, 3
   economic, 53
character type, 69–70, 169, 221–223
   definition of, 52–53
   levelled *were*, 76, 108–110
   negative concord, 134–135
   right dislocation, 169
   tag questions, 173
characterological figure. *See* character type
chav, 50
Cheshire, Jenny, 9–10, 76, 138, 168

child-directed speech, 78, 85
child language acquisition, 11, 77–80, 86, 106, 228
   morphosyntax, 80
clarification. *See* discourse function
cognition
   automaticity, 230
   cognitive primacy, 11, 110
   language variation, 227–228
   social meaning, 224, 232
commonness
   construal of, 51
   levelled *were*, 212
   negative concord, 111, 134–136
   right dislocation, 139, 160, 167
community of practice
   definition of, 28, 44, 87
compound indefinites
   levelled *were*, 94, 101–102
conduciveness. *See* discourse function
conjecture. *See* interpretant
creaky voice, 58
cultural studies, 27
Cushing, Ian, 225–227

Definite Article Reduction (DAR), 7, 8
delinquency
   negative concord, 112, 124, 125
   persona, 124
   social class, 112
   social meaning, 49
   Townie, 106, 124, 129–133, 165, 192, 205
demonstratives
   pragmatic meaning, 63
   right dislocation, 141, 153–155, 161–162
discourse function
   afterthoughts
      right dislocation, 144
   clarification
      right dislocation, 144–146, 148, 161

Index

discourse function (cont.)
  conduciveness, 206
    tag questions, 5, 56–58, 65, 173, 180, 181, 195–196
  emphasis
    negative concord, 116, 129–131, 214–216, 221
    right dislocation, 146
  evaluation, 159–160, 167–168, 218–219
    historic present, 70
    innit, 57
    right dislocation, 147–148, 150–151, 161–163, 169, 215, 216
    tag questions, 5
  exit devices
    tag questions, 180
  focusing, 214
    negative concord, 116
    right dislocation, 146–147, 161, 215–216
  intensification, 114, 116
    negative concord, 8, 137
    right dislocation, 12
discourse markers, stigma, 140, 196
discourse new/given
  existential *there*, 143–144
  marking of, 9–10
  right dislocation, 146–147

Eckert, Penelope, 27, 28, 53–54, 56, 80, 116, 169, 208, 227
Eden Village
  definition of, 29–33
education
  language perceptions, 11, 81, 212
  levels, 87
  policy, 14, 209–210, 225–231
embodiment. *See* persona, stance, style
emphasis. *See* discourse function
enregisterment, 59–61
  of grammar, 212
  tag questions, 205, 218–220
erasure, 59, 112
ethnicity
  body size, 54
  and grammar, 212
  in schools, 18
  social class, 17
ethnography, 74
  dilemmas, 208
  fieldwork, 13
  in schools, 16–17, 18, 27
evaluation. *See* discourse function
existentials
  discourse function, 9, 143–144
  existential BE, 84, 96
  levelled *were*, 94, 102

f0. *See* pitch
face-threat
  negative concord, 114
  right dislocation, 53, 159, 161–162, 216
  tag questions, 218–219
Fens English, 83
fractal recursivity, 17
frequency code (Ohala), 54

Gal, Susan, 17, 22, 49–51, 54, 59–60, 74
gatekeepers, 3, 31
Geeks
  definition of, 33–37
gender
  delinquency, 126–131
  study participants, 26–28
  styles, 168–169
  tag questions, 172, 218
  vernacular culture, 76–77
goth, social type, 32, 139–140
  Geek intersection, 37, 138
grammar
  definition of, 7
  perception of. *See* methods, experimental
grammatical variation
  types of, 7

habitus, 2, 86
Head-driven Phrase Structure Grammar (HPSG), 213
heterosexual market, 27, 127
historic present, 69–70

icon. *See* sign
implicit bias, 3
indeterminate, 111, 115
  definition of, 117–118
index. *See* sign
indexical field
  definition of, 56–57
  intersecting variables, 206
  lifespan development, 108–110
  negative concord, 133–136
indexicality
  chain of associations, 66
  character type, 58
  definition of, 52, 212
information structure, 214, 215
  negative concord, 221
  right dislocation, 161
  sociolinguistic variation, 9
  tag questions, 219, 224
innit, 54–59, 174
  character type, 55, 57–59
  commonness, 55, 59, 64
intensifier, *totally*, 61–63, 68, 220, 223
Interface Principle, 212–213, 223

Index

interpretant, 113
  class distinction, 50–51, 59–61, 64–66
  definition of, 49
Irvine, Judith T., 17, 22, 45, 49–51, 54, 59–60, 74

kernel of similarity, 51, 56
knowledge about language (KAL), 230

Labov, William, 8, 11, 69, 71, 87, 116, 212, 226
Lancashire English, 83–84, 123
language ability, 72, 229
legitimate peripheral participation, 3–4
Lexical Functional Grammar (LFG), 213
literacy, 14, 210, 229
London English, 83

Mandarin, Beijing, 54
markedness
  definition of, 5–6
  discourse new, 9
  negative concord, 112, 116, 134
  right dislocation, 142, 169, 216
  social salience, 62–63
  standard English, 230
  tag questions, 219
Mass Observation archive, 142
metalinguistic awareness
  levelled *were*, 108
  negative concord, 115
  right dislocation, 218
  social justice, 230
  tag questions, 197
methods
  ethnographic, 73–74
  experimental, 71–73
  variationist, 71
Middlesbrough English, 65
modal verbs, 63–64
morpholexis. *See* variable, morpholexical
morphosyntax. *See* variable, morphosyntactic
Myhill, Debra, 14, 230

National Curriculum, 80, 228
negation
  acquisition of, 77
  in Scots, 8, 78, 112–113, 215, 227
  semantic, 115
  syntactic, 115
negative concord
  perceptions of, 72
Northern Subject Rule, 71
NURSE-SQUARE merger, 75

Ochs, Elinor, 52
Ofsted, 18, 225, 230
othering, 51

Peirce, Charles, 49, 53–54, 61, 74
persona
  definition of, 50
  embodiment, 136
pitch, 54, 58, 79, 168, 170, 211
place, 84
Podesva, Robert J., 173–174, 196–197, 211, 219
policing, of language, 225–226
politeness, 114
  norms, 162
  right dislocation, 218
  subversion of, 106
  tag questions, 172
Populars
  definition of, 37–41
possessive *me*, 65–66, 211
pragmatic meaning
  definition of, 5, 6, 216
prestige, covert/overt, 11
principle of error correction, 226
progressive SIT/STAND/LIE, 95–96

qualia, 65
  definition of, 54
  rhematisation, 59
quotatives, 95–96

raciolinguistics, 225
Reading English, 83
rebelliousness. *See* delinquency
referential meaning. *See* semantic meaning
repetition
  intensification, 116
  negative concord, 8, 12, 214
  right dislocation, 146
rheme. *See* sign
rhoticity, 54
Rosen, Michael, 230

Scots, Buckie, 78–79, 112, 116, 134, 215, 227
semantic meaning
  definition of, 5, 115, 215
Sharma, Devyani, 11, 224
sign
  icon
    definition of, 53–54
    innit, 58–59
    negative concord, 112, 113, 129, 136–137
    possessive *me*, 66
    Townie, 42
    working class, 60
  index, 53
  mutability, 52
  object, 49, 52, 53–54
  Peircean, 49

sign (cont.)
　rheme
　　definition of, 54, 205
　　innit, 65
　　negative concord, 113, 135–136
　　right dislocation, 218
　　working class, 58–61
　Saussurian, 53
　symbol, 53
　vehicle, 8, 49, 51, 52–54
Silverstein, Michael, 52, 53, 66
Smith, Jennifer, 78–80, 112–113, 227
Smoothies, 198–201
Snell, Julia, 65–66, 142, 147, 161, 167, 225–230
social class, 1–4, 10–11
　adolescent, 105
　at Midlan High, 87–88
　definition of, 86–87
　mobility, 107–108
　perceptions of working class, 50–51, 65–66, 112, 212
　right dislocation, 161
social meaning
　acquisition of, 78, 109–110
　definition of, 6, 216
　rooted in character type, 64–65, 204, 217–220
　rooted in semantics, 61–64, 214–215
　rooted in sound symbolism, 65, 211
social type
　definition of, 50
sociolinguistic vitality, 77
sound symbolism, 54, 58
speech and language therapy, 229
Spencer, Sarah, 225, 229
stance
　accretion, 57, 135
　acquisition of, 79–80
　adverbials, 167
　definition of, 52
　embodiment, 58
　measuring, 150
statistics
　Estimated Marginal Means (EMMs), 100–104
　General Linear Mixed Effects, 97–100
　terminology, 88
style
　definition of, 45
　embodiment, 37, 50, 52
　reification, 49–50
subject–verb agreement
　perceptions of, 71
　salience, 79
　sociolinguistic variable, 217
symbol. *See* sign
syntax. *See* variable, syntactic

tags
　clause-terminal, 140
　levelled *were*, 94
teaching. *See* education
third wave variationism, 208
topic
　negative concord, 125–129
　tag questions, 174, 184–185
topicalisation. *See* discourse function, focusing
Townies
　definition of, 41–44
Type CT meanings. *See* social meaning, rooted in character type
Type SM meaning. *See* social meaning, rooted in semantics
Type SS social meaning. *See* social meaning, rooted in sound symbolism

Universal Grammar, 213
unmarked plurality, 225

variable
　definition of, 7–10
　morpholexical, 8, 70, 220
　　demonstratives, 61–63
　　levelled *were*, 67–68, 220
　　negated verbs, 187–190
　　negation, 7
　　totally, 223
　morphophonemic
　　Definite Article Reduction (DAR), 7
　　innit, 58
　　possessive *me*, 211
　morphosyntactic, 220–222
　　historic present, 69
　　negative concord, 7, 8–9, 68, 220
　　perception of, 71
　phonetic, 12–13
　　(th)-fronting, 7–8
　　socially-restricted, 68, 220–223
　syntactic, 9–10, 222–223
　　marking discourse new, 7
　　right dislocation, 68–69, 220
　　widespread, 68, 223
verb processes (Halliday), 149–150
vernacular universal, 85, 123

word-final (t), 175, 188, 224
word-initial (h). *See* /h/-dropping
writing, as distinct from speech, 81, 138, 212, 226, 227, 231

York English, 83
youth culture, 27

For EU product safety concerns, contact us at Calle de José Abascal, 56–1°,
28003 Madrid, Spain or eugpsr@cambridge.org.

www.ingramcontent.com/pod-product-compliance
Ingram Content Group UK Ltd.
Pitfield, Milton Keynes, MK11 3LW, UK
UKHW022001030326
468620UK00021B/849